PRAISE FOR THE FIRST EDITION

"This is an important book. Once and for all, we get put before us the facts of the Carroll-Tenniel relationship along with the pictures that materialized from the association."
—Morton N. Cohen, *Victorian Periodicals Review*

"Hancher's coffee-table-sized volume with more than two hundred illustrations is a methodical study. . . . Hancher convincingly shows how familiar Alice's world, as viewed through Tenniel's illustrations would have seemed to Victorian readers, since many details are recycled from cartoons produced for *Punch*."
—Jan Susina, *Victorian Studies*

PRAISE FOR THE SECOND EDITION

"This vastly enlarged and splendidly illustrated new edition of Michael Hancher's already indispensable book is a must-read, not merely for those who relish the work of John Tenniel and Lewis Carroll, but for anyone interested in how the surprisingly complex processes of nineteenth-century illustration actually worked during the golden age of wood engraving. The book's appearance is cause for rejoicing—for Victorianists everywhere."
—Patrick Leary

"Michael Hancher's significantly updated and revised study of the collaboration between John Tenniel and Lewis Carroll on the creation and production of the *Alice* books is essential reading for scholars in book history, Victorian studies, and children's literature. Given Hancher's meticulous eye for detail, I think even Carroll would approve."
—Jan Susina

THE TENNIEL ILLUSTRATIONS TO THE "ALICE" BOOKS

THE TENNIEL ILLUSTRATIONS TO THE "ALICE" BOOKS

Second Edition

Michael Hancher

THE OHIO STATE UNIVERSITY PRESS
COLUMBUS

For Linda and Matthew
and
in memory of my parents

CONTENTS

ILLUSTRATIONS

FIGURES

PLATES

Plates follow page 114.

PREFACE TO THE SECOND EDITION

*T*he first edition of this book was the first major account of Tenniel's *Alice* illustrations. It drew selectively on the materials that were available in print at the time, and did not investigate archival resources. This new edition is better informed by the archive, and also benefits from the large scholarly literature that has illuminated the *Alice* books and their illustrations in the last several decades. The discovery of the original Dalziel wood blocks of the Tenniel illustrations was a find that virtually coincided with the publication of this book in 1985. Now at the British Library, they are a major addition to the record, as are the many electrotype replicas that are housed in the archives of Macmillan Publishing in Basingstoke, Hampshire. I have been able to consult both sets and also albums of proofs of Dalziel wood engravings in the British Museum, and annotated proofs and related materials held by the following institutions: St. Bride Foundation and Library, London; The Rosenbach, Philadelphia; The Newberry Library, Chicago; The Morgan Library and Museum, New York; The Berg Collection and George Arents Collection at The New York Public Library; Special Collections and University Archives, Stony Brook University; The Beinecke Rare Book & Manuscript Library, Yale University; the Houghton Library, Harvard University; and the Children's Literature Research Collections, University of Minnesota Libraries. I thank the following people for their help and advice in accessing these collections, and for their responses to other inquiries: Gordon Anderson, Alexandra Ault, Sophia Dahab, Molly Dotson, Cheryll Fong, Elizabeth E. Fuller, Jill Gage, Alex Hailey, Clare Imholtz, Lorraine Janzen, Tim Johnson, P. J. MacDougall, Caitlin Marineau, Hope Mayo, John Monahan, Kristen J. Nyitray, Helen Peden, Samantha Porter, Mark Richards, Bob Richardson, Angela Roche, Alysoun Sanders, Kim Sloan, Ingrid Smits, Bethan Stevens, Krystal Thomas, Robert Tyrwhitt, Deborah K. Ultan, Carolyn Vega, and Jessica Wolfe. Melissa Merte has been immensely helpful in gathering materials that inform this second edition and in helping to refine the results. Lindsay Martin at The Ohio State University Press gave early guidance and encouragement.

Scholarship on Lewis Carroll and John Tenniel has greatly advanced in recent decades. Roger Simpson's monograph on Tenniel (1994) sheds light on many of the topics discussed here. Major biographies of Lewis Carroll by Morton Cohen (1995) and Edward Wakeling (2015) have proved particularly helpful, as have biographies of Tenniel by Rodney Engen (1991) and Frankie Morris (2005). Other important new resources include Edward Wakeling's edition of Carroll's diaries (1993–2003), Morton Cohen's later editions of Carroll's letters (1987, 2003), Charlie Lovett's catalogue of Carroll's personal Library (2005), Justin G. Schiller and Selwyn H. Goodacre's monograph on the first edition of *Alice's Adventures* (1990), histories of *Punch* by Richard Altick (1997) and Patrick Leary (2010), recent editions of the *Alice* books, and many journal publications.

Work on the second edition was made possible by a sabbatical leave and by funding provided by the Office of the Vice President for Research and also the Office of the Executive Vice President and Provost, University of Minnesota, and by the Department of English.

The manuscript for the first edition of this book was produced on an IBM electric typewriter, floated by many ounces of Wite-Out correction fluid and bandaged by yards of white correction tape. Correspondence was conducted via the United States Post Office. The World Wide Web had not yet been spun. No Gopher, no Google. Today's literary historian has many advantages, including digital facsimiles of millions of books served up by Google Books, HathiTrust, and the Internet Archive, not to mention word-processing software and email. In some ways discovery and writing is easier now than it was then. In some important ways the data for literary scholarship are now digital.

But not in all ways. Actual, material books still matter. Having spent time scrutinizing many different copies of the "same" editions of the *Alice* books I remain persuaded by the "Statement on the Significance of Primary Records" that the Modern Language Association of America (MLA) published in 1995, as the digital age was dawning. One passage is particularly apt:

> Not only do editions differ from one another, but also copies within an edition (of any period) often vary among themselves; as a result, every copy is a potential source for new physical evidence, and no copy is superfluous for studying an edition's production history. Furthermore, since the shape, feel, designs, and illustrations of books have affected, and continue to affect, readers' responses (some of which have been recorded in the margins of pages), access to the physical forms in which texts from the past have appeared is a fundamental part of informed reading and effective classroom teaching; if that access is to be as widespread as it can be, the number of available copies of past editions, held in libraries of all kinds, must be as large as possible.

Habent sua fata libelli, "books have their fates"; and the fate of actual books in research libraries remains in doubt. Digital facsimiles are not surrogates. As much as possible, primary records should be preserved. Appreciation is due to the many hundreds of people who over the last century and a half helped to preserve the primary records on which much of the following account is based.

All the original chapters have been updated; some have been expanded. The first two chapters present general frames of reference: Tenniel's work as a staff cartoonist for *Punch* and its effect on the illustrations; and Lewis Carroll's own illustrations for the original manuscript version of *Alice's Adventures*. The next four chapters concentrate on details of illustration in *Alice's Adventures in Wonderland*; three further chapters focus on illustrations for *Through the Looking-Glass*. The three following chapters return to general considerations: the nature of the Carroll–Tenniel collaboration; the practical and aesthetic conditions of Victorian woodblock illustration, especially as they exemplified the always problematic relation of illustration to text; and the merits of the original layout of the *Alice* books. Six new chapters provide information about how the wood blocks were engraved and revised; how the blocks were copied by the electrotyping process; how the early editions were printed, with what consequences; how later editions were colored; how certain limited editions signed by "the original Alice" were illustrated; and how *looking* as such figures in the two *Alice* books.

FROM PREFACE TO THE FIRST EDITION

*M*any people have given help and encouragement to the writing of this book. I especially want to thank the following: Chester L. Anderson, Mary Ann Bonney (*Punch*), Honor Dexter, Joan Digby, Margery Durham, Félix Alfaro Fournier, John GilMartin (City of Birmingham Museums and Art Gallery), Donald J. Gray, Edward Guiliano, Elizabeth L. Hirsch, Gordon Hirsch, Park Honan, Kenneth Keller, Janis Lull, William Madden, J. Lawrence Mitchell, Angelina Morhange (The National Gallery, London), Frankie Morris, Alan F. Nagel, Stephen Prickett, Phyllis M. Rogers (Palace of Westminster, London), John B. Smith, III, Phoebe Stanton, and Michael Steig.

My wife Linda first pointed out to me the resemblance of young John Bull to Tweedledum and Tweedledee, and so confirmed my curiosity about the Tenniel illustrations. Matthew, our son, has grown almost to Alice's age in the time it has taken to write this book. It is for them both, as well as for my parents—who, along with much else, gave me my first set of the *Alice* books when I was about Matthew's age.

Cathy Aunan patiently repaired and maintained the text after it was read into a word processor by a troublesome optical scanner. Among the staff members of the University of Minnesota Libraries, Robert Jevne, Jennifer Lewis, Erika Linke, Dennis Skrade, and Herbert Scherer have been especially helpful.

I owe a special debt to Elizabeth Martin, who edited this book with great skill and forbearance.

Versions of chapters 1, 7, and 12 have appeared previously in *Lewis Carroll: A Celebration* (New York: Clarkson N. Potter, 1982); *Jabberwocky: The Journal of the Lewis Carroll Society* 8 (1979); and the *Harvard Library Bulletin* 30 (1982). Thanks are due to the editors (Edward Guiliano, Selwyn H. Goodacre, and Kenneth E. Carpenter) for their initial support and for their kind permission to reprint.

Much of the work on this book was made possible by a sabbatical leave from the University of Minnesota and a summer research grant from the Graduate School. Some of the research for chapter 12 was funded by a McMillan Travel Grant from the College of Liberal Arts. The cost of preparing many of the illustrations was underwritten by a grant from the Graduate School.

INTRODUCTION

*T*he *Times*, the chief newspaper of Victorian England, first reported the existence of *Alice's Adventures in Wonderland* toward the end of an unsigned omnibus review that appeared the day after Christmas in 1865. Nineteen "Christmas books" were discussed; and in keeping with the current gift-book fashion most of them featured woodcut illustrations. Seven "children's books" were relegated to the last paragraph of the review, where the reviewer discussed *Alice* immediately after a now forgotten volume of fantastic tales by James Greenwood, *The Hatchet Throwers*, which had been illustrated by Ernest Griset.[1] Griset's illustrations were "clever and funny."

> His drawing of animals is remarkable, and amid all the freedom of extravagance he manages to adhere to truth. His truthfulness, however, in the delineation of animal forms reminds us of Mr. Tenniel, who has illustrated a little work—*Alice's Adventures in Wonderland,* with extraordinary grace. Look at the first chapter of this volume; and note the rabbit at the head of it. His umbrella is tucked under his arm and he is taking the watch out of his pocket to see what o'clock it is. The neatness of touch with which he is set living before us may be seen in a dozen other vignettes throughout the volume, *the letterpress of which is by Mr. Lewis Carroll, and may best be described as an excellent piece of nonsense.*[2]

The italics are mine, not the reviewer's: note the minor credit that Carroll received. For *The Times* reviewer, as for other contemporary readers of *Alice's Adventures,* it was not Carroll's text but the set of illustrations by John Tenniel that made the book worth noticing. Three days earlier *The Pall Mall Gazette* had praised the story as well as the illustrations, but it emphasized the illustrator's name, not the author's. Later the children's journal *Aunt Judy's Magazine* would begin its review of the book with a concise and telling statement of priorities: "Forty-two

1. Set in Africa, *The Hatchet Throwers* was conventionally imperialist and racist. Lionel Lambourne reproduces several of Griset's illustrations for the book in *Ernest Griset: Fantasies of a Victorian Illustrator* (London: Thames & Hudson, 1979), 43–45; see also 13, 42.

2. *The Times,* 26 December 1865, 5.

illustrations by Tenniel! Why there needs nothing else to sell this book, one would think."[3]

The Reverend C. L. Dodgson probably had some such thought in mind himself when he sought out the professional artist John Tenniel to illustrate his amateur children's story. At that time "Lewis Carroll," the pseudonymous author of some fugitive light verse, was virtually unknown; and he was not much better known in proper style as "Charles Lutwidge Dodgson, M. A.," the author of several obscure mathematical works. But Tenniel was one of the most popular artists in England. His political cartoons attracted general comment as they appeared each week in *Punch,* then the establishment humor magazine; and his drawings had decorated—and helped to sell—more than a dozen books in the previous decade. His sixty-nine exotic illustrations for Thomas Moore's Oriental romance *Lalla Rookh* (1861) had been described by *The Times* as "the greatest illustrative achievement of any single hand."[4] No wonder that *The Times* noticed *Alice's Adventures* mainly on account of its Tenniel illustrations.

Eventually Carroll's fame as the author of the two *Alice* books eclipsed that of his artist-collaborator. For a mix of reasons, Lewis Carroll, like Alice herself, has become a creature of popular legend. And yet Tenniel's own contribution to the books is probably as well-known as Carroll's—perhaps more widely known, for there must be thousands of persons (children and adults alike) who are familiar with reproductions of some of the illustrations, despite never having actually read the text. In a ghostly way, Tenniel retains something of his original precedence over Carroll.

This is not the place for a full account of Tenniel's life or career. His career involved so many hundreds—indeed, thousands—of published drawings as to greatly outweigh, if not overshadow, the crucial work on Carroll's two books. Also, substantial biographies by Rodney Engen and Frankie Morris now supply much valuable information.[5] But the outlines can be simply sketched.

Tenniel was born on 28 February 1820, in London, where he lived for the rest of his life; he was the third son of a dancing and fencing master of Huguenot descent, John Baptist Tenniel. Twenty years later, in a fencing match with his father, Tenniel was accidentally blinded in his right eye. In later years he would minimize the incident; and it is hard to say how it affected his artistic career, which was already well under way.

Largely self-taught, Tenniel may have benefited from his childhood friendship with the sons of John Martin, the painter. He quit his studies at the Royal Academy Schools "in utter disgust of there being no teaching," as he recalled some years later.[6] Instead he joined the Clipstone Street Artists' Society to practice life drawing, and frequented the British Museum to study classical sculpture and (encouraged by Sir Frederic Madden) books and prints of costume and medieval armor. At age sixteen he exhibited, and sold, his first oil painting, at the Society of British Artists. In 1837 he successfully submitted a narrative painting—a scene from Scott's *The Fortunes of Nigel*—for exhibition at the Royal Academy, and he continued for several years to exhibit there. After submitting a large-scale cartoon, *The Spirit of Justice,* in the national competition for fresco designs to decorate the new Houses of Parliament, Tenniel was awarded a premium and was actually commissioned to do a

3. The *Alice* notices in *The Pall Mall Gazette* and *Aunt Judy's Magazine* are among many early reviews reprinted in *Jabberwocky* 9:1–4 (1979–80). See also Elizabeth A. Cripps, "*Alice* and the Reviewers," *Children's Literature* 11 (1983): 32–48; and *Lewis Carroll's Alice's Adventures in Wonderland: A Documentary Volume,* ed. Carolyn Singer, *Dictionary of Literary Biography* 373 (Detroit: Gale Cengage Learning, 2014), 153–69.

The review in *Aunt Judy's Magazine* was not disinterested. The editor and presumable reviewer, Mrs. Alfred Gatty, had published a series of successful children's books called *Parables from Nature,* the third (1861) including an illustration by Tenniel; and she had been on friendly terms with Carroll in Oxford at least since the early sixties.

4. "Mr. Tenniel's *Lalla Rookh,*" *The Times,* 31 October 1860, 9. See also 24 December 1860, 10. Though dated "1861" on the title page, *Lalla Rookh* was published in time for the Christmas trade, 1860.

5. Rodney Engen, *Sir John Tenniel: Alice's White Knight* (London: Scolar Press, 1991). Frankie Morris, *Artist of Wonderland: The Life, Political Cartoons, and Illustrations of Tenniel* (Charlottesville: University of Virginia Press, 2005).

6. M. H. Spielmann, *The History of "Punch"* (London: Cassell and Company, 1895), 461.

fresco, although on a different theme, Dryden's *St. Cecilia*—one of eight illustrations of British poetry.[7]

To learn fresco technique, Tenniel took his first (and all but last) trip abroad, to Munich, where he studied briefly with Peter von Cornelius, whose somewhat schematic draftsmanship reinforced a tendency in Tenniel's own work toward clarity and simplicity of line. In later years Tenniel would gently mock his youthful ambitions for "High Art," and certainly he prospered in the relatively lower reaches of illustration and political caricature. As a boy he had impressed his father with a set of drawings he had done for Bunyan's *Pilgrim's Progress*—drawings since lost, that one would like to compare to the drawings he did later of Alice's progress. Before long he was publishing book illustrations: first, several for S. C. Hall's *Book of British Ballads* (1842); then the set of eleven drawings for a new edition of *Undine,* by Friedrich de la Motte Fouqué (1845); and then over a hundred illustrations for the Reverend Thomas James's new version of *Æsop's Fables* (1848), a book that confirmed Tenniel's reputation, and that led to his being offered a position on the art staff of *Punch* two years later.

Tenniel at first contributed a few relatively small black-and-white illustrations to that comic weekly, then more numerous and more important cuts, until he was relied upon to supply a full-page cartoon each week, and had become the virtual equal on the staff of John Leech. When Leech died in 1864, Tenniel became the chief artist, a position he kept until he retired in 1901. In the early decades, he continued to accept commissions to illustrate books, including the well-received *Lalla Rookh* and the *Alice* books.

Tenniel married in his early thirties, but was widowed within two years; after that he lived a quiet domestic life, at first with his mother-in-law and then with a sister. The Victorian *Punch* was as much a men's club as a magazine; it provided Tenniel with social amenities not unlike those that the Reverend Dodgson enjoyed at Christ Church.

Tenniel was knighted on Prime Minister Gladstone's recommendation in 1893, and lived almost until the age of ninety-four. He died on 25 February 1914, only months before the Great War destroyed the world that he had known and in a way epitomized.

QUOTATIONS FROM *Alice's Adventures in Wonderland* and *Through the Looking-Glass* usually follow the text of the first editions (London: Macmillan, 1866 and 1872, respectively). Most of the Tenniel illustrations are reproduced from the People's Editions of the two books (London: Macmillan, 1887). Most quotations and illustrations from *Punch* are taken from a reprinted set of the first hundred volumes published by the *Punch* office in 1891, and again by *The Times* in 1900; see R. G. G. Price, *A History of Punch* (London: Collins, 1957), 346. The date of publication for a given issue often appears in a running head; when not, it is supplied by *Punch Historical Archive, 1841–1992,* a database published by Gale Cengage.

7. For accounts of Tenniel's fresco projects and their contexts see Engen, *Sir John Tenniel,* 17–21; Roger Simpson, *Sir John Tenniel: Aspects of His Work* (Madison, NJ: Fairleigh Dickinson Press, 1994), 25–47; L. Perry Curtis's review of that book, *Victorian Studies* 40 (1996): 168–71; Michael Hancher, "Tenniel's Allegorical Cartoons," *The Telling Image: Explorations in the Emblem,* ed. Ayers Bagley, Edward M. Griffin, and Austin McLean (New York: AMS Press, 1996), 139–70; Morris, *Artist of Wonderland,* 37–45; and Janice Carlisle, *Picturing Reform in Victorian Britain* (Cambridge: Cambridge University Press, 2012), 85–116.

CHAPTER 1

Punch and *Alice*

Through Tenniel's Looking-Glass

*B*y now Tenniel's illustrations have become perfect mirror images of the world that Alice discovered down the rabbit hole and through the looking-glass. They make up the other half of the text, and readers are wise to accept no substitutes, not even those drawn by Arthur Rackham, certainly not those by Salvador Dali.[1] This parity of word and image, unmatched in any other work of literature, fulfills the rules of symmetry set out in the second of Carroll's two *Alice* books, which is itself a reflection on the first. It also satisfies our modern and Romantic need to see in literature a hall of mirrors that gives no outlook on the world.

Nonetheless, like Alice herself, I can't help wondering if there isn't something of interest to be found on the other side of the mirror, behind (or before) the impassive surface of Tenniel's realistic fantasies. And so, like her, I will venture back and through.

The first discovery to be made on the other side is that things look much the same: Tenniel shared a world of imagery with Alice. In this respect, as in others, the *Punch* career was crucial. It was through a friend on the *Punch* staff, the dramatist and humorist Tom Taylor, that Carroll first approached Tenniel to do the *Alice* illustrations.[2] More importantly, Tenniel's growing success as the chief cartoonist of *Punch* guaranteed for his work the esteem of thousands of middle-class readers.

Like us, Victorian readers would find much of Alice's strange world to be reassuringly familiar. For them, however, the familiarity would not come from having read the books and studied the pictures at age six, or from having been overexposed to the reproduction and adaptation of Tenniel's images in novel contexts (such as advertisements[3]), but from having been granted frequent previews of Wonderland in images drawn for *Punch* by Tenniel and his colleagues on the staff.

Some years ago Frances Sarzano noted in passing that the *Alice* books "harvest the work of early days on *Punch*." Before that, Marguerite Mespoulet had shown that the humanized animals of Carroll's text

1. *Alice's Adventures in Wonderland*, illustrated by Arthur Rackham (London: Heinemann, 1907); illustrated by Salvador Dali (New York: Maecenas Press, 1969); illustrated by Salvador Dali, ed. Mark Burstein (Princeton, NJ: Princeton University Press, 2015). The recent Princeton University Press facsimile edition is an attractively produced book, more approachable than the original Maecenas Press limited-edition portfolio.

2. *The Letters of Lewis Carroll*, ed. Morton N. Cohen, 2 vols. (New York: Oxford University Press, 1979), 1:62 (20 December 1863). Apparently Carroll chose Tenniel on the advice of Robinson Duckworth. A fellow of Trinity College, Duckworth had accompanied Carroll and the three Liddell sisters on the river outing during which Carroll first improvised his story about Alice. See *The Lewis Carroll Picture Book*, ed. Stuart Dodgson Collingwood (London: T. Fisher Unwin, 1899), 358.

3. For a selection of vintage advertisements that recycle Tenniel's imagery, see "Beyond Wonderland: Business and Technology," part of "Alice 150 and Counting: The Legacy of Lewis Carroll; Selections from the Collection of August and Clare Imholtz," University Libraries, University of Maryland, www.lib.umd. edu/alice150.

FIGURE 1.1. Tenniel. Alice encounters Tweedledum and Tweedledee. From *Through the Looking-Glass.*

and of Tenniel's illustrations must have evolved from the grotesqueries drawn by J. J. Grandville for the French prototype of *Punch*, the journal *Charivari*.[4] Humanoid and fashionably dressed animals multiply in the pages of *Punch* both immediately before and throughout Tenniel's career there. What I want to draw attention to are certain *Punch* illustrations by Tenniel and others that are not so obviously in Grandville's tradition, but that reflect light also on the pages of Carroll's books.

Since image reflection is our inevitable topic, Tweedledum and Tweedledee are obvious subjects (fig. 1.1, which was drawn, like all the *Looking-Glass* illustrations, sometime between the end of 1869 and the middle of 1871). Here, on the far side of the looking-glass, each identical twin represents only the other. But on the near side, where Alice begins and ends her journey, both resemble John Bull, that embodiment of everyday England, at an age when he might be styled Master John Bull (fig. 1.2; 27 April 1861, 173). Under the anxious eyes of his mother, Britannia (judging from the unusual crest on the ordinary bonnet), Master Bull is accepting an anodyne of a small reduction in the income tax from his considerate dentist, William E. Gladstone, then chancellor of the exchequer. He looks almost as distressed as Tweedledum (fig. 1.3).

Like many of the *Punch* drawings by Tenniel to be cited in this book, the Gladstone tax cartoon is unsigned; it does not bear the familiar monogram ☙. Tenniel signed his work occasionally from early 1851 (shortly after he joined the *Punch* staff) until early 1853, and more regularly from August 1862 on; but during the intervening decade his abundant work for *Punch* bore no signature, and much of the early work is unsigned also. Still, there is rarely any question whether a particular drawing is his; the styles in which he worked are distinctive enough.

Like the twins, Tenniel's young John Bull wears a "skeleton suit," standard for schoolboys early in the century: a high-waisted, tight-fitting jacket, usually dark, decorated in front with two or three vertical rows of buttons, with the shirt collar worn out, and ankle-length high-waisted trousers, usually light in color, buttoned over the jacket and worn with white socks and black shoes. The frilled shirt collar of figure

4. Frances Sarzano, *Sir John Tenniel, English Masters of Black-and-White* (New York: Pellegrini & Cudahy, 1948), 18. Marguerite Mespoulet, *Creators of Wonderland* (New York: Arrow Editions, 1934).

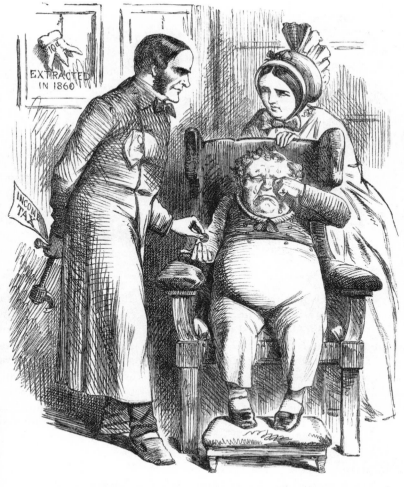

MASTER BULL AND HIS DENTIST.

Dentist. "DON'T CRY, MY LITTLE MAN! I'M NOT GOING TO DRAW ANY MORE THIS TIME, AND
THERE'S A PENNY FOR YOU!"

FIGURE 1.3. Tenniel. Tweedledum enraged. From *Through the Looking-Glass*.

FIGURE 1.4. Tenniel. Young John Bull in Mr. Punch's classroom. From *Punch,* 28 June 1856.

5. Phillis Cunnington and Anne Buck, *Children's Costume in England* (London: Adam & Charles Black, 1965), 172–75; Doreen Yarwood, *The Encyclopedia of World Costume* (New York: Charles Scribner's Sons, 1978), 78; Elizabeth Ewing, *History of Children's Costume* (New York: Charles Scribner's Sons, 1977), 46–48, 63–64.
In 1836 Charles Dickens meditated nostalgically on "a patched and much-soiled skeleton suit" found in a used-clothing market:

> . . . one of those straight blue cloth cases in which small boys used to be confined, before belts and tunics had come in, and old notions had gone out: an ingenious contrivance for displaying the full symmetry of a boy's figure, by fastening him into a very tight jacket, with an ornamental row of buttons over each shoulder, and then buttoning his trousers over it, so as to give his legs the appearance of being hooked on, just under the armpits.

"Meditations in Monmouth Street," first published in 1836; included in *Sketches by Boz,* part 4 (1838). *Sketches by Boz,* ed. Dennis Walder (London: Penguin Books, 1995).
In 1852 Dickens added that a skeleton suit "gave the wearer something of a trussed appearance, like a young fowl ready for the spit. It was a dreadful fashion, as offering irresistible temptations to the schoolmaster to use his cane." *Charles Dickens' Uncollected Writings from Household Words, 1850–1859,* ed. Harry Stone, 2 vols. (Bloomington: Indiana University Press, 1968), 2:413. Compare Alice's magisterial response to the twins' outfits.

1.2 was out of fashion by 1830, when the twins' flat, turned-down collar replaced it. The whole outfit, common during Tenniel's boyhood, was archaic by the time he started drawing *Punch* cartoons—not to mention the pictures for *Through the Looking-Glass.* If the twins, "two fat little men," are about forty years old, they are still wearing the clothes that they knew when they were children. Alice is so struck by their looking "exactly like a couple of great schoolboys"—from the past, as Tenniel drew them—that she immediately takes on the role of schoolmistress, calling out "First Boy!" and "Next Boy!" starting off their relationship on the wrong foot.[5]

A few years before the Gladstone cartoon, Tenniel had shown little John Bull dressed as a schoolboy in Mr. Punch's schoolroom of western nations, where he is being defied by a rambunctious Jonathan (the United States) for having tried to take some toy soldiers (fig. 1.4, from the preface to volume 30, dated 28 June 1856). During the previous months the Pierce administration had sharply cooled its relations with Great Britain, partly because British agents had actively recruited soldiers for the Crimean War in the United States. (Master Bull's Tweedle-twin in the background, wearing the paper hat labeled "BOMBA," is Ferdinand II, King of the Two Sicilies, popularly known as "King Bomba," who had been censured by England and France for committing atrocities against his own subjects. Among other things he had ordered the bombardment of major cities in Sicily—hence the nickname.)

As late as 1882, ten years after *Looking-Glass* was published, Tenniel's young John Bull still looks like a prototype for Tweedledee and Tweedledum (see fig. 1.5, the New Year's cartoon published 7 January 1882, 7). Tenniel's political cartoons were conservative artistically as well as politically; he did not change his stock of imagery much during his long career. The first historian of *Punch,* M. H. Spielmann, noticed that the way Tenniel drew a locomotive hardly changed, even as actual locomotives evolved into more and more modern forms. Tenniel's persistent image of the fat, skeleton-suited schoolboy is another instance. The new, realistic style of black-and-white illustration that emerged in

THE LATEST ARRIVAL.

FIGURE 1.5. Tenniel. "The Latest Arrival." From *Punch,* 7 January 1882.

FIGURE 1.6. Tenniel. Tweedledum and Tweedledee armed for combat. From *Through the Looking-Glass.*

the sixties, inspired in part by the work of J. E. Millais, put great stock in the close observation of concrete detail, usually contemporary, and the conscientious use of models; but after his apprenticeship Tenniel would have nothing to do with models, and relied instead on what he remembered of what he had seen.[6] The result was that his drawings, including his illustrations for the *Alice* books, tended to conserve and renew the imagery of the recent and not-so-recent past. In particular, Tenniel renewed in the *Alice* books imagery that was already established in *Punch.*

When relations between Carroll's Tweedledum and Tweedledee deteriorate to the point where the two have to be armed for battle, Tenniel pictures the scene (fig. 1.6) in a way that not only responds to Carroll's description but also recalls the supposed mock-heroics of the Chartist movement as they were interpreted for *Punch* by John Leech (fig. 1.7; 2 September 1848, 101).[7] The Chartist included in one suit of armor the dish-cover breastplate of Tweedledum and the coal-scuttle helmet of Tweedledee. Tweedledum's own saucepan-helmet closely

6. Spielmann, 471. George du Maurier, another *Punch* artist, commented that Tenniel's *Alice* illustrations "belong to the old school. . . . Perhaps we, of the new school, are too much the slaves of the model." "The Illustrating of Books from the Serious Artist's Point of View: I," *The Magazine of Art* 13 (1890): 351.

7. Though Leech, like Tenniel, did not sign all his work, this cartoon is recognizably his.

Carroll's text specifies much of the detail in Tenniel's illustration: "their arms full of things—such as bolsters, blankets, hearth-rugs, table-cloths, dish-covers, and coal-scuttles"; also the saucepan-helmet. Though the twins strangely enough find these things in a "wood," they are the household items that a Victorian child would most readily convert into armor for war games.

A PHYSICAL FORCE CHARTIST ARMING FOR THE FIGHT.

8. Figure 1.9 is from chapter 18 in the series "Punch's Book of British Costumes," which ran from 4 February to 29 December 1860. Henry Silver wrote the letterpress; Tenniel did the illustrations (Spielmann, 347–48). Tenniel had made a special study of costume when an art student.

From time to time, the series cites the authority of (among others) F. W. Fairholt, who wrote *Costume in England* (London: Chapman & Hall, 1846; 2nd ed., 1860). Several of the illustrations for the *Punch* series are silently copied (with ironic commentary) or adapted from illustrations in Fairholt's history. Figure 1.9 obviously derives from figure 1.10.

9. From about 1839 a member of the Whig party in the United States might be called a "coon" because of the raccoon emblem of the party; Lincoln had been a Whig until the party disintegrated after the 1856 election. There may also be a racist slur implied.

Tenniel was not the sole author of his political cartoons. The basic "idea" for each cartoon was usually invented by the *Punch* editorial staff at their weekly meeting; see Patrick Leary, *The Punch Brotherhood: Table Talk and Print Culture in Mid-Victorian London* (London: The British Library, 2010), 37–43. Tenniel illustrated the ideas of others—for *Punch* as for *Alice*.

resembles the new hat for London bobbies that *Punch* proposed in 1865 (fig. 1.8; 25 February 1865, 81, by an anonymous artist). A few years before that, Tenniel had illustrated the transformation of utensils into helmets, as part of a parody of nineteenth-century researches into the history of costume (fig. 1.9; 9 June 1860—a specific parody of fig. 1.10).[8]

The mild hostility between England and the United States that marked the mid-fifties had worsened a good deal by the early years of the Civil War. When the *USS San Jacinto* stopped the British steamer *Trent* and seized two Confederate envoys, the British responded with threats of war that in the end forced the Lincoln administration to release them (the so-called "Trent affair"). Tenniel depicted the outcome for *Punch* by showing Abraham Lincoln as a raccoon treed by John Bull—who is now his adult self, and an honorary "Colonel" as well (fig. 1.11; 11 January 1862, 15).[9] The vertical relation of the two figures in this cartoon is the same as in the famous illustration, drawn some three years later, of Alice and the Cheshire Cat (fig. 1.12); and the

. HELMETS. TEMP. RICHARD THE FIRST AND JOHN.
4, 5, 6. THE SAME IN THEIR PRIMITIVE SHAPE.
FROM MR. PUNCH'S ARCHÆOLOGICAL MUSEUM.

FIGURE 1.8. Saucepan-hat for London bobby. From *Punch*, 25 February 1865.

FIGURE 1.9. Tenniel. Helmets and utensils; a parody of figure 1.10. From *Punch*, 9 June 1860.

FIGURE 1.10. F. W. Fairholt. Medieval helmets. From *Costume in England* (1846; 2nd ed., 1860).

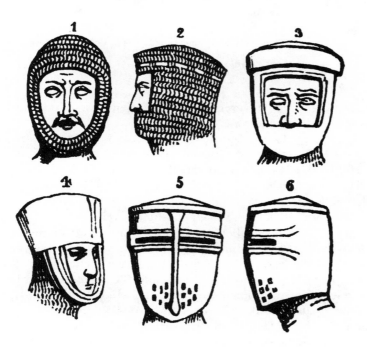

FIGURE 1.11. Tenniel. "'Up a Tree':
Colonel Bull and the Yankee
'Coon." From *Punch,* 11 January
1862.

"UP A TREE."
Colonel Bull and the Yankee 'Coon.
'COON. "AIR YOU IN ARNEST, COLONEL?"
COLONEL BULL. "I AM."
'COON. "DON'T FIRE—I'LL COME DOWN."

perspective is precisely reversed, as is the orientation of the tree branch on which each animal is perched.

Tenniel may have based the design of the Lincoln cartoon on Gillray's rendering of Francis Russell, the duke of Bedford, as a hapless squirrel falling from an aristocratic height into entanglement with the predatory snake Charles James Fox (fig. 1.13). The caricature, originally published in 1795, would have been readily available to Tenniel in a collection of Gillray's work published in 1851.[10]

One of the simpler reflections in the *Alice* books of Tenniel's work for *Punch* is the drawing of Humpty Dumpty addressing the messenger (fig. 1.14). Especially as regards the character on the left, it mirrors Tenniel's contemporary illustration of a giant Grandvillian gooseberry addressing an even more Grandvillian frog (fig. 1.15; 15 July 1871, 15), who in turn anticipates the demeanor of the Frog-Footman in *Alice's Adventures* (fig. 1.16).[11] (The gigantic gooseberry and the background shower of frogs allude to stock "filler" items, reporting supposed wonders of

10. *The Works of James Gillray* (London: Henry G. Bohn, 1851; rpt. New York: Benjamin Blom, 1968), 136. See also Mary Dorothy George, *Catalogue of Political and Personal Satires Preserved in the Department of Prints and Drawings in the British Museum,* vol. 7 (London: British Museum, 1942), 198–99, no. 8684.

11. Mespoulet compares Tenniel's drawing of the Frog-Footman to two drawings by Grandville (44–45).

FIGURE 1.12. Tenniel. Alice and the Cheshire Cat. From *Alice's Adventures in Wonderland.*

FIGURE 1.13. James Gillray. "The Republican Rattle-Snake fascinating the Bedford Squirrel." Engraving. From *The Works of James Gillray* (1851; rpt. 1968).

The Republican Rattle-Snake fascinating the Bedford-Squirrel.

FIGURE 1.14. Tenniel. Humpty
Dumpty and the messenger. From
Through the Looking-Glass.

FIGURE 1.15. Tenniel. "The
Gigantic Gooseberry." From
Punch, 15 July 1871.

THE GIGANTIC GOOSEBERRY.

G. G. "HERE'S A PRECIOUS GO, FROGGY! I THOUGHT BIG GOOSEBERRIES AND SHOWERS O' FROGS UD HAVE A HOLIDAY THIS 'SILLY SEASON,'
ANYHOW. BUT THE PRECIOUS TICHBORNE CASE HAVE BEEN ADJOURNED, AND WE'LL HAVE TO BE ON DUTY AGAIN."

nature, which filled the popular press during the slow summer months, when there was usually a dearth of official news, and which *Punch* never tired of ridiculing.)

Perhaps more subtle reflections would have caught the Victorian reader's eye more immediately. Some early readers may have noticed how Tenniel's White Queen and Red Queen (fig. 1.17) renew the association in *Punch* of Mrs. Gamp and her imaginary friend Mrs. Harris—the besotted pair from *Martin Chuzzlewit*—who served as emblems of the look-alike *Morning Herald* and *Evening Standard* (fig. 1.18, by John Leech; 9 April 1864). Note the crinoline apparatus displaying itself beneath the White Queen's dress, and beneath Mrs. Gamp's. *Punch* waged a relentless war against the vanity and vulgarity of crinolines, then the current fashion.[12] *Punch* also disdained the Pope (Pius IX), and loved to show him effeminate and helpless in crinolines (fig. 1.19, by Tenniel; 20 September 1862, 121). In general posture this Pope is every inch a White Queen (fig. 1.20, drawn nine years later).[13]

That *Punch* thought the Papacy to be a caterpillar on the English landscape can be judged from the conjunction of two more or less irreverent images, figure 1.21, by Tenniel (17 February 1855, 67), and figure 1.22, by Leech (25 January 1851, 35): taken together, they yielded the

12. The joke on the *Morning Herald* and *Evening Standard,* newspapers that were much the same because under the same management, dates back to a series of attacks launched in 1845, including a squib accompanied by a cartoon by Leech, published on 20 December 1845, 262; see Spielmann, 210–13. The crinoline was a later addition, calculated to keep Mrs. Gamp in the rear guard of fashion, and Tenniel perpetuated this detail in cartoons of Mrs. Gamp published 16 July 1864, 11 August 1866, and 22 August 1868.

In figure 1.18, "The Idle Gossips," Mrs. Gamp and Mrs. Harris are complaining of Palmerston's failing health, and looking forward to his replacement as prime minister by either Benjamin Disraeli or the earl of Derby.

13. Pius IX was made uneasy by the prospect of the French emperor, Napoleon III (right), withdrawing his forces from Italy and leaving Rome to the mercy of Victor Emmanuel II (left, trying to remove traces of Garibaldi's recent unsuccessful campaign). In this and many similar cartoons, Tenniel reduces the Pope's triple crown to a mobcap, to go with the crinoline. David Lockwood discusses this cartoon and related illustrations in "Tenniel, Alice and the Pope," *The Carrollian* 11 (2003): 23–30. See also Simpson, 75–88.

FIGURE 1.17. Tenniel. Alice with the White Queen and the Red Queen. From *Through the Looking-Glass*.

FIGURE 1.18. John Leech. "The Idle Gossips." From *Punch*, 9 April 1864.

THE IDLE GOSSIPS.

FIGURE 1.19. Tenniel. "Relieving Guard." From *Punch*, 20 September 1862.

RELIEVING GUARD.

Mrs. Pope. "OH, MR. POLICEMAN, I HOPE YOU AIN'T A-GOIN' TO LEAVE A POOR OLD 'OMAN?"
Mr. Nap. "YES, M'M, I AM—YOU WILL BE QUITE SAFE WITH YOUR FRIEND, VICTOR, YONDER. HE'S A CAPITAL OFFICER."

FIGURE 1.20. Tenniel. The White Queen and Alice. From *Through the Looking-Glass*.

FIGURE 1.21. Tenniel. Nicholas
Cardinal Wiseman. From *Punch*,
17 February 1855.

FIGURE 1.22. John Leech. "The
Pope in His Chair." From *Punch*,
25 January 1851.

THE POPE IN HIS CHAIR.

With Mr. Punch's Compliments to Lady Morgan.

now well-known image of the arrogant Caterpillar savoring his hookah on a toadstool (fig. 1.23).[14]

The hookah was a common motif in the fantasies of the *Punch* staff, which often boasted Arabian or Oriental decor; in one instance it was accompanied by a psychedelic mushroom (fig. 1.24, by H. R. Howard; 20 October 1860, 159).

Even as in the *Alice* books, orality in *Punch* could take more aggressive forms than placid hookah-smoking. A trope shared by both publications, very common in *Punch,* shows animated foodstuffs in danger. The well-known scene of the Walrus and the Carpenter addressing the Oysters (fig. 1.25), for example, is a recasting of Tenniel's cartoon of the English beef admonishing the German sausages under the gaze of

14. Figure 1.22, which represents the pope as a Mohammedan, alludes to an extended controversy about sacred authenticity that involved Nicholas Wiseman and Lady Sydney Morgan, which was renewed in 1850 when he became cardinal archbishop of Westminster. See Brian H. Murray, "The Battle for St. Peter's Chair: Mediating the Materials of Catholic Antiquity in Nineteenth-Century Britain," *Word & Image* 33 (2017): 317–23. Figure 1.21 is Tenniel's caricature of Wiseman, sitting atop his cardinal's red hat.

FIGURE 1.24. H. R. Howard. Mushroom and hookah. From *Punch*, 20 October 1860.

FIGURE 1.25. Tenniel. The Walrus, the Carpenter, and the Oysters. From *Through the Looking-Glass*.

THE ENGLISH BEEF, THE FRENCH WINE, AND THE GERMAN SAUSAGES.

The Beef. " NOW, LOOK HERE, YOU 'SMALL GERMANS,' DON'T JUMP OUT OF THE FRYING-PAN INTO THE FIRE—THAT'S ALL!"

an Oyster shell   A lady's Bonnet

ORIGINAL SKETCH BY MR. PUNCH'S LITTLE BOY.

the French wine (fig. 1.26; 9 January 1864, 15).[15] Oysters had been personified before in a *Punch* drawing, perhaps by Tenniel (fig. 1.27; 10 December 1853, 244). The personified beef and wine look forward, also, to the disturbing dinner-party that concludes *Looking-Glass*, especially to the personified leg of mutton (fig. 1.28), the bottles that turn into birds, and the recalcitrant pudding.

When Alice tries to treat the pudding as just an ordinary pudding, and takes a slice out of it, Carroll has it talk back to her much like the pudding in a cartoon that was probably drawn by Frank Bellew, figure 1.29 (19 January 1861, 30).[16] Tenniel pictures Alice's pudding only

FIGURE 1.26. Tenniel. "The English Beef, the French Wine, and the German Sausages." From *Punch,* 9 January 1864.

FIGURE 1.27. Oyster shell and bonnet. From *Punch,* 10 December 1853.

15. Caption: "THE ENGLISH BEEF, THE FRENCH WINE, AND THE GERMAN SAUSAGES. | THE BEEF. 'Now, look here, you "small Germans," don't jump out of the frying-pan into the fire—that's all!'" The frying pan is labelled "SCHLESWIG and HOLSTEIN."

The Beef is John Bull; the bottle is Napoleon III. Bavaria and the other lesser German states (here the "small Germans"—small German sausages) were at that time opposing, more aggressively than Prussia or Austria, Danish claims on the duchy of Schleswig ("The Schleswig-Holstein Question," *The Times,* 2 January 1864, 10). England here warns them of the dangers of interference.

16. Despite the apparent initials "EB," the flattened triangle was Frank Bellew's hallmark; see Spielmann, 500–01, 573–74 (no. 27). Roger Lancelyn Green notices the cartoon and ascribes it to Edward Bradley in *Lewis Carroll* (London: Bodley Head, 1960), 48; but according to Spielmann, 495, Bradley contributed nothing to *Punch* after 1856.

FIGURE 1.30. Tenniel. End of
the banquet. From *Through the
Looking-Glass*.

17. Caption: "THE DUKE OF CAM-
BRIDGE RECEIVING AN INVITATION TO
A CHARITY DINNER ON HIS BIRTHDAY."
On the table, a stack of papers marked
"INVITATIONS"; beside it, a box marked
"DINNER PILLS." Framed paintings of a
pig and a hare are on the wall. 24 February 1844 was the seventieth birthday
of Adolphus Frederick, duke of Cambridge, a son of George III and uncle
of Queen Victoria. The duke was "most
generous with his time . . . to an almost
incredible number of charitable causes."
Roger Fulford, *Royal Dukes: The Father
and Uncles of Queen Victoria*, 2nd ed.
(London: Collins, 1973), 300. Apparently much of that time was spent ban-
queting, at the expense of the various
foods shown here presenting an invitation inscribed "I. O. U."

18. *The Comic Almanack for 1841* (London: Tilt & Bogue, 1841), facing 41; rpt.
*The Comic Almanac . . . First Series, 1835–
1843* (London: Chatto & Windus, 1912),
facing page 289. For a dozen years,
Punch's Almanack imitated and competed
with Cruikshank's *Comic Almanack*, and
in the end it was the survivor.
Caption: "DECEMBER—'A Swallow at
Christmas' (Rara avis in terris)." Since
swallows are proverbially associated with
summer, "a swallow at Christmas" was a
proverb for rarity—here given a punning interpretation. Note the walking
roast and pudding.

once, as part of the general confusion that ends the banquet (fig. 1.30);
it is easy to miss in the lower left-hand corner, opposite the mutton
(appropriately), upside down, with a look of perplexity appearing on
its face/body.

A prototype for all the *Punch* cartoons cited here (and others, similar) is a drawing by Leech for *Punch's Almanack for 1844* (fig. 1.31, on
the page for February).[17] George Cruikshank had published a drawing
with similar details in his *Comic Almanack for 1841* (fig. 1.32, December).[18] No doubt this tradition of illustration was as influential on Carroll as it was on Tenniel.

THE DUKE OF CAMBRIDGE RECEIVING AN INVITATION TO A CHARITY DINNER ON HIS BIRTHDAY.

FIGURE 1.31. John Leech. "The Duke of Cambridge Receiving an Invitation to a Charity Dinner on His Birthday." From *Punch's Almanack for 1844.*

DECEMBER—"A Swallow at Christmas" (Rara avis in terris)

FIGURE 1.32. George Cruikshank. "December: 'A Swallow at Christmas.'" From *The Comic Almanack for 1841* (rpt. 1912).

19. The cartoon is reprinted and the case identified in John Tenniel, *Cartoons from "Punch"* (London: Bradbury & Evans, n.d.), 82. The ultimate source of the epigram may be "The Benefit of Going to Law," a poetic squib printed by Benjamin Franklin in *Poor Richard's Almanack* (Philadelphia, 1733), 21.

When the Carpenter finally sets to work devouring the Oysters (fig. 1.33), he strikes a pose identical to that of an oyster-eating lawyer in Tenniel's cartoon "Law and Lunacy," drawn almost a decade earlier (fig. 1.34; 25 January 1862, 35). A satire on the way that court costs were consuming the large inheritance of an heir said by his guardian to be insane, the drawing alludes to an old epigram on the injustice of the law in the matter of court costs: "A shell for him, a shell for thee, / The oyster is the lawyer's fee."[19]

This proverb, which associates oysters with the sharp practices of lawyers, occasions a complaint by some high-minded oysters to the

FIGURE 1.33. Tenniel. The Walrus and the Carpenter devouring the Oysters. From *Through the Looking-Glass.*

LAW AND LUNACY :
Or, a Glorious Oyster Season for the Lawyers

FIGURE 1.34. Tenniel. "Law and Lunacy." From *Punch,* 25 January 1862.

reform-minded lord chancellor Lord Bethell, in a doggerel fable in the manner of John Gay's *Fables* (1727), called "Reversing the Proverb." This fable, which was illustrated by Tenniel (fig. 1.35; 4 June 1864, 233) even while he was working on the illustrations for *Alice's Adventures,* probably was noticed by Carroll at the time, and had its echo years later in the pathetic colloquy of the Oysters, the Walrus, and the Carpenter. As Lord Bethell was about to enjoy a luncheon of oysters, ale, bread, and butter,

FIGURE 1.35. Tenniel. "Reversing the Proverb." From *Punch*, 4 June 1864.

REVERSING THE PROVERB.

"The Oyster where it ought to be, | And Shell and Shell the Lawyer's Fee."

An Oyster thus addressed my Lord,
Not in a whistling timid key,
But in a voice well-trained at sea.

    "Ho! Equity's great guard and friend!
Attention and assistance lend."

· ·

    "My Lord," the Oyster said again,
(Edging away from the Cayenne)
"We ask relief, nor singly come,
But in the name of Oysterdom.
Too long, my Lord, a proverb old
Links us with justice missed, or sold,
Too long we've been the ribald type
Of all who'd give the law a wipe,
And now we hold it fitting time
That you should quite reverse the rhyme."

After some discussion Bethell tells the Oyster that he has already accomplished the desired reforms.

"Henceforth the rhyme that carries smart
To my poor Oyster's oozy heart,
Shall in another fashion run,
And thus be passed by sire to son:
'The Oyster where it ought to be,
And shell and shell the lawyer's fee.'"

    Again he smiled, so says the fable,
And drew his chair up near the table,
When all the Oysters, seen and hid,
Cried, "Eat, and welcome." And he did.

FIGURE 1.36. Tenniel. "The Strike. "Hitting Him Hard." From *Punch,* 22 June 1861.

THE STRIKE.—HITTING HIM HARD.

Non-Unionist. "AH, BILL! I WAS AFRAID WHAT *YOUR* UNION WOULD END IN"

So ends "Reversing the Proverb," on much the same note as Carroll's own fable of oysters, pepper, bread, and butter:

"O Oysters," said the Carpenter,
    "You've had a pleasant run!
Shall we be trotting home again?"
    But answer came there none—
And this was scarcely odd, because
    They'd eaten every one.

The Carpenter's hat (figs. 1.25, 1.33) is, of course, the standard paper cap of the mid-Victorian workingman, which Tenniel had occasion to draw many times; for example, figure 1.36 (22 June 1861, 253).[20] Tenniel's habit of drawing carpenters may have determined his choice of that character type when Carroll put the choice to him. (Having at first objected to the Carpenter, Tenniel finally preferred him to either of the two dactylic replacements that Carroll had obligingly offered, "baronet" or "butterfly.")[21]

20. See also 22 October 1853, 169; 6 April 1861, 141; 5 September 1863, 99; and 4 August 1866, 51. For instructions on how to make such a hat out of folded paper see *The Workwoman's Guide,* 2nd ed. (London: Simpkin, Marshall, 1840), 157–58 and plate 19—reproduced by Jeffrey Stern and Edward Wakeling in "The Workwoman's Guide to 'The Working Man's Cap,'" *The Carrollian* 15 (Spring 2005): 15–17.

21. *Lewis Carroll & His Illustrators: Collaborations and Correspondence, 1868,* ed. Morton N. Cohen and Edward Wakeling (Ithaca, NY: Cornell University Press), 170–71.

FIGURE 1.37. Tenniel. Father William doing a headstand. From *Alice's Adventures in Wonderland*.

FIGURE 1.38. Tenniel. Mr. Punch and his family. From *Punch,* 5 July 1856.

As well as the foreground figures in *Alice,* the backgrounds too sometimes derive from *Punch.* Two of the four Tenniel drawings that illustrate the poem "Father William" are landscapes, and both have their prototypes in the magazine. The field in which Father William does his headstand (fig. 1.37) had already served as a resort for Mr. Punch and his family (fig. 1.38, by Tenniel; 5 July 1856; note the hay rakes and pitchforks). When Father William balances an eel on the end of his nose (fig. 1.39), he does so before a background that may perplex the modern reader, but that would have been familiar to anyone who had frequented a riverbank in the middle of the nineteenth century or, failing that, who had read *Punch* or looked at certain lesser nineteenth-century landscape paintings. The structure in the right

FIGURE 1.39. Tenniel. Father William balancing an eel on his nose. From *Alice's Adventures in Wonderland.*

MR. BRIGGS STARTS ON HIS FISHING EXCURSION.

FIGURE 1.40. John Leech. "Mr. Briggs Starts on His Fishing Excursion." From *Punch,* 31 August 1850.

background is an eel weir or set of eel bucks, wicker baskets used to trap eels—a detail appropriate to a scene in which a man balances an eel on his nose. Leech made eel bucks the dominant elements in the design of his cartoon of Mr. Briggs, the sports enthusiast, setting out on a doomed fishing expedition (fig. 1.40; 31 August 1850, 94). Eel weirs are pictured in *Punch* in 1 October 1853, 142, and 23 April 1859, 168, as well; Tenniel himself used one again as a background motif as late as 22 April 1876. William Müller did several paintings and drawings that exploit the picturesque qualities of this rustic architecture, and a painting by Frederick Richard Lee, *Morning in the Meadows* (fig. 1.41), shows this minor genre at its most pleasant.[22]

22. William Müller, *Eel Bucks at Goring, 1843, with Boys Fishing,* reproduced by Walter Shaw Sparrow in *Angling in British Art through Five Centuries: Prints, Pictures, Books* (London: John Lane, The Bodley Head, 1923), facing 116; see also Art UK, artuk.org. For related works see Sparrow, 282; and C. G. E. Bunt, *The Life and Work of William James Müller of Bristol* (Leigh-on-Sea, Eng.: F. Lewis, 1948).

Morning in the Meadows was Lee's diploma painting, given to the Royal Academy in 1869, the year he was elected to membership; see www.racollection.org.uk.

FIGURE 1.41. Frederick Richard Lee. *Morning in the Meadows.* Oil on canvas. Reproduced by permission of the Royal Academy of Arts, London.

FIGURE 1.42. Tenniel. Mr. Punch distributing bound volumes of *Punch.* From *Punch,* 1 July 1853.

FIGURE 1.43. Tenniel. Queen Alice demanding admission. From *Through the Looking-Glass.*

One final background, displayed in figure 1.42 (1 July 1853, title page), may suggest how nearly equivalent *Punch* and *Alice* were for Tenniel. The Romanesque doorway from which Mr. Punch distributes his largesse (bound volumes of *Punch*) is virtually the same door at which Alice demands admission to her royal prerogatives (fig. 1.43). These are not the only Romanesque doorways that Tenniel drew; he had an antiquarian fondness for the style. Still, the resemblance is striking.[23]

And what of Alice herself? What place does she have in *Punch*'s England? She plays essentially the same role there as her usual role in the *Alice* books, that of a pacifist and noninterventionist, patient and polite, slow to return the aggressions of others. At the end of June 1864, when he had read Carroll's manuscript but probably had not yet begun drawing the illustrations for *Alice's Adventures*, Tenniel put Alice in the center of a patriotic *Punch* title page (fig. 1.44; 1 January 1864, title page). Only a few days had passed since Palmerston's cabinet had decided not to intervene against Bismarck in the deteriorating Schleswig-Holstein affair, which had become a war between the German states and Denmark.[24] The decision, which Parliament quickly confirmed, proved Palmerston's earlier vague threats to be empty, but the British press in general greeted it with "relief at having escaped the horrors of war."[25] In this cartoon Tenniel fittingly images that relief in domestic terms. The English cannon stands at the ready, but only to protect the domestic scene; and the British lion is

23. Simpson perceptively compares the two images (68). In 1980 Mavis Batey proposed that the doorway is "clearly" that of the medieval Chapter House at Christ Church, Oxford, which was close by the residences of Alice Liddell and Lewis Carroll. Martin Gardner reiterated this proposal in 2000 (*The Annotated Alice: The Definitive Edition*, ed. Martin Gardner, 3rd ed. [New York: W. W. Norton, 2000], 259), and the doorway is now known locally as "the Queen Alice door" (Charlie Lovett, "Finding Alice's 'Wonderland' in Oxford," *The New York Times*, 13 November 2015; nyti.ms/2jMPlKu). The Chapter House doorway, which dates from the twelfth century, is pictured in *An Inventory of the Historical Monuments in the City of Oxford* (London: H. M. Stationery Office, 1939), 106. The design of that doorway only roughly resembles that shown in Tenniel's *Looking-Glass* illustration, which much more closely resembles the title-page doorway that Tenniel drew for *Punch*.

24. "Denmark and Germany: The Conference," *Hansard's Parliamentary Debates* 176 (27 June 1864): 337–51.

25. Keith A. P. Sandiford, *Great Britain and the Schleswig-Holstein Question, 1848–64: A Study in Diplomacy, Politics, and Public Opinion* (Toronto: University of Toronto Press, 1975), 118.

FIGURE 1.44. Tenniel. Alice figure garlanding the British lion. From *Punch*, 1 January 1864.

FIGURE 1.45. Tenniel. Alice and the Dodo. From *Alice's Adventures in Wonderland*.

BOMBA'S BIG BROTHER.

Emperor of Russia. "THEY SHAN'T TAKE AWAY HIS PLAYTHINGS, THAT THEY SHAN'T."

changed from a ferocious agent of war to a noble household pet, suitable to amuse boys or girls.

   In decorating that militant animal with the garlands of peace, Alice is much more at her ease than she is later in *Alice's Adventures*, when she confronts the officious Do-Do-Dodgson (fig. 1.45). But though her demeanor is thus subtly different in the two images, the figure and the posture are essentially the same. Of course, no reader in the middle of 1864, when this *Punch* frontispiece appeared, could have recognized Alice in this her first appearance. And by the time, a year and a half later, she finally appeared as herself in *Alice's Adventures*, the old image from *Punch* would have slipped from memory. Yet, like the absent-minded White Rabbit, the Victorian reader might well suppose that he already knew who Alice was.

FIGURE 1.47. Tenniel. "Leo" and "Virgo." From *Punch's Almanack for 1865.*

Alice is not the only veteran from *Punch* to appear in figure 1.45: the ape peering out from behind the Dodo shows the same face as the villainous King Bomba, who in figure 1.46 (11 October 1856, 145) seeks the support of Russia after having been censured by England and France.[26]

Conversely, figure 1.44 is not Alice's only appearance in *Punch*. *Punch's Almanack for 1865,* published a year before *Alice's Adventures,* contains a page for July and August on which Alice figures as the astrological sign Virgo, in the form of a statue of the modest and long-suffering Joan of Arc (fig. 1.47). The facial aspect and Pre-Raphaelite hair are virtually the same as in figure 1.48, which shows Alice undergoing one of her early ordeals. A late-summer harvest scene is depicted in the tapestry hanging behind this statue, and Tenniel plays wittily with the frames of these disparate art objects by having the virtual reality of the statue impinge on the virtual reality of the tapestry. The mower closest in the foreground appears amazed to discover, behind a sheaf of wheat, this heroic image of maidenhood. The amazement may be in part the shock of recognition, for this mower and his colleagues look much like the gardeners who painted the Queen's roses red (fig. 1.49), whom Alice protected. Opposite this Virgo stands Leo, the British lion, already seen paired with Alice in the peace cartoon (fig. 1.44). But unlike the mowers in the tapestry, this figure does not put in an appearance in *Alice's Adventures.* When he does appear in *Looking-Glass,* opposite the Unicorn (fig. 1.50), he wears a bemused look, which is called for in the text, and a pair of spectacles, which are not. ("The Lion had joined them . . . he looked very tired and sleepy, and his eyes were half shut.

26. The Russian bear has the spindly legs and military boots that Tenniel regularly gave to Czar Alexander II. The bandaged paw alludes to setbacks suffered in the Crimean War.

FIGURE 1.48. Tenniel. Alice outgrowing the room. From *Alice's Adventures in Wonderland*.

FIGURE 1.49. Tenniel. The gardeners painting the Queen's roses. From *Alice's Adventures in Wonderland*.

FIGURE 1.50. Tenniel. The Lion and the Unicorn. From *Through the Looking-Glass.*

FIGURE 1.51. Tenniel. The British lion and the Scottish unicorn. From *Punch,* 5 February 1853.

'What's this!' he said, blinking lazily at Alice.") The spectacles are an old attribute, dating from 1853 at least (5 February 1853, 57), some twenty years before: in figure 1.51 the English lion protests to a Scottish unicorn that he should not be displaced from the royal arms of the United Kingdom by "an obsolete quadruped calling itself the Lion of Scotland," despite a recent proposal by some Scotsmen. The squib

FIGURE 1.52. Tenniel. "Constantine Pry's Visit to England." From *Punch,* 13 June 1857.

CONSTANTINE PRY'S VISIT TO ENGLAND.

accompanying this drawing is cast in the form of a letter from "The British Lion" to the lord responsible for the royal arms.[27] The tone is one of formal indignation, like that of a typical letter to *The Times;* evidently this lion is at home in his study, so the pair of spectacles is quite in order. A few years later they help in reading a newspaper, no doubt *The Times* (fig. 1.52; 13 June 1857, 237).[28]

It is unlikely that Alice, before or after her visits to Wonderland and through the looking-glass, ever paid much attention to *The Times;* for her standard for a worthwhile book, at least, called for an ample stock of "pictures" and "conversations." *The Times* during this period was long on parliamentary debates and law reports—which involve conversations of a peculiar sort—but it was very short on pictures. This lack was in large part supplied by *Punch,* which, after its salad days of radicalism, settled down to provide a comic and largely visual supplement to the somber and verbal newspaper of record—so that Tenniel gradually became the quasi-official political cartoonist of England. If indeed Alice would not have looked at *The Times,* she might well have looked at *Punch* now and again, not so much for the conversations as for the pictures, in some of which she would have recognized herself and her world, as in a looking-glass.

27. "Outheralding Heraldry," *Punch,* 5 February 1853, 57, responding to "An Heraldic Grievance," *The Times,* 27 January 1853, 8.
28. The Grand Duke Constantine, brother of Czar Alexander II, had paid a perfunctory courtesy visit to Queen Victoria, one "divested of any show or state," on 1 June 1857 (*The Times,* 29 May 1857, 10; 1 June 1857, 9). The surname is taken from the hero of John Poole's farce, *Paul Pry* (1825), who was constantly making a nuisance of himself, and forever saying "I hope I don't intrude."

CHAPTER 2

The Carroll Illustrations

1. *Alice's Adventures under Ground, Being a Facsimile of the Original MS. Book Afterwards Developed into "Alice's Adventures in Wonderland"* (London: Macmillan, 1886); the edition used in this chapter. Selwyn H. Goodacre and Denis Crutch described various editions in "The 'Alice' Manuscript, and Its Facsimiles: An Annotated Hand List," *Jabberwocky* 7 (1978): 89–99. Other editions followed, from Mayflower Books, New York (1980); Pavilion Books, London (1985); Holt, Rinehart & Winston, New York (1985); and The British Library, London (2008, 2014). The British Library has also posted digital images of the manuscript online, at www.bl.uk/onlinegallery/ttp/alice/accessible/introduction.html.

2. Sidney Herbert Williams and Falconer Madan, *A Handbook of the Literature of the Rev. C. L. Dodgson (Lewis Carroll)* (London: Oxford University Press, 1931), 110. This judgment was perpetuated in the two later editions of the *Handbook*, passing muster with two more editors; see *The Lewis Carroll Handbook*, ed. Roger Lancelyn Green (London: Oxford University Press, 1962), 134; further revised by Denis Crutch, *The Lewis Carroll Handbook* (Folkestone, Kent: Dawson-Archon, 1979), 145. Martin Gardner, too, expressed doubt about the connection in his introduction to *Alice's Adventures under Ground* (New York: Dover Publications, 1965), xi. For positive judgments see the following: Gordon N. Ray, *The Illustrator and the Book in England from 1790 to 1914* (New York: The Pierpont Morgan Library, 1976), 117. Edward Hodnett, *Image and Text: Studies in the Illustration of English Literature* (London: Scolar Press, 1982), 175 ("A comparison of the two sets of designs shows too many similarities for them to be unrelated"). Citing the first edition of the present book: Will Brooker, *Alice's Adventures: Lewis Carroll in Popular Culture* (New York: Continuum, 2004), 113–15. David Lockwood, review of Frankie Morris, *Artist of Wonderland*, *The Lewis Carroll Review* 33 (May 2006): 2–10; 5–6. Zoe Jaques and Eugene Giddens, *Lewis Carroll's Alice's Adventures in Wonderland and Through the Looking-Glass: A Publishing History* (Farnham, Eng: Ashgate, 2013), 12.

The first of the many illustrators of Lewis Carroll's *Alice* books was not John Tenniel but Carroll himself. Before he had elaborated his children's story into the fully developed version that was published as *Alice's Adventures in Wonderland*, Carroll prepared a hand-lettered and -illustrated manuscript of an earlier version, titled *Alice's Adventures under Ground*, as a gift for Alice Liddell. It is clear from the first paragraph of this manuscript that the Alice of the story disliked books that lacked pictures: "'What is the use of a book,' thought Alice, 'without pictures or conversations?'" By this logic Carroll's gift book had to have illustrations. Fortunately Carroll, though not a trained nor even skilled draftsman, had done such work before; as a boy he had illustrated several manuscript "magazines" that he had composed to entertain his brothers and sisters.

More than twenty years after Carroll presented his illustrated manuscript to Alice Liddell, he arranged for it to be published in facsimile, and it has been reprinted several times since. In recent decades the manuscript has received much publicity as a treasured possession of the British Library.[1]

It used to be thought that Carroll's illustrations to *Alice's Adventures under Ground* were not an important influence on Tenniel's drawings for *Alice's Adventures in Wonderland*. The opinion of one of Carroll's early bibliographers, Falconer Madan, was influential: "In spite of some inevitable similarities, it may be doubted whether Tenniel derived any ideas directly from this book, though he may have seen it."[2] However, it is very likely that Tenniel did indeed see the Carroll illustrations, and, furthermore, that they helped shape his drawings for the book.

In 1979 a letter of Carroll's was published that sheds some light on the question. Writing to Tom Taylor, the popular dramatist who was on the staff of *Punch*, he raised for the first time the question whether Tenniel could be persuaded to do the illustrations for *Alice's Adventures*. "If he should be willing to undertake them, I would send him the book to look over, not that he should at all follow my pictures, but simply to give him an idea of the sort of thing I want."[3]

The excuse that Carroll gave in this letter for turning to a professional artist was that he could not be bothered to learn the demanding skill of drawing on wood blocks before they were engraved: "I have tried my hand at drawing on the wood, and came to the conclusion that it would take much more time than I can afford, and that the result would not be satisfactory after all." The eminent art critic John Ruskin, his friend and colleague at Christ Church, is said at some point to have discouraged Carroll from trying to draw, recommending that he pursue photography instead: "he had not enough talent to make it worth his while to devote much time to sketching, but every one who saw his photographs admired them."[4] Credit for recommending that Carroll invite Tenniel to do the *Alice* illustrations was later claimed by Robinson Duckworth, who had been present on the fateful boating expedition the afternoon of 4 July 1862, when Carroll improvised the first *Alice* story to entertain Alice Liddell and her two sisters. After Carroll wrote up the story and asked Duckworth for his opinion, "I assured him that, if only he could induce John Tenniel to illustrate it, the book would be perfectly certain of success, and at my instance he sent the MS. to Tenniel, who soon replied in terms of warm admiration, and said that he should feel it a pleasure to provide the illustrations for so delightful a story."[5]

Carroll made the proposal to Tenniel during a visit on 25 January 1864, armed with a letter of introduction from Taylor, who had already "applied" to him on Carroll's behalf. Carroll recorded in his diary that Tenniel "was very friendly, and seemed to think favourably of undertaking the pictures, but must see the book before deciding."[6] On 5 April he added this entry: "Heard from Tenniell [*sic*] that he consents to draw the pictures for 'Alice's Adventures Under Ground.'"[7]

The book that Tenniel would have seen at that time could not have been precisely the same book that Carroll ultimately gave to Alice Liddell on 26 November, for Carroll did not finish the pictures in that manuscript until 13 September (*Diaries*, 5:9).

Either the manuscript that Carroll showed Tenniel that spring was incomplete, with only some illustrations, or else it was a preliminary illustrated version, since lost. (In early 1863 Dodgson had lent to the family of George MacDonald a manuscript version of *Alice's Adventures*; it is not known whether this had any illustrations, or what its relation was to the gift manuscript.) However, Tenniel may have had an opportunity to see the completed gift manuscript when Carroll visited him in October, a month after Carroll finished it and more than a month before he gave it to Alice. During that visit Carroll and Tenniel "discussed the book, and agreed on about 34 pictures," only eight short of the final total. Presumably Carroll had the major say in deciding which narrative moments to illustrate—if his practice in this case was like his typical practice in commissioning illustrations for his later books.[8]

Many years after the fact, Alice Liddell herself recalled that "as a rule Tenniel used Mr. Dodgson's drawings as the basis for his own illustrations."[9] When she sold the manuscript at auction the sales catalogue spoke of "the author's drawings (many of which Sir John Tenniel followed very closely)."[10] This testimony finds support in a comparison of the pictures themselves.

One basis for comparison is the synchronization of picture to narrative. A large proportion of the Carroll illustrations, eighteen of the

3. *Letters*, 1:62 (20 December 1863).

4. Harry Furniss, "Recollections of 'Lewis Carroll,'" *The Strand Magazine* (British edition) 35:205 (January 1908): 48–52; 32, evidently paraphrasing what Carroll once recalled. It is uncertain when Ruskin gave this advice, and whether it pertained to illustrations for *Alice* or just to Carroll's general interest in drawing.

5. Carroll, *Picture Book*, 360.

6. *Lewis Carroll's Diaries: The Private Journals of Charles Lutwidge Dodgson (Lewis Carroll)*, ed. Edward Wakeling, 10 vols. (Luton, Eng.: The Lewis Carroll Society, 1993–2007), 4:271–72.

7. *Diaries*, 4:284. Presumably in the interval Tenniel had seen "the book."

8. *Diaries*, 5:16 (12 October 1864). Hodnett, 173–74, citing the opinion of Morton N. Cohen. The letter from Tenniel to Martin F. Tupper quoted below (chapter 3, note 4), suggests that Tenniel was willing to seek guidance in such matters.

9. "Alice's Recollections of Carrollian Days: As Told to Her Son, Caryl Hargreaves," *The Cornhill Magazine* n.s. 73 (1932): 1–12; 9.

10. *Catalogue of Important Literary, Historical and Geographical Manuscripts, Valuable Printed Books, Autograph Letters, &c.* (London: Sotheby, 1928), 46, lot 319.

FIGURE 2.1. Carroll. Alice in the pool of tears. From *Alice's Adventures under Ground*.

FIGURE 2.2. Tenniel. Alice in the pool of tears. From *Alice's Adventures in Wonderland*.

thirty-eight, illustrate the same or almost the same moment in the story as does a Tenniel illustration. Another nine illustrate moments in the story that are fairly close to ones that Tenniel illustrated. The remaining eleven are unique to the Carroll manuscript; they lack counterparts in the published book.

Altogether, then, some three-quarters of the Carroll illustrations synchronize more or less closely with the Tenniel illustrations. Admittedly this agreement could result just from Carroll's authority over both projects; but that Tenniel actually studied the Carroll illustrations is apparent from some striking resemblances.

For example, the two illustrations that show Alice just after her fall into the pool of tears look very much alike (fig. 2.1 by Carroll; fig. 2.2 by Tenniel). Although Alice's facial expressions differ, neither her posture nor the observer's point of view changes much. What change there

is involves a more closely observed realism of Alice's posture in the water. Despite the text, which describes Alice as "up to her chin in salt water," and also despite the law of gravity, Carroll's Alice floats with much of her body out of the water. But Tenniel's Alice has to exert herself to keep her chin above water, as would realistically be the case—even in salt water.

Other differences between these two images, including the difference in Alice's expression, follow from this basic physical difference. Carroll's Alice lifts her left arm high, in what looks to be as much a gesture of some sort as an athletic maneuver. But in Tenniel's picture the arm is closer to the water, about to stroke it. Tenniel also shows the other arm already engaged in the water; Carroll does not. The face of Carroll's Alice is perfectly composed, but the open mouth of Tenniel's Alice suggests breathlessness and alarm. The moods of the two pictures are quite different. Carroll's drawing is tranquil, even mysterious; Tenniel's approaches closer to panic.

A case can be made against Tenniel's naturalizing of this scene. Although the text justifies his showing Alice sunk deep in the water, nothing that Carroll wrote suggests that her response was a frantic one. (The sole remark that Alice "swam about, trying to find her way out," suggests diligence more than a life-and-death struggle.) Also, Carroll's serene if impossible picture is very attractive. Whichever image one prefers, however, it is obvious that Tenniel took Carroll's into account when he drew his own.

A less complex example is the relation between figures 2.3 and 2.4, Carroll's and Tenniel's renderings of Bill the Lizard being propelled from the chimney by Alice's foot. Tenniel has drawn a much more

FIGURE 2.6. Tenniel. Alice at croquet. From *Alice's Adventures in Wonderland*.

plausible lizard, improved upon Carroll's two chimneys, and added some appropriate smoke. However, the angle of view is almost the same, and so is Bill's posture. It is apparent that Tenniel set out to draw in more accurate detail what Carroll had already drawn.

From early in his career, when he illustrated *Aesop's Fables* (1848), Tenniel gained a reputation for the skillful illustration of animals; he later acknowledged spending much time at the Zoological Gardens in London, making mental notes (not sketches) of how various animals actually looked.[11] This expertise may explain the major difference between Carroll's and Tenniel's drawings of Alice preparing to play croquet (figs. 2.5, 2.6). Carroll's Alice uses an ostrich for a croquet mallet, in keeping with the description given in the manuscript; but Tenniel's Alice holds a flamingo, which accords with a revision that Carroll made in the published text. Ostriches grow up to eight feet tall and weigh up to three hundred pounds—too much for a girl to hold in her arms! The revision is more realistic. If Carroll asked Tenniel to show Alice carrying an ostrich, Tenniel may have asked him to change the text to something more plausible—even as he later persuaded Carroll to drop the wasp-in-a-wig episode from *Through the Looking-Glass* (discussed in chapter 10).

However, aside from the difference in birds, figures 2.5 and 2.6 are alike to an extent that can hardly be accidental. In each picture, in front of a nondescript background, the girl and the bird face each other in profile or close to it; their general orientation in Tenniel's

11. Cosmo Monkhouse, *The Life and Work of Sir John Tenniel, R.I.* (London: The Art Journal Office, 1901), 28. Monkhouse credits Tenniel with some of his biographical information (10).

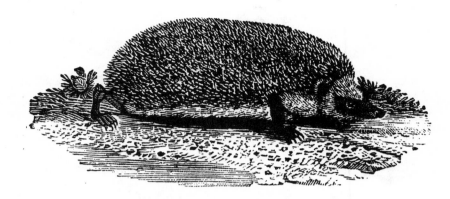

FIGURE 2.7. Thomas Bewick. Hedgehog. Wood engraving. From *A General History of Quadrupeds* (1790; rpt. 1824).

picture mirrors that in Carroll's. The hedgehog does not change its orientation, and hardly changes otherwise. Carroll is known to have borrowed an illustrated book of natural history from the deanery at Christ Church, to improve the accuracy of his drawings.[12] It may have been Thomas Bewick's well-known *General History of Quadrupeds* (1790, often reprinted), which contains illustrations of a jerboa and a guinea pig that approximate animals in one of Carroll's full-page drawings.[13] It also includes a hedgehog illustration (fig. 2.7) that roughly anticipates Carroll's drawing and more closely anticipates Tenniel's (note especially the treatment of the right rear leg). Whether or not Carroll consulted the Bewick cut, Tenniel probably did, or at least one derived from it—besides consulting Carroll's drawing.[14]

Tenniel's drawing of Alice in conversation with the Caterpillar departs considerably from Carroll's (figs. 2.8, 2.9), but it still shows a dependence upon it. Tenniel depicts a slightly later moment, the start of chapter 5 rather than the end of chapter 4, where the Caterpillar was first glimpsed (as Carroll tried—unconvincingly—to show it) "with its arms folded." Tenniel's Caterpillar "at last . . . took the hookah out of its mouth, and addressed her in a languid, sleepy voice"—a moment of increased dramatic interest. Tenniel keeps the general scale of Carroll's drawing and makes only a minor change in the angle of view. That change is the necessary accompaniment to Tenniel's redeployment of the two figures, so that the Caterpillar is viewed almost from behind. By arranging the characters this way Tenniel is able to suggest, in trompe-l'oeil fashion, that the Caterpillar has a human face. The implied mouth, nose and brow arise from actual caterpillar feet seen in silhouette. The result is a mood of personification without the unconvincing explicitness of Carroll's version.[15] On this improved arrangement, Alice, if she is to face the Caterpillar, also must face the viewer, and vice versa; this requires the elevation of the point of view if Alice is not to be hidden entirely by the mushroom. Tenniel's Alice stands as the text describes her, "stretched . . . up on tiptoe," just "peep[ing] over the edge of the mushroom." Her expressive eyes are framed by the edge, and we can see them peering at the Caterpillar—a more striking arrangement than the one in Carroll's picture. Tenniel also improved the hookah—called for by the text—which Carroll had ineptly made into a pipe. In general, Tenniel's view of Alice and the Caterpillar recognizably derives from Carroll's, but it improves the realism and psychological interest of significant details.

Carroll included in *Alice's Adventures under Ground* several full-page drawings, set sideways to the text, which mimic landscape-oriented

12. Stuart Dodgson Collingwood, *The Life and Letters of Lewis Carroll (Rev. C. L. Dodgson)* (London: T. Fisher Unwin, 1899), 96.

13. *Alice's Adventures under Ground*, 44.

14. Two of Tenniel's pencil drawings for figure 2.6 are in the Houghton Library at Harvard, and have been published by Eleanor Garvey and William H. Bond in *Tenniel's Alice* (Cambridge, MA: Houghton Library, 2005), 35. In the earlier of these two drawings, the hedgehog is almost as round as that in Carroll's illustration, figure 2.5; in the later one it is sleeker, more like Bewick's rendition in figure 2.7.

A likely intermediate source is William Harvey's drawing of a hedgehog, closely modeled on Bewick's image, which Dalziel engraved for J. G. Wood, *The Illustrated Natural History* (London: George Routledge, 1853), 82. Tenniel may have resorted to this book more than once in preparing the *Alice* illustrations; see Rose Lovell-Smith, "The Animals of Wonderland: Tenniel as Carroll's Reader," *Criticism* 45 (2003): 383–415.

15. Carroll was impressed with Tenniel's resourcefulness here; he drew attention to the device in commenting on the picture in *The Nursery "Alice"* (London: Macmillan, 1890), 27.

FIGURE 2.8. Carroll. The
Caterpillar and Alice. From *Alice's
Adventures under Ground.*

FIGURE 2.9. Tenniel. The
Caterpillar and Alice. From *Alice's
Adventures in Wonderland.*

FIGURE 2.10. FIGURE 2.10. Carroll. Alice and the Mouse in the pool of tears. From *Alice's Adventures under Ground.*

FIGURE 2.11. Tenniel. Alice and the Mouse in the pool of tears. From *Alice's Adventures in Wonderland.*

plates in a published book. The only full-page illustration in *Alice's Adventures in Wonderland* is the frontispiece—which will receive separate discussion in the next chapter. Several of the *Under Ground* plates synchronize more or less closely with several of Tenniel's drawings; for example, the encounter of Alice with the Mouse in the pool of tears (figs. 2.10, 2.11), and the scene in which Alice grows too big for the little room (figs. 2.12, 2.13). The moments of figures 2.10 and 2.11 are slightly different: in figure 2.10 Alice is just greeting the Mouse, whereas in figure 2.11 their conversation has deteriorated to the point where Alice is talking "half to herself," and the Mouse is on his way out of the scene. Tenniel's drawing captures better than Carroll's the ultimately unsatisfactory nature of this encounter—not to mention the more accurate rendering of the Mouse buoyant in the water—but it copies the disposition of Alice's legs and arms very closely. The ornamental fish that Carroll added, Tenniel left out, perhaps as distracting.

Carroll's full-page illustration of Alice growing too large for the small room (fig. 2.12) has been praised, as compared to Tenniel's version (fig. 2.13), for more powerfully evoking fetal claustrophobia.[16] By placing Alice's foot and head at opposite corners of the picture frame, Carroll suggests that she has completely exhausted the available space—a suggestion absent from the Tenniel illustration, which does

16. William Empson, *Some Versions of Pastoral* (London: Chatto & Windus, 1935), 271; Donald Rackin, "Laughing and Grief: What's So Funny about *Alice in Wonderland?*" in *Lewis Carroll Observed: A Collection of Unpublished Photographs, Drawings, Poetry, and New Essays,* ed. Edward Guiliano (New York: Clarkson N. Potter, 1976), 12.

FIGURE 2.12. Carroll. Alice outgrowing the room. From *Alice's Adventures under Ground*.

FIGURE 2.13. Tenniel. Alice outgrowing the room. From *Alice's Adventures in Wonderland*.

not show her feet. Tenniel shows the actual location of walls, floor, and ceiling; that is a more realistic if less effective approach than Carroll's "naive" substitution of the picture frame for the physical structure of the room. Furthermore, by showing the actual room, Tenniel has occasion to show the window through which Alice thrusts her arm, in a first effort to escape her confinement; the moment here is slightly later than in the Carroll illustration, and the scene of confinement is less absolute. Despite these considerable differences, the basic composition and general proportions of the two pictures are much the same; this similarity is especially obvious if one is viewed in a mirror. Tenniel altered Carroll's drawing considerably, but he did not ignore it.

Carroll drew two consecutive illustrations that show, first, Alice swimming in the water with various birds and other creatures (fig. 2.14), and, then, Alice with one of the birds on the bank, dripping wet (fig. 2.15). Tenniel combined these two illustrations into one that shows Alice and all the creatures as "a queer-looking party . . . assembled on the bank—the birds with draggled feathers, the animals with their fur clinging close to them, and all dripping wet, cross, and uncomfortable" (fig. 2.16). Although it has been said that the picture unfortunately "shows everybody dry," Alice's hair and dress look wet enough, and the

FIGURE 2.14. Carroll. Alice swimming with the creatures. From *Alice's Adventures under Ground.*

FIGURE 2.15. Carroll. Alice and a bird on the bank. From *Alice's Adventures under Ground.*

FIGURE 2.16. Tenniel. Alice with the creatures on the bank. From *Alice's Adventures in Wonderland.*

FIGURE 2.17. Carroll. The creatures fleeing from Alice. From *Alice's Adventures under Ground.*

feathers on the parrot do seem "draggled."[17] Still, some puddles would improve the effect. The two crabs, not to be seen in Carroll's illustration, are included in this one because they have speaking roles later in the chapter.[18] The monkey on the left, the owl in the middle, and the rodent-like animals on the right are all characters that are not mentioned in the text; they come from Carroll's illustration. By moving the group out of the water onto dry land, Tenniel managed to show the creatures to better advantage: he also gave the illustration a motivation and a focus in the Mouse's recitation of English history.

From these examples and others that could be cited, it is clear that Tenniel was respectful of his pictorial source as well as of the text that he was illustrating. He departs selectively from Carroll's prototype, usually in the interests of greater realism. Readers have long approved the way that Tenniel creates a realistic counterpart to the fantastic world that Carroll describes. In a few instances, as has already been remarked, the primitivism of Carroll's drawings hints at subtleties and sophistications more interesting for the modern reader than anything that Tenniel's literalism can express. And Tenniel, needing the space to illustrate the additions that Carroll made to the text of the published version, ignored some of Carroll's drawings, quite possibly on Carroll's own recommendation. One or two of these may be regretted, such as the poignant scene of Alice being left behind by the frightened creatures (fig. 2.17). But these are exceptional cases. By and large Tenniel improved, as he was supposed to do, upon the model presented by Carroll's illustrations for *Alice's Adventures under Ground.*

17. Selwyn H. Goodacre, "Lewis Carroll's 1887 Corrections to *Alice,*" *The Library,* 5th ser., 28 (1973): 131–46; 138.

18. As Lovell-Smith points out (413n36), these crabs were probably modeled on Wenceslas Hollar's full-page engraved illustration for John Ogilby, *The Fables of Aesop Paraphrase'd in Verse* (London, 1665), part 2, facing 20. Two decades later Tenniel would place such crabs in the foreground of his remarkable but previously unremarked cover illustration for *The Official Handbook to the Royal Aquarium and Summer and Winter Garden* (London: Royal Aquarium, 1876).

CHAPTER 3

"Look at the Frontispiece"

"*T*he judge, by the way, was the King; and as he wore his crown over the wig, (look at the frontispiece if you want to see how he did it,) he did not look at all comfortable, and it was certainly not becoming." Some readers, looking at the frontispiece to *Alice's Adventures in Wonderland* (fig. 3.1), have interpreted the King's odd countenance as showing anger at the Knave; but according to the text all that it shows is the King's awkward discomfort under his double burden.

FIGURE 3.1. Tenniel. Trial scene. Frontispiece to *Alice's Adventures in Wonderland.*

The self-absorption of the King contrasts to the other-directed emotion of the Queen beside him, who has a more personal reason to be angry at the Knave, and who shows her anger by glaring at him and crossing her arms defensively.[1]

The Knave, in his disgrace, is relegated to the inferior half of this carefully bisected picture. The smug expression on his face has no textual authority; Carroll does not even establish that the Knave is guilty as charged, let alone that he is unrepentant. The red nose (indicated by hatching in the original black-and-white engraving, and actually colored red in *The Nursery "Alice"*) is not mentioned in the text either. Nonetheless, the red nose does have a textual explanation: the Duchess's cook testifies, under cross-examination, that tarts are made of "pepper, mostly." The pepper-box that she carries with her to the trial makes bystanders sneeze; evidently the pepper tarts had the same effect on the thieving Knave. To be red-nosed in this case is to be red-handed: guilty. It is in keeping with the rest of the Knave's disorderly trial that no one notices this incriminating evidence, as plain as the nose on his face.[2]

The Knave shares the lower half of the picture with two guards, several bird-barristers seated at a table, and an expectant executioner lurking in the background. Carroll does mention two guards, but not any barristers—the King, the Queen, and some jurymen ask all the questions—nor any executioner. Conversely, Tenniel ignores the background details of the scene that Carroll describes at the start of chapter 11:

> The King and Queen of Hearts were seated on their throne when they [Alice and the Gryphon] arrived, with a great crowd assembled about them—all sorts of little birds and beasts, as well as the whole pack of cards: the Knave was standing before them, in chains, with a soldier on each side to guard him; and near the King was the White Rabbit, with a trumpet in one hand, and a scroll of parchment in the other. In the very middle of the court was a table, with a large dish of tarts upon it.

The beginning of this passage better describes Carroll's own illustration of the scene (fig. 3.2) than Tenniel's.

All that is missing from Carroll's illustration are the two guards, who in fact were not mentioned in the briefer manuscript account: "The King and Queen were seated on their throne when they arrived, with a great crowd assembled around them: the Knave was in custody: and before the King stood the white rabbit, with a trumpet in one hand, and a scroll of parchment in the other." Here Carroll did not specify, either, that the "great crowd" includes "all sorts of little birds and beasts"; these creatures appeared for the first time in figure 3.2, Carroll's manuscript illustration—which in turn served as the basis for the amplified description that Carroll finally wrote for *Alice's Adventures*. In illustrating this new scene, Tenniel ignored the crowd altogether. Not only would it have cluttered up the picture, but it would have required space, and space is scarce in this boldly foreshortened picture. Except for the pasteboard body of the Knave and the flat face of the uncomfortably stiff King, the individual characters are plausibly three-dimensional; and yet the total picture space is very shallow. Tenniel most obviously foreshortened the runway or platform on which the White Rabbit is standing; it seems to be hardly as wide as he is.

1. Carroll explains the King's expression even more clearly in *The Nursery "Alice,"* a simplified version for very young children. After suggesting that the reader "look at the big picture, at the beginning of this book," he comments: "The King is very grand, *isn't* he? But he doesn't look very *happy*. I think that big crown, on the top of his wig, must be *very* heavy and uncomfortable" (50).

2. Tenniel colored the illustrations for *The Nursery "Alice"* himself (see chapter 16). In the illustration of the royal procession in the garden (see chapter 6, figure 6.1), which takes place before the trial, the Knave has the same shaded nose—conspicuously red in *The Nursery "Alice."* It can also be seen later in the trial (fig. 3.4). The pepper-tart explanation was suggested to me by Kris Timian. In her review of the first edition of the present book Frankie Morris noted instead that a red nose conventionally signified overindulgence in alcohol; *Jabberwocky* 15 (1986): 45–51; 46.

FIGURE 3.2. Carroll. Trial scene. From *Alice's Adventures under Ground.*

The text of the manuscript version makes no mention of any larger background for the trial, and Carroll's illustration seems to be set indifferently out of doors. But the published text sets the trial in a "court" with a "roof," and the compression that Tenniel brings to the scene befits this indoor setting.

By minimizing depth Tenniel draws attention to the two-dimensional geometry of the picture, which is quartered as neatly as the royal coat of arms on the arras behind the King and Queen. The vanishing point, at the very center of the picture, lies behind the front edge of the royal dais, which marks a bold boundary between the top and bottom halves. In this foreshortened space, the royal couple above and the Knave below seem almost to occupy the same vertical plane.

The basic elements of this composition were present in Carroll's drawing; Tenniel intensified them by suppressing the third dimension (and the crowd with it), and by not letting the top and bottom halves of the scene overlap. He also reversed the positions of the King and Queen, giving a diagonal force to the Queen's baleful glare at the Knave.

FIGURE 3.3. Tenniel. The White Rabbit as herald. From *Alice's Adventures in Wonderland.*

FIGURE 3.4. Tenniel. The Knave on trial. From *Alice's Adventures in Wonderland.*

There is a slight difference in the timing of these two pictures. In Tenniel's version the White Rabbit is reading the accusation (the first half of the nursery rhyme "The Queen of Hearts"). For the manuscript version, Carroll had chosen a less important moment just before, when the White Rabbit gives a preliminary flourish on his trumpet. Tenniel showed that moment too, fixing it in a small but very popular drawing (fig. 3.3). There is no reason in the text why the White Rabbit's trumpet should be so tiny as it is in figures 3.1 and 3.3; it may be that Tenniel was playing a private joke, parodying Carroll's clumsily exaggerated drawing of the trumpet in figure 3.2.

Tenniel supplies a table, as does Carroll, and outfits it with tarts that look more like tarts and less like cupcakes. The birds sitting at the table—three bewigged barristers on the right and at least two on the left (the tops of their wigs barely visible in figure 3.4)—are not called for in the text. They may descend from the bewigged dog and birds in an enigmatic frontispiece by Tenniel's *Punch* colleague Charles H. Bennett, depicting "Man tried at the Court of the Lion for the Ill-treatment of a Horse" (fig. 3.5).

FIGURE 3.5. Charles H. Bennett. "Man tried at the Court of the Lion." Wood engraving by Swain. From *The Fables of Æsop and Others, Translated into Human Nature* (1857).

3. Charles H. Bennett, *The Fables of Æsop and Others, Translated into Human Nature* (London: W. Kent, 1857). Falconer Madan mentioned the "very remarkable and suggestive resemblance" in Williams and Madan, 18. Jeffrey Stern compared the various expressions and postures in a letter to the editor of *Jabberwocky* 7 (1978): 49.

4. Martin F. Tupper, *Proverbial Philosophy* (1854; rpt. London: Thomas Hatchard, n.d.), [64]. Tenniel was one of several illustrators for the book. In *Martin Tupper: His Rise and Fall* (London: Constable, 1949), 160, Derek Hudson remarked that this engraving "is parodied in the comic trial of the Knave of Hearts." Hudson also printed a letter from Tenniel (then aged 32) to Tupper, accepting the commission to do illustrations for the book:

> . . . long ago, when I read the "Proverbial Philosophy" I felt it to be the subject of all others that I should like to illustrate, and I assure you that the feeling is greatly increased on a second reading. . . . As far as I have at present gone in the book *almost every subject suggests a picture,* so that I foresee considerable difficulty as regards selection—should the affair be definitely arranged, perhaps you will kindly assist me, by naming those that you would most wish to be illustrated. (159)

This last comment exemplifies Tenniel's collaborative approach to illustration, discussed in chapters 2 and 10.

5. On title pages, in advertisements, and in a memoir the firm was identified under different names, as "the Brothers Dalziel" and also as "Dalziel Brothers." Macmillan's ads for *Alice's Adventures* in *The Publishers' Circular,* 15 November 1865 (665) and 8 December 1865 (Illustrations 91), credit "Dalziel Brothers."

Other resemblances suggest that Tenniel consulted this engraving: the owl and the King look alike; also the lion and the Queen; and the dog and the Knave.[3] Furthermore, Bennett's picture is organized in the same tight space as Tenniel's, and it too is divided in half horizontally. One of Bennett's barristers has the hooked beak of a bird of prey, as does one of Tenniel's. Tenniel took this joke against the legal profession one step further by making the most prominent of the barristers a veritable parrot of the law. (There may also be another, private joke involved, for in chapters 2 and 3 an eaglet and a lory—that is, parrot—represent Alice Liddell's two sisters, Edith and Lorina.) When Tenniel drew the second illustration of this scene (fig. 3.4), he showed all the barristers nodding, indifferent to the defendant's fate.

The most curious prototype for the *Wonderland* frontispiece is Tenniel's own illustration for Martin Tupper's poem "Of Estimating Character" (fig. 3.6), one of the several that he did for the illustrated edition of Tupper's uplifting *Proverbial Philosophy* (1854).[4] This drawing was engraved by Dalziel Brothers, who later engraved all the *Alice* illustrations.[5]

The passage that this particular engraving illustrates has to do with the murder trial of a man who killed impulsively after repeated

FIGURE 3.6. Tenniel. "Of Estimating Character." Wood engraving by Dalziel Brothers. From Martin F. Tupper, *Proverbial Philosophy: Illustrated* (1854; rpt. n.d.).

OF ESTIMATING
CHARACTER.

RASHLY, nor ofttimes truly,
doth man pass judgment on
his brother;
For he seeth not the springs of
the heart, nor heareth the
reasons of the mind.

insults and provocations. Society ("man") judges this act to be a capital offense; but God ("the Righteous Judge") knows that the deed is less guilty than the conduct of the victim who maliciously provoked it. Tenniel's illustration of this little homily on the deficiency of human justice shows an arrangement much like that of the frontispiece to *Alice's Adventures*, with the judge occupying the upper half of the picture, and the defendant in chains (like the Knave) at the lower left, in right profile, his head held back and his arms held high. The court's evidence of the evil deed rests on a cloth-covered table before him, as in the frontispiece; and an eager executioner loiters on the scene—though not in the background.[6] The young scribe on the judge's left prefigures the White Rabbit. The close, foreshortened space of this scene of judgment is essentially the same as in Tenniel's frontispiece. A major difference is in the demeanor of the defendant, who here pleads for mercy (to an indifferent court), unlike the Knave, who is complacent in his sins. The troubled gaze of the youth shows that he, like Tupper, views the scene with greater misgivings than the rest of the court, and feels an unexpected compassion for death's next victim. Unlike Wonderland, this is not a world where every arbitrary judgment entails an arbitrary pardon.

6. A condemned man in chains, a draped corpse, and an executioner also dominate the left foreground of the cartoon *The Spirit of Justice,* which won Tenniel a premium in the House of Lords competition (1845). See Monkhouse, facing page 12.

CHAPTER 4

The Lineage of the Ugly Duchess

*E*arly in 1920 Christie's, the London auction house, sold a painting of a grotesque old woman which they described as a "Portrait of the Duchess of Carinthia and Tyrol, in jewelled head-dress," and which they attributed to the sixteenth-century Flemish artist Quintin Matsys (fig. 4.1; the name has also been spelled Quinten Massys, among other variants). Later that year the popular *Illustrated London News* devoted a two-page spread to the Duchess and the painting, including a full-page reproduction. The article, by William A. Baillie-Grohman, had the eye-catching headline "The Ugliest Woman in History"; over the illustration was a headline almost as remarkable, at least for readers of *Alice*: "Tenniel's Model for the Duchess in 'Alice': The Ugliest Woman." The paragraph below the illustration repeated this claim: "The portrait has . . . interest as having been the original from which Sir John Tenniel drew the familiar and hideous countenance of the Duchess in his illustrations to 'Alice in Wonderland'" (figs. 4.2, 4.3).[1]

In the article proper, Baillie-Grohman did not mention Tenniel; indeed, he had little to say about the painting, mainly confining himself to the scandalous biography of the supposed subject. Baillie-Grohman was doubly qualified to discuss the portrait, for he was a connoisseur of some prestige, and also a frequent chronicler of "Tyrol and the Tyrolese"—the title that he gave his first book, published forty-five years earlier. In a subsequent book *The Land in the Mountains* (1907), Baillie-Grohman had devoted eight pages to the Duchess Margaret (1318–1369), who was nicknamed "Maultasche"—usually rendered "pocket-mouthed." He commented, with some regret, "Of the truth of the legends relating to the monstrously ill-shaped mouth of Margaret, we have no means of judging, for there is no contemporary portrait of her in existence."[2] In this book Baillie-Grohman noted another explanation for the nickname, according to which it meant a box on the ears—alluding to a family incident with political consequences. And in the *Illustrated London News* article he preferred that explanation.

1. *Catalogue of Pictures of Old Masters, the Property of Miss Seymour . . . Which Will be Sold by Auction by Messrs. Christie, Manson & Woods . . . January 23, 1920,* lot 92. William A. Baillie-Grohman, "The Ugliest Woman in History," *The Illustrated London News,* 25 December 1920, 1080–81.

2. W. A. Baillie-Grohman, *The Land in the Mountains: Being an Account of the Past & Present of Tyrol, Its People and Its Castles* (London: Simpkin, Marshall, Hamilton, Kent, 1907), 78. Baillie-Grohman's main expertise was in the iconography of field sports.

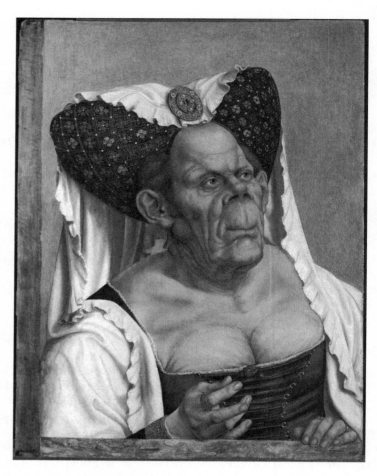

FIGURE 4.1. Quinten Massys. *An Old Woman ("The Ugly Duchess")*. Oil on oak. © National Gallery, London / Art Resource, NY.

FIGURE 4.2. Tenniel. The Duchess. From *Alice's Adventures in Wonderland*.

Nonetheless, in the article he did mention "her fame as the ugliest woman of her day." Presumably the newly found portrait substantiated that reputation—though indirectly, since it was painted over a hundred years after her death.

Baillie-Grohman next wrote a more scholarly article for the art journal *The Burlington Magazine,* in which he discussed the painting itself in some detail. He now emphasized an aspect that had only been mentioned before: the painting closely resembled a drawing in the collection of Windsor Castle that had been attributed to Leonardo (fig. 4.4, eventually deemed a copy). Baillie-Grohman concluded that Tenniel "must . . . have been acquainted with one or the other"—the painting or the drawing—"when he drew his famous Duchess in 'Alice in Wonderland.'" Perhaps Tenniel had seen the painting "in the collection of Alfred Seymour," the father of the woman from whose estate Christie's had sold it.[3]

3. W. A. Baillie-Grohman, "A Portrait of the Ugliest Princess in History," *The Burlington Magazine* 38 (1921): 172–78.

FIGURE 4.4. Francisco Melzi, after Leonardo da Vinci. Head and shoulders of a hideous old woman. Red chalk on paper. Royal Collection Trust / © Her Majesty Queen Elizabeth II 2018.

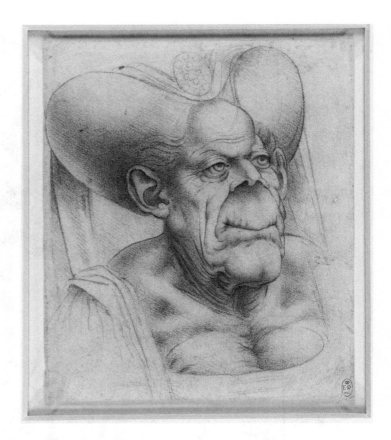

4. Langford Reed, *The Life of Lewis Carroll* (London: W. & G. Foyle, 1932), 45. Lion Feuchtwanger, *The Ugly Duchess, A Historical Romance,* trans. Willa and Edwin Muir (London: M. Secker, 1927). Falconer Madan mentioned the drawing, the painting, and the novel on page 16 of the pamphlet *Supplement* (London: Oxford University Press, 1935) that he issued to Williams and Madan's *Handbook.* There Carroll's "Duchess" became "the Ugly Duchess." See also Empson, 273, 275, 276, and especially 288.

5. *The Lewis Carroll Centenary in London 1932,* ed. Falconer Madan (London: J. & E. Bumpus, 1932), 108a–108b. For more recent historical information about Margaret and relevant illustrations see *Margarete Gräfin von Tirol* (exhibition catalogue), ed. Julia Hörman-Thurn und Taxis (Innsbruck: StudienVerlag, 2007).

6. Florence Becker Lennon, *Victoria through the Looking–Glass: The Life of Lewis Carroll* (New York: Simon and Schuster, 1945), 112.

7. *The Annotated Alice: Alice's Adventures in Wonderland & Through the Looking-Glass,* ed. Martin Gardner (New York: Clarkson N. Potter, 1960), 82; expanded in the 3rd ed., 60.

8. Martin Davies, *Early Netherlandish School,* 2nd ed., National Gallery Catalogues (London: National Gallery, 1955), 70–73, no. 5769. This article is not much enlarged in the third edition (1968), 92–95, to which the following account refers. Davies preferred the spelling "Quinten Massys"; it will be used here except in quotation from other sources. See also Hugh T. Broadley, "The Mature Style of Quinten Massys" (Ph.D. diss., New York University, 1961), 138–40; Andrée de Bosque, *Quinten Metsys* (Brussels: Arcade, 1975), 230; Larry Silver, *The Paintings of Quinten Massys with Catalogue Raisonné* (Montclair, NJ: Allanheld & Schram, 1984), 220–21; and the publications by Lorne Campbell cited in note 13 below.

Eleven years later, in his centennial biography of Carroll, Langford Reed repeated the original claim, without mentioning Leonardo. Opposite a plate reproducing the painting, he remarked, "for his studies of the Duchess [Tenniel] took as his model the famous portrait of the hideous Duchess of Corinthia [sic] and Tyrol, painted about the year 1520 by the Flemish artist, Quentin Metsys." In a footnote he referred to *The Ugly Duchess,* a recent historical novel that Lion Feuchtwanger had based on Margaret's life. First published in Germany as *Die hässliche Herzogin Margarete Maultasch* (1923), the novel appeared in English translation four years later. It was under the influence of its English title *The Ugly Duchess, A Historical Romance* that the Carroll–Tenniel character would gradually come to be known as "the Ugly Duchess." Carroll simply called her "the Duchess."[4] When the painting, still in private hands, was exhibited in London as part of the Lewis Carroll Centenary Exhibition, the catalogue entry, edited by Falconer Madan, described it as "representing an 'Ugly Duchess,'" and paired it with the Windsor drawing as a possible source, while casting doubt on the Feuchtwanger thesis.[5]

Florence Becker Lennon thought the painting a more likely source than the drawing, because Tenniel "uses the detail of costume in that painting."[6] In his popular and influential edition *The Annotated Alice* (1960), Martin Gardner cited the painting only—which he called "the portrait of the *Ugly Duchess.*"[7] Meanwhile, the painting had passed into the collection of the National Gallery, London, where it was catalogued by Martin Davies in 1955.[8]

Davies doubted that Massys himself painted the work (thinking that it was a copy after a painting by Massys now lost), and he rejected the

supposed connection to the Duchess Margaret. Taking up the question whether Tenniel had used the painting as a source, he suggested that besides the painting there are other possibilities just as plausible: (1) other painted versions; (2) the Windsor drawing; (3) an early nineteenth-century engraving after the Windsor drawing; and (4) various seventeenth- and eighteenth-century engravings of a similar subject.

Davies supposed that the lost Massys original had been modeled after the Windsor Castle drawing—or rather after the original of the Windsor Castle drawing, itself judged to be a copy. Massys would have supplied the additional details of costume, most obviously the embroidery in the headdress.

In this respect Davies followed Kenneth Clark, formerly director of the National Gallery, who attributed the Windsor Castle drawing to Francesco Melzi, a pupil of Leonardo's.[9] As regards subject matter, Clark saw no reason to believe that either the drawing or the painting represented the Duchess Margaret. "The tradition to this effect is of no antiquity," he remarked citing by way of contrast a "free engraving" of the picture by the seventeenth-century artist Wenzel Hollar, in which the corresponding figure is identified as the Queen of Tunis (fig. 4.5). Davies, dismissing both alternatives as equally fanciful, simply entitled the painting *A Grotesque Old Woman*, paraphrasing the earliest published reference to the painting, made by Gustav Waagen in 1854, a decade before Tenniel prepared his drawings. ("The great art-critic, Waagen," as Carroll called him in a different context.[10])

Davies doubted a proposal by Erwin Panofsky, according to which the Leonardesque drawing did not represent any actual woman, but rather was a general satire on lascivious old women, in the tradition of Erasmus's *Praise of Folly*. The question of Leonardo's purposes in sketching his many grotesque portraits or caricatures, including others similar to the original of the Windsor Castle drawing, has engaged art historians from Vasari on down to Ernst Gombrich, and is beyond the scope

9. Kenneth Clark, *A Catalogue of the Drawings of Leonardo da Vinci in the Collection of His Majesty the King at Windsor Castle*, 2 vols. (New York: Macmillan, 1935), 1:70–71, no. 12492. Kenneth Clark and Carlo Pedretti, *The Drawings of Leonardo da Vinci in the Collection of Her Majesty the Queen at Windsor Castle*, 2nd ed., 3 vols. (London: Phaidon, 1968), 1:83.

10. Gustav Friedrich Waagen, *Treasures of Art in Great Britain*, 3 vols. (London: John Murray, 1854), 2:243. Waagen had seen the painting in the collection of Henry Danby Seymour during his visit to England in 1850. He reported it as follows:

Quentin Matsys.—A frightful old woman; half-length figure, larger than life, painted with fearful truth in his later brown flesh-tones. Greatly resembling a caricature of a similar kind drawn by Leonardo da Vinci.

For Carroll's remark see *The Russian Journal and Other Selections from the Works of Lewis Carroll*, ed. John Francis McDermott (1935; rpt. New York: Dover Publications, 1977), 78.

of this discussion.[11] Massys's intentions for his painting likewise remain uncertain.

In 1989 J. Dequeker proposed that both the Massys painting and the Leonardo drawing accurately represented visible symptoms associated with Paget's disease of bone, *osteitis deformans,* which was not identified as such until the nineteenth century.[12] Lorne Campbell, Martin Davies's successor at the National Gallery, accepted that diagnosis in his recent reanalysis of the painting—which he now titles, with a parenthetical bow to tradition, *An Old Woman ("The Ugly Duchess").*[13] Campbell also strengthened the attribution of the painting to Massys, despite Davies's doubts, citing details of underpainting now revealed by infrared reflectography, the provenance of part of the oak panel on which it was painted, characteristic subtleties of the brushwork, and a companion portrait of a man, also attributed to Massys.

As regards the Duchess in *Alice's Adventures,* acknowledged to be in some respect a "copy," Campbell is no more specific than Davies: "it has not been possible to discover whether Tenniel had seen" the painting now in the National Gallery "or whether he worked from one of the copies," of which there were several, "or from one of the Leonardesque drawings, or from John Chamberlaine's engraving of the Windsor drawing" (an eighteenth-century publication).

Of these possibilities not all seem equally probable. The several painted copies were housed abroad, in France. Many of the relevant drawings and engravings lack the detailed treatment of the headdress (cruciform floral embroidery) that characterizes both the painting and Tenniel's two illustrations. It was on this ground that Lennon favored the London painting as a likely source, rather than the Windsor drawing. A similar point can be made about the treatment of the woman's hair. In the Windsor drawing and its copies, the hair at the temples is wispy; but in the painting it has a wave; and in the Tenniel illustrations it has been obviously crimped. Tenniel elaborated a hint of vanity from the painting that is not in any of the versions of the Windsor drawing. The Hollar engraving (fig. 4.5) is in the tradition of the painting, not the drawing; the headdress is embroidered, and the treatment of the hands also conforms to that of the painting. But in size and in detail the headdress is emphasized less in the engraving than in the painting, which makes it a less likely source for Tenniel.

In her monograph on Massys, Andrée de Bosque reproduces two French engravings of the painting (or paintings), one engraved by Gilles-Antoine Demarteau (1750–1802) and the other by Ephraïm Conquy (1809–1843). The first identifies the sitter as "Marguerite surnommée Maltasche." This tradition of identification, which probably influenced the cataloguer for the Christie's sale, was apparently French; and as early as 1879 a French connoisseur dissented from it.[14] Of the two engravings, the Demarteau is closer both to the National Gallery painting and to the Tenniel illustration, especially as regards the embroidery of the headdress (fig. 4.6). Demarteau copies the cruciform embroidery flowers displayed in the painting, which Tenniel registers but renders more abstractly as a quatrefoil pattern. Assuming that Tenniel had access to a copy of the engraving, it could have served him for a model as well as the painting.

The question remains whether Tenniel might have had access to the painting itself. Lennon follows Baillie-Grohman in suggesting that Tenniel saw it in the collection of Alfred Seymour; but according to Davies,

11. Erwin Panofsky, *Early Netherlandish Painting: Its Origins and Character,* The Charles Eliot Norton Lectures, 1947–1948, 2 vols. (Cambridge, MA: Harvard University Press, 1953), 1:356. Ernst Gombrich, "Leonardo's Grotesque Heads," *Leonardo: Saggi e ricerche* (Rome: Instituto Poligrafico dello Stato, 1954), 199–219.

12. J. Dequeker, "Paget's Disease in a Painting by Quinten Metsys (Massys)," *BMJ: British Medical Journal* 299 (1989): 1579–81.

13. Lorne Campbell, *The Sixteenth Century Netherlandish Paintings with French Paintings before 1600,* 2 vols. (London: National Gallery, 2014), 2:446–63. See also the catalogue entry in Lorne Campbell et al., *Renaissance Faces: Van Eyck to Titian* (London: National Gallery, 2008), 228–31.

14. "Champfleury" (Jules Fleury-Husson), "Anatomie du laid, d'après Léonard de Vinci," *Gazette des Beaux-Arts,* ser. 2, 19 (1879): 190–202; 198–99.

FIGURE 4.6. Gilles-Antoine Demarteau. "Marguerite surnommée Maltasche." Etching. Circa 1787. Bibliothèque nationale de France.

Marguerite surnommée Maltasche, c'est-à-dire, Gueule de Sac étoit fille de Henri X.ᵉ du nom Duc de Carinthie, Comte de Tirol ensuite Roi de Bohême mort en 1331. et d'Anne fille de Wenceslas IV surnommé le Bon Roi de Bohême. Elle naquit en 1300 et après la mort de son Pere, ayant eu en partage le Comté de Tirol, elle epousa en premieres noces en 1329 Jean Henri Duc de Moravie frere de l'Empereur Charles IV. dont elle se sépara en 1341. L'année suivante 1342 elle epousa en secondes noces Louis fils de l'Empereur Louis de Baviere qui mourut en 1361. De son second mariage elle n'eut qu'un fils nommé Maynard IV dernier Comte de Tirol né en 1344 et qui epousa à 14 ans Marguerite fille de l'Empereur Albert II dont il n'eut point d'enfans. Maynard IV étant mort en 1363, Marguerite Maltasche sa mere céda l'année suivante 1364 le Comté de Tirol à la Maison d'Autriche. Elle mourut en 1366.

Alfred did not inherit it from his brother, Henry Danby Seymour, until 1877. Waagen reported having seen it in the older brother's collection in London in 1850. Might Tenniel have seen it there some fifteen years later?

There is a possible connection. Henry Danby Seymour, like Dodgson, studied at Christ Church, Oxford. He graduated in 1842, eight years before Dodgson matriculated, so they were not contemporaries.[15] But a classmate of Seymour's, John Ruskin, became acquainted with Carroll in the late fifties, both still having rooms in Christ Church. And there are records from the seventies of Ruskin's advising Carroll on illustrating his later books.

During their undergraduate years, Ruskin and Seymour socialized often.[16] Given the young Ruskin's interest in painting, it is likely that he knew Seymour's respectable collection. There is no record of contact between Seymour and Ruskin (let alone Carroll) in the sixties, but Seymour's standing as a member of parliament would not have made such contact unlikely.

15. Joseph Foster, *Alumni Oxonienses,* later series, 4 vols. (Oxford: James Parker, 1888–91), 4:1277.

16. *The Ruskin Family Letters,* ed. Van Akin Burd, 2 vols. (Ithaca: Cornell University Press, 1973); see index.

17. Lionel Cust, "Notes on Pictures in the Royal Collections—XXIII: *The Misers* at Windsor Castle Attributed to Quentin Matsys," *The Burlington Magazine* 20 (1912): 252–53, 256–58. "Quintin Messys, or Matsys," *The Penny Magazine,* 28 December 1833, 497–98. "Observations on Painting," *The Gentleman's Magazine* n.s. 9 (1838): 244–46; 245–46. J. Dixon, "'The Misers' of Quentin Matsys," *Notes and Queries,* 21 January 1860, 55.

18. *The Visitants' Guide to Windsor Castle and its Vicinity,* 4th ed. (Windsor, Eng.: C. Andrews, 1828), 77.

19. According to Monkhouse, Tenniel told him that he had been "very much interested in costume and armour, and studied them in the reading room and print room of the British Museum, where he laid the foundation of that knowledge of both, which has been of such great advantage to him as the cartoonist of *Punch*" (10).

20. Fig. 4.7: 24 January 1852, 42. Fig. 4.8: 26 July 1856, 39. Fig. 4.9: 3 November 1860, 178. The prototype for fig. 4.9 is the monumental effigy of Beatrice, Countess of Arundel (d. 1439), in the church at Arundel. Drawings of the head and headdress appear in the anonymous *History of British Costume* (London: Charles Knight, 1834), 189, and Fairholt's *Costume,* 182. Both derive from plate 105 in C. A. Stothard, *The Monumental Effigies of Great Britain* (London: privately printed, 1817), which may be Tenniel's immediate source. Both the anonymous historian and Fairholt emphasize how "ugly" the style was. A photograph of the effigy appears in Arthur Gardner's *Alabaster Tombs of the Pre-Reformation Period in England* (Cambridge: Cambridge University Press, 1940), fig. 188. "The countess wears the most marvellous spreading head-dress . . . some 22 in. across" (59).

Massys had a certain popularity in mid-Victorian England. A painting known as *The Misers* was a prized and well-publicized painting in the royal collection at Windsor Castle. Although described in the seventeenth century as "a copy after Quintin," in the nineteenth century it was widely discussed—even in popular journals—as a work by Matsys himself.[17] Early in the nineteenth century a Windsor guide book reported that it was "one of the most noted paintings in the royal collection at the Castle, a reputation it has acquired in part from its merits as a work of art, which are unquestionably great as to design and colouring, and partly from the romantic tale connected with it."[18]

According to that tale, Matsys, originally a mere blacksmith, had courted the daughter of a painter, who withheld consent to their marriage until Matsys had demonstrated, by producing an impressive painting, that he was qualified to join the more elevated artistic fraternity. The Austrian novelist Caroline Pichler had embroidered this tale in a novella that was published in translation by James Burns (London) as *Quentin Matsys; or, The Blacksmith* (1845). (In her version of the story the painting was an Annunciation.) That same year Burns published Fouqué's *Undine,* which Tenniel illustrated with eleven designs; Tenniel probably knew of the Matsys book, if indeed he did not design the (anonymous) frontispiece for it.

The overlapping associations of Seymour, Ruskin, Carroll, and Tenniel may have resulted in Tenniel's consulting Seymour's painting, created by an artist who was publicized by Tenniel's early publisher James Burns—a painting by different traditions supposed to represent either "a frightful old woman" (Waagen's phrase) or a particular ugly duchess—as a detailed model for his own Duchess, who is described in the text simply as being "*very* ugly" (132). The most likely alternative source is the Demarteau engraving. Whichever the source was, Tenniel may have alluded to the tradition of the ugly duchess Margaret Maultasche.

Of course, Tenniel mitigates the grotesqueness of the tradition. He replaces the emblematic rose in the Duchess's hand with a sprawling baby, who covers up any immodest neckline. Carroll would have disliked the sexual satire of the Massys painting, and Tenniel managed to make little of it. Instead, he drew attention to the Duchess's remarkable headdress.

In his apprenticeship years, Tenniel closely studied medieval costume, and that interest enlivened many of the minor drawings that he produced during his early years on the staff of *Punch*.[19] Especially at the start Tenniel did many ornamental initials, a neo-medieval form of illustration that invited the use of medieval motifs. Two of these initials use elaborate women's headdresses to shape the capital letter *M* (figs. 4.7, 4.8). When Tenniel illustrated, and perhaps wrote, the series called "Punch's Book of British Costumes," which ran in 1860, he used the same ornamental device (fig. 4.9). This drawing carries a joke caption, but the drawing itself hardly exaggerates its prototype, a fifteenth-century monumental effigy.[20] Contemporary writers had ridiculed the extravagance of such headdresses, and nineteenth-century historians renewed the ridicule. The author of this chapter in the *Punch* series refers to old jokes about them, "mostly far too coarse to quote"—probably about horns and cuckoldry.

FIGURE 4.7. Tenniel. Woman in medieval headdress. From *Punch*, 24 January 1852.

FIGURE 4.8. Tenniel. Woman in medieval headdress. From *Punch*, 28 July 1856.

FIGURE 4.9. Tenniel. Woman in medieval headdress. From *Punch*, 3 November 1860.

FIGURE 4.10. F. W. Fairholt. Misericord: woman in medieval headdress. Wood engraving by Fairholt. From Thomas Wright, *A History of Caricature & Grotesque in Literature and Art* (1865).

21. Thomas Wright, *A History of Caricature & Grotesque in Literature and Art* (London: Virtue Brothers, 1865), 102. (Published in January 1865, according to *The Publishers' Circular*, a few copies have "1864" on the title page.) *The Art-Journal*, n.s., 2 (1863): 143. A photograph of the misericord appears in Francis Bond, *Wood Carvings in English Churches: Misericords* (London: Oxford University Press, 1910), 180.

In his *History of Caricature & Grotesque in Literature and Art,* chapters of which first appeared in the prestigious *Art-Journal,* the antiquarian Thomas Wright cited one such headdress as typifying the extravagance of late medieval costume. The record of this headdress was a fifteenth-century misericord from Shropshire, which Wright reproduced as drawn and engraved by F. W. Fairholt (fig. 4.10).[21] Panofsky later used this illustration to document the satirical tradition in which he would place the Massys painting. Possibly the Fairholt engraving has a more direct relation to Tenniel's Duchess. In the frontal aspect of the face, and certain details of the nose and chin, it more closely resembles Tenniel's Duchess than the Massys portrait does. Given its venues and subject matter, Tenniel would almost certainly have seen, perhaps owned, a copy of Wright's work. It is likely that Tenniel's ugly Duchess reflects aspects of both the Massys painting (perhaps mediated by Demarteau) and the Fairholt engraving.

CHAPTER 5

Sign of Madness

Shakespeare to Tenniel

1. Lewis Carroll, *The Nursery "Alice"* (London: Macmillan, 1890), 37–38. The past-tense verbs suggest that Carroll thinks of the sign as operating *within* the world of the fiction, as well as—or before—operating on the reader. That is, the other characters in the story could know, thanks to the straw on his head, that the March Hare was mad.

Tenniel adapted the colored illustration of the tea-party in *The Nursery "Alice"* from the original black-and-white wood engraving that the Dalziel Brothers prepared after his design. Tenniel's other drawing of the March Hare, near the end of the tea-party chapter in *Alice's Adventures,* shows the same view of his head with every straw in place.

*T*he Nursery *"Alice"* (1890), which Lewis Carroll wrote specifically for "Children aged from Nought to Five," is not only simpler in its plot and language than *Alice's Adventures in Wonderland* (1866), on which it is based; it also emphasizes the illustrations more. They are enlarged, even more than the pages are, and colored; furthermore, Carroll repeatedly draws attention to them in the text. Occasionally he glosses some detail of illustration that he thinks might be difficult for young readers, as when he comments on Tenniel's depiction of the March Hare at the mad tea-party (fig. 5.1): "That's the March Hare, with the long ears, and straws mixed up with his hair. The straws showed he was mad—I don't know why."[1] This chapter will con-

FIGURE 5.1. Tenniel. March Hare at tea-party. From *Alice's Adventures in Wonderland.*

MANIAC MARCH HARES.

FIGURE 5.2. "Maniac March Hares." From *Punch's Almanack for 1842*.

firm Carroll's observation that the straws showed that the March Hare was mad (many readers miss this point), and it will also review some of the history of this signification.

The straw was probably Tenniel's idea, not Carroll's, even though Tenniel drew all the illustrations for *Alice* on commission from Carroll and under his supervision. The device had served as a conventional sign of madness in many illustrations drawn for *Punch* before and during Tenniel's employment on the art staff there; indeed, Tenniel had drawn quite a few of these illustrations himself. The use of this detail in the mad tea-party illustration was probably a conventional embellishment by the artist.[2]

The first of the many *Punch* drawings to use the sign, possibly drawn by H. G. Hine or Hablot Browne, appeared in the first of the series of "almanacks" that *Punch* published, the one for 1842—eight years before Tenniel joined the staff. At the top of the page devoted to March is a drawing titled "Maniac March Hares" (fig. 5.2). The hare in the center, wearing a dress, is strewing flowers from the basket held in her right hand; and she is crowned with wisps of straw.

The general mad-hare motif for March is introduced by the *Almanack* entry for the last day of February, on the previous page: "HARE-HUNTING ENDS, and Hares run mad for joy." (A euphemistic account of the rutting season.) *Almanack* entries for other days in March continue the theme; for example, 7 March, "The Society for the Prevention of Cruelty to Animals proposes to erect a Lunatic Asylum for insane hares." Lewis Carroll was only ten years old when this *Almanack* was published; given his interest in comic magazines, it may be that he came across it later, and that the personified maniac March hares there contributed to his mad tea-party.

The central hare in the illustration—a madwoman strewing flowers and crowned with weeds—recalls the best-known madwoman in English literature. When Ophelia strews rosemary, fennel, columbines, and rue there is no mention in the text that she is crowned with wild plants (*Hamlet* IV.v), but Gertrude later describes her, at the time of her death, as carrying "fantastic garlands" and "coronet weeds" (IV.vii). Hence Nicholas Rowe's influential stage direction for the earlier mad scene: "Enter Ophelia, fantastically drest with Straws and Flowers" (1709; perpetuated by later editors). Benjamin West, in the scene he painted for

2. Simpson (145–52) touches on this aspect, citing some of the images discussed below.

FIGURE 5.3. Benjamin West. "*Hamlet*. Act IV. Scene V." Engraving by Francis Legat (detail). From *A Collection of Prints, from Pictures Painted for the Purpose of Illustrating the Dramatic Works of Shakespeare by the Artists of Great Britain* (1803 [1805]). Boston Public Library.

John Boydell's Shakespeare Gallery, took care to include a few wisps of straw in Ophelia's hair (figure 5.3, a detail of the engraving after West by Francis Legat).[3] The second *Punch* illustration to be considered here was done by Tenniel himself—it bears his monogram—within a year or so of his joining the *Punch* staff. It is an initial letter *C*, which introduces a letter supposedly written by "An English Dramatist" who specialized in aping contemporary French theatrical fashions. (By his own account, the opening of one of his plays coincided with the irreparable cracking of "the statue of SHAKESPEARE over Drury Lane portico.") He proposes a crazy scheme of simultaneous translation in which the French text of a play would be spoken aloud by the prompter, and translated into English by the actors on stage (31 May 1851, 223).

The Tenniel illustration that introduces this nonsense shows an old man in a dressing gown and slippers, riding an umbrella for a hobby-horse, crowned with straw, and holding a clutch of straws for a scepter (fig. 5.4). The hints of royal regalia, the offhand dress, the man's grizzled old age, and his distracted yet dignified air suggest a version of King Lear, especially next to a paragraph that mentions Shakespeare. This particular image evidently derives from figure 5.5, a portrait engraving of Lear "after a study by Sir Joshua Reynolds," which appeared in Charles Knight's *Pictorial Edition of the Works of Shakspere* (1839–43, often reprinted). There may also be an element or two borrowed from the James Barry illustration for Boydell's Shakespeare Gallery.[4] These earlier images of Lear lack both the crown of straw and the scepter supplied by Tenniel; and when Cordelia describes the mad Lear she does not mention any scepter; but her account of Lear's crown is famous:

> Crown'd with rank fumiter, and furrow weeds,
> With bardocks, hemlock, nettles, cuckoo-flowers,
> Darnel, and all the idle weeds that grow
> In our sustaining corn. (IV.iv)

3. John Boydell, *A Collection of Prints, from Pictures Painted for the Purpose of Illustrating the Dramatic Works of Shakespeare*, 2 vols. (London, 1803), 2: plate 45 (detail).

4. *Pictorial Edition of the Works of Shakspere*, ed. Charles Knight, 8 vols. (London, n.d.), 1:464. Boydell, *Collection of Prints*, 2: plate 40.

FIGURE 5.4. Tenniel. King Lear. From *Punch,* 31 May 1851.

FIGURE 5.5. Joshua Reynolds. King Lear. Wood engraving attributed to Stephen Sly. From *Pictorial Edition of the Works of Shakspere,* ed. Charles Knight (c. 1840).

FIGURE 5.6. Tenniel. "Poor TOM's a-cold." From *Punch*, 13 October 1855.

Evidently in theatrical performance this crown might be made entirely of straw; David Garrick, at least, seems to have worn a "crown of straw." And a stage convention before Garrick's time gave the actor playing Lear a "straw scepter." As a young man, Tenniel frequented the London theaters, accompanied by his sketchbook; he probably knew such conventions at first hand.[5] In any case figure 5.4 does caricature Shakespeare's King Lear, even as it looks forward to Carroll's March Hare.

Four years later Tenniel produced several dozen cartoons for *Punch* under the general title "Punch's Illustrations to Shakespeare." The cartoons are unsigned, like much of Tenniel's early work for *Punch*; but the style obviously continues from the signed work of 1850 and 1851.[6] This series, which during its run appeared almost every week, satirized the persistent vogue for pious illustrations of brief excerpts from Shakespeare's plays. Instead of ornamenting the text in the usual manner, Tenniel's illustrations subvert it by playing on some punning sense. The gag for each cartoon may have been concocted by the *Punch* editorial staff, even as they later supplied Tenniel with the ideas for his political cartoons. It is also possible, given Tenniel's early familiarity with the theater, that he framed the puns himself.

Tenniel's only illustration for *King Lear* in this series glosses a remark made by Edgar while impersonating the mad Tom o' Bedlam: "Poor Tom's a-cold." Construing this to mean not that Tom is cold but that he *has* a cold, Tenniel shows a madman (crowned in straw, with a straw-wrapped staff near at hand) trying to cure his cold in a crazy fashion (fig. 5.6; 13 October 1855, 150). The gruel and hot water are conven-

5. Frederick Hawkins, "*Lear on the Stage*," *The English Illustrated Magazine* 10 (1892–93): 161. Marvin Rosenberg, *The Masks of King Lear* (Berkeley: University of California Press, 1972), 267. Jacqueline Knight, "The Theatre of John Tenniel," *Theatre Arts Monthly* 12 (1928): 111–18.

6. Forrest Reid credits the "Illustrations to Shakespeare" to Tenniel in *Illustrators of the Eighteen Sixties* (1928; rpt. New York: Dover Publications, 1975), 27.

FIGURE 5.7. Tenniel. "There's
fennel for you, and columbines."
From *Punch,* 17 November 1855.

7. John Bright as a mad jackass
crowned with straw: *Punch,* 26 February
1853, 85. A cabdriver in a madhouse: 6
August 1853, 53. Big Ben "cracked": 15
October 1859, 154. Fig. 5.89: 4 March
1854, 93. Nicholas I as a mad dog: 11
March 1854, 100. For theatrical associations and two more illustrations, see 24
June 1843, 254; and 19 April 1845, 172.

8. Edward Geoffrey O'Donoghue,
*The Story of Bethlehem Hospital from Its
Foundation in 1247* (London: T. Fisher
Unwin, 1914), 257 (Fox—"The Incur-
able," erroneously attributed to Gillray);
284 (Burke). Frederic George Stephens
and M. Dorothy George, *Catalogue of
Political and Personal Satires,* 12 vols.
(London: The British Museum, 1938),
6:81, no. 6495; 7:52, no. 8367.

9. W. Harrison Ainsworth, *Jack Sheppard* (1839; rpt. London: George Routledge & Sons, 1854), facing page 214.

tional treatments, but applied unconventionally. Presumably Tom rubs
a candle against his sinuses because he remembers but misunderstands
a snatch from the old ballad "Waly, Waly," on the subject of "love": "But
when 'tis auld it *waxeth cauld,* / And fades awa' like morning dew."

Hamlet provided two texts for Tenniel's "Illustrations," one of them
being a line from Ophelia's mad scene, "There's fennel for you, and
columbines." Tenniel's mad Ophelia has herbs in her hand and ferns
in the folds of her gown—not to mention straw in her hair (fig. 5.7;
17 November 1855, 204). But instead of passing out the herbs when
she says this line, she gestures with them toward the scene she is commenting upon; and what she points out are three dancers from English
pantomime, each impersonating the inamorata Columbine; they are
busy flattering Claudius. (As early Shakespearean commentators had
pointed out, fennel was a traditional emblem of flattery.)

Shakespeare did not invent all the madmen caricatured in *Punch*;
the weekly news turned up others. John Leech and other staff cartoon-
ists showed the likes of the pacifist John Bright, striking cabdrivers, and
even the newly "cracked" Big Ben (the great bell of the Palace of Westminster) as crowned with straw. Figure 5.8 is one of two Tenniel cartoons showing Czar Nicholas I as insane at the time of the Crimean
War. In the other he is shown as a mad dog. Both use the straw device.[7]

That device was a standard weapon in political caricature well before
the founding of *Punch* in 1841. Rowlandson had applied it to both Fox
and Burke, associating it with "Bedlam" (Bethlehem Hospital), where
pallets stuffed with straw supplied the mad with ornamental material.[8]
When George Cruikshank drew an engraving, "Jack Sheppard visits his
Mother in Bedlam," for W. Harrison Ainsworth's popular novel *Jack
Sheppard* (1839), he followed tradition by putting her on a bed of straw,
with straw on her head (fig. 5.9).[9] "Cowering in a corner upon a heap

FIGURE 5.8. Tenniel. Czar Nicholas I. From *Punch,* 4 March 1854.

of straw, sat his unfortunate mother. . . . Her head had been shaved, and around it was swathed a piece of rag, in which a few straws were stuck" (214). A letter from Cruikshank to Ainsworth indicates that this passage—like much of Ainsworth's fiction—was composed under Cruikshank's direction: "For fear you might not recollect the attire of Jack's Mother I will just state that her head which is *shaved* is bound round with a *rag* in which some straws are stuck for ornament."[10]

The straw device seems to have lost currency not long after Tenniel drew illustrations for *Alice's Adventures.* I don't know that any examples can be found in *Punch* after 1870. When other artists illustrated *Alice's Adventures* on the expiration of the copyright in 1907, some followed Tenniel's prototype illustrations closely enough to retain the straw device for the March Hare; but a sampling suggests that most did not. Arthur Rackham is one well-known artist who omitted the straw; he may have thought that the sign had become obsolete, or possibly he did not know that it *was* a sign.

10. Quoted by J. R. Harvey, *Victorian Novelists and Their Illustrators* (New York: New York University Press, 1971), 37.

FIGURE 5.9. George Cruikshank. "Jack Sheppard visits his Mother in Bedlam." Etching. From W. Harrison Ainsworth, *Jack Sheppard* (1839; rpt. 1854).

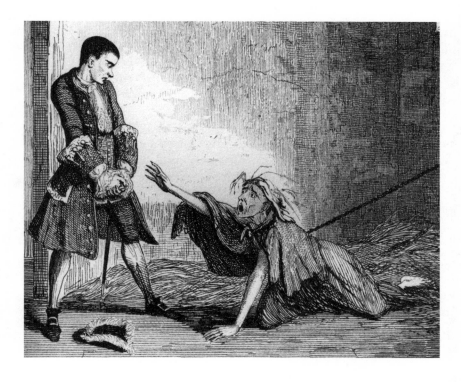

FIGURE 5.10. Walt Disney. March Hare at tea party. From *Alice in Wonderland*. © 1951 Disney.

The most telling vestige of the tradition, precisely because it is so obviously vestigial, is the revision of Tenniel's March Hare that The Walt Disney Studios made for their animated version of *Alice*, released in 1951. On the top of the March Hare's head there is a definite patch of yellow something; but the viewer would be hard put to say what exactly it was; it might as well be fur as straw (fig. 5.10). If few viewers can tell what that yellow patch is supposed to be, not many will know (in Carroll's words) what it "showed," let alone "why."

CHAPTER 6

Alice and the Queen of Spades

"The Queen turned crimson with fury, and, after glaring at her for a moment like a wild beast, began screaming, 'Off with her head! Off—'" In the early editions of *Alice's Adventures in Wonderland* this sentence is all the text there is on page 117, where it appears directly below figure 6.1, as much a caption to that picture as a continuation of the story.[1] Looking up from that caption the

1. Such crisp juxtaposition of text and illustration is common throughout the early editions, but often neglected in later editions. See chapter 12.

FIGURE 6.1. Tenniel. Alice and the Queen of Hearts. From *Alice's Adventures in Wonderland.*

reader will focus at least some attention on the tip of the Queen's out-stretched index finger, partly because the gesture of pointing conventionally commands attention, but also because Tenniel has centered the whole composition of the picture on this point. The Queen who stands behind this threatening gesture takes up roughly a quarter of the picture space; and the bold geometry of the pattern that she presents—especially the black vertical bar at the base of her coronet, and the directed curves at the back of her gown—strengthens the vector of her outstretched arm. But Alice is not moved. She stands her ground with arms crossed in a comfortably self-protective posture, insulated from disturbances by an umbral halo (all the other characters have to compete against a cluttered background to be seen at all), her head cocked just enough to look her accuser defiantly in the eye. She virtually ignores the accusing finger.

Aside from being the only character to stand out clearly against the background, Alice is the character closest to the picture plane, and the only character entirely modeled in three dimensions. The farther back from the picture plane (and the farther back from Alice), the flatter the character: this is an ordinary effect of perspective, which Tenniel has pointedly exaggerated. The Queen, almost as far forward as Alice, has a fully modeled face and arm, and her foot protrudes forward convincingly; but the rest of her is all one plane, as flat as the playing card she derives from. The Knave has somewhat less three-dimensional reality than the Queen, and a good deal less than the pillow that he holds in his hands. The King's left arm and scepter cast shadows on his robe; that is the only detail that saves him from being a mere pasteboard figure, like the other court cards to be glimpsed farther back. Behind those stand ranks of faceless cards, whose flatness, parallel to the picture plane, is reinforced by the flat planes of the topiary hedges behind them.

And yet those hedges are obviously thick and rounded, at least as three-dimensional as the fountain that plays in front of them. And behind the hedges, masses of trees imply considerable depth, as do the birds in the air; and hovering in the midst of the background is the sizable spaciousness of the glass conservatory. So the perspectival flattening that controls the social foreground of Tenniel's picture does not control the horticultural background, where, on the contrary, things resume a fully dimensioned reality.

Clearly Alice, the exceptional figure in the foreground, belongs more to the world of the garden (where indeed she has wanted to go since chapter 1) than to the world of the social figures who are blocking her path and walling her out.

The hierarchy of reality according to which Tenniel ranks the figures in the foreground corresponds to the degrees of complexity that the figures present in Carroll's story in general, or at this particular point in the story. Alice is the only character in the book who might be called a "round" character in E. M. Forster's sense; that is, one who is "capable of surprising in a convincing way."[2] The Queen is relatively inflexible and predictable; like the Mrs. Micawber of Forster's example, she can easily be summarized in a phrase; and yet she has a certain capacity to surprise, at least on this first encounter, and so gets a degree of modeling. The Knave is even more completely defined by his simple knavish role in the history of the tarts. What complexity he has he gets not from

2. E. M. Forster, *Aspects of the Novel* (1927; rpt. New York: Harcourt, Brace, n.d.), 103–18.

FIGURE 6.2. Carroll. Royal procession to the garden. From *Alice's Adventures under Ground.*

FIGURE 6.3. Thomas de la Rue. Knave of Hearts playing card (1834). Photograph © Museo Fournier de Naipes de Álava.

Carroll but from Tenniel, who allows him a rounded countenance (here as in the frontispiece, figure 3.1) suggestive of a smug satisfaction in his knavery. The King at this point of the story is the least independent of all the principal characters, useful to swell the Queen's progress, and little else. (He becomes a more rounded character when he presides at the trial in chapter 12; see figure 3.4.) Aside from Alice the only fully rounded character to be seen in this garden is the White Rabbit, who can just be glimpsed behind the Knave, almost out of the picture. Again, two images later, he can be seen more fully as a rounded witness of the royal conference, which is even more foreshortened (fig. 6.8).

Tenniel's assigning to the characters in this garden scene various degrees of solidity is an elegant solution to a problem that evidently daunted Carroll when he illustrated the story himself, in the gift manuscript for Alice Liddell. Figure 6.2 is Carroll's drawing of the end of the royal procession to the garden: it can be seen here, as in other illustrations in the manuscript, that he had trouble reconciling the two-dimensional patterning of the costumes of standard nineteenth-century court cards with the three-dimensional quality that those cards as characters would have in Alice's dream. (Figure 6.3 shows a representative actual card, a Knave of Hearts printed in England in 1832.[3]) Tenniel, a professional artist, could interpret figure and pattern in any degree of three-dimensionality that he chose. In the frontispiece to *Alice's Adventures* (fig. 3.1), the body of the Knave of Hearts is as flat as it is in the garden scene, but the Queen and her formally patterned gown are both presented in a conventionally modeled, foreshortened three-dimensionality.

Carroll's illustration of the procession is an obvious prototype for Tenniel's garden illustration. From it Tenniel got, besides the principal characters, some details that are not specified at this point in the text: the fountain (although fountains were included in Alice's first glimpse of the garden, in chapter 1), the low fencing, the enlarged crown, and the reduction of the gardeners to playing cards (aptly revealed by Tenniel in fig. 1.49 to be inferior pips of Spades). For the parasol that Carroll put in the Queen's hand Tenniel substituted a fan, because he could render it emblematically heart-shaped. Otherwise, nothing in Carroll's original picture has been left out.

3. From a pack of cards printed by Thomas de la Rue in 1832, which conformed to the traditional "Rouen" pattern, now in Museo Fournier de Naipes de Álava, Vitoria-Gasteiz, Spain. See *Playing Cards* by Roger Tilley (London: Octopus Books, 1973), 2, 67–69; *Museo de Naipes* (Vitoria, Spain: Heraclio Fournier, n.d.), 109, no. 176. Figures 6.16, 6.17, and 6.22 are from the same set; their history can be traced in Félix Alfaro Fournier, *Playing Cards: General History from Their Creation to the Present Day* (Vitoria, Spain: Heraclio Fournier, 1982), 130, 133 (French, 1675); 217–33 (English, various dates). Although double-headed court cards appeared in England in the 1850s they were at first disfavored in conservative circles, and the traditional format remained a persistent cultural memory. Sylvia Mann, *Collecting Playing Cards* (Worcester, UK: Arco Publications, 1966), 65.

FIGURE 6.4. Carroll. Alice and the Queen of Hearts. From *Alice's Adventures under Ground.*

A great deal has been added, however, and from several sources. Alice and the Queen do not confront each other in Carroll's drawing of the procession, but they do in his last illustration to the story proper, when Alice rejects as "nonsense" the Queen's idea of courtroom procedure ("Sentence first—verdict afterwards"). Figure 6.4 shows the Queen responding angrily to this rejection: "'Hold your tongue!' said the Queen . . . 'I won't!' said Alice . . . 'Who cares for you? . . . You're nothing but a pack of cards!'"

This is a highly charged moment in the story, indeed so highly charged that it fast brings the dream to an end. The fact that it turns on Alice's rejection of the Queen's discourse as "nonsense" allies it with the moment in the garden that occurs just after the moment illustrated in figure 6.1, when Alice rejects the Queen's order of execution. "'Nonsense!' said Alice, very loudly and decidedly, and the Queen was silent." These two moments of rejection by Alice are structurally the same, which explains why Tenniel incorporated Carroll's visualization of the final scene into his representation of the quarrel in the garden.

Certain aspects of figure 6.4 have already been noticed in figure 6.1: the fact that the Queen admonishes Alice from a superior height, and the fact that Alice cocks her head up to face down the Queen's anger. And though Tenniel has turned the Queen to show her in profile, it is obvious that his rendition of Alice's impassive head (the more impassive because her expression is not shown) is modeled closely on Carroll's.

Certain other details Tenniel drew not from Carroll's example but from his own experience as a staff cartoonist for *Punch.* The topiary arched hedges in the garden, for example, derive from the Fragonardesque garden scene that Tenniel provided the British royal family in *Punch's Pocket Book for 1857* (fig. 6.5), directly above a listing of their birth dates. This scene is the contrary of the garden scene in *Alice's Adventures.* The Queen (Victoria) here looks benignly on the pastime

FIGURE 6.5. Tenniel. "The Royal Family of England." From *Punch's Pocket Book for 1857*. Beinecke Rare Book and Manuscript Library, Yale University.

THE STATE.

THE ROYAL FAMILY OF ENGLAND.

	Born
QUEEN ALEXANDRINA VICTORIA (Acc. June 20, 1837) .	May 24, 1819
Prince Albert Francis Augustus Charles Emanuel . . .	Aug. 26, 1819
Albert Edward, Prince of Wales	Nov. 9, 1841
Albert Ernest Alfred	Aug. 6, 1844

B

of her daughter (Mary Louisa, the Princess Royal), who amuses herself by making a pet of the ferocious British lion (compare figure 1.44). All terror is here sublimated in play; even the stolen bird's nest, a dreaded loss in chapter 5 ("You're looking for eggs, I know *that* well enough," the Pigeon tells Alice), makes a pleasant gift for a little girl in this pastoral landscape.

The connection between these two scenes is secured by the detail of the crown which surmounts the lower border of figure 6.5. It is the same crown, *mutatis mutandis,* that the Knave of Hearts carries on his pillow: St. Edward's crown, the state crown of England, complete with fleurs-de-lys and quadruple arches. The cross that tops St. Edward's crown is hard to make out in figure 6.5; in figure 6.1 it is replaced by a more fitting heart. (A minor cross at the base of the central arch is missing from both versions.) From the early eighteenth century on, a representation of St. Edward's crown appeared on every Ace of Spades printed in England, to certify payment of a special duty on playing cards. Figure 6.6 shows a late eighteenth-century example, in which the artist has made the arches about as angular as Tenniel does. Figure 6.7 shows an early Victorian version of the crown, ornamenting a book label for a dealer who specialized in children's literature.[4] In nineteenth-century England St. Edward's crown was a ubiquitous piece of iconography, as common as the lion and unicorn who fought for it in the nursery rhyme.

4. M. O. Grenby, *The Child Reader, 1700–1840* (Cambridge: Cambridge University Press, 2011), 150.

FIGURE 6.6. J. Hardy. Ace of Spades playing card. By permission of the Worshipful Company of Makers of Playing Cards, London.

FIGURE 6.7. Bookseller label, showing St. Edward's crown. Private collection.

5. Derek Hudson, *Lewis Carroll* (London: Constable, 1954), 157.

6. *Letters,* 1:44. The photograph, part of "the whole set of the Royal Family" that Carroll possessed and promised to show his siblings, has not been identified. The most likely candidate is the full-length portrait of Victoria taken at Buckingham Palace on 25 June 1857 by Leonida Caldesi, two months after he had taken portraits of four of her children and a month after he had photographed her with nine of them (see *Queen Victoria's Journals,* http://qvj.chadwyck.com). A late print from the negative of her portrait is reproduced by Anne M. Lyden, *A Royal Passion: Queen Victoria and Photography* (Los Angeles: J. Paul Getty Museum, 2014), plate 88.

Tenniel's incorporation of St. Edward's crown into Alice's fantasy would have made that fantasy a familiar one for any Victorian child reader. It has sometimes been suggested that the Queen of Hearts looks a bit like Queen Victoria, and Tenniel's drawing of Victoria in figure 6.5 provides a sketchy ground for comparison. The three-quarters profile of the Queen of Hearts in figure 6.8 compares more directly to that of Queen Victoria in figure 6.9 (*Punch,* 23 September 1865, 117). Tenniel drew this cartoon the same year as the *Alice* illustrations, as part of a general campaign to bring the widowed queen back into public life. The Queen of Hearts is older and uglier than this obviously idealized figure, but there is a clear resemblance.

Carroll, a fervent admirer of Queen Victoria, once pretended that she had invited him to one of her garden parties; figure 6.10 shows the handwritten invitation from Victoria that he forged for the entertainment of some child friends.[5] Victoria and her entourage did make a surprise visit to Christ Church on 12 December 1860, after which Carroll reported to his brothers and sisters, "I had never seen her so near before, nor on her feet, and was shocked to find how short, not to say dumpy, and (with all loyalty be it spoken), how *plain* she is. She is *exactly* like the little full-length photograph published of her."[6] Apparently their next encounter was on 1 July 1865, at Windsor, while *Alice's Adventures* was being readied for the press. "Walked in the Park in the afternoon, and met the Queen driving in an open carriage, and got a bow from her all to myself" (*Diaries,* 5:83).

QUEEN HERMIONE.

PAULINA (BRITANNIA) UNVEILS THE STATUE. "'TIS TIME! DESCEND; BE STONE NO MORE!"

Winter's Tale, Act V., Scene 3.

Aside from the Queen, the most imposing Victorian motif in figure
6.1 is the hemispherical glass conservatory looming in the background,
an unprecedented triumph of nineteenth-century engineering. Green-
house architecture had culminated in the spectacular Crystal Palace of
1851, which Tenniel illustrated for *Punch* as an epitome of British progress (figs. 6.11 and 6.12).[7] However, no purely hemispherical green-
house like that shown in figure 6.1 had ever been attempted. In 1815
Sir George Mackenzie had identified "the sphere" as "the *ne plus ultra*"
of "form for the glass," because the sun's rays would fall perpendicu-
larly upon "*some part of it,* during the whole period of the sun's shining,
not twice, but every day in the year." Only in Wonderland would such
an ideal form be practicable; and indeed Mackenzie "[left] it to hor-
ticulturalists to choose any intermediate degree of perfection, which
may suit their purposes."[8] The Antheum (or Antheum) at Hove was
planned by Henry Phillips to be an immense unsupported glass dome,
but more than twice as broad as tall, and topped off with a cupola; it
collapsed before completion in the summer of 1833. The same archi-
tect had recently completed a more modest squat dome, which for
many years was a popular attraction at the Surrey Zoological Gardens.[9]

A careful reader of *Punch* might have recognized in Tenniel's Queen
of Hearts the identity of another queen than Queen Victoria, a kind of
anti-Victoria, a queen notorious for her "frailty": Queen Gertrude, the
wife of Claudius and mother of Hamlet. Gertrude dominates one of the
two "Illustrations to Shakespeare" that satirize *Hamlet*. It takes its text

7. Figure 6.11: 1 January 1851, title
page. Figure 6.12: 19 July 1851, 38;
pointing with pride at the spectacle are
Mr. Punch and Prince Albert. Albert
had proposed the international exhibition that the Crystal Palace was built to
house, and he saw the idea through to
completion.

8. George Stuart Mackenzie, "On the
Form which the Glass of a Forcing-house
Ought to Have, In Order to Receive the
Greatest Possible Quantity of Rays from
the Sun," *Transactions of the Horticultural
Society of London,* 2 (1818): 171–77; 173.

9. *The Gardener's Magazine* 7 (1831):
693; see John Hix, *The Glass House* (Cambridge, MA: MIT Press, 1974), 112. See
also Stefan Koppelkamm, *Glasshouses
and Wintergardens of the Nineteenth Century,* trans. Kathrine Talbot (New York:
Rizzoli, 1981), 19, for contemporary
comments on the style.

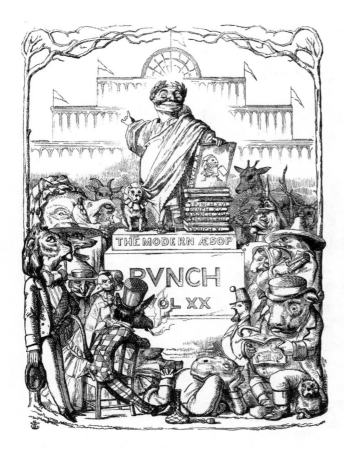

THE HAPPY FAMILY IN HYDE PARK.

from the closet scene, as Hamlet eulogizes his father, King Hamlet, for having possessed superlative attributes:

> Hyperion's curls, the front of Jove himself,
> An eye like Mars, to threaten and command,
> A station like the herald Mercury
> New lighted on a heaven-kissing hill—
> A combination and a form indeed
> Where every god did seem to set his seal
> To give the world assurance of a man. (III.iv)

Taking the second of these lines for a caption and punning from "Mars" to "Ma's," Tenniel drew the curiously familiar scene of figure 6.13 (*Punch,* 22 September 1855, 120), in which Queen Gertrude threatens and commands quite in the attitude of the Queen of Hearts, if with more emphasis upon her evil eye and less upon shouting. By transferring the royal prerogatives of threat and command from King Hamlet to his wife Queen Gertrude, and by reducing them in the process to the arbitrary bluster of a querulous middle-aged woman, the *Punch* editors and Tenniel foreshadowed the decay of the authority of the King of Hearts into the petty willfulness of his Queen. Furthermore, Tenniel's cartoon on the closet scene, in which Hamlet decried his mother's sensuality, corroborates what many readers have suspected: that the threat which the Queen of Hearts presents to Alice is chiefly maternal and sexual.

FIGURE 6.11. Tenniel. "The Modern Æsop," showing the Crystal Palace. From *Punch,* 1 January 1851.

FIGURE 6.12. Tenniel. "The Happy Family in Hyde Park," showing the Crystal Palace. From *Punch,* 19 July 1851.

FIGURE 6.13. Tenniel. "An eye like MARS (Ma's) to threaten and command." From *Punch*, 22 September 1855.

FIGURE 6.14. Thomas de la Rue. King of Hearts playing card (1834). Photograph © Museo Fournier de Naipes de Álava.

FIGURE 6.15. Thomas de la Rue. Queen of Hearts playing card (1834). Photograph © Museo Fournier de Naipes de Álava.

Another ominous element of this Queen's identity would have been available not only to readers of *Punch* but to anyone who had ever played with an early nineteenth-century set of playing cards. Tenniel's image of the King of Hearts is taken directly from the standard playing card pattern (fig. 6.14); this adoption is most obvious in figure 6.1. We have already seen that Tenniel's Knave of Hearts conforms to this pattern. But Tenniel obviously did not draw his Queen of Hearts after the usual prototype (fig. 6.15). (For one thing, the bold checkered collar of the playing card is missing from figure 6.1; instead a scarf crosses in

The King of Hearts

FIGURE 6.16. William Mulready. "The King of Hearts." From *The King and Queen of Hearts* (1806); rpt. *The Works of Charles and Mary Lamb* (1903).

FIGURE 6.17. Thomas de la Rue. Queen of Spades playing card (1834). Photograph © Museo Fournier de Naipes de Álava.

front of the bodice.) Nor is Tenniel's Queen of Hearts dressed like the Queen in nineteenth-century illustrations of the nursery rhyme, who usually wears her proper attire—as in figure 6.16.[10] Instead, Tenniel has dressed her in the clothes of her playing-card rival and nemesis, the Queen of Spades, the queen of death (fig. 6.17).

10. *The King and Queen of Hearts*, a booklet for children published anonymously in London in 1806, and reprinted in *The Works of Charles and Mary Lamb*, ed. E. V. Lucas, 7 vols. (New York: G. P. Putnam's Sons, 1903), 3:336–50; illustrations attributed to William Mulready. See also Iona and Peter Opie, *Three Centuries of Nursery Rhymes and Poetry for Children* (London: National Book League, 1973), item 462.

11. Ermine fur, used to line royal robes, had long figured in French and English heraldry as the precise pattern that Tenniel displays in fig. 6.1 and also fig. 3.1; John Guillim, *A Display of Heraldry*, 6th ed. (London, 1724), 10, 15. Nineteenth-century English court cards such as figs. 6.14 and 6.17, which derived from relatively crude eighteenth-century French woodcuts, used a much simplified notation for the ermine pattern—which Tenniel restored.

12. For a more conservative account of the difference, published the same year as *Alice's Adventures*, see E. S. Taylor, *The History of Playing Cards, With Anecdotes of Their Use in Conjuring, Fortune-Telling, and Card-Sharping* (London: Camden Hotten, 1865), 473. In fortune-telling the Queen of Hearts "is a model of sincere affection, devotion, and prudence"; the Queen of Spades "is a person not to be provoked with impunity, never forgetting an injury, and having a considerable spice of malice in her composition." Strictly speaking, "sickness and death" are attributes not of the Queen but of the Ace of Spades (472). But widows (Queen Victoria, Gertrude) are always represented by the Queen of Spades (471); and the suit generally connotes hazard, disaster, and death. See "The Folk-Lore of Playing Cards," *The Book of Days: A Miscellany of Popular Antiquities in Connection with the Calendar,* ed. R. Chambers, 2 vols. (London: W. & R. Chambers, 1862), 1:281–84; 283.

Carroll's own drawing of the Queen (fig. 6.4) bears reexamination in this context. The bodice design matches that of the Queen of Hearts, though without the checkered patterning. The triangular panel at the back of the gown may derive from the Queen of Spades. It is hard to say what Carroll was doing; but Tenniel took a full ensemble of details from the Queen of Spades.

It may be that Tenniel preferred the robes of the Queen of Spades for purely formal reasons, so as to incorporate the triangular back panel of her gown, with its array of pointed "ermine spots," into the sweeping vectors that he focused onto the Queen's pointing finger.[11] Or it may be that he dressed Carroll's Queen of Hearts like the Queen of Spades because the quality that she brings to Alice's nightmare is not love but the fear of death.[12] If Tenniel's gesture was not merely formal but serious, Alice's response to the Queen's savage command, "Off with her head! Off—," is the more eloquently effective. "'Nonsense!' said Alice, very loudly and decidedly, and the Queen was silent."

CHAPTER 7

The Invention of the White Knight

"It's my own invention."

*I*n *The History of "Punch"* (1895), M. H. Spielmann incidentally publicized a belief that John Tenniel's drawings of the White Knight in Lewis Carroll's *Through the Looking-Glass* (figs. 7.1, 7.2, and 7.3, drawn about 1870), were also caricatures of Tenniel's friend and colleague, Horace "Ponny" Mayhew.[1] Presumably this belief had been held by some members of the *Punch* staff. Since the mid-sixties Tenniel had been the chief cartoonist at *Punch*; and Horace Mayhew, younger brother of the cofounder Henry Mayhew, was a well-liked factotum on the staff.

Even as he publicized this notion, Spielmann took pains to discredit it. He quoted a denial that Tenniel had made, probably in a letter written to Spielmann in the early nineties, responding to enquiries. This is Spielmann's whole account:

> "Ponny's" portrait, it has often been said, may be seen in the White Knight in "Alice in Wonderland" [a casual reference to the sequel, *Through the Looking-Glass*]; but "the resemblance," says Sir John Tenniel, "was purely accidental, a mere unintentional caricature, which his *friends,* of course, were only too delighted to make the most of. P. M. was certainly handsome, whereas the White Knight can scarcely be considered a type of 'manly beauty.'"[2]

Spielmann does say that Mayhew "was a strikingly good-looking man." Evidently, too, he was a bon vivant and man-about-town, unlike Carroll's Knight. "Bright, good-natured, and lively, not very clever, but always letting off little jokes," according to one friend; "a social butterfly, who never fulfilled the promise of his youth," according to another.[3]

Some readers of Spielmann's *History* have taken Tenniel's disclaimer into account. In his memoirs Harry Furniss, who followed Tenniel both on the staff of *Punch* and as an illustrator for Lewis Carroll (*Sylvie and Bruno*), quoted Tenniel's reply as definitive. And in her monograph on Tenniel, Frances Sarzano mentioned both the theory and the denial.

1. Tenniel may have begun work on *Looking-Glass* in January 1870; he finished the latter half of 1871. See his letter to Dalziel, 11 January 1870 (*The Brothers Dalziel,* 128); and Carroll's *Diaries,* 6:79, 112, 178–79.

2. Spielmann, 329. Spielmann had interviewed Tenniel in 1889 about his general procedures working for *Punch* (461–66); they may have dealt with the supposed caricature then. But the phrase, "says Sir John Tenniel," suggests that Spielmann is quoting from writing. In his preface, written late in 1895, Spielmann reports that he had spent "four years . . . engaged upon this book," corresponding with "hundreds" of informants; so if Tenniel responded in writing he probably did so in the early nineties. Either way, he would have made this disclaimer to Spielmann some two decades after he drew the illustrations in question.

3. Spielmann, 328–29. See also Leonée Ormond, *George du Maurier* (Pittsburgh, PA: University of Pittsburgh Press, 1969), 164, 168–69; and Deborah Vlock, "Mayhew, Horace (1816–1872)," *Oxford Dictionary of National Biography* (Oxford University Press, 2004), online.

FIGURE 7.1. Tenniel. The White Knight and Alice. Frontispiece to *Through the Looking-Glass.*

4. Harry Furniss, *The Confessions of a Caricaturist,* 2 vols. (London: T. Fisher Unwin, 1901), 1:300. (Furniss thought that others had been too quick to find personal caricatures in his own cartoons, and so he appreciated Tenniel's disclaimer.) Sarzano, 21. Price, 74. Arthur Prager, *The Mahogany Tree: An Informal History of "Punch"* (New York: Hawthorn Books, 1979), 81. See also Leary, 22.

But two historians of *Punch* who wrote after Spielmann are more casual about the matter. R. G. G. Price offers the unqualified report that Tenniel sketched a "picture of his colleague Ponny Mayhew as Carroll's White Knight." And Arthur Prager writes that Mayhew's "friend and drinking companion John Tenniel used Ponny as his model for the White Knight in Lewis Carroll's *Through the Looking-Glass.* Today Ponny Mayhew is probably the only Punchite whose features would be instantly recognizable to literate people."[4]

Given these two conflicting traditions, both derived from Spielmann's book, one wonders what Ponny Mayhew actually looked like, why the *Punch* staffers assumed that Tenniel's White Knight caricatured him, and whether Tenniel's denial, made some twenty years after the fact, is plausible.

FIGURE 7.2. Tenniel. The White Knight and the aged man. From *Through the Looking-Glass.*

FIGURE 7.3. Tenniel. Alice and the White Knight. From *Through the Looking-Glass.*

Spielmann's *History* itself provides enough evidence to judge these questions. It includes a small photograph of Mayhew, taken at an uncertain date (fig. 7.4),[5] and also two caricature sketches by Tenniel's colleagues on the *Punch* art staff, John Leech and Richard Doyle. Figure 7.5 is a detail from an 1847 Leech cartoon that represents the *Punch*

5. The National Portrait Gallery, London, owns a contemporary copy of this photograph, a carte-de-visite credited to Alexander Bassano in the 1860s. See https://goo.gl/UUYvV7.

FIGURE 7.4. Alexander Bassano. Photographic portrait of Horace Mayhew. From M. H. Spielmann, *The History of "Punch"* (1895).

FIGURE 7.6. Richard Doyle. Sketch of John Leech, Tom Taylor, and Horace Mayhew. From M. H. Spielmann, *The History of "Punch"* (1895).

FIGURE 7.5. John Leech. *Punch* staff as musical band. From M. H. Spielmann, *The History of "Punch"* (1895).

FIGURE 7.7. Tenniel. The *Punch* staff at play. From *Punch*, 8 July 1854.

staff as a musical band; according to Spielmann (261–62), the cornetist at the extreme left is Mayhew. Figure 7.6 is a sketch by Richard Doyle, probably drawn before 1850 (when he left the magazine). Spielmann credits Mayhew with the minimal profile on the extreme right (337). It is obvious from these two caricatures, if not from the photograph, that Mayhew had a pronounced, hooked nose, rather like that of the White Knight, which is displayed prominently in Tenniel's frontispiece (fig. 7.1). But the Leech cartoon shows a relatively young Mayhew, and the Doyle caricature is less than sketchy. Altogether, the evidence of these three images is inconclusive.

The matter is not settled even by a caricature of Mayhew that Tenniel drew himself, in 1854 (fig. 7.7; 8 July 1854, 1).[6] Mayhew is playing leapfrog just to the right of center. (The other *Punch* staffers shown here include the artist, who is decorating a wall with a graffito of Mr. Punch—who is, as often in *Punch*, a knight-at-arms himself.) Here Mayhew does look as the White Knight conceivably might have looked in his younger days. But again the age difference prevents any definite identification.

Fortunately, Spielmann's book includes one more relevant image, which seems to be decisive. Late in 1869 or early in 1870 George du Maurier, Tenniel's junior colleague on the art staff, drew a caricature of Mayhew that confirms, and indeed may have inspired, the old supposition that the White Knight bears more than an accidental resemblance to Mayhew. This caricature was part of a printed invitation form sent out each week to summon *Punch* staff members to their elaborate dinner meetings, at which much of the week-to-week planning was done (fig. 7.8). According to Spielmann (69) the winged head responding to the call on the right represents Tenniel, who was, of course, a regular

6. An illustrated volume rubric from *Punch*, reproduced and analyzed by Prager, 30.

FIGURE 7.8. George du Maurier. *Punch* dinner invitation card. From M. H. Spielmann, *The History of "Punch"* (1895).

10, Bouverie Street, E.C.

July 15ᵗʰ 1871

The pleasure of your Company is requested on Wednesday next, the 19ᵗʰ inst. at half-past Six sharp.

An answer, if unable to come, will oblige

guest at these dinners; and that in the center is Mayhew, another regular guest (with du Maurier himself in tow). In almost all its details, this profile caricature of Ponny Mayhew closely matches Tenniel's frontispiece profile of the White Knight (fig. 7.1). No wonder the *Punch* staff saw Mayhew in the *Looking-Glass* antihero.

As for Tenniel's disclaimer, there is the broadly discrediting fact that two decades had passed between his *Looking-Glass* drawings and his reply to Spielmann. The specific objection that Mayhew was too handsome may have been based on old memories of Mayhew in his youth. And, as Tenniel almost hints himself, he need not have caricatured Mayhew consciously and directly. He may have unconsciously assimilated du Maurier's profile sketch of him, which, because of its context, he would have seen dozens of times, week after week, during the months when he was preparing the *Looking-Glass* illustrations.

Tenniel took pride in the fact that he usually drew the visual imagery of his cartoons from the visual imagery in his head, hardly ever having to resort to the direct study of objects or models of any kind. But what made this possible, as he once remarked to Spielmann, was that "anything I see I remember."[7] He certainly saw du Maurier's sketch of Mayhew, and in some sense "remembered" it when he sat down to illustrate chapter 8 of *Through the Looking-Glass.*

Carroll strongly objected to the image of the White Knight that resulted. "The White Knight must not have whiskers; he must not be made to look old," he insisted in a letter—but to little or no effect.[8] To overcome such objections Tenniel must have had more than a casual commitment to what he had drawn.

Aside from Mayhew the only other person thought to be a possible prototype for Tenniel's White Knight is Tenniel himself. John Pudney,

7. Spielmann, 463, 466. Tenniel did concede that he would study photographs to capture an unfamiliar face or uniform "and so on."

8. Collingwood, *Life and Letters,* 130. Presumably Carroll used the word *whiskers* in the old sense, denoting *moustache,* not in the new Victorian sense, denoting hair grown "on the cheeks or sides of the face" (*OED*). If he did mean the latter, Tenniel did comply with this suggestion—though not with the suggestion about the Knight's age.

FIGURE 7.9. Unidentified photographer. Portrait of John Tenniel. Circa 1895. Location unknown; formerly British Museum.

FIGURE 7.10. Tenniel. Self-portrait. Pen and ink. From M. H. Spielmann, *The History of "Punch"* (1895).

FIGURE 7.11. John & Charles Watkins. Photographic portrait of John Tenniel, circa 1867–71 (detail). Metropolitan Museum of Art, New York. Accession Number: 1970.659.766. The Albert Ten Eyck Collection. Gift of the Centennial Committee, 1970. Public domain.

FIGURE 7.12. Elliott & Fry. Photographic portrait of John Tenniel, "late 1860s–early 1870s" (detail). © National Portrait Gallery, London.

citing an apparently undated portrait photograph then in the British Museum (fig. 7.9), commented that "the features of the White Knight bear a remarkable resemblance to the illustrator's own."[9] That photograph looks to be contemporary with a pen-and-ink self-portrait that Tenniel dated "1889" (fig. 7.10).[10] If so, the resemblance that Pudney saw is a matter of life imitating art. Two decades earlier, at the time Tenniel was actually drawing the White Knight, he did not much resemble his subject. Du Maurier's contemporary sketch (fig. 7.8), shows that Tenniel still had a distinct thatch of hair, unlike the bald knight. A portrait photograph of Tenniel taken by John & Charles Watkins around 1867–71 shows him to be decades younger than the White Knight, garnished with whiskers, and moustache-free (fig. 7.11). Another portrait photo, by Elliot & Fry, perhaps taken a few years later, shows drooping moustache and whiskers and dark hair (fig. 7.12)—not the head of Alice's aged guide, philosopher, and friend.

In his biography of Tenniel, Rodney Engen styled the artist as "Alice's White Knight," adducing as evidence a Tenniel drawing of a knight on horseback, armed (like the White Knight) with an umbrella, which he took to be a self-portrait (fig. 7.13).[11] However, in her biography of the artist, Frankie Morris dates that drawing to 1866 and quotes Tenniel's verse inscription on the back to identify it as a satire on tippling, not on Tenniel.[12]

9. John Pudney, *Lewis Carroll and His World* (New York: Charles Scribner's Sons, 1976), 77; reproduced also by Engen, *Sir John Tenniel*, 96. In *Lewis Carroll: A Biography* (London: J. M. Dent & Sons, 1979), Anne Clark also characterizes Tenniel's White Knight as "a self-portrait of the artist" (173).

10. A full-page portrait in Spielmann, 462.

11. Rodney Engen, *Sir John Tenniel: Alice's White Knight* (London: Scolar Press, 1991), 96 and front cover of dust jacket.

12. Morris, *Artist of Wonderland*, 379n3.

FIGURE 7.13. Tenniel. Plumed knight in armor on horseback with umbrella. Pen and ink, 1866. From Rodney Engen, *Sir John Tenniel: Alice's White Knight* (1991).

This is all too bad, for Pudney's suggestion (and Engen's) is very appealing. We know that Carroll's White Knight is something of an autobiographical satire; it would be fitting if Tenniel's White Knight were too.

But art isn't always that pat. Prager seems closer to the truth than Pudney. Ponny Mayhew, and not John Tenniel, "is probably the only Punchite whose features"—although mediated by du Maurier's pen—"would be instantly recognizable to literate people."

THE LITERATE PERSON who reviewed *Through the Looking-Glass* for *The Spectator* noticed two other prototypes for Tenniel's White Knight: "Mr. Tenniel has added to his interest by throwing in reminiscences of Albert Dürer's Knight and Don Quixote."[13] The Quixote reminiscences were probably mediated by Gustave Doré's wood engravings of Cervantes's impractical hero for *The History of Don Quixote,* published in London in 1864–67 and in later editions, especially several illustrations that show Quixote in armor astride his steed Rozinante, both horse and rider in profile facing left, as in Tenniel's frontispiece.[14]

The Dürer reminiscence is more specific. Not long before it published *Through the Looking-Glass* Macmillan published the first biography in English of the German artist, by Mary Margaret Heaton, who acknowledged that "the print known by the titles of 'The Knight, Death,

13. "Through the Looking-Glass," *The Spectator,* 30 December 1871, 1607–09; 1609.

14. Cervantes, *The History of Don Quixote,* ed. J. W. Clark (London: Cassell, Petter & Galpin, n.d.), plates 15, 36, 68, 81. (*Rocinante* in the original Spanish.)

The Knight,
Death, and Satan.

FROM ALBT DURER.

FIGURE 7.14. Albrecht Dürer. "The Knight, Death, and Satan." Trimmed inset wood engraving probably by William James Linton. Frontispiece to Fouqué, *Sintram and His Companions* (London: Edward Lumley, 1855, rpt. 1861).

and the Devil,' 'The Horse of Death,' and 'The Christian Knight' . . . is perhaps the most celebrated of all Dürer's engravings."[15] An accompanying illustration reproduced "the Engraving in the British Museum"— where Tenniel could have seen it.

A wood engraving adapted from that print served as the frontispiece to an edition of *Sintram and His Companions* (fig. 7.14), a translation of the romance that Friedrich de la Motte Fouqué had confected to provide a backstory for Dürer's image. Edward Lumley published the tale and its frontispiece around 1855 in a one-volume collection of four of Fouqué's tales titled *The Four Seasons*. (The printer for that volume was Richard Clay, who would later print the approved early editions of the *Alice* books.) Included was a reprint of *Undine* (1845)—the first book for which Tenniel prepared all the illustrations. Looking through *The Four Seasons* Tenniel would see Dürer's copperplate engraving as reengraved on wood (probably by William James Linton, then the dean of British wood engravers), after contemplating his own chivalric drawings for *Undine,* which John Bastin had engraved.[16]

One of these drawings, heading chapter 14, "The Black Valley," shows a knight, his horse, and a maiden in a dark wood (fig. 7.15), as in the frontispiece to *Through the Looking-Glass*—except that here the

15. Mrs. Charles Heaton, *The History of the Life of Albrecht Dürer of Nürnberg* (London: Macmillan, 1870), 168.

16. In this Lumley edition the Dürer image is not signed, aside from a line crediting him. Set within an ornamental frame, it appears to be a slightly cropped electrotype replica of a wood block that Linton had engraved (and signed) for the edition of Fouqué's *Four Seasons* that James Burns published in 1846. In 1847 Burns consigned much of his backlist to "the remainder market"; the Fouqué titles, including Tenniel's *Undine,* went to Edward Lumley, who reissued them at various times under his own imprint. Brian Alderson, "Some Notes on James Burns as a Publisher of Children's Books," *Bulletin of The John Rylands University Library* 76 (1994): 103–26; 122.

CHAPTER XIV.

The Black Valley.

HE Black Valley lay deep within the
mountains. None know how it is called

FIGURE 7.15. Tenniel. "Drawing on the horse by the bridle, the knight supported the falling maiden with his other arm." Wood engraving by John Bastin. *Undine* in *The Four Seasons* (London: Edward Lumley, 1855, rpt. 1861).

FIGURE 7.16. Unidentified artist. "The three travellers." Fouqué, *Undine* in *The Four Seasons* (London: James Burns, 1845).

17. Facing page 49. Advertised in *The Publisher's Circular*, 1 August 1845, 236, as "lately published," part of "Burns' Fireside Library; a Series of Cheap Books for Popular Reading, suited for the Fireside, the Lending Library, the Steamboat, or the Railway Carriage, elegantly printed and done up, with numerous illustrations." This edition of *Undine* had only four illustrations; it was priced at nine pence—unlike the five shillings charged for the Burns edition that included eleven illustrations by Tenniel.

18. Gleeson White, "Children's Books and Their Illustrators," *The Studio* special number (Winter 1897): 3–67; 20, 26.

maiden is fainting, and the horse, having been maddened by a looming goblin, is not fit to ride.

The goblin has not yet arrived on the scene in a similar illustration that was made for a different edition of *Undine* that Burns published, probably at first separately and then as part of *The Seasons: Four Romances* (1843; fig. 7.16).[17]

> The three travellers had reached the thickest shades of the forest without interchanging a word. It must have been a fair sight, in that hall of leafy verdure, to see this lovely woman's form sitting on the noble and richly ornamented steed, on her right hand the venerable priest in the white garb of his order, on her left the blooming young knight, clad in splendid raiment of scarlet, gold, and violet, girt with a sword that flashed in the sun, and attentively walking beside her. (48)

This picture, too, is composed along the lines of the Dürer engraving— and also like the *Looking-Glass* frontispiece, except that here the positions of the knight and the maiden are reversed. Gleeson White, an early expert on mid-Victorian black-and-white illustration, credited the picture to Tenniel, perhaps confusing this book with the later Burns edition of *Undine*.[18] Whoever did draw it, Tenniel probably saw it, adding another reflection of this Düreresque scene to his resourceful memory bank.

Tenniel could also have recalled another such forest scene that he designed (and signed) as the frontispiece for another book, Froissart's *Chronicles of England*, volume 2 (fig. 7.17). Another early commission

FIGURE 7.17. Tenniel. "King, ride no further, but return; for thou art betrayed." Frontispiece to volume 2 of Froissart's *Chronicles* (London: James Burns, [1847]).

Vol. II. page 244.

by the publisher James Burns, this frontispiece was printed, along with the rest of the book, by Richard Clay, the same firm that Tenniel would later recommend to Carroll for the *Alice* books. The only illustration in the volume, Tenniel's frontispiece marks a pivotal moment in the madness of King Charles VI of France, who is startled by an ominous encounter in the forest of Le Mans:

> A man, bareheaded, with naked feet, clothed in a jerkin of white-russet, rushed out from the trees, and boldly seized the reins of his horse, saying, "King, ride no further, but return; for thou art betrayed." The men-at-arms beat the man off, and he escaped; but his speech made such an impression on the king's mind, that his understanding was shaken.[19]

Charles's ensuing madness had political consequences, including the pretension to the French throne of the infant King Henry VI of England.

19. Jean Froissart, *The Chronicles of England, France, Spain, Etc. Etc.*, trans. Henry Peter Dunster, 2 vols. (London: John Burns, [1847]), 2:244. Tenniel also designed the frontispiece to volume 1.

FIGURE 7.18. Tenniel. "The Knight and His Companion." *Punch,* 5 March 1887.

THE KNIGHT AND HIS COMPANION.

(Suggested by Albert Dürer's famous picture.)

Many years after he drew the *Looking-Glass* frontispiece, in 1887, Tenniel returned, for *Punch,* directly to Dürer's rocky landscape. In "THE KNIGHT AND HIS COMPANION. (*Suggested by Albert Dürer's famous picture.*)" the knight is Bismarck, his steed is Liberty, and the lurking menace is Socialism (fig. 7.18).[20] Alice has left the forest.

On 22 January 1898, a week after the death of Charles Lutwidge Dodgson, a writer for *The Saturday Review,* possibly the art critic D. S. MacColl, published an appreciation of the literary achievements of "Lewis Carroll" in an article titled with that pseudonym in quotation marks. He claimed for Carroll's work "much purpose and seriousness"; and also "pathos":

Take, as an instance, the Fawn that has forgotten its name and accompanies Alice fearlessly till the wood is cleared; then, crying, "I am a fawn, and you—you are a human child!" springs startled away. So, also, the whole episode of the White Knight, of so much wisdom gone foolishly astray, has about it almost the same charm as Millais' "Sir Isumbras," now delighting all who make Burlington House their mild wintry resort.[21]

20. *Punch,* 5 March 1887, 115.

21. "Lewis Carroll," *The Saturday Review,* 22 January 1898, 102–03; 103. See also August A. Imholtz, Jr., and Charlie Lovett, eds., *In Memoriam Charles Lutwidge Dodgson 1832–1898: Obituaries of Lewis Carroll and Related Pieces* (New York: Lewis Carroll Society of North America, 1998), 139–42.

FIGURE 7.19. John Everett Millais. *A Dream of the Past, Sir Isumbras at the Ford.* Oil on canvas. 1857. © National Museums Liverpool, Lady Lever Art Gallery.

Burlington House was the home of the Royal Academy, where an exhibition of paintings by John Everett Millais, the late president of that organization, was then on display.[22] (Millais had been a close friend of Carroll's, figuring often in his diaries and photographs.) MacColl, reviewing that exhibition the previous week for *The Saturday Review,* had found fault with *Sir Isumbras at the Ford* (fig. 7.19), comparing that painting unfavorably to Millais's painting *Autumn Leaves,* which he thought displayed formal self-sufficiency: "Here is no search for explanatory incident; the figures are present by a lyrical correspondence and necessity." *Sir Isumbras,* on the other hand, though it, too, had merits as regards landscape and facial expression, nonetheless faltered: "the attempt to give greater resonance to the emotion by the furniture of romance in the golden armour and legendary incident disturbs and puzzles rather than intensifies."[23]

The "legendary incident" in question was an event told in some pseudo-medieval English verse, attributed to a "Metrical Romance of Sir Ysumbras," which was printed in the exhibition catalogue when the painting was first shown at the Royal Academy, in 1857.[24] As the 1898 catalogue entry noted, this quotation, "which was supposed at the time to have been taken from the ancient romance . . . was really written for the occasion by the late Mr. Tom Taylor." It was Taylor who had recommended Tenniel to Carroll for the *Alice* illustrations, and Taylor's involvement with the painting was likely to deepen their interest in its notoriety.

That notoriety had been spurred by John Ruskin, Carroll's colleague in Christ Church—who would later teach drawing to Alice Liddell and her sisters, and then be transmogrified in *Wonderland* as the Mock Turtle. "The Drawling-master was an old conger-eel, that used to come once a week: *he* taught us Drawling, Stretching, and Fainting in Coils." Ruskin had once been the chief advocate for Millais's career and the Pre-Raphaelite Brotherhood generally, but in his *Academy Notes* Ruskin faulted many aspects of this new painting, including careless brushwork, misjudged illumination, and the "clever mystification" of Taylor's mock-medieval text, forged in "bad English."[25]

22. Royal Academy, *Exhibition of Works by the Late Sir John Everett Millais* (London: William Clowes, 1898).

23. D. S. MacColl ("D. S. M."), "Millais," *The Saturday Review,* 15 January 1898, 73–75; 74.

24. *The Exhibition of the Royal Academy of Arts, MDCCCLVII: The Eighty-Ninth* (London: The Royal Academy, 1857), 15–16 (no. 283). The catalogue entry was titled "Sir Isumbras at the ford." A significant alternative title, cited by *The Art-Journal* in its review of the exhibition (vol. 19, p. 170), was *A Dream of the Past—Sir Isumbras at the Ford.* That duplex title has become traditional.

25. John Ruskin, *Notes on Some of the Principal Pictures Exhibited in the Rooms of The Royal Academy* (London: Smith, Elder, & Co., 1857), 24. Carroll owned a copy of this booklet. Charlie Lovett, *Lewis Carroll among His Books: A Descriptive Catalogue of the Private Library of Charles L. Dodgson* (Jefferson, NC: McFarland, 2005), 265, no. 1734.

There really was a metrical romance of "Sir Ysumbras," which had been published in 1844 by the Camden Society.[26] And it did tell the story of the knight's effort to rescue by horseback, across a river, some children—but there were three children to save in repeated ventures (his own children, all sons—no daughter), as well as his wife, and he lost them all until a happy ending reunited them. Millais used artistic license to simplify the drama and to introduce a girl—license warranted by Taylor's bogus verses, which mentioned "a mayden."[27] Ruskin objected to this fakery, but the scandal of the painting only increased its fame. A parodic print by Frederick Sandys converted Sir Isumbras into Millais, the two children into Millais's Pre-Raphaelite Brothers William Holman Hunt and Dante Gabriel Rossetti, and the horse into an ass branded on its ass with Ruskin's initials. It was titled "A Nightmare."[28]

Carroll recorded his own misgivings about the painting on 1 July 1857, when he visited the exhibition. There he saw:

> Many fair pictures, none, I think, remarkable, except perhaps Millais' two "Sir Isumbras at the Ford," and "The Escaped Heretic," which were remarkably ugly. In the first of these there are three people on a horse, but so much smaller than the average human stature as to be hardly any load at all; an additional gigantic effect is given to the animal by its being partly out of the picture. The girl's face is earnest, but coarse, and her eyes unnaturally large; the knight is good, though with an expression like an honest old gardener; the face of the boy behind is lubberly and wooden to a degree. . . . The details of both pictures are wonderfully good, as one might expect. (*Diaries*, 3:74–75)

Carroll would not have forgotten *A Dream of the Past* and its "honest old gardener" when he invented Alice's White Knight, nor would Tenniel when he designed the *Looking-Glass* frontispiece.

Arguably the similarities between these two images are as remarkable as their differences. Both illustrate dream romances; indeed, in Millais's case the "dream" aspect may explain and even justify the liberties that he and Taylor took with the text of the original romance. Both show in profile a late-middle-aged, bearded, bare-headed but otherwise armored knight riding his steed from right to left in the center of the picture, accompanied by a girl approaching adolescence. Both horses bear some odd appurtenances on their left flanks: large peacock feathers in the Millais; many household implements and vegetables in the Tenniel (these are discussed in chapter 10). Both knights stare straight ahead, as if unaware of, or indifferent to, their immediate surroundings. But there are important differences. The settings are quite different: a river under the open sky in the painting; a dark forest side-lit by "the setting sun" in the frontispiece. The boy in the painting, a kind of chaperone, is absent from the engraving. The relations of the knight and the girl are different, too: the girl held close in the knight's armed arms in the painting, but standing apart in the engraving; and the two girls' aspects are different: wary in the Millais, aloof in the Tenniel. The girl in the painting may wonder what will happen next, but Tenniel's heroine knows she is well on her way to becoming Queen Alice, once she has seen the knight on his solitary way. Despite these differences, both scenes share a certain brooding "charm," as MacColl remarked in 1898.

26. *The Thornton Romances: The Early English Metrical Romances of Perceval, Isumbras, Eglamour, and Degrevant,* ed. James Orchard Halliwell-Phillips (London: Camden Society, 1844).

27. *The Exhibition of the Royal Academy of Arts* (London: The Royal Academy, 1857), 16.

28. Zincotype print, Department of Prints and Drawings, The British Museum, no. 1859,0709.848; https://goo.gl/FtQfU5. Betty Elzea, *Frederick Sandys, 1829–1904: A Catalogue Raisonné* (Woodbridge: Antique Collectors' Club, 2001), 131. Julie F. Codell traces the popular reception of Millais's painting in "Sir Isumbras, M. P.: Millais's Painting and Political Cartoons," *The Journal of Popular Culture* 22:3 (December 1988): 29–47. See also Richard Altick, *Paintings from Books: Art and Literature in Britain, 1760–1900* (Columbus: Ohio State University Press, 1985), 234–35, where the work is seen to signal the decline of literary painting in England.

Several later critics have also noticed the resemblance. Timothy Hilton simply called Tenniel's drawing "a caricature of Sir Isumbras."[29] Robert M. Polhemus was more expansive:

This painting, which John Tenniel obviously used in illustrating Lewis Carroll's *Through the Looking-Glass* (1871), is surely a main source of the White Knight in Carroll . . . and it helped Dodgson-Carroll, who admired and photographed Millais, to imagine a comic yet noble role for himself as a literary knight-errant to Alice and to children generally. He identified completely with this figure and the quest of serving children. Given Carroll's well-known passion and pure love for little girls, we can infer from *Sir Isumbras* the broad cultural phenomenon that faith in children and the mission both to feature and protect them goes along with their eroticization and its dangers. The good knight will rush to their rescue, but may look a bit foolish and faintly compromised.[30]

In his edition of the two *Alice* books for the Penguin Classics series Hugh Haughton reiterated that Tenniel's frontispiece is "clearly a parody of one of the most famous Pre-Raphaelite paintings of the time."[31] Frederick Sandys's scandalous print is just such a parody. Tenniel's chivalric invention imagines something more complex than that.

Other aspects of the *Looking-Glass* frontispiece figure in chapters 11 and 13.

29. Timothy Hilton, *The Pre-Raphaelites* (New York: Oxford University Press, 1970), 82.

30. Robert Polhemus, "John Millais's Children: Faith and Erotics—*The Woodman's Daughter* (1851)," *Victorian Literature and the Victorian Visual Imagination*, ed. Carol T. Christ and John O. Jordan (Berkeley: University of California Press, 1995), 289–302; 296.

31. Lewis Carroll, *Alice's Adventures in Wonderland and Through the Looking-Glass*, ed. Hugh Haughton (London: Penguin Books, 1998), 325; see also xlviii, 349.

CHAPTER 8

The Descent of the Jabberwock

*T*he day after Christmas in 1868, *Punch* published a nightmarish vision drawn by Tenniel's friend and colleague on the art staff, George du Maurier. This cartoon, titled "A Little Christmas Dream" (fig. 8.1; 26 December 1868, 272), is in several respects a prototype for Tenniel's famous *Looking-Glass* illustration of a young knight confronting the Jabberwock (fig. 8.2). As striking as the sameness of the subject matter—a boy menaced by a monster—is the basic similarity of the organization of these two pictures, with the boy in each one placed in a foreground corner, looking diagonally across towards the monster farther back, who almost fills the opposite half of the picture. Though the different monsters descend from different stock (du Maurier's is mainly a mammoth, Tenniel's mainly a dragon), they carry their tusks, claws, and heads in the same menacing configuration (secondary head, in the du Maurier). The city street and the path in the woods too are much the same, with the houses, lamp posts, and picket fence of the one replaced by the thicket of trees of the other.

Originally planned as the frontispiece to *Through the Looking-Glass*, Tenniel's drawing was relegated to the middle of chapter 1 when Lewis Carroll decided, after consulting the mothers of representative potential readers, that it was indeed (as had been suggested to him) "too terrible a monster, and likely to alarm nervous and imaginative children."[1]

Of course, nervous and imaginative children would be terrified as much by the weakness of the protagonist as by the power of the monster. They would identify with Tenniel's seemingly frail, childlike knight—"Childe," in the nomenclature of the old ballads, which the poem "Jabberwocky" parodies. This child knight seems the androgynous projection of Alice's own fears: he closely resembles the Alice of figure 8.3, leaning back with long hair hanging down. (In that picture, having mastered the monstrous poem "Jabberwocky" by interpreting it for Alice, Humpty Dumpty has taken the monster's place.) Neither Alice nor her chivalric counterpart looks strong enough for

1. Crutch, 61. This is the best-known instance of Carroll's custom of showing the Tenniel illustrations to friends before publication. For other instances see Carroll, *Picture Book*, 360; and *Diaries*, 6:120–21 (25 June 1870).

A LITTLE CHRISTMAS DREAM.

FIGURE 8.1. George du Maurier.
"A Little Christmas Dream." From
Punch, 26 December 1868.

FIGURE 8.2. Tenniel. The
Jabberwock and the young knight.
From *Through the Looking-Glass*.

FIGURE 8.3. Tenniel. Alice and Humpty Dumpty. From *Through the Looking-Glass.*

self-defense. As one viewer has commented, Tenniel's little hero "could not possibly galumph," let alone slay dragons.[2]

In its way the du Maurier picture is even more alarming. The terror of the Jabberwock is at least partly undercut by its myopic expression and middle-class waistcoat and spats, but the terror of the du Maurier monster is unmitigated. The doubled heads and gaping mouth are obviously threatening; more subtle is the carelessness of the extra figure of the policeman, who twirls his baton as he patrols the street, unseeing. The snow freezing to the boy's feet realizes the anxious dream motif of arrested flight that Freud would soon study in *The Interpretation of Dreams* (1900).[3] It does not take much analysis to recognize the unknowing bobby as a neglectful father figure—the antitype of the supportive father to whom Carroll's hero will report his surprising victory over the Jabberwock. In du Maurier's nightmare such a happy ending is unimaginable.

Like the Tenniel drawing, the du Maurier cartoon is a kind of book illustration, but displaced. It is a satiric comment on *The World before the Deluge* by Louis Figuier, a book of popular paleontology that had achieved five editions in the original French and two editions (1865, 1866) in English translation. The cartoon's caption is largely self-explanatory:

> Mr. L. Figuier, in the Thesis which precedes his interesting work on the world before the Flood, condemns the practice of awakening the youthful mind to admiration by means of fables and fairy tales, and recommends, in lieu thereof, the study of the natural history of the world in which we live. Fired by this advice, we have tried the experiment on our eldest, an imaginative boy of six. We have cut off his "Cinderella" and his "Puss in Boots," and introduced him to some of the more peaceful fauna of the preadamite world, as they appear restored in Mr. Figuier's book.
>
> The poor boy has not had a decent night's rest ever since!

Although Figuier writes as if his proposals were new, they are in the tradition of Rousseau's *Émile* (1762). Figuier wants to deny children fables, fairy tales, myths, and all such "purely imaginative" readings, because such stories condition "weak and irresolute minds, given to credulity, inclined to mysticism—proselytes, in advance, to chimerical conceptions and to every extravagant system." He acknowledges that "the imaginative faculty, which permits of ideality and of the abstract,— which forms poets, inventors, and artists,—is inherent in the mind, and cannot be suppressed; it can only perish with it. It is the integral part of intelligence." But he maintains that that faculty can best be exercised on the things of this world, in "the study of nature." The works of the Creator are marvelous enough for any childish or adult imagination, and their study both educates the reasoning faculty and leads to a proper reverence for the Creator. Even geology, if properly understood,

2. Alexander L. Taylor, *The White Knight: A Study of C. L. Dodgson (Lewis Carroll)* (Edinburgh: Oliver & Boyd, 1952), 80.

3. Sigmund Freud, *The Interpretation of Dreams,* 3rd ed., trans. A. A. Brill (New York: Macmillan, 1913), 461.

FIGURE 8.4. Édouard Riou. "Ideal scene of the Lias with Ichthyosaurus and Plesiosaurus." Wood engraving by Laurent Hotelin and Alexandre Hurel. From Louis Figuier, *The World before the Deluge* (1865; rpt. 1866).

FIGURE 8.5. Édouard Riou. "Ideal Landscape of the Liasic Period." Wood engraving by Antoine Valérie Bertrand. From Louis Figuier, *The World before the Deluge* (1865; rpt. 1866).

will strengthen piety; and it has the advantage over fairy tales that it is scientifically true, and good for the mind.[4]

What Figuier seems not to notice, but what du Maurier seizes upon as the basis for his cartoon, is the fact that his essay in "science" carries with it a large number of fantastic woodcut illustrations, not factual and pietistic but imaginative and profane. A conjectured monster is no less fabulous for having a scientific name, and several of the illustrations in *The World before the Deluge* could do just what Figuier feared, that is, "cultivate and excite that inclination for the marvellous which is already excessive in the human mind."

Not that there is anything very extravagant about the illustrations of the mammoth skeleton and reconstructed mammoth in Figuier's book, which are the immediate prototypes for du Maurier's monster. But they were not part of the main series of illustrations by the artist Édouard Riou, called "ideal landscapes" or "ideal scenes," which together made up the chief interest of the book. These pictures included visions of some remarkably sublime monsters: for example, figures 8.4 and 8.5. Instead of becoming extinct, these monsters had progeny that still flourish in sensational (and profitable) "dinosaur books" for children.

4. Louis Figuier, *The World before the Deluge* (London: Chapman & Hall, 1865), 2, 4, 5, 7.

FIGURE 8.6. Tenniel. Ornamental initial. From *Punch*, 1 March 1851.

FIGURE 8.7. Tenniel. Ornamental initial (St. George and the dragon). From *Punch*, 21 August 1852.

FIGURE 8.8. Tenniel. Ornamental initial. From *Punch*, 15 October 1853.

5. Riou's fantastic illustrations proved to be very popular; redrawn, and without attribution, they appeared in Alexander Winchell's *Sketches of Creation* (New York: Harper, 1870; often reprinted—in London, by Sampson Low, Son, & Marston, 1870). Martin J. S. Rudwick devotes a chapter to Figuier's book in *Scenes from Deep Time: Early Pictorial Representations of the Prehistoric World* (Chicago: University of Chicago Press, 1992), 173–218.

Appropriately, Riou's high-Romantic penchant for the fabulous side of science later made him an authorized illustrator of the scientific fantasies of Jules Verne.[5]

The haberdashery that Tenniel used to humanize the Jabberwock recalls the outfits of several dragons that he had drawn for *Punch* early in his career, all ornamental initials (figs. 8.6, 8.7, 8.8). Figure 8.7 varies the stock *Punch* theme of St. George and the dragon (figs. 8.9, 8.10,

FIGURE 8.9. Tenniel. Ornamental initial (St. George and the dragon). From *Punch,* 9 August 1851.

FIGURE 8.10. Tenniel. Ornamental initial (St. George and the dragon). From *Punch,* 20 September 1851.

FIGURE 8.11. Tenniel. Ornamental initial (St. George and the dragon). From *Punch,* 13 March 1852.

8.11).[6] The culmination of this motif was the title page that Tenniel drew for volume 37 (1859), in which Mr. Punch, armed not as a medieval but as a Greek warrior, triumphs over the monster of "cant," "folly," and "humbug" (fig. 8.12; 1 July 1859, title page). When this image is held upside down in front of a mirror, the kinship between the dragon and the *Looking-Glass* Jabberwock becomes more obvious, especially in the wings and the trailing tail. And, of course, Mr. Punch's polka-dotted

6. Figure 8.6: 20 (1 March 1851), 91. Figure 8.7: 23 (21 August 1852), 85. Figure 8.8: 25 (15 October 1853), 161. Figure 8.9: 21 (9 August 1851), 67. Figure 8.10: 21 (20 September 1851), 133. Figure 8.11: 22 (13 March 1852), 105. Simpson sheds light on Tenniel's refinement of the neo-medieval tradition at *Punch* of inventing ornamental initials (114–19).

FIGURE 8.12. Tenniel. Mr. Punch as a Greek warrior. From *Punch,* 1 July 1859.

hobbyhorse will also reappear in *Looking-Glass,* not much metamorphosed, as the Rocking-horse-fly (fig. 8.13).

Hobbyhorses in this style, as drawn by John Leech and others as well as by Tenniel, were standard props in *Punch;* figure 8.12 is only the most striking example.

In addition to the du Maurier and Tenniel cartoons that prefigure the Jabberwock, there is also an Old Master painting. Francis Huxley drew attention to an engraving after a painting by Salvator Rosa, which had been printed in William Hone's *Every-Day Book and Table Book*—a Regency almanac, elaborately annotated and illustrated, which was often reprinted. Carroll himself owned a copy.[7] The entry for 17 January is devoted to the life of St. Anthony, the patron saint of monks, whose religious retreat had been tested repeatedly by devils in many guises, including that of an exceptionally hideous monster. The engraving by Samuel Williams with which Hone illustrates this hagiography (fig. 8.14) is a simplified rendering of Rosa's *The Temptation of St. Anthony,* long in the Pitti Palace in Florence. The perspective of this engraving does indeed anticipate that of the Jabberwock; the monsters have several features in common; and the old saint's cross and young knight's sword are functionally as well as visually equivalent.

Whether or not Tenniel knew this particular engraving or the painting on which it is based, he certainly knew the topic that they illustrate. One of his first large drawings for *Punch,* an illustration to an

7. Francis Huxley, *The Raven and the Writing Desk* (New York: Harper & Row, 1976), 68. William Hone, *Every-Day Book; or, The Guide to the Year,* 2 vols. (London: Hunt & Clarke, 1826–27). Lovett, *Lewis Carroll among His Books,* 157, no. 973.

FIGURE 8.13. Tenniel. Rocking-horse-fly. From *Through the Looking-Glass.*

FIGURE 8.14. Salvator Rosa. *The Temptation of St. Anthony.* Wood engraving by Samuel Williams. From William Hone, *Every-Day Book and Table Book* (n.d.).

FIGURE 8.15. Tenniel. "The Saints of Old." From *Punch*, 22 March 1851.

8. "The Saints of Old. *(That is, of the Dark Ages.)* A Chant for the Times," *Punch*, 22 March 1851, 122. This satiric verse, by staff writer Percival Leigh, is an instance of the anti-Catholic feeling provoked by the so-called "Papal Aggression" of 1850, in which Nicholas Wiseman was made cardinal archbishop of Westminster.

Richard Altick deemed the unsigned drawing to be "characteristic work of [Richard] Doyle, one of the last pieces he did while on the *Punch* staff"; *"Punch": The Lively Youth of a British Institution, 1841–1851* (Columbus: Ohio State University Press, 1997), 165. But Doyle had resigned from *Punch* three months earlier, in November 1850; and Tenniel was quickly hired as his replacement, at first mimicking Doyle's style (Engen, *Sir John Tenniel*, 25–27). Leigh's role, identified from a ledger of contributors, is noted in the *Punch Historical Archive 1841–1992* database.

9. Wright, 299; previously published in *The Art-Journal*, n.s. 3 (1864): 117. In drawing St. Anthony, Fairholt may have copied Williams. For discussions of the "outline style" of drawing, see William Vaughan, *German Romanticism and English Art* (New Haven: Yale University Press, 1979), 123–54; and Altick, *"Punch,"* 676–79.

anticlerical travesty called "The Saints of Old," shows (in the upper left-hand corner) St. Anthony, asleep, being menaced by an ineffectual dragon as loutish as the Jabberwock (fig. 8.15; 22 March 1851, 122). Two stanzas in the *Punch* ballad motivate this vignette and also the one opposite:

> Talk of Jumpers, talk of Shakers, and their antics queer and quaint!
> They are all nothing; none but Fakirs can approach your ancient Saint.
> Thus he lived without a neighbour, or a soul to love or please,
> Working not, and giving labour only to industrious fleas.
> > [Sing the cock-bird is the gander, and the goose the gander's hen;
> > And these, my bucks, were your holy men!]
>
> Now he lay in trances snoring—now his occupation dull
> Was to sit intently poring on an image or a skull;
> With these employments interfered the Fiend, with imps in various shapes,
> Who, to annoy the Saint, appeared as dragons, owls, wild beasts, and apes.
> > Sing, &c.[8]

Just as likely as the Williams engraving to have caught Tenniel's attention is the engraving of the same painting, by F. W. Fairholt, in Thomas Wright's *A History of Caricature and Grotesque* (fig. 8.16). Despite the shadows of the forest, Tenniel's monster is a brighter and firmer image than Williams's; it has more in common with Fairholt's more analytic "outline" version.[9]

FIGURE 8.16. Salvator Rosa. *The Temptation of St. Anthony.* Wood engraving by F. W. Fairholt. From Thomas Wright, *A History of Caricature & Grotesque in Literature and Art* (1865).

It happens that Lewis Carroll's later advisor on artistic matters, John Ruskin, had strongly mixed emotions about Salvator Rosa. He feared, and condemned as meretricious, Salvator's penchant for the terrible and the Sublime: "The base and vicious painters, of whom Salvator stands far ahead the basest—unapproachably and inexpressibly detestable—a very abyss of abomination—these as a class—and Salvator chiefly as representative of them, are attracted by terror—and skillful in arousing it in others." But Salvator's *St. Anthony*, which Ruskin studied in the Pitti Palace, had a great appeal for him; he thought that in it "such power as the artist possessed is fully manifested, and less offensively than is usual in his sacred subjects." The painting showed Salvator to be "capable of fear"—fear of damnation. In the following account, Salvator seems to merge with St. Anthony himself—who also shares the perspective of the onlooker and art critic: "The gray spectre, horseheaded, striding across the sky . . . its bat wings spread, green bars of the twilight seen between its bones; it was no play to him—the painting of it. Helpless Salvator! A little early sympathy, a word of true guidance, perhaps, had saved him."[10]

10. *Modern Painters,* in *The Works of John Ruskin,* ed. E. T. Cook and Alexander Wedderburn, 39 vols. (London: George Allen, 1903–12), 4:373 (from a manuscript), 86; 7:309.

Ruskin's responses to this picture may serve as proxy for what Carroll's own responses would have been. Collegiate monastics at Christ Church, Ruskin and Carroll suffered many of the same temptations (including affection for Alice Liddell), and much the same sense of guilt. Ruskin's guilt eventually gave way to madness; Carroll evaded his by constructing intellectual puzzles in the sleepless hours of night, to ward off the torment of evil thoughts. It could as well be said of each of them what the art historian Carl Linfert has said of St. Anthony, whom Bosch and many others besides Salvator painted in his distress: "What attracted Bosch was the true content of this man's life: the resistance he put up to onslaughts against his virtue which, admittedly, came mostly as visions, so that the saint scarcely had much occasion to become familiar with the real world, the flesh, and real devils."[11] During his visit to the Royal Museum in Berlin in 1867 Carroll noticed "several [paintings] well known from engravings, such as St. Anthony's temptation" (*Russian Journal*, 78).

Perhaps when he relegated Tenniel's monstrous frontispiece to the inside of his book, Carroll was protecting himself as well as "nervous and imaginative children." The mock-heroic note that Tenniel struck was not an adequate defense. Descending from Salvator's sublime demon—the tormentor of an ascetic saint—Tenniel's Jabberwock could indeed be "too terrible a monster."

11. Carl Linfert, *Hieronymus Bosch,* trans. Robert Erich Wolf (New York: Harry N. Abrams, 1971), 74.

PLATE 1. Dalziel Brothers. Proof of wood engraving of the Sheep's shop interior in *Through the Looking-Glass*, annotated by Tenniel. Photographic credit: The Pierpont Morgan Library, New York.

PLATE 2. Carroll. Title page to gift manuscript for Alice Liddell, *Alice's Adventures under Ground* (1864). British Library / Granger. All Rights Reserved.

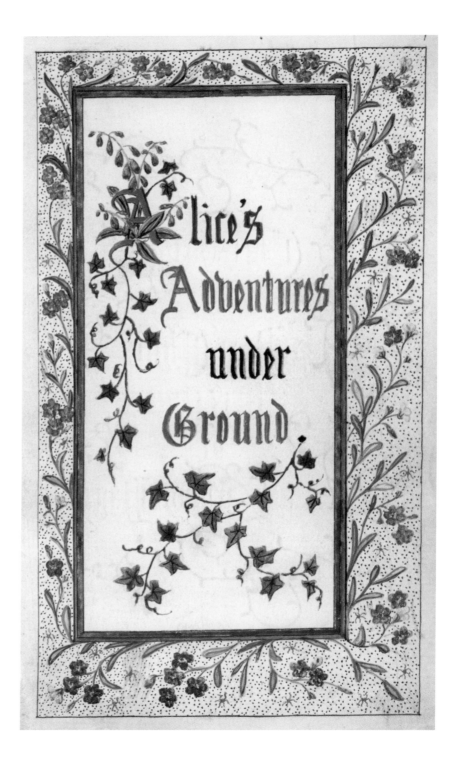

PLATE 4. Tenniel. Hand-colored supplementary frontispiece to *Alice's Adventures in Wonderland* (1866), tipped in. *EC85.D6645.865a.1866a. Houghton Library, Harvard University.

PLATE 5. Tenniel. "*The Queen has come!* And *isn't* she angry?" From *The Nursery "Alice"* (1890), printed by Edmund Evans. *EC85.D6645.865a.1890. Houghton Library, Harvard University.

PLATE 7. Tenniel; colored by Fritz Kredel. Chess-board landscape. From *Through the Looking-Glass* (New York: Random House, 1946).

PLATE 8. Tenniel, colored by Fritz Kredel. Trial scene, part of title page to *With Alice in Wonderland*, the first story in *Best in Children's Books* 12 (New York: Nelson Doubleday, 1958).

"Looking-Glass Insects"

he most commonly cited link between *Punch* and *Alice* is the supposed presence in *Through the Looking-Glass* of two stock characters from Tenniel's political cartoons, Benjamin Disraeli and William Ewart Gladstone. Chapter 3, "Looking-Glass Insects," includes Tenniel's illustration of Alice in a railway compartment; by an established convention the man across from her, wearing a paper hat and otherwise "dressed in white paper," is Benjamin Disraeli (fig. 9.1). This idea may belong to William Empson, who introduced it casually in his influential study of the *Alice* books, a chapter in *Some Versions of Pastoral* (1935):

FIGURE 9.1. Tenniel. Alice in the railway carriage. From *Through the Looking-Glass.*

In the *Looking-Glass* too there are ideas about progress at an early stage of the journey of growing up. Alice goes quickly through the first square by railway, in a carriage full of animals in a state of excitement about the progress of business and machinery; the only man is Disraeli dressed in newspapers—the new man who gets on by self-advertisement, the newspaper-fed man who believes in progress, possibly even the rational dress of the future. (256)

Empson apparently was looking at the picture here, not the text; for the text does not specify newspapers, but Tenniel's passenger does hold a newspaper—whatever he may be wearing.

On the next page, Empson hazarded that Disraeli "turns up again as the unicorn when the Lion and the Unicorn are fighting for the Crown." Probably this too refers to an illustration (fig. 1.50) which shows the combatants more clearly than the illustration of them actually at fisticuffs but somewhat in the background, a few pages before. In any case both of Empson's suggestions have been applied to the Tenniel illustrations.

Even Frances Sarzano, who was skeptical about other supposed "models" for various figures in *Alice,* was not prepared "to deny that the paper-clad passenger in the railway compartment is Benjamin Disraeli." As Martin Gardner put it in *The Annotated Alice,* "A comparison of the illustration of the man in white paper with Tenniel's political cartoons in *Punch* leaves little doubt that the face under the folded paper hat is Benjamin Disraeli's." Gardner went on to suggest that "Tenniel and/or Carroll may have had in mind the 'white papers' (official documents) with which such statesmen are surrounded." Donald J. Gray ambivalently observed that "although Tenniel's drawing unmistakably resembles him, there is nothing in the text to suggest that man dressed in paper is intended to represent Benjamin Disraeli"—aside from the possibility that his advice to "take a return ticket" at each stop may reflect Disraeli's frequent returns to office as a government minister.[1]

As regards the later illustration (fig. 1.50), if the Unicorn was Disraeli then the Lion might as well be Gladstone; and in 1945 Florence Becker Lennon suggested that he was, citing as evidence Tenniel's "cartoons of the two alternating Prime Ministers in *Punch*" (184). Martin Gardner gave this idea some currency in the first edition of *The Annotated Alice* (1960, page 288), but criticized it in the third edition (2000, page 230), citing the first edition of the present work.[2]

In 2007 Richard Aldous appropriated the supposed identities of the Lion and the Unicorn to construct the title of his comparative history of the rival prime ministers, *The Lion and the Unicorn: Gladstone vs Disraeli.*[3] In the text he asserted, without citing evidence, that when *Looking-Glass* appeared chapter 7 ("The Lion and the Unicorn") "had been widely interpreted as a subtle depiction of Gladstone and Disraeli" (244). The appearance of Aldous's book prompted Richard Scully to search for evidence to support the identity thesis, and, finding none, he concluded that the argument that I presented in the first edition of this book is correct: specifically, that neither Carroll nor Tenniel identified the Lion or the Unicorn with Gladstone or Disraeli, and, furthermore, that the identification of Disraeli with the Unicorn was not a Victorian understanding but a figment of William Empson's twentieth-century imagination.[4]

1. Sarzano, 21. *Annotated Alice,* 3rd ed., 172. *Alice in Wonderland,* ed. Donald J. Gray, Norton Critical Edition, 3rd ed. (New York: W. W. Norton, 2013), 128.

2. Michael Patrick Hearn, in his essay "*Alice*'s Other Parent: John Tenniel as Lewis Carroll's Illustrator," *American Book Collector* n.s. 4:3 (May–June 1983), attributed the Disraeli and Gladstone interpretations to "some early reviewers" (18)—not identified. Two related suggestions have not been widely accepted. Roger Lancelyn Green compared the Mad Hatter of *Alice's Adventures* (fig. 5.1) to Tenniel's Gladstone; and Alison Lurie saw the contrast between the dapper Walrus and the proletarian Carpenter (fig. 1.25) to be a contrast between Disraeli and Gladstone. *The Diaries of Lewis Carroll,* ed. Roger Lancelyn Green, 2 vols. (1954; rpt. Westport, CT: Greenwood Press, 1971), 1:237; 2:277. Alison Lurie, "On the Subversive Side," *Times Literary Supplement,* 28 March 1980, 353.

3. Richard Aldous, *The Lion and the Unicorn: Gladstone vs Disraeli* (New York: W. W. Norton, 2007).

4. Richard Scully, "The Lion and the Unicorn: William Gladstone and Benjamin Disraeli through William Empson's Looking Glass," *International Journal of Comic Art* 15 (2013): 323–37; 334.

Most of the identity claims invite the reader to compare the *Alice* illustrations to typical Tenniel caricatures of the two prime ministers, so I selected some representative cartoons from 1871 (the year that Tenniel finished drawing the *Looking-Glass* illustrations) as a basis for comparison. Figures 9.2, 9.3, 9.4, and 9.5 are details from contemporary cartoons that show the faces of both Disraeli (with the goatee) and

FIGURE 9.2. Tenniel. Disraeli and Gladstone (cartoon detail). From *Punch*, 20 May 1871.

FIGURE 9.3. Tenniel. Disraeli and Gladstone (cartoon detail). From *Punch*, 27 May 1871.

FIGURE 9.4. Tenniel. Disraeli and Gladstone (cartoon detail). From *Punch*, 1 July 1871.

FIGURE 9.5. Tenniel. Disraeli and Gladstone (cartoon detail). From *Punch*, 5 August 1871.

FIGURE 9.6. Tenniel. Sketch of
Alice in the railway carriage. From
Phillip James, *Children's Books of
Yesterday* (1933).

5. Fig. 9.2: 20 May 1871, 203. Fig. 9.3:
27 May 1871, 215. Fig. 9.4: 1 July 1871,
269. Fig. 9.5: 5 August 1871, 49. Tenniel had begun work on *Looking-Glass*
by January 1870, but apparently had not
finished by August 1871; see chapter 7,
note 1.

6. Reproduced from Phillip James,
Children's Books of Yesterday (London:
The Studio, 1933), 113; see also Justin
G. Schiller, "Census: Sir John Tenniel's
Original Drawings to *Alice's Adventures
in Wonderland* and *Through the Looking-
Glass*," *Alice's Adventures in Wonderland:
An 1865 Printing Re-Described* (Kingston, NY: privately printed, 1990), 92. A
similar reverse drawing of this scene is
reproduced by Garvey and Bond, 53.
Tenniel included a very rough sketch of
this scene in a letter to Carroll, reproduced in Collingwood, 147; see figure
10.5 below.

7. Odell Shepard, *The Lore of The Unicorn* (New York: Barnes & Noble, 1967),
70. Figure 9.7 is from *Burke's Peerage and
Baronetage*, 31st ed. (London: Harrison,
1869), xv.

8. *Punch*, 7 October 1871, 147. The
cartoon and a poem on the facing page
make swimming instruction a matter
of patriotic duty. The quotation in the
caption, "And teach the young idea how
to—*swim!*" plays on the words of James
Thomson's *The Seasons*, "Spring," 1153.

9. Fig. 9.9: 15 June 1861, 246. Fig.
9.10: 23 October 1858, 170.

Gladstone.[5] Disraeli's profile in these cartoons does roughly match the
profile of the man in the paper hat; but in all of Tenniel's political cartoons there is a definite chin under the goatee, which itself is fairly well
developed, whereas in the railway-car illustration the man in the paper
hat has a receding chin and the merest wisp of a goatee. If Tenniel
had wanted the engravers (the Dalziel Brothers) to produce a likeness
consistent with his *Punch* caricatures of Disraeli, he could easily have
controlled these details. An early drawing of this scene shows the man
in white paper both chinless and beardless (fig. 9.6).[6] It is unlikely that
he is a deliberate caricature of Disraeli.

Of course, the Unicorn in figure 1.50 does have a conspicuous goatee; and I suspect that it was this detail that first prompted the identification with Disraeli. Certainly in no other respect does the Unicorn
look much like Disraeli. But a goatee is part of the nature of the beast.
According to tradition a unicorn is partly goat-like; and in British heraldry unicorns have goat beards, as in figure 9.7, a contemporary rendering of the royal arms.[7] So there is nothing peculiarly Disraeliesque
about the Unicorn in figure 1.50.

The case for Gladstone is no better. The Lion in figure 1.50 is as
dour as the Gladstone of figures 9.2, 9.3, and 9.4, but there is little else
to compare. However, the Lion in figure 1.50 is indistinguishable from
the adult lion in figure 9.8, also drawn by Tenniel in 1871, who represents not Gladstone but the ideal English paterfamilias.[8]

To allegorize the Lion and the Unicorn into Gladstone and Disraeli
is a pleasant idea, but it was not Tenniel's or Carroll's.

The man in white paper, the goat, and the guard's use of binocu-
lars are all bizarre details in figure 9.1; and yet Tenniel's drawing of the
interior of the railway compartment presents, nonetheless, a more or
less ordinary view. The lack of privacy to be had in even a first-class railway compartment was the basis for countless *Punch* cartoons during the
fifties and sixties. For example, figure 9.9 (drawn by Gordon Thompson
in 1861) shows a bohemian artist affronting a straitlaced clergyman in a
compartment much like Alice's. And figure 9.10 (unsigned, 1858) has
a guard intrude on the privacy of the passengers almost as effectively
as Tenniel's guard does in figure 9.1.[9] The indignities of railway travel
are not much worse in the *Looking-Glass* illustration than they could be
in fact.

FIGURE 9.7. The royal arms. From Burke, *Peerage and Baronetage*, 31st ed. (1869).

A LESSON WORTH LEARNING.

"AND TEACH THE YOUNG IDEA HOW TO—*SWIM!*"

FIGURE 9.8. Tenniel. "A Lesson Worth Learning." From *Punch*, 7 October 1871.

And yet privacy was possible in such a setting, as can be seen in the handsome genre painting by Augustus Leopold Egg, *The Travelling Companions* (1862; fig. 9.11). The girl sleeping and the other girl reading are each in a private world, comfortably protected by yards of luxurious fabric, oblivious even to the picturesque foreign landscape passing outside their window. No guard menaces them, and no goat,

FIGURE 9.9. Gordon Thompson. "Enthusiastic Artist." From *Punch*, 15 June 1861.

ENTHUSIASTIC ARTIST. *" My dear Sir, keep that Expression for one moment ! You 've got such a splendid Head for my Picture of the ' Canting Hypocrite ! ' "*

FIGURE 9.10. "A Fact. Three Gentlemen Smoking in a Railway Carriage." From *Punch*, 23 October 1858.

A FACT.

Three Gentlemen Smoking in a Railway Carriage—Guard puts in his head, and loquitur : *" There are two things not allowed on this Line, Gentlemen ; Smoking, and the Servants of the Company receiving Money."* The result, a metallic pass from Gentlemen to Guard.

and no dubious man in white paper. But their compartment is virtually the same as Alice's, the posture of the girl on the right is the same, and even their little black hats on their laps are the same, each ornamented with a red feather, like Alice's white one.

FIGURE 9.11. Augustus Leopold Egg. *The Travelling Companions.* Oil on canvas. Photo by Birmingham Museums Trust.

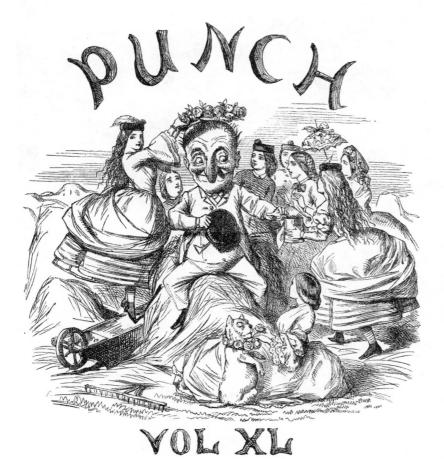

FIGURE 9.12. Tenniel. Fashionable young women with Mr. Punch. From *Punch,* 1 January 1861.

FIGURE 9.13. John Everett Millais. *My First Sermon*. Mixed mezzotint engraving by T. O. Barlow, 1865. Crown Copyright Victoria and Albert Museum.

10. Raymond Lister, *Victorian Narrative Paintings* (London: Museum Press, 1966), 52–53. For Egg's friendship with Leech and Lemon see *A Victorian Canvas: The Memoirs of W. P. Frith, R. A.*, ed. Nevile Wallis (London: Geoffrey Bles, 1957), 60–61. Egg died the year after he painted *The Travelling Companions*, and it was not exhibited at the Royal Academy. Sold at auction by Christie's in May 1863, and purchased by a dealer, .at some point before 1876 it became part of the large art collection of Albert Levy, who owned other paintings by Egg. "Hilaire Faberman, Augustus Leopold Egg, R. A. (1816–1863)" (Ph.D. dissertation, Yale University, 1983), 504. Hilarie Faberman, "Egg, Augustus Leopold (1816–1863)." *Oxford Dictionary of National Biography* (Oxford University Press, 2004), online.

11. Millais painted a sequel, *My Second Sermon* (1864), which was also engraved and published in 1865; it showed the same sitter (Millais's daughter, Effie), in the same setting and costume, with her hat at her side, drowsing off. *PRB Millais PRA: An Exhibition* (Liverpool: Walker Art Gallery, 1967), 46–47. Hilary Guise, *Great Victorian Engravings: A Collector's Guide* (London: Astragal Books, 1980), 134. Rodney K. Engen, *Pre-Raphaelite Prints: The Graphic Art of Millais, Holman Hunt, Rossetti and Their Followers* (London: Lund Humphries, 1995), 63, 122. Both paintings are reproduced by Geoffroy Millais, *Sir John Everett Millais* (London: Academy Editions, 1979), 72–73.

As Raymond Lister suggests, Tenniel may have known this painting. A possible connection would be through John Leech or Mark Lemon of *Punch*, both mutual friends of Egg and Tenniel.[10] However, neither the mass-produced railway compartment nor the stylish porkpie hat were unusual sights in mid-Victorian times. Tenniel's title-page illustration for the first *Punch* volume of 1861 shows two such hats adorning young women several years older than Alice (fig. 9.12; 1 January 1861, title page). Alice's hat—including a white feather—her barrel muff, her shoes, her skirt, and her general posture, all figure in J. E. Millais's sentimental and vastly popular genre painting *My First Sermon*, which was exhibited at the Royal Academy in 1863 and published as an engraving (fig. 9.13) in 1865.[11] In 1868 Tenniel put a similar hat on a girl he drew for *Punch* who could pass for Alice (fig. 9.14; she is shown on the edge of a crowd at the Zoological Gardens). This girl already has the striped stockings that Alice will wear in *Through the Looking-Glass*,

a change from the plain ones of *Alice's Adventures*; and, like the Alice of figure 9.1, she still has the porkpie hat that had passed from adult fashion some years before. It is hard to say when this style ceased to be fashionable for little girls. A photograph of three young aristocratic sisters taken in 1871 (fig. 9.15) shows larger hats with bigger feathers; but otherwise Alice's traveling outfit was very much up to date when Tenniel drew it, despite his old-fashioned habits. The girl on the left could be Alice herself.[12]

TWO ILLUSTRATIONS in the same chapter of *Through the Looking-Glass* draw attention to an old-fashioned decorative motif that may seem mysterious if noticed out of historical context. Tenniel shows two of Carroll's "looking-glass insects" against a background of relatively large ivy leaves (figs. 8.13, 9.16). This compositional device draws attention to the ivy that flourishes elsewhere in this book: there is ivy on the oak tree in the frontispiece, ivy on the tree behind Tweedledum and Tweedledee, and a spray of ivy on Humpty Dumpty's wall. Ivy being an ancient symbol—variously of love, wine, victory, or mourning—one might wonder whether Tenniel was using ivy symbolically in *Through the Looking-Glass,* and, if so, how.

12. Figure 9.14 is from *Punch's Almanack for 1868*. The fashion for porkpie hats lasted approximately from 1855 to 1865 (*OED*); the hat was fashionable for children before it was for adults. Anne Buck, *Victorian Costume and Costume Accessories* (New York: T. Nelson & Sons, 1961), 117. The photograph was previously published by Adeline Hartcup, *Children of the Great Country Houses* (London: Sidgwick & Jackson, 1982), 131.

In his children's book *Little Annie and Jack in London* (1869), Walter Crane included a drawing of a brother and sister and their parents seated in a railway compartment. The point of view is the same as in figure 9.1. The girl, about Alice's age, sits in the same corner, though turned to her left; she wears a similar hairdo, and hat (though without the feather), and bow tie, and muff. Reproduced in Rodney K. Engen, *Walter Crane as a Book Illustrator* (London: Academy Editions, 1975), 30; see also 29.

FIGURE 9.16. Tenniel. Snap-dragon-fly. From *Through the Looking-Glass.*

FIGURE 9.17. Tenniel. Ornamental initial. From *Punch,* 11 January 1851.

FIGURE 9.18. Tenniel. Ornamental initial. From *Punch,* 8 February 1851.

In fact the abundant ivy in *Through the Looking-Glass* is only decorative and not symbolic, a vestige of Tenniel's early graphic repertoire. Figures 9.17 and 9.18, early ornamental initials for *Punch,* integrate ivy and calligraphy in a way that recalls the little vines or "vinets" (vignettes) that decorate the borders and illustrated capitals of illuminated medieval manuscripts. Tenniel, having studied in Munich, was as susceptible as any Victorian artist to the vogue for German design, which in the second quarter of the nineteenth century revived elements of archaic page layout, including borders made up of ivy and

FIGURE 9.19. Henry Anelay.
Illustrated title page. Wood
engraving by James Johnston.
From Mrs. T. D. Crewdson, *Aunt
Jane's Verses for Children* (1851).

other vines. (The various L-shaped illustrations in the *Alice* books,
which integrate closely with the text alongside, are a product of the
same design tradition.)[13]

The German influence was widespread; figure 9.19 shows a representative engraved title page from the early fifties, framed with posts
that are entwined with ivy. Tenniel used a similar framing device in
illustrations for *Aesop's Fables* (1848; fig. 9.20) and Martin Tupper's
Proverbial Philosophy (1854; fig. 9.21). This illustration, to Tupper's poem
"Of Education," borrows more than the grape-arbor motif from Dante

13. Figures 9.17 and 9.18 are from 11
January 1851, 20; 8 February 1851, 61.
For an account of the decorated page
in Germany and England see Vaughan,
155–76.

FIGURE 9.20. Tenniel. "The Stag at the Pool." Wood engraving by Leopold Martin. From *Æsop's Fables,* trans. Thomas James (1848).

FABLE CXCVII.

THE STAG AT THE POOL.

A STAG one summer's day came to a pool to quench his thirst, and as he stood drinking he saw

FIGURE 9.21. Tenniel. "Of Education." Wood engraving by Dalziel Brothers. From Martin Tupper, *Proverbial Philosophy* (1854; rpt. n.d.).

FIGURE 9.22. Dante Gabriel Rossetti. *The Girlhood of Mary Virgin*. Oil on canvas, 1848–49. © Tate, London 2018.

Gabriel Rossetti's famous first Pre-Raphaelite painting, *The Girlhood of Mary Virgin* (exhibited 1849; fig. 9.22).[14]

By the time, some two decades later, that Tenniel came to draw the illustrations to *Through the Looking-Glass,* the supporting posts were gone, and the ivy had become a more natural part of the landscape; but it remained a vestige of an essentially ornamental tradition.

14. In the Rossetti painting, of course, the grape vines are emblematic, prefiguring the Passion. And in figure 9.21 they connote husbandry and harvest, aspects of the work of education. But these are exceptional uses of the ornamental motif.

Conventional flourishes of ivy also ornament the cover to the illustrated manuscript of *Alice's Adventures under Ground,* which Carroll specially prepared for Alice Liddell in 1863 and 1864, and which Tenniel evidently knew. See Plate 2.

CHAPTER 10

Carroll and Tenniel in Collaboration

*H*ow much control did Carroll exercise over Tenniel's illustrations for the *Alice* books? What elements of the pictures did Tenniel determine himself? The historical record is relatively thin; furthermore, parts of it are ambiguous, and others are apocryphal. I will review it in this chapter; and in the next will consider some practical and theoretical aspects of Victorian book illustration, before assessing there the implications of the previous chapters.

Most of what is certain about Tenniel's work on the first book, *Alice's Adventures,* is recorded in Carroll's diaries. Tom Taylor gave Carroll a letter of introduction to the artist on 25 January 1864, having already "applied" to him, on Carroll's behalf, "about pictures for *Alice's Adventures*" (*Diaries,* 4:271). Armed with this letter of introduction, Carroll found Tenniel at home that same day. "He was very friendly, and seemed to think favourably of undertaking the pictures, but must see the book before deciding" (4:272). Presumably having seen some version of the manuscript, Tenniel notified Carroll that "he consents to draw the pictures for 'Alice's Adventures Under Ground'" (5 April 1864; *Diaries,* 4:284). (No terms are mentioned in Carroll's diaries at this point, but a later record indicates that Carroll paid Tenniel £138 for drawing the illustrations—a significant sum for a college lecturer salaried at "about £450 a year."[1])

Carroll next mentions "Tenniell"—his regular misspelling for several months, not corrected until 17 July (4:338)—on 2 May 1864: "Sent Tenniell the first piece of slip set up for *Alice's Adventures,* from the beginning of Chap. III" (4:297). A surviving portion of a marked-up proof sheet in the Lewis Carroll Collection of Christ Church Library shows that Carroll had the text of *Alice's Adventures under Ground* set up in type, and that he used galley proofs as the basis for revision.[2] Evidently Carroll gave Tenniel a set of those unrevised proof sheets to work from, and then supplemented them with proofs of new and revised sections as they became available. The diary entry quoted above

1. Payment to Tenniel, 26 June 1865; *Lewis Carroll in His Own Account: The Complete Bank Account of The Rev. C. L. Dodgson,* ed. Jenny Woolf (London: Jabberwock Press, 2005), 47. Jenny Woolf, *The Mystery of Lewis Carroll: Discovering the Whimsical, Thoughtful, and Sometimes Lonely Man Who Created Alice in Wonderland* (New York: St. Martin's Press, 2010), 271.

2. "Proof sheet of the last chapter of Alice in Wonderland," Christ Church Carroll A8, Modern Archives and Manuscripts, Digital Bodleian, https://goo.gl/H2wLUZ. Evidently such proof sheets were prepared by Oxford University Press: the typeface matches that of the suppressed first printing of *Alice's Adventures in Wonderland,* and some unrevised passages are typographically identical.

may refer to galleys of chapter 3 of the manuscript text thus set up in type (including the Puppy and Caterpillar episodes); or it may have been chapter 3 of the revised version, *Alice's Adventures in Wonderland* ("A Caucus-race and a Long Tale"). Whichever it was, by 20 June 1864 Tenniel had "not begun the pictures yet" (4:310). The first drawing, on a wood block, that Tenniel was able to show Carroll—on 12 October 1864—was "of Alice sitting by the pool of tears, and the rabbit running away" (5:16), a scene in chapter 2 of the book pictured by Tenniel rather differently from the corresponding scene in chapter 1 of the manuscript, which shows the rabbit returning to Alice with a nosegay in his right hand.

The only known letter from Tenniel to Carroll surviving from this early period speaks to differences in the text at stages of revision: "Could you manage to let me have the text of 'A Mad Tea-party' for a day or two? There is much more in it than my copy contains."[3] "A Mad Tea-party," chapter 7 in *Alice's Adventures in Wonderland,* was an entirely new section for the book, not represented in the original *Under Ground* text; apparently Tenniel already had an early set of galleys for this new chapter, knew that Carroll had continued to revise it after it was set up in type, and wanted to see the current version. More about that below.

Carroll's diaries for 1864 and 1865 report several excursions by Carroll to consult with Tenniel, some of which found him at home. For example, on 21 June 1864, Carroll visited his publisher, Alexander Macmillan, "who strongly advised my altering the size of the page of my book, and adopting that of the *Water Babies*," by Charles Kingsley—published by Macmillan the previous year. That same day Carroll "called on Tenniell, who agreed to the change of page."[4] Evidently Carroll was willing to be advised by Tenniel about details of book design at this early stage of their collaboration, even before Tenniel had started work on the pictures.

Draft title pages in the Lewis Carroll Collection at Christ Church Library show that at one time or another Carroll planned for there to be 20 illustrations by Tenniel, or 24—fewer in either case than the 38 illustrations that he had himself prepared for the shorter *Under Ground* manuscript.[5] Eventually the title page for the book proudly boasted, "WITH FORTY-TWO ILLUSTRATIONS | BY JOHN TENNIEL."

Although Carroll originally wanted to publish the book in time for Christmas 1864, Tenniel was slow to begin work. As we have seen, on 20 June 1864, more than two and a half months after Tenniel had accepted the commission, Carroll found that he had "not begun the pictures yet." On 20 November Carroll wrote to Macmillan: "I fear my little book *Alice's Adventures in Wonderland* cannot appear this year. Mr. Tenniel writes that he is hopeless of completing the pictures by Xmas. The cause I do not know, but he writes in great trouble, having just lost his mother, and I have begged him to put the thing aside for the present." Carroll now hoped for publication in time for Easter, if not sooner (*Letters,* 1:74). Within a month Tenniel did send Carroll the first twelve proofs from the engraved blocks (16 December 1864).

Tenniel's letter of 8 March 1865 gives evidence of the close working relationship between the two men. Apropos the enlarged revision of the "Mad Tea-party" chapter, which he had seen and asked to borrow, Tenniel reported,

3. *Lewis Carroll & His Illustrators,* 12.

4. *Diaries,* 4:311–12. In the end, however, Carroll settled on a smaller page size than that of Kingsley's book. Jaques and Giddens, 16.

5. Christ Church Carroll-A4–A7; https://goo.gl/pPt154. Christ Church Carroll-A14; https://goo.gl/kC7koe. See also Crutch, plate II, facing 132.

The subjects I have selected from it are—The Hatter asking the riddle; which will do equally well for any other question that he may ask, and can go anywhere; and—The March Hare and the Hatter, putting the Dormouse into the tea-pot.

We now want an intermediate one, but I don't think "Twinkle, twinkle" will do, as it comes close upon the first subject, i.e. in *my copy*.[6]

It is significant that Tenniel speaks of "the subjects I have selected": evidently Carroll did not completely control the selection of the scenes to illustrate. As we saw above in chapter 2, when he illustrated a scene that Carroll had already illustrated in *Alice's Adventures under Ground* Tenniel usually was content to follow Carroll's lead, often quite closely; but for illustrating new material his initiative was at least as strong as Carroll's. Carroll may have proposed the Mad Hatter singing "Twinkle, twinkle" as an intermediate illustration; Tenniel objects that it is too close to the riddle scene in his copy, but in the end (thanks to new material?) it appears a comfortable six pages later in the book. It may be that Carroll offered Tenniel a list of scenes to choose from—of which Tenniel mentions only the two he chose and the one he had doubts about. In any case, Tenniel did choose the scenes.

It is almost shocking to see Tenniel casually suggest that the illustration of "The Hatter asking the riddle . . . will do equally well for any other question that he may ask, and can go anywhere," given how well that tea-party illustration captures in body language the "severity" of Alice's response to the Hatter's "personal remarks" uttered just before. Fortunately the layout of this image in the book as published does show both Alice's chagrin and the Hatter blandly and irrelevantly responding to it with a riddle. At the start of this letter Tenniel is less casual about the question of where to place the picture of the Fish-Footman and Frog-Footman in chapter 6. "I cannot see your objection to the page as at present arranged, but if you think it would be better to place the picture further on in the text, do it by all means. The 'two Footmen' picture is certainly too large to head a chapter." As published the picture appears at the top of the page facing the opening of the chapter, perfectly placed. Tenniel concludes this letter with an appreciative postscript: "I am very glad you like the new pictures."

Tenniel completed his work on the illustrations by the middle of June 1865; and by 15 July there were "twenty or more" copies of the printed book available to Carroll at Macmillan's, which he inscribed to friends with a feeling of satisfaction that can be guessed at. Four days later Carroll heard from Tenniel that the printing was unacceptable[7]—precipitating a crisis that is detailed in chapter 15 below.

THREE OFTEN REHEARSED STORIES would shed light on Carroll's guidance regarding Tenniel's drawings for *Alice's Adventures*. They require scrutiny.

In 1931 H. W. Greene wrote a letter to *The Times* asserting that Carroll had Tenniel model his drawing of the Mad Hatter on one Theophilus Carter, an Oxford cabinetmaker and furniture dealer, who was remembered as the inventor of a "clockwork bed" displayed at the Exhibition of 1851. This bed, an invention worthy of the White Knight him-

6. *Lewis Carroll & His Illustrators*, 12, 14.
7. See Carroll's own chronology, reproduced in *Letters*, 1:72; and also *Diaries*, 5:9–10.

self, "tipped up and threw the occupant out at the appointed hour." According to Greene, Carter "was the doubtless unconscious model for the Mad Hatter in 'Through the Looking-Glass' [sic] as depicted by Tenniel, who was brought down to Oxford by the author, as I have heard, on purpose to see him. The likeness was unmistakable."

A few days later, the Reverend W. Gordon Baillie insisted that Carter must have known he had been the model for the Mad Hatter. And as a cap to this correspondence, W. J. Ryland, who had originally mentioned Carter in connection with the clockwork bed, testified that he had not known "that Carter was the original of the 'Mad Hatter,' but on looking again at the Tenniel drawing I see it is he to the life. To me," he went on, introducing a red herring, "he was the living image of the late W. E. Gladstone, and, being well aware of the fact, was always careful to wear the high collar and black stock so often depicted in *Punch* in cartoons of the 'Grand Old Man.'"[8]

All three reporters agreed that Carter looked like Tenniel's Mad Hatter, and according to Baillie the resemblance was widely noticed. But these accounts rely heavily on hearsay ("as I have heard"; "the story went"). No evidence has come to light, in Carroll's diaries, letters, or elsewhere, that Carroll ever brought Tenniel to Oxford to see Carter.

Tenniel did visit Oxford on occasion, to join rowing expeditions.[9] Williams and Madan proposed in 1931 that Tenniel's two illustrations of the interior of the Sheep's shop in *Looking-Glass*, chapter 5, were closely modeled on the interior of a shop across the street from Christ Church, where Carroll lived (page 239; plates XV, XVI). However, I know of no evidence that before drawing the illustrations for the first volume, *Alice's Adventures*, "Tenniel was invited to Oxford to explore the background of the story, the familiar scenes and objects," as Sally Brown has asserted.[10]

Mad Hatter matters become complicated when biographers take into account an enigmatic remark that S. D. Collingwood made in his early *Life and Letters of Lewis Carroll* (1898). According to Collingwood, during Carroll's undergraduate days at Christ Church he was assigned to a dining table along with an unidentified person who was to become the prototype of the Mad Hatter. "In those days the undergraduates dining in hall were divided into 'messes.' Each mess consisted of about half a dozen men, who had a table to themselves. . . . In Mr. Dodgson's mess were Philip Pusey [son of Edward Pusey, the theologian], the late Rev. G. C. Woodhouse, and, among others, one who still lives in 'Alice in Wonderland' as the 'Hatter.'" This account has proven difficult to square with the Theophilus Carter legend. There is no evidence that either Collingwood or Greene was right about the Mad Hatter, let alone that they both were.[11]

Shortly after Greene publicized the Carter story Falconer Madan publicized the more interesting and even more influential claim that Tenniel modeled his drawings of Alice on a young girl named Mary Hilton Badcock. Carroll, supposedly taken with a photograph of Miss Badcock (fig. 10.1), was thought to have purchased a copy in January 1865, which he "recommended" to Tenniel. (We now know what Madan may not have known: that Tenniel and Dalziel had by this time already completed a dozen engravings; see note 7.) According to Madan, Tenniel "subsequently paid visits" to the girl's home at Ripon "and adopted the suggestion." For this information as well as for a copy of

8. *The Times*, 7 March 1931, 9; 10 March 1931, 10; 13 March 1931, 10; 19 March 1931, 10; 20 March 1931, 10; see also 12 March 1931, 8. The *Official Descriptive and Illustrated Catalogue of the Great Exhibition of the Works of Industry of All Nations, 1851*, 5 vols. (London: Spicer Brothers, 1851), reports two different "alarum bedsteads" on display: one by Theodore Jones, 28 Lombard Street, "Inventor and Proprietor"; and another by Robert Watson Savage, 15 St. James Square, "Inventor"; 1:xxxvi, 466*; 2:598; Carter is not mentioned. (It happens that Tenniel designed the allegorical frontispiece and gilt-stamped covers for this impressive publication.) Falconer Madan appropriately hedged his report about Carter as the Mad Hatter (Williams and Madan, 21); Martin Gardner was less cautious (*Annotated Alice*, 3rd ed., 69). Citing a shilling guide to the exhibition, Robert Douglas-Fairhurst discredits Carter in favor of Savage in *The Story of Alice: Lewis Carroll and the Secret History of Wonderland* (London: Harvill Secker, 2015), 57.

9. Engen, *Sir John Tenniel*, 81; Morris, *Artist of Wonderland*, 72; *The Young George du Maurier: A Selection of His Letters*, ed. Daphne du Maurier (Garden City, NY: Doubleday, 1952), 262, reporting an excursion in June 1865.

10. Sally Brown, *The Original Alice: From Manuscript to Wonderland* (London: The British Library, [1997]), 39.

11. Collingwood, *Life and Letters*, 47. Hudson, *Lewis Carroll*, 144. Roger Lancelyn Green, ed., *Alice's Adventures in Wonderland and Through the Looking-Glass* (1971; rpt. London: Oxford University Press, 1976), 258. Hudson quotes extensively from an obituary article by the Reverend G. J. Cowley-Brown, one of Carroll's classmates, which was evidently Collingwood's source for the anecdote. The context of Cowley-Brown's reference to the Mad Hatter is a roll call of undergraduate colleagues (60–61).

the photograph, Madan was indebted to the adult model (now Mrs. W. G. C. Probert) and to her husband. "The resemblance," Madan wrote with circumspect indefiniteness, "is stated to be even closer in the *Looking-Glass* than in the earlier volume."[12]

This story has had a mixed reception. Roger Lancelyn Green and Denis Crutch silently dropped it—photograph and all—from their later editions of Madan's *Handbook*. Carroll's biographers have taken it up with more or less caution, ignored it, or rejected it. Florence Becker Lennon, John Pudney, Derek Hudson, and Anne Clark all say or imply that Carroll did send Tenniel this photograph, which all publish as an illustration (Hudson, in the second edition of his Carroll biography; Clark, in her biography of Alice Liddell). Hudson, partly because of the chronological problem, doubts that Tenniel paid the photograph any attention. Clark sees little resemblance "except for the long blonde hair," though in the Liddell biography she implies that Tenniel did make Alice a blonde because of the photograph. Cohen ignores the claim in his biography; Wakeling discredits this "popular myth."[13]

In the first edition of *The Illustrators of Alice* Graham Ovenden printed the photograph too, with the caption, "Mary Hilton Badcock, the model for Tenniel's Alice."[14] Florence Becker Lennon not only saw a resemblance between the photograph and the picture but repeated the story of Tenniel making "several trips to Ripon to sketch" the girl. And yet, later in her book Lennon quotes from a letter that Carroll wrote to Gertrude Thomson, an artist and illustrator with whom he began to correspond in 1878:

> Mr. Tenniel is the only artist, who has drawn for me, who has resolutely refused to use a model, and declared he no more needed one than I should need a multiplication table to work a mathematical problem! I venture to think that he was mistaken, & that for want of a model, he drew several pictures of "Alice" entirely out of proportion—head decidedly too large and feet decidedly too small.[15]

So Tenniel didn't travel to Ripon to sketch any model. I think that Roger Lancelyn Green was right to drop the whole Badcock story from his edition of the *Handbook* (followed also by Crutch in his edition). There is no disinterested authority for it, and the photograph does not look any more like Alice than do Tenniel's other renderings of young English girls (see figs. 1.44, 9.12, 9.14).

IF TENNIEL'S ALICE had any prototype, aside from Tenniel's customary representations of middle-class girls, it was Carroll's Alice: not the historical Alice Liddell, of course, who was dark-haired and wore bangs (fig. 10.2), but the Alice that Carroll himself drew in the gift

FIGURE 10.1. Photographic portrait of Mary Hilton Badcock. From S. H. Williams and F. Madan, *A Handbook of the Literature of the Rev. C. L. Dodgson (Lewis Carroll)* (1931).

12. Williams and Madan, 22.

13. Lennon, 112, 314. Pudney, 77. Hudson, *Lewis Carroll*, 2nd ed., 119. Clark, *Biography*, 135; also Anne Clark, *The Real Alice: Lewis Carroll's Dream Child* (London: Michael Joseph, 1981), 105, 106. Morton Cohen, *Lewis Carroll: A Biography* (New York: Alfred A. Knopf, 1995). Edward Wakeling, *Lewis Carroll: The Man and His Circle* (London: I.B. Tauris, 2015), 68.

14. *The Illustrators of Alice in Wonderland and Through the Looking Glass,* ed. Graham Ovenden (London: Academy Editions, 1972), [103]. In his introduction to this book John Davis says that Tenniel's illustrations were "undoubtedly" based on Miss Badcock, though he "probably worked straight from the photograph" (8).

15. Lennon, 314; for a full transcription of this letter (31 March 1892), different in minor details, see *Lewis Carroll & His Illustrators*, 246–47.

FIGURE 10.2. Carroll. Photographic portrait of Alice Liddell. Detail cut from a larger photograph, appended at the end of Carroll's gift manuscript of *Alice's Adventures under Ground* (1864). British Library / Granger. All Rights Reserved.

manuscript (see illustrations in chapter 2). Jeffrey Stern showed that the Alice of Carroll's drawings embodies Pre-Raphaelite notions of feminine beauty, especially as expressed by the painters Arthur Hughes and Dante Gabriel Rossetti.[16] Some of this influence carries over to Tenniel's conception, though he moderates it considerably. Tenniel combs Alice's abundant hair back, instead of parting it, and he minimizes the Pre-Raphaelite wave. (In *Looking-Glass* he adds a hairband—which, thanks to him, became known as an "Alice band.") Aside from the long hair, the most important trait that Tenniel takes from Carroll's drawings of Alice is the impassive, almost pouty expression. Another mark of Pre-Raphaelite style, it suits the sober child described in the text.

WITHIN A YEAR of the publication of *Alice's Adventures,* Carroll confided to Macmillan that he had "a floating idea of writing a sort of sequel to *Alice*" (*Letters,* 1:94; 24 August 1866). His first task was to commission an illustrator. Presumably he approached Tenniel first—most likely in the fall or winter of 1866. As late as April 1868, Tenniel was still resisting the idea, pleading lack of time (*Diaries,* 6:20).

Early in 1867 Carroll turned to Richard Doyle, a popular illustrator, whom Tenniel had long since replaced on the staff of *Punch.* Falconer Madan says that Carroll wrote to Doyle on 22 January 1867, "by Tenniel's advice."[17] Two days later Carroll visited Doyle, who was interested in the project but uncertain that he could do it in time. "We left the matter unsettled for the present," Carroll recorded (*Diaries,* 5:192). A year later he was writing to Mrs. George MacDonald, "Doyle isn't good enough (look at any of his later pictures)."[18] By then he was in real difficulty, having just been turned down by Sir Joseph Noël Paton, the illustrator of Kingsley's *Water-Babies* (Macmillan, 1863), and a well-known painter of fairy and allegorical subjects. Paton, pleading ill health, insisted in any case that Tenniel was the man for the job (*Diaries,* 6:22). Carroll wrote to Tenniel once more, making the remarkable offer to "pay his publishers for his time for the next five months. Unless he will undertake it, I am quite at a loss" (*Diaries,* 6:30–31; 19 May 1868). A month later Carroll recorded with some relief that Tenniel agreed to do the illustrations to the new book, "at such spare times as he can find" (*Diaries,* 6:37; 12 June 1868).

Some months later Carroll noted that Tenniel "reluctantly consented, as his hands are full: I have tried Noël Paton and Proctor in vain" (*Diaries,* 6:59; 1 November 1868). "Proctor" is John Proctor, an artist now almost entirely forgotten, who from September 1867 until December 1868 was the chief cartoonist for *Judy, or the London Serio-Comic Journal.* This new weekly magazine, which very closely mimicked the format of *Punch,* featured a large political cartoon drawn by Proctor

16. Jeffrey Stern, "Lewis Carroll the Pre-Raphaelite: 'Fainting in Coils,'" *Lewis Carroll Observed,* 161–80.

Alice Liddell was aware of a deliberate difference between Tenniel's Alice and herself, according to Hargreaves, "Recollections," 9. "One point, which was not settled for a long time and until after many trials and consultations [between Carroll and Tenniel], was whether Alice in Wonderland should have her hair cut straight across her forehead as Alice Liddell had always worn it, or not. Finally it was decided that Alice in Wonderland should have no facial resemblance to her prototype."

Figure 10.2 is the photograph of Alice Liddell by Lewis Carroll that Carroll affixed to the end of the gift manuscript of *Alice's Adventures.*

17. Williams and Madan, 238.

18. *Letters,* 1:120 (19 May 1868). In the same sentence, Carroll goes on to rule out the Pre-Raphaelite painter Arthur Hughes, because he "has not, so far as I know, any turn for grotesque." For Hughes's relationship to George MacDonald and Carroll, see Stern, 172–75.

in Tenniel's heroic-allegorical style. Carroll must have hoped that Proctor's knack for imitating Tenniel could be applied to the second *Alice* book. But Proctor turned down this chance to enter literary history, and in the end the real Tenniel agreed to do the job.[19]

As Tenniel had warned, progress was slow. Although Carroll had sent the first chapter of *Looking-Glass* to the printer in January 1869, Tenniel had not started on the drawings by early April. "Rough sketches of about ten of the pictures" were available for inspection in January of the following year, and printed proofs of seven by late June. On 15 January 1871, Carroll sent the last proofs of *Looking-Glass* to Tenniel, noting that "it all now depends upon him, whether we get the book out by Easter or not." After more delays on Tenniel's part forced Carroll to defer his hopes from Easter to midsummer, and then to Michaelmas, he finally reconciled himself to Christmas, when the book did appear.[20]

The information on record about Carroll's and Tenniel's negotiations over the second book is more specific than that for the first. Collingwood preserved two details as examples of how closely Carroll controlled—or tried to control—Tenniel's work: "Mr. Dodgson was no easy man to work with; no detail was too small for his exact criticism. 'Don't give Alice so much crinoline,' he would write, or 'The White Knight must not have whiskers; he must not be made to look old'— such were the directions he was constantly giving."[21]

Carroll's remark about excessive crinoline probably refers to the crinoline-supported chessman-like skirt of the dress that Tenniel originally gave Alice on her becoming Queen; it has the general shape of the carved skirts worn by the Red Queen and the White Queen, though it is more obviously made of soft fabric, real clothing for a real person. Proofs survive of all five *Looking-Glass* engravings that show Queen Alice, in both the uncorrected and the corrected states of the woodblocks. Figures 10.3 and 10.4 typify what Carroll was objecting to, and figures 1.43 and 1.17 what Tenniel supplied instead. The replacement is a more conventional formal dress for a young girl of the period (compare figure 9.15), and not so full as the chessman outfit.[22]

Tenniel ignored the other instruction that Collingwood cites. Despite Carroll's objections, Tenniel's White Knight looks quite old— not a flattering self-image for Carroll, who modeled much of the Knight's character on himself. Collingwood's general point, that Carroll strictly supervised Tenniel's work, was later amplified, not to say exaggerated, in the published recollections of Harry Furniss, a younger *Punch* colleague of Tenniel's, who illustrated Carroll's two *Sylvie and Bruno* books (1889, 1893). To Furniss, Carroll was "a captious critic."

> He subjected every illustration, when finished, to a minute examination under a magnifying glass. He would take a square inch of the drawing, count the lines I had made in that space, and compare their number with those on a square inch of illustration made for "Alice" by Tenniel! And in due course I would receive a long essay on the subject from Dodgson the mathematician.[23]

One such dispute led Carroll to tell Furniss that he intended to write an article or pamphlet called "Authors' Difficulties with Illustrators." This pamphlet was never written, and one wonders how Tenniel would have figured in it. As it happens, Carroll's letter to Furniss, in which

19. It has sometimes been said that Carroll also approached W. S. Gilbert, later famous as the librettist for the Savoy operas. Carroll did admire some of Gilbert's magazine illustrations, signed "Bab"; and after Tenniel provided the identification, Carroll made inquiries about Gilbert; but Carroll never actually approached him. See *Letters*, 1:120.

Tenniel also identified Georgina Bowers as the artist who had recently begun publishing "sporting pictures" in *Punch* (*Diaries*, 6:21); but there is no evidence that Carroll offered her the commission.

20. Wakeling, *Carroll*, 83–85.

21. Collingwood, *Life and Letters*, 130. Carroll loathed "the unapproachable ugliness of 'crinoline,'" as he later described it to Harry Furniss; "I *hate* crinoline fashion." Furniss, *Caricaturist*, 1:107.

22. Tenniel's *Looking-Glass* chessmen are modifications of the English "Staunton" pattern, designed by Nathaniel Cook in 1835; it became the international standard. A representative Victorian set and the illustrations from the pattern book published by the original manufacturer are reproduced by A. E. J. Mackett-Beeson in *Chessmen* (New York: Putnam, 1968), 34–35. Tenniel's Knights follow the Staunton type closely, especially in the illustrations early in the book, and so stand only two generations removed from the classical horses' heads of the Elgin marbles. But the skirts of Tenniel's chessmen are more corrugated and more voluminous than the bases in that pattern—less tapered and more like skirts. Tenniel also deprived the Kings of their crowns (significantly?), substituting instead coronets like those worn by the Queens.

The proofs reproduced by figures 10.3 and 10.4 are in the British Museum, MS. C247, vol. 28, folio 148 recto; Edward Guiliano first brought them to my attention. Other proofs highlight the revisions made on these same wood blocks; see https://goo.gl/8urBnj. Sketches for figure 10.3 are reproduced in Schiller, 104; see also Sarzano, 68.

For detailed accounts of Alice's changing wardrobe in the Tenniel illustrations, see F. Gordon Roe, *The Victorian Child* (London: Phoenix House, 1959), 81–84; and Ewing, 96–98.

23. Furniss, "*Recollections,*" 51.

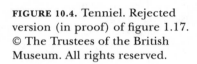

he edgily announces this whimsical project, shows how much Carroll appreciated Tenniel's cooperativeness. Carroll rejects Furniss's sweeping assertion that "John Tenniel, George du Maurier, or Harry Furniss, must be accepted as they are—as the public are willing to accept them: you cannot alter them." Not so, Carroll responds:

> *I* also am going to quote Tenniel as an instance of the direct *contrary!* By a most curious coincidence, the very thing, which has upset all your plans, happened in *his* case! There was a *face,* and that's the face of the *heroine,* to which I objected. But instead of saying, as you would have expected, "you cannot alter John Tenniel: I cannot illustrate your book," he kindly consented to re-draw it, though this required the block to be "plugged."[24]

"The heroine" here must, of course, be Alice, and there are indeed two Dalziel wood blocks for *Looking-Glass* that show substantial alterations of her hairdo. Details of how that was done will be discussed below, in chapter 13. The point that Carroll makes here is that Tenniel was an exemplary illustrator because he was willing and able to cooperate in representing Alice as her author wished.

After Carroll had died, but even while Tenniel was still alive, Furniss claimed that Tenniel lost all patience with Carroll's niggling interfer-

24. *Lewis Carroll & His Illustrators,* 159 (26 August 1889). The crucial final sentence here supplements the version of this otherwise fragmentary letter that was published in *Letters,* 2:754.

ence, dismissing him as "that conceited old Don." "When I told Tenniel that I had been approached by Dodgson to illustrate his books, he said, 'I'll give you a week, old chap; you will never put up with that fellow a day longer. . . . Lewis Carroll is impossible.'"[25] It's a good story, which has often been repeated (as in the first edition of the present book), but there are reasons to doubt Furniss's credibility.[26]

In fact, Carroll was willing to make major and minor changes in *Looking-Glass* to satisfy Tenniel. He told Furniss himself about another instance. Tenniel unaccountably "remonstrated against 'The Walrus and the Carpenter' as a hopeless combination, and begged to have the 'carpenter' abolished. I remember offering 'baronet' and 'butterfly' . . . but he finally chose 'carpenter.'"[27] Tenniel had a more decisive effect on the lines, "The Walrus and the Carpenter / Were walking close at hand," which Carroll revised, "to suit the artist," from the original reading: "Were walking hand-in-hand" (*Letters*, 1:222). Carroll doesn't mention Tenniel's reason for objecting; but the Walrus, as Tenniel drew him, has flippers that look like flippers—not hands.

Collingwood records two letters in which Tenniel suggested other changes that Carroll adopted. The more important of these concerned an extended passage in *Looking-Glass,* one that both Tenniel and Collingwood called a "chapter," perhaps mistakenly. It featured a wasp in a wig. At some point Tenniel objected that "a *wasp* in a *wig* is altogether beyond the appliances of art." And toward the end of a letter dated 1 June 1870, which Collingwood reproduced in facsimile (fig. 10.5), Tenniel expanded on his feelings: "Don't think me brutal, but I am bound to say that the '*wasp*' chapter doesn't interest me in the least, & I can't see my way to a picture. If you want to shorten the book, I can't help thinking—with all submission—that *there* is your opportunity." Whether Carroll thought Tenniel brutal or not, he took his advice, and there is no wasp in any wig in *Through the Looking-Glass.* However, Carroll's own marked-up galleys of the episode were later discovered and published, and the slackness of the entire episode justifies Tenniel's critical judgment, and Carroll's willingness to go along with it.[28]

At the start of the same letter, Tenniel provided Carroll with a rough sketch of the railway-carriage illustration, and suggested that when the carriage suddenly leaps into the air Alice should grab hold of the goat's beard, "instead of the old lady's hair." Tenniel left the old lady out of his sketch, and Carroll obligingly dropped her from the chapter.

Taken together, all the evidence suggests that the Carroll–Tenniel collaboration was by no means one-sided. Both men could be demanding, and both sensibly found ways to accommodate the other's demands.

After *Looking-Glass,* both men remained active and continued to do successful work: Tenniel, his *Punch* cartoons; Carroll, *The Hunting of the Snark* (1876). But after collaborating with Tenniel, Carroll's gift for storytelling flagged—despite the great length of *Sylvie and Bruno* and its sequel. And Tenniel, who before working for Carroll had contributed illustrations to dozens of books—five of them illustrated entirely by him—did little such work after 1872. When Carroll approached him to illustrate some new book of his (not since identified), Tenniel responded with detachment: "It is a curious fact that with 'Through the Looking-Glass' the faculty of making drawings for book illustration departed from me, and, notwithstanding all sorts of tempting inducements, I have done nothing in that direction since."[29]

25. Furniss, "Recollections," 50. Furniss varied the story slightly in *Caricaturist,* 1:103: "Tenniel and other artists declared I would not work with Carroll for seven weeks!"

26. Morris, *Artist of Wonderland,* 140–41. *Lewis Carroll & His Illustrators,* 103–04.

27. *Lewis Carroll & His Illustrators,* 170–71.

28. Collingwood, *Life and Letters,* 146, 148–49. Lewis Carroll, *The Wasp in a Wig: A "Suppressed" Episode of Through the Looking-Glass and What Alice Found There,* ed. Martin Gardner (New York: Lewis Carroll Society of North America, 1977). The quality and authenticity of this text are debated in a special issue of *Jabberwocky,* 7:3 (Summer 1978).

29. Collingwood, *Life and Letters,*146. Carroll's *Diaries* record that in 1875 Tenniel "consented" to draw a frontispiece for "a little book of original puzzles etc. which I think of calling *Alice's Puzzle-Book,*" but little came of this project (6:381–82). Edward Wakeling, "Recreational Mathematics," in *The Mathematical World of Charles L. Dodgson (Lewis Carroll),* ed. Robin J. Wilson and Amirouche Moktefi. (Oxford: Oxford University Press, 2019), 141–75; 167–68.

FIGURE 10.5. Letter from Tenniel to Carroll, 1 June 1870. From S. D. Collingwood, *The Life and Letters of Lewis Carroll (Rev. C. L. Dodgson)* (1898; rpt. 1899).

Interior of Railway carriage.
(1st Class). Alice on seat
by herself. Man in white
paper. reading, & Goat.
very shadowy & indistinct
sitting opposite. (with opera glass)
Guard looking in at windows.

My dear Dodgson.

I think that where
the *jump* occurs in the

Railway Scene you might
very well make Alice lay
hold of the Goat's beard
as being the object nearest
to her hand – instead of
the old lady's hair. The
jerk would naturally
throw them together.
Don't think me brutal. but
I am bound to say that
the 'wasp' chapter doesn't
interest me in the least; &
that I can't see my way
to a picture. If you
want to shorten the book.

I can't help thinking —
with all submission —
that there is your oppor-
tunity.
In an agony of haste
Yours sincerely
J Tenniel.

Portsdown Road.
June 1. 1870

Tenniel was exaggerating here, but not much. He did contribute a drawing to a versified temperance tract by his old acquaintance S. C. Hall, *The Trial of Sir Jasper* (1873); another to Hall's *An Old Story* (the same genre, published in 1875); and a pair of new illustrations for Walter Thornbury's *Historical & Legendary Ballads & Songs* (1876). He prepared a single cover illustration for Bernard H. Becker's *Official Handbook to the Royal Aquarium and Summer and Winter Garden* (1876); it shows a curvaceous mermaid coifing her Pre-Raphaelite hair while balancing a merchild on her thigh, who toys with one of many ambient sea creatures. But these were minor efforts, mostly one-off, hardly comparable to Tenniel's work for *Lalla Rookh* or the *Alice* books. Frankie Morris has pointed out that Tenniel had begun to reduce his work as an illustrator even before *Looking-Glass,* which stands out as an energetic exception against a gradual decline. She speculates that Tenniel's renewed commitment to fine art was a factor (he was elected to membership in the Royal Institute of Painters in Water Colours in 1874), and also that he wanted to limit demands on his diminished eyesight.[30] In any case Tenniel did continue to produce his distinctive large "cuts" for *Punch* each week, not retiring from the staff there until 1900—by which time he had produced more than 2,500 of them. After *Alice,* as before, there was always *Punch.* And yet it is for his ninety-two *Alice* illustrations that Tenniel is best remembered.

Carroll and Tenniel continued to cooperate until shortly before Carroll's death. Carroll was careful to seek Tenniel's approval for proofs of the pages of the new editions of *Alice's Adventures* and *Through the Looking-Glass* that were published in 1897. Details of Tenniel's comments at the proof stage have not survived. In any case, Carroll was not happy with the results. "The pictures seem to *me* some under and some over done; but I must get Tenniel's opinion," he wrote in his diary.[31] Carroll was then able to report to Macmillan that the artist was generally satisfied with the results: "I find Sir John Tenniel is well pleased with the new *Alice* books, and can only find, 'here and there,' pictures that are slightly too dark."[32] But such guarded approval from his collaborator was not enough to satisfy Carroll, who had a higher standard in mind. "My hopes had been high that the new books would be *faultless,* and I was much disappointed with the result," he wrote to Macmillan on 23 November 1897:

Some sheets seem to have taken the ink better than others. If you turn over the leaves you will find places in which one of two opposite pages is pale compared with the other. It might be well to see to the *ink* also, and to make sure that, next time the *Alice* books are printed, it is the *blackest* ink procurable. I feel quite sure that more brilliant copies *can* be produced.

To which Frederick Macmillan replied:

I do not recognize the faded appearance of which you complain. Of course, the woodcuts would look blacker if the paper on which they were printed was a dead white instead of being a creamy tone, and it would be possible to have a dead white paper if you care about it, but the creamy paper, if you will remember, was made specially at your request to imitate that used for the first edition.[33]

30. Morris, *Artist of Wonderland,* 146–47.

31. *Diaries,* 9:340 (24 September 1897).

32. *Lewis Carroll and the House of Macmillan,* ed. Morton N. Cohen and Anita Gandolfo (Cambridge: Cambridge University Press, 1987), 357.

33. *Lewis Carroll and the House of Macmillan,* 359; see also 341, 341–42n, 352n2.

To appreciate the subtleties at stake in such an exchange it will be necessary to consider Tenniel's notorious rejection of the first printing of *Alice's Adventures in Wonderland,* and the practical realities that conditioned the printing of wood engravings in the nineteenth century, topics that will be taken up in chapter 15.

CHAPTER 11

Illustration and Difference

*A*lice's Adventures in Wonderland* and *Through the Looking-Glass* are the most popular illustrated books to come down to us from the nineteenth century. Indeed, they are probably the only such books to have kept a very wide audience. But in their day they were not so remarkable. The publishing era called "the Sixties," which actually spanned two decades, from 1855 to about 1875, was the golden age of illustration in England for both books and magazines; and in such a context the publication of each *Alice* book was a relatively minor event.[1]

Most Sixties illustrations were produced by a century-old process known as wood engraving; more precisely, by a modern version of that process that was geared to the commercial production of printed fac-similes of ink or pencil drawings. There was usually a division of labor: the artist would prepare a drawing for the professional engraver to cut into the end grain of a hardwood block (usually boxwood). The cutting would be done so that the lines of the drawing would stand out on the block in relief against the cut-away background; after being inked these relief lines would print black on a white ground, reproducing the original drawing. Usually printing would be done not from the original wood blocks but from stereotype or electrotype replicas.

This procedure had real commercial advantages, making its use widespread. And it did contribute to some illustrated books of remarkable merit. But despite its commercial and aesthetic vogue, John Ruskin harshly criticized the technique, for the apparently continuous, freehand lines in such engravings, including the many squiggles and cross-hatchings that closely mimicked the shaded areas of drawings, were cruelly deceptive. They resulted not from continuous cuts by the engraver's chisel but rather, as a sort of residue, from scores of minute, cramped, repetitive gouges into the surface of the block. Examining a small patch of cross-hatched shadow in a typical wood engraving of the period (it happened to be a *Punch* cartoon by Tenniel), Ruskin

1. See Gleeson White, *English Illustration "The Sixties": 1855–1870* (London: Archibald Constable, 1897), 127; Reid, 28–29; Percy Muir, *Victorian Illustrated Books* (New York: Praeger Publications, 1971), 109–10; Eric de Maré, *The Victorian Woodblock Illustrators* (London: Gordon Fraser, 1980), 146.

calculated more than a thousand interstices, each requiring ten or so individual cuts. With characteristic moral fervor, he decried the mechanical, alienated nature of such work, and compared its commercial exploitation to the slave trade. Ruskin raised this cry in 1872, the same year *Looking-Glass* was published. Certainly few readers of the *Alice* books, then or now, have supposed that each illustration cost a craftsman hours and hours of niggling and tedious hand labor.[2]

In facsimile engraving of this sort it was usual for the artist to draw the intended picture—reversed left to right—directly onto the woodblock. (To heighten contrast the surface of the block would have been painted with whitewash.) The engraver then cut away the unmarked areas of the wood. It was Tenniel's custom first to prepare a sketch on regular paper, and then to transfer the outlines of that sketch (in reverse) onto the whitewashed block using tracing paper, before elaborating the drawing on the block with a hard lead pencil.[3] Many of Tenniel's preliminary sketches for *Alice* have survived, and are catalogued by Schiller (54–109); several of these will be discussed in chapter 13.

The resulting engraved block was so durable as to make possible mass reproduction of the image—an improvement on the engraved copperplates that were common in eighteenth-century printing, which quickly suffered wear. (Nonetheless, for various reasons, from the early 1840s on it became standard practice to make electrotype replicas of the wood blocks, which were used in the actual printing of commercial books; this aspect of the process will be discussed in chapter 14.) Furthermore, being a relief and not an intaglio process, wood engraving did not need special treatment. A copper or steel engraving had to be printed separately on a special cylindrical press that exerted great pressure on the paper, forcing its surface into the inked shallow grooves of the engraved plate; but a relief wood engraving—or an electrotype replica of such a wood block—could be printed in the same press as the composed type, right next to it, making it much easier for the printer to integrate the pictures into the text. It will be seen in chapter 12 how the early editions of the *Alice* books took advantage of this flexibility.

For publishers, much of the appeal of wood engraving was economic; but from the time of Thomas Bewick the artistic possibilities of the medium were also attractive. "Serious" artists were not above drawing for it, and many engravers raised the mechanical side of the business almost to a high art. The most distinguished firm of engravers was commonly known as the Brothers Dalziel—George and Edward Dalziel, assisted by two other brothers, a sister, and other employees. The firm engraved pictures for hundreds of illustrated books during the second half of the nineteenth century, and often produced and printed illustrated books for others to publish.[4] It was the Dalziels who prepared Tenniel's wood blocks for the *Alice* books.

The most celebrated book of "the Sixties" is the illustrated edition of Tennyson's *Poems,* a deluxe reprint of the text of 1842, which Edward Moxon published in 1857. The book was not a great financial success, and it was not a uniform artistic success either. Although one of the virtues of wood engraving was the contribution it could make to a unified layout, it was too common to waste this opportunity by commissioning drawings by different artists for the same book, and to have them engraved by different engravers. Such was the case with the Moxon illustrated Tennyson, which included illustrations by established artists

2. John Ruskin, *Ariadne Florentina: Six Lectures on Wood and Metal Engraving* (delivered in 1872); *Works*, 22:359–60. Ruskin preferred, as more authentic and less mechanical, the wood-engraving technique of Thomas Bewick, who designed most of his own work and modeled his pictures directly with the white lines cut by the chisel.

See also Chatto 1861, 561–62, 599–601. The account there, probably by Jackson, is similar to Ruskin's, if less impassioned.

3. Spielmann, 463–68. Monkhouse, 8. A similar procedure was followed by Dickens's illustrator, Hablot Browne ("Phiz"); Edgar Browne, *Phiz and Dickens* (London: James Nisbet, 1913), 164, cited by Michel Steig, *Dickens and Phiz* (Bloomington: Indiana University Press, 1978), 6. The tracing-paper technique was also used by engravers, who probably devised it; see Thomas Gilks, *The Art of Wood Engraving: A Practical Handbook* (London: Winsor and Newton, 1866), 23–24.

4. See their memoir, *The Brothers Dalziel: A Record of Fifty Years' Work in Conjunction with Many of the Most Distinguished Artists of the Period, 1840–1890* (London: Methuen, 1901). See also Simon Houfe's introduction to *The Dalziel Family: Engravers and Illustrators* (London: Sotheby's Belgravia, 1978). Percy Muir devotes chapter 6 of *Victorian Illustrated Books* to "The Dalziel Era." See also research by Bethan Stevens reported in chapter 13.

FIGURE 11.1. William Holman Hunt. "The Lady of Shalott." Wood engraving by John Thompson. From Moxon's illustrated edition of Tennyson's *Poems* (1857; rpt. 1859).

(Thomas Creswick, William Mulready, Daniel Maclise, Clarkson Stanfield), and also work by younger, more remarkable members of the Pre-Raphaelite Brotherhood: John Everett Millais, William Holman Hunt, and Dante Gabriel Rossetti. The fifty-four engravings were done by six firms, with fifteen being produced in the Dalziel workshop.[5]

According to tradition Tennyson recommended the three Pre-Raphaelite artists to Moxon, and Maclise also; but beyond that, unlike Lewis Carroll, he had little if anything to do with designing the illustrations. However, he did criticize some of them after the fact; and his criticisms express one contemporary standard by which Sixties book illustrations might be judged.

Tennyson's opinion has been recorded most fully as regards William Holman Hunt's illustration for "The Lady of Shalott," which was engraved by John Thompson (fig. 11.1). It became the best known illustration in the book, and indeed is one of the most remarkable engravings of the century. Hunt shows the Lady at the climactic moment of Tennyson's poem, when she has just renounced her world of innocent, dreamy, and artistic shadows for an unmediated and fatal view of the real world, a world made attractive by the erotic figure of Sir Lancelot. At that moment the tapestry she has been weaving tears asunder, and the mirror, which until then has mediated all her worldly experience, is also broken:

> Out flew the web and floated wide;
> The mirror crack'd from side to side.

It happens that the Lady's crisis resembles three different crises in the *Alice* books: one at the end of *Alice's Adventures*, when the deck of cards flies apart and Alice wakes abruptly from her dream (fig. 11.2); another at the end of *Through the Looking-Glass,* when Alice tears the

5. The Moxon illustrated Tennyson has attracted detailed study since the nineteenth century, starting with George Somes Layard, *Tennyson and His Pre-Raphaelite Illustrators* (London: Elliot Stock, 1894). Recent accounts include Lorraine Janzen Kooistra, *Poetry, Pictures, and Popular Publishing: The Illustrated Gift Book and Victorian Visual Culture, 1855–1875* (Athens: Ohio University Press, 2011), 34–78; and Jim Cheshire, *Tennyson and Mid-Victorian Publishing: Moxon, Poetry, Commerce* (London: Palgrave Macmillan, 2017), 137–58.

tablecloth off the table and the candelabra explode into Roman candles, ending another dream (fig. 1.30); and the preliminary crisis in *Alice's Adventures* when Alice upsets the jury box—the crisis which, as drawn by Tenniel (fig. 11.3), approaches most closely to the style and composition of Hunt's engraving.[6]

When Tennyson visited Hunt's studio sometime after the book appeared, he objected to the way that Hunt had drawn the broken tapestry: "Why did you make the web wind round and round her like the threads of a cocoon?" Hunt quoted the couplet given above as a justification. Tennyson insisted: "But I did not say it floated round and round her." He was offended also by Hunt's treatment of the Lady's hair, "wildly tossed about as if by a tornado." Hunt argued that this effect communicated her experience of the event, so that "while she recognised that the moment of the catastrophe had come, the spectator might also understand it"—and also, presumably, understand that she understood it. But Tennyson was not to be persuaded: "I didn't say that her hair was blown about like that." He thought it a general rule that "the illustrator should always adhere to the words of the poet," and that he "ought never to add anything to what he finds in the text." It was no use for Hunt to plead that poetry and drawing operated under different constraints, and that an illustration could not express anything like the same content as a poetic text except by interpreting it freely. "May I not urge that I had only half a page on which to convey the impression of weird fate, whereas you use about fifteen pages to give expression to the complete idea?"[7] Hunt's apology for artistic license in illustration recalls Joshua Reynolds's defense of idealization in history painting: "A Painter must compensate the natural deficiencies of his art. He has but one sentence to utter, but one moment to exhibit. He cannot, like the poet or historian, expatiate."[8] When Hunt reconstructed his conversation with Tennyson, some fifty years after the fact, he had just completed a painting of the Lady of Shalott that derived freely from the engraving. It would have amazed Tennyson in its elaboration of iconographic details unprecedented in either the poem or the engraving.[9]

Dante Gabriel Rossetti, who contributed five illustrations to Tennyson's *Poems*, including the other illustration to "The Lady of Shalott," differed from Tennyson even more sharply than Hunt as regards the proper relation of illustration to text. Before he had started work on any of the illustrations, he commented to a friend that he wanted to illustrate poems whose meaning was implicit rather than explicit, poems like Tennyson's "*Vision of Sin* and *Palace of Art*, etc.,—those where one can allegorize on one's own hook on the subject of the poem, without killing, for oneself and everyone, a distinct idea of the poet's."[10] The vaguer the poem, the better the potential for a picture.

Rossetti's mentor and ally John Ruskin expressed a similar but even bolder theory in a letter that he wrote to Tennyson after the book was published:

> Many of the plates are very noble things, though not, it seems to me, illustrations of your poems.
>
> I believe, in fact, that good pictures never can be; they are always another poem, subordinate but wholly different from the poet's conception, and serve chiefly to show the reader how variously the same verses may affect various minds (Ruskin, 36:264–65).

6. Tenniel's Alice and Hunt's Lady are also related by collateral descent. According to family tradition, Hunt's model for his drawing of the Lady was his mistress, Annie Miller. Miller, as represented in a drawing by Dante Gabriel Rossetti that Carroll photographed, strongly influenced Carroll's Pre-Raphaelite-esque drawings of Alice—which in turn had their influence on Tenniel's drawings. Carroll's photograph of Rossetti's drawing of Miller is reproduced by Stern, "Lewis Carroll," 169; there it is juxtaposed to a remarkably similar drawing by Carroll for *Alice's Adventures under Ground*. Regarding Miller as the model for Hunt's Lady see Diana Holman-Hunt, *My Grandfather, His Wives and Loves* (London: Hamish Hamilton, 1969), 205.

7. W. Holman Hunt, *Pre-Raphaelitism and the Pre-Raphaelite Brotherhood*, 2 vols. (London: Macmillan, 1905), 2:124–25.

8. Joshua Reynolds, *Discourses on Art*, ed. Robert R. Wark, 2nd ed. (New Haven: Yale University Press, 1975), 60 (Discourse 4; 1771).

9. Judith Bronkhurst, *William Holman Hunt: A Catalogue Raisonné*, 2 vols. (New Haven: Yale University Press, 2006), 1:262–63.

10. *Letters of Dante Gabriel Rossetti*, ed. Oswald Doughty and John Robert Wahl, 4 vols. (Oxford: Clarendon Press, 1965–67), 1:239.

FIGURE 11.3. Tenniel. Alice upsetting the jury box. From *Alice's Adventures in Wonderland.*

FIGURE 11.4. Dante Gabriel
Rossetti. St. Cecilia. Wood
engraving by Dalziel Brothers.
From Moxon's illustrated edition
of Tennyson's *Poems* (1857; rpt.
1859).

Although Ruskin has poetry specifically in mind here, his argument
applies just as well to prose fiction.

If taken yet one more step, however, the case for interpretive freedom can turn, ironically, against the illustrator—who then appears not
as an imaginative reader of the author's text but rather as a usurper
of the actual reader's own imaginative claims. So Graham Greene has
regretted the "disservice" done to Dickens by illustrators such as George
Cruikshank: "for no character any more will walk for the first time into
our memory as we ourselves imagine him, and *our* imagination after all
has just as much claim to truth as Cruikshank's."[11] Such a complaint
could be made against any illustration of Tennyson's poetry, Rossetti's
included. And Tenniel's *Alice* illustrations: are they objectionable on
these grounds? They do compel the reader's imagination. In any case
illustrations for the *Alice* books will always be privileged, thanks to Alice's
own instinctive demand that a worthwhile book must have "pictures."

True to his prediction Rossetti did draw two illustrations for Tennyson's visionary poem "The Palace of Art." One of these greatly per-
plexed the poet. Figure 11.4 is his interpretation of a tapestry that hung
in the palace:

> . . . in a clear-wall'd city on the sea,
>   Near gilded organ-pipes, her hair
> Wound with white roses, slept St. Cecily;
>   An angel look'd at her.

Aside from Rossetti's invention of much detail that is not mentioned by the text, there is the obvious discrepancy between the angel
described in the poem, who merely "look'd at" St. Cecilia, and his
counterpart in the engraving, who is vigorously kissing her forehead.
Rossetti's brother and biographer, William Michael Rossetti, years later

11. Graham Greene, introduction to
Charles Dickens, *Oliver Twist* (London:
Hamish Hamilton, 1950), vii; as cited by
Jane R. Cohen, *Charles Dickens and His
Original Illustrators* (Columbus: Ohio
State University Press, 1980), 234.

conceded that in preparing the Moxon illustrations Rossetti "himself only, and not Tennyson, was his guide. . . . The illustration of *St. Cecilia* puzzled [Tennyson] not a little, and he had to give up the problem of what it had to do with his verses."[12]

Besides the topical discrepancy between the text and the engraving, there was another kind of discrepancy, between what Rossetti actually drew on the block and what Dalziel engraved there. It happens that Lewis Carroll was an early critic of the difference between Rossetti's drawing and the Dalziel engraving. In 1859, before he met Rossetti, Carroll visited the artist's studio, and he reported his visit in a letter to Tennyson's wife: he "saw photographs from the original drawings of *St. Cecily* and *The Lady of Shalott*. The difference between them and the woodcuts is certainly very striking."[13] Carroll's perception may have been colored by Ruskin's complaint, published in *The Elements of Drawing* (1857), about the poor quality of the engraving for the Moxon edition, especially the engraving of the St. Cecilia drawing. The drawings had been "terribly spoiled in the cutting, and generally the best part, the expression of feature, [was] *entirely* lost. . . . This is especially the case in the St. Cecily . . . which would have been the best in the book had it been well engraved" (Ruskin, 15:224).

IN THEIR MEMOIR the Dalziels themselves acknowledged that when the *Alice* books were being prepared Carroll would find fault with both the drawings and the engravings; but they also implied that there was no lasting dissatisfaction on his part. When Carroll sent the Dalziels payment for their work on *Looking-Glass,* he did compliment them in terms that seem to be more than *pro forma,* despite being cast in the formal third-person idiom of business correspondence: "Mr. Dodgson encloses to Messrs. Dalziel a cheque for £203 16s., in payment of their account, and takes the opportunity of thanking them for the great pains which have evidently been bestowed on the pictures. He thinks them quite admirable and (so far as he is a judge) first-rate specimens of the art of wood-engraving."[14] A decade later Carroll again commissioned the Dalziels to engrave illustrations for one of his books, the illustrations by A. B. Frost for *Rhyme? and Reason?* (1883). Apparently he was satisfied with their engravings for *Alice.*

Rossetti was harder to please. "I have . . . designed five blocks for Tennyson," he wrote to a friend in 1857, "some of which are still cutting and maiming."

> It is a thankless task. After a fortnight's work my block goes to the engraver, like Agag, delicately, and is hewn to pieces before the Lord Harry!
>
> Address to the D——l Brothers
>
> > O woodman, spare that block,
> > O gash not anyhow;
> > It took ten days by clock,
> > I'd fain protect it now.
>
> Chorus, wild laughter from Dalziel's workshop.

12. *Dante Gabriel Rossetti: His Family-Letters,* ed. William Michael Rossetti, 2 vols. (London: Ellis and Elvey, 1895), 1:189–90. W. M. Rossetti later offered a supposedly authoritative account of "what Rossetti meant," distinguished from the description of St. Cecilia given by the poem. Virginia Surtees, *The Paintings and Drawings of Dante Gabriel Rossetti (1828–1882): A Catalogue Raisonné,* 2 vols. (Oxford: Clarendon Press, 1971), 1:48.

13. *Letters,* 1:39 (4 June 1959). Moxon illustrated "The Lady of Shalott" with two engravings, the one by Hunt already discussed, and another by Rossetti, which is evidently the one referred to here.

Presumably what Carroll saw in Rossetti's studio was not a photograph of any preliminary drawing of "St. Cecilia" but rather one made from Rossetti's drawing on the block: late in 1856 Rossetti sent a copy of such a photograph to William Allingham (Rossetti, *Letters,* 1:315). Two of Rossetti's preliminary paper drawings for this illustration survive (Surtees, 1:48).

14. Harold Hartley quotes from Carroll's letter in "Lewis Carroll and His Artists and Engravers," *The Lewis Carroll Centenary in London, 1932,* ed. Falconer Madan (London: J. & E. Bumpus, 1932), 109–16; 115. For the Dalziels' recollection of their dealings with Carroll see *The Brothers Dalziel,* 126.

Rossetti once virtually acknowledged that the problem was his fault for using chalk and wash to model his drawings, instead of distinct pencil or ink lines.[15] And yet he allowed the engraver no artistic license, despite claiming large freedom for himself as an illustrator of Tennyson's text. Millais cooperated with the Dalziels on the Tennyson project more closely than Rossetti did, and he was lavish in praising their work on later commissions.[16] But William Holman Hunt brought a painter's prejudices to his work for the medium. Years later he recalled "the disappointment I felt when at first I saw my designs in Moxon's volume. A certain wirelike character in all the lines was to me, as to all artists with like experience, eminently disenchanting."[17]

TO RETURN to the artist's role: Rossetti did distinguish between visionary poems that gave the illustrator broad artistic license, and those others—those "absolutely narrative as in the old ballads, for instance"—that he thought were so literal as to keep the artist from allegorizing on his own hook. "Are we to try the experiment ever in their regard?" he wondered, coveting for himself yet another degree of artistic freedom.[18] Ruskin more decisively liberated *all* "good pictures" from their poetic texts. His reference to the nominally "subordinate" nature of illustration, in the letter to Tennyson, was probably just a courtesy to the poet. In any case a variety of arguments can free illustration from subordination to the text.

Some illustrations have literal priority over the text that they are supposed to illustrate, because they were drawn before the text was written. If any question of subordination affects such illustrations, it is the other way around. Rowlandson's illustrations of William Combe's *Dr. Syntax* books (1812–21) were of this sort; and Charles Dickens was hired to write letterpress that would annotate plates for *The Pickwick Papers*, though in fact he very quickly seized control from the unfortunate artist, Robert Seymour. (Late in his life George Cruikshank claimed, without much justification, that Dickens wrote *Sketches by Boz* and *Oliver Twist* to complement his drawings for these works. He made similar claims for some of W. Harrison Ainsworth's novels, apparently with better cause.) The popular annual gift books of the early Victorian period could be explicit about the secondary status of the text: one such book advertised its poems and prose pieces as being "no unfit companions to the beautiful Engravings which they are intended to illustrate."[19]

Even less closely related than texts "written up to" illustrations in this way are texts and illustrations that have independent origins, and that gain the appearance of shared reference only through editorial intervention. For example, in the nineteenth century it was common for Bewick's many small woodcuts to be reused to "illustrate" a variety of textual scenes. In effect they were treated as stock printer's blocks. And the same frugal use could be made of more elaborate designs. The Dalziel Brothers in particular would shamelessly "botch" things this way—so Eric de Maré has complained. He cites as examples their strikingly irrelevant reuse of a handsome block by Frederick Sandys, and similar treatment of two blocks by J. M. Whistler, all for Walter Thornbury's *Historical & Legendary Ballads & Songs* (1876).[20]

Tenniel himself did not escape such recycling: the same block that illustrated the death of the heroine Zelica in Moore's *Lalla Rookh* (1861) was used again to represent, in Thornbury's book, the death of a

15. Rossetti, *Letters,* 1:243. For the quotation see page 318, and also page 310.

16. Mary Lutyens, "Letters from Sir John Everett Millais, Bart., P.R.A. (1829–1896) and William Holman Hunt, O.M. (1827–1910) in the Henry E. Huntington Library, San Marino, California," *The Forty-Fourth Volume of the Walpole Society, 1972–1974* (1974), 1–93, especially 17–45.

17. William Holman Hunt, introduction to *Some Poems by Alfred, Lord Tennyson* (London: Freemantle, 1901), xxiii.

18. Rossetti, *Letters,* 1:239.

19. Harvey, 34–43, 199–210; Steig, 7. Sybille Pantazzi outlines the nineteenth-century tradition of authors "writing up to" preexisting illustrations in "Author and Illustrator: Images in Confrontation," *Victorian Periodicals Newsletter* 9 (1976): 38–49, especially 39–41. On page 40 she gives the quotation noticed here, from *Finden's Tableaux . . . of National Character,* ed. Mary Russell Mitford (1838). Allan R. Life discusses the tradition (which he believes was minor and atypical) in "'Poetic Naturalism': Forrest Reid and the Illustrators of the Sixties," *Victorian Periodicals Newsletter* 10 (1977): 47–68; 56–58. See also Kooistra, 98.

20. De Maré, 57–58, 64, 133–34. Reid wryly notices how Thornbury glossed over this practice (17). According to Life there were "numerous volumes, mostly issued in the seventies, wedding new texts to illustrations reprinted from books and periodicals" (58). The practice suggests decline, and indeed the era of "the Sixties" was coming to an end.

FIGURE 11.5. Tenniel. The death of Zelica. Wood engraving by Dalziel Brothers. From Thomas Moore, *Lalla Rookh* (1861).

nameless Persian bride (fig. 11.5). No matter that in his text Moore mentioned the soldiers standing by "with pity in their eyes," but that Thornbury did not: the Dalziels found the block as appropriate for the new text as for the old.[21]

Cruikshank's notorious claim to have originated *Sketches by Boz* and *Oliver Twist* is not usually taken seriously, but J. Hillis Miller has shown how, in the experience of the reader, it might as well be true. Cruikshank's pictures, being more conspicuous than the text, are likely to be "read" first, making the text a belated adjunct to the pictures. "Within the atemporal realm of the finished works Cruikshank's drawings seem prior, originating. They appear to be the radiant source beside which Dickens' words are secondary, from which they appear to have derived." Miller goes on to call into question ordinary assumptions about the mimetic or referential function of illustration. His analysis has a bearing on the problematic aspects of illustration that were debated by Tennyson, Hunt, Rossetti, and Ruskin, and that necessarily affect the Tenniel illustrations.

On the standard assumption, as Miller describes it, text and pictures reflect the same reality—or the same fiction—so that the partial information supplied by the text can be filled out with complementary information supplied by the pictures. In the picture we are commonly supposed to be able to "see more exactly what a character or scene 'really looked like.'" On this assumption the criterion for good illustration is that the pictures give a faithful rendition of the world that the text mirrors also.

A cruder version of this assumption takes for granted the mimetic adequacy of the text, and asks of the pictures only that they faithfully mirror the text itself. For obvious reasons authors—such as Tenny-

21. Thomas Moore, *Lalla Rookh: An Oriental Romance* (London: Longman, Green, 1861), 117, an illustration for the versified story "The Veiled Prophet of Khorassan." Walter Thornbury, *Historical & Legendary Ballads & Songs* (London: Chatto and Windus, 1876), 120; for the poem "A Tartar Foray." It is true that Thornbury's melodramatic Persian exoticism is a lot like Moore's.

son—will incline toward this view. The popular idea that illustration is secondary and belated has some justification in the early history of the word *illustrate*. Derived from the Latin noun *lux* ("light"), *illustrate* originally had to do with shedding light on things: illuminating, elucidating previously existing things or concepts. Although in that respect fundamentally visual, the verb *illustrate* did not acquire specifically pictorial meanings until the seventeenth century—and the noun *illustration* did not acquire pictorial force until early in the nineteenth century (*OED*). When the words *illustrate* and *illustration* did get applied to pictorial illustration, they kept their flavor of secondariness. The ordinary assumption would be that an illustration of a text is a belated and dependent illumination of it.

Miller thoroughly deconstructs that ordinary assumption:

> The relation between text and illustration is clearly reciprocal. Each refers to the other. Each illustrates the other, in a continual back and forth movement which is incarnated in the experience of the reader as his eyes move from words to picture and back again, juxtaposing the two in a mutual establishment of meaning. Illustrations in a work of fiction displace the sign-referent relationship assumed in a mimetic reading and replace it by a complex and problematic reference between two radically different kinds of sign, the linguistic and the graphic. Illustrations establish a relation between elements within the work which short-circuits the apparent reference of the literary text to some real world outside. . . . Such an intrinsic relation between text and picture sets up an oscillation or shimmering of meaning in which neither element can be said to be prior. The pictures are about the text; the text is about the pictures.[22]

Furthermore, the presupposition of such mutual reference is *difference*—a difference between the two kinds of sign ("linguistic" vs. "graphic"), and a consequent difference in the contents of the signs. It is impossible to say something the same way in pictures as in words; therefore, impossible to say quite the same thing. Such was the argument that Hunt made to Tennyson. What Tennyson failed to understand is that there is no question of discrepancy between text and illustration, only of difference. As Ruskin said in his letter, "good pictures . . . are always another poem . . . *wholly different*" (emphasis added). The ultimate and surprising implication of the old axiom *traduttore, traditore* is to absolve the "translator" (whether in words or pictures) of any guilt. Some artists, like Rossetti, will gladly exploit this absolution.

Whatever the general truth of the claim that text has no priority over illustration, it seems to fit *Alice's Adventures in Wonderland* particularly well. Alice's dual requirements for a useful book—"pictures" and "conversations"—are remarkable not only for putting pictures first but also for not mentioning descriptions. Young readers are easily bored by scenic descriptions; Carroll wisely let the pictures that he commissioned from Tenniel do much of his descriptive work for him. Twice in *Alice's Adventures* Carroll refers the reader to an illustration for some descriptive detail—and thereby recognizes a kind of priority for the illustrations over the text. (In *The Nursery "Alice"* outfitted with enlarged and colored pictures to make up for a greatly reduced text, Carroll often interrupts his story to discuss the pictures.) Furthermore, as Richard

22. J. Hillis Miller, "The Fiction of Realism," *Victorian Subjects* (Durham, NC: Duke University Press, 1991), 152–55.

Kelly has pointed out, the physical appearances of the major characters of *Alice's Adventures* can hardly be guessed from what Carroll says in the text: to visualize clearly how most of them look, the reader must first look at the pictures.[23] Much the same is true of *Through the Looking-Glass*. And, of course, the text of *Through the Looking-Glass* was written under the influence of the earlier illustrations to *Alice's Adventures*, especially as regards the continuing character and image of Alice.

Granting that Carroll's text and Tenniel's pictures are virtually simultaneous and "about" each other, and also that such mutual reference presupposes not identity but difference, in what general ways does the basic difference reveal itself? And what is the reader to make of any particular difference?

MOST GENERALLY, and least subtly, illustrations will differ from the text in the matter of narrative emphasis. Even when the scene of the illustration corresponds directly to a specific scene in the narrative—which is usually the case for both Carroll's own illustrations to *Alice's Adventures* and Tenniel's—the illustration, as an illustration, is foregrounded, and therefore more emphatic than the corresponding passage by itself. By italicizing the passage, so to speak, the illustration heightens it, changing the whole narrative from what it would be without the illustration. That is why what Hodnett calls "the moment of choice" is so important (6–10).

As Lessing put the matter in the eighteenth century, "it is to a single moment that the material limits of [spatial and visual] art confine all its imitations. . . . the artist, out of ever-varying nature, can only make use of a single moment."[24] His remarks were influentially prescriptive although not descriptive; he disparaged and so acknowledged the simultaneous representation of different narrative moments in certain paintings by Parmigianino and Titian, for example.[25] And early modern book illustration also sometimes depicted different narrative moments within the same picture space.[26] However, by the nineteenth century Lessing's requirement that a history painting depict—and emphasize—but one moment had become normal for a narrative book illustration as well; save for general, scene-setting images, the artist would use the picture to illustrate and thus highlight a moment in the story. There might be occasional exceptions to this rule; for example, Tenniel's illustration for Aesop's fable "The Stag at the Pool" (fig. 9.20) integrated in one illustration, if not quite in the same picture space, three key moments from the narrative (the stag admiring his horns reflected in a pool; the stag pursued by hounds; the stag at bay, his horns entangled in the brush). But the usual practice was to illustrate a single moment, providing a "visual embodiment" of a "dramatic flash point."[27]

Carroll made several effective choices of moments to illustrate when he prepared the manuscript of *Alice's Adventures under Ground* for Alice Liddell and, as has been seen in chapter 2 above, Tenniel respected Carroll's framework by selecting many of the "same" moments to illustrate in the more fully developed narrative of *Alice's Adventures in Wonderland*. As Carroll expanded the first narrative into the second, he supplied the new material to Tenniel as he wrote it, and it appears from the letter quoted above that it was Tenniel who chose the moments to illustrate in the new material.[28]

23. Richard Kelly, "'If You Don't Know What a Gryphon Is': Text and Illustration in Alice's Adventures in Wonderland," *Lewis Carroll: A Celebration—Essays on the Occasion of the 150th Anniversary of the Birth of Charles Lutwidge Dodgson*, ed. Edward Guiliano (New York: Clarkson N. Potter, 1982), 62–74. Revised as "Alice Pictured" in Kelly's introduction to *Alice's Adventures in Wonderland*, Broadview Editions, 2nd ed. (Peterborough, Ont.: Broadview Press, 2011), 35–46. John Davis was wrong to assert that "the various characters are meticulously described by Carroll[,] who left little scope for the artist to do much more than embellish the story" (14). Brooker (104–49) discusses the opportunities offered by Carroll's underdetermining text—noting that many later illustrators were nonetheless constrained by Tenniel's illustrative precedents.

24. Gotthold Ephraim Lessing, *Laocoon: An Essay on the Limits of Painting and Poetry*, trans. E. C. Beasley (London: Longman, Brown, Green and Longmans, 1853), 16.

25. "Fr[ancesco] Mazzuoli" (Lessing, 120)—more commonly spelled *Mazzola*—was the birth name of Parmigianino. For a general account of the practice see Lew Andrews, *Story and Space in Renaissance Art: The Rebirth of Continuous Narrative* (Cambridge: Cambridge University Press, 1995).

26. Gyöngyvér Horváth cites many instances in "From Sequence to Scenario: The Historiography and Theory of Visual Narration," Ph.D. thesis, University of East Anglia School of World Art Studies and Museology, 2010.

27. Q. D. Leavis, "The Dickens Illustrations: Their Function," in F. R. Leavis and Q. D. Leavis, *Dickens the Novelist* (London: Chatto & Windus, 1970), 332–71; 336.

28. *Lewis Carroll & His Illustrators*, 12, 14 (8 March 1865). See also Morris, *Artist of Wonderland*, 142–45.

The moment of an illustration is one thing, its perspective is another. In illustrating the early and late versions of *Alice* Carroll and then Tenniel saw to it that what can be called the "point of view" of the illustration faithfully matched the corresponding point of view of the narration. The omniscient third-person narrator who tells the story of Alice varies his attention from scenes in which Alice is an important protagonist and the main object of our observation, to scenes in which she figures mainly as an observer, and in which the narration foregrounds instead the things that Alice sees. Tenniel varies his pictorial point of view in a similar way. The contrast of the trial scene (fig. 3.1) and the garden scene (fig. 6.1)—otherwise alike in many details—shows the use of such rhetorical variation. The trial scene is a remarkable scene in itself, something that holds Alice's attention and ours, without Alice's participation. But the power of the garden scene, as narrated and as shown in the illustration, lies in the threat that it poses to Alice and the resistance that she summons against that threat. At this critical moment she properly plays a leading role both in the narration and in the picture. (Alice appears and disappears like this in Carroll's own illustrations—for example, figures 6.4 and 3.2.) In this respect Tenniel's illustrations "differ" from the text less than do those that Barry Moser produced for the impressive Pennyroyal Edition of *Alice's Adventures,* where all the illustrations between Alice's falling asleep and her waking leave Alice herself literally out of the picture.[29]

Moser justifies this innovation by complaining that all previous illustrators "have intruded on the privacy of Alice's adventure, standing apart and observing Alice in her dream. They have been voyeurs, and yet there can be no voyeurs to dreams. In *The Pennyroyal Alice* [on the other hand] . . . the images of Alice's dream are always seen from Alice's point of view, for after all, the dream *is* Alice's dream" (143). Moser's point is a double one: the view from outside is both impolite and impossible. But by that logic, the whole of Carroll's narration of Alice's dream is an impolite impossibility.[30]

Given a narrative scene underscored by a corresponding illustration, typically in the same rhetorical mode, several other kinds of difference might be involved. These can be classed roughly as differences of style and differences of content—not a subtle or precise distinction (the matter of point of view, for example, straddles it), but one that does capture a habit of Victorian comment on illustration. The dispute between Tennyson and Hunt about the Lady of Shalott is typical in focusing on matters of content, not style—in part because it is hard to articulate visual nuance. Most of the paragraphs that follow consider, in Victorian fashion, differences of content between text and illustration; but some stylistic differences also call for comment.

Of course, the most general aspect of the "style" of the Tenniel illustrations has less to do with Tenniel than with the medium in which he worked, black-and-white wood engraving. The general impression made by the *Alice* illustrations would be quite different if they were chromolithographs, or even hand-colored black-and-white engravings—two other Victorian options. Economics and the Sixties vogue for "black-and-white" together determined Carroll's choice of technology, which had its consequences.

As a series of visions in black and white, the Tenniel illustrations inevitably differ from the sometimes colorful details of Alice's dreams.

29. *Lewis Carroll's Alice's Adventures in Wonderland,* illustrated by Barry Moser (West Hatfield, MA: Pennyroyal Press, 1982; rpt. Berkeley, CA: University of California Press, 1982).

30. That said, I would recommend Moser's *Alice* illustrations as the most worthy successor to Tenniel's. For further discussion of point of view see chapter 18.

The red chessmen, the red paint on the white roses, the green hedges of the checkerboard landscape, the golden key and the golden crown: Tenniel reduces all of these to combinations of black and white.

And yet the reduction is not a major loss, for color does not saturate Alice's dreams. Scenes are more likely to be "bright" or "dark" than specifically colored. Alice sees "the bright flower-beds and the cool fountains"; or, finding herself in "a little dark shop," she is attracted to "a large bright thing, that looked sometimes like a doll and sometimes like a work-box." In *Alice's Adventures* the Caterpillar may be "blue," the King's crown may rest on "a crimson velvet cushion," and the Queen may turn "crimson with fury," but there are not many other striking details of color in either book. Even "the little golden key"—a much-repeated phrase—is more a nominal formula than a vivid perception; and the red chessmen are easily imagined as their conventional black equivalents—significant because not white. (The Red Queen herself is a transformation of a black kitten.) Carroll's hobby as a photographer may have something to do with the understatement of color in the two books.

If Tenniel's illustrations were brightly colored they would differ more than they now do from Carroll's narrative style, which usually avoids particularizing, and is more conceptual than visual. Nonetheless, long-standing popular desire for color in illustration made it inevitable that Tenniel's black-and-white pictures would eventually—and more than once—be "colorized." Details of that prolonged process are discussed in chapter 16.

Aside from the matter of color constraint, black-and-white wood engraving accommodates a large variety of artistic styles. The several John Leech engravings that have already been cited are sufficiently close to Tenniel's work historically and stylistically to throw some of Tenniel's traits into relief.[31] Leech's line is more casual and calligraphic; by contrast Tenniel's mature style can seem precise, literal-minded, "wooden" (as it has sometimes been called). Even the strain of youthful caricature that survives in Tenniel's *Alice* drawings—most apparent in the supernumeraries, like Father William and his son (fig. 1.39) or the messenger (fig. 1.14)—has been domesticated into a kind of literal explicitness. Tenniel may have prided himself on not using any models, but his image of the Gryphon looks as if it were drawn from the life.

The straightforward sobriety of the Tenniel illustrations befits Carroll's deadpan narration of Alice's adventures. What is wonderful about Wonderland is not that the dream is fantastic but that it feels real; and the pictures convey this matter-of-fact actuality as effectively as the text. By contrast, Carroll's own illustrations show the quirkiness of an incredible homemade world.

The Tenniel illustrations differ in content from Carroll's narrative as modestly as they differ in style. Hardly any of the differences involve positive *contradiction* of the text. Most involve either *supplementation* (the addition of details not specified in the text), or *neglect* (the occasional omission of textual details that might be expected to appear within the picture frame), or *selection* (the framing of the picture to focus on some things rather than others).[32]

Tenniel's Duchess exemplifies both contradiction and supplementation. It is a *contradiction* of the text (noticed by Richard Kelly) for

31. Figs. 1.7, 1.18, 1.22, 1.31, 1.40, and 7.5; also 11.8.

32. For a similar, more elaborate account of such possible differences, see Joseph H. Schwarcz, *Ways of the Illustrator: Visual Communication in Children's Literature* (Chicago: American Library Association, 1982), 16–18, 93–94. *Supplementation* in any case is inevitable: "no verbal description can ever be as particularized as a picture must be." E. H. Gombrich, *Symbolic Images: Studies in the Art of the Renaissance* (London: Phaidon, 1972), 3.

Tenniel to show the Duchess as having a broad and bulky chin: Carroll three times describes it as a "sharp little chin"—one that Alice doesn't want to have pressed onto her shoulder. And Tenniel's rendering of the Duchess's headdress goes beyond or *supplements* what the text specifies. Indeed, no matter how Tenniel had shown the top of the Duchess's head, he could not have avoided going beyond the description in the text—which is nil. George Somes Layard made this general point in his late Victorian essay on the Moxon illustrated Tennyson. He shared Tennyson's dislike of any illustrators coming "into direct collision with his author," but believed that it was

> quite another thing for the artist to import into his work particulars that have been ignored in, but are not inconsistent, with the author's production. Indeed, when we consider the matter closely, it is inevitable throughout that this should be the case. To take an obvious example, Tennyson does not even mention the Lady of Shalott's hair; but that would hardly preclude Mr. Hunt from representing her other than bald.[33]

By the same token, Tenniel had to picture the Duchess's head in *some* way not specifically authorized by the text.

Nonetheless, though supplementation is necessary to illustration, it will be more or less remarkable depending upon how well it jibes with the reader's expectations. Tenniel's basic image of Alice supplements what the text specifies, but it would not have been remarkable for Victorian readers, because it conformed so much to the expected type. (The type, as we have seen, was familiar to Tenniel; and it is not special to him. See, for example, figure 11.6, a characteristic cartoon by Leech.[34])

The supplementary image of the Duchess, however, is quite remarkable: the reader would have had no reason to expect such grotesquely disproportionate features in a duchess, even an "ugly" one, nor any outsized headdress, nor indeed any medieval headdress at all. By being unexpected the supplementary image calls attention to itself and raises the question of motivation. Perhaps, as we have already considered, the image of the Duchess refers to the iconographic tradition of the supposedly hideous duchess Margaret Maultasche. The reference may have been Carroll's idea; or possibly Tenniel was allegorizing on his own hook, greatly elaborating the sole mention of the Duchess as "ugly." (Of course, the contemporary audience for such a recherché reference would not have been very large; it verges on a private joke. But private jokes do occur in these two books.)

The work of this image as a supplement to the text is more typical than is its work as a contradiction. For aside from the blunt chin that Tenniel gave the Duchess, there are not many contradictory images in the *Alice* books. Perhaps appropriately ("Contrariwise!"), Tweedledee and Tweedledum supply two instances. In figure 1.6 it should be Tweedledum who has the wooden sword, not Tweedledee.[35] And Carroll, who should know, judged the "rattle" depicted in the left corner of figure 1.3 to be the wrong kind: not a young child's hollow toy (as he understood the nursery rhyme) but a ratcheted "watchman's rattle" used to sound an alarm.[36]

Sometimes an illustration will differ not from the text but from another illustration as regards something not mentioned in the text:

33. Layard, 40. Compare Meyer Schapiro, *Words and Pictures: On the Literal and the Symbolic in the Illustration of a Text* (The Hague: Mouton, 1973), 11: "Sometimes the text itself is not specific enough to determine a picture, even in the barest form. Where the book of Genesis tells that Cain killed Abel, one can hardly illustrate the story without showing how the murder was done. But no weapon is mentioned in the text and the artists have to invent the means."

34. *Punch*, 27 February 1864, 90.

35. So noted by an anonymous reviewer for The Ohio State University Press.

36. C. L. Dodgson to Henry Savile Clarke, 29 November 1886, autograph letter in The Alfred C. Berol Collection of Lewis Carroll, Bobst Library, New York University; quoted by Charles C. Lovett, *Alice on Stage: A History of the Early Theatrical Productions of Alice in Wonderland* (Westport, CT: Meckler, 1990), 44. Tenniel was committed to this "visual pun" (as Peter Hunt called it): he added the bulky watchman's rattle to the impedimenta that hang upon the White Knight's horse in the *Looking-Glass* frontispiece (fig. 7.1). Peter Hunt, introduction to *Alice's Adventures in Wonderland and Through the Looking-Glass*, Oxford World Classics (Oxford: Oxford University Press, 2009), 287. See also *Annotated Alice*, 3rd ed., 191.

FIGURE 11.6. John Leech. "Little Darling." From *Punch*, 27 February 1864.

Grandpapa. " HEYDAY ! WHAT MAKES MY LIITLE DARLING SO CROSS?"
Little Darling. "WHY, GRANDPA, MAMMA WANTS ME TO GO TO A PANTOMIME IN THE DAY TIME, AS IF I WAS A MERE CHILD!"

iconic inconsistency. For example, the White Rabbit, on his first appearance, wears a solid-colored waistcoat; but two chapters later, as he crashes into the cucumber-frame, the waistcoat matches his checked jacket. There are several ways to explain this: the Rabbit changed his waistcoat; Alice changed her dream; Tenniel or Dalziel forgot what the Rabbit was wearing. Similar accounts might explain why the Mad Hatter's bow tie points to the left in three illustrations but to the right in one—or there may just have been some mix-up in imposing Tenniel's drawing onto the woodblock, which reverses left/right relationships.

The frontispiece to *Alice's Adventures* (fig. 3.1) diverges from the text in a way that might seem contradictory of the text but that is in fact more a matter of selection than of contradiction. Carroll sets the scene for the trial by mentioning "a great crowd assembled about" the King and Queen: "all sorts of little birds and beasts, as well as the whole pack of cards." Tenniel omits most of this from his frontispiece, selecting only the central details; but the reader can imagine the crowd as extending beyond the picture frame.

In fact, Tenniel will often be extremely selective, deemphasizing background and setting altogether, focusing instead on one or two characters. Anne Clark has suggested that this close visual focus matches Carroll's narrative interest: "Both author and illustrator were concerned primarily with characters, and very little with setting. Tenniel's background is rarely more than a little cross-hatching."[37] It is true

37. Clark, *The Real Alice*, 105–06. See also her *Biography*, 135.

that many of the vignettes are like that: what we see is a character or two at a significant moment of action, with most other details omitted (for example, figures 1.14, 1.20, and 3.3). But Tenniel also drew some fully developed backgrounds—which usually show a good deal more than the narrative specifies. He was likely to enlarge his focus to take into account a distinctive landscape setting (for example, figures 1.37, 1.39, 6.1), but he could also provide fully detailed genre interiors (for example, the two interiors in the "Father William" series; the scene of Alice and the Sheep in the shop). Most of the illustrations have a moderately close focus, showing enough background detail to anchor the scene (for example, figures 5.1, 7.1, 8.2, 9.1).

Not all omissions can be explained as a matter of selective close focus; some result from mere neglect. For example, the jug of milk that the March Hare upsets at the tea-party does not show in figure 5.1: it should be there, close to the March Hare and the Dormouse (while moving to take the Dormouse's place, the March Hare "upset the milk-jug into his plate")—not offstage, at the imaginable other end of the table.[38] In most cases, like this one, the detail (usually a minor detail) gets mentioned several pages away from the narrative moment that the picture illustrates; no wonder that Tenniel and Carroll overlooked it. Even Homer nods.

The frontispiece to *Looking-Glass* (fig. 7.1) is harder to "place" in its narrative than the frontispiece to *Alice's Adventures,* so its fidelity is harder to judge. There is a passage of high sentiment in chapter 8, which frames the moment when the White Knight sings "A-sitting On A Gate," to a tune of his own invention:

> Years afterwards she could bring the whole scene back again, as if it had been only yesterday—the mild blue eyes and kindly smile of the Knight—the setting sun gleaming through his hair, and shining on his armour in a blaze of light that quite dazzled her—the horse quietly moving about, with the reins hanging loose on his neck, cropping the grass at her feet—and the black shadows of the forest behind—all this she took in like a picture, as, with one hand shading her eyes, she leant against a tree, watching the strange pair, and listening, in a half dream, to the melancholy music of the song.

"Like a picture," but not quite like *this* picture; for though the sunlight and shadows are there, Alice is not shading her eyes, not leaning against any tree, and the White Knight is not singing, and the horse is not free to crop grass.

But there is no contradiction if the picture shows a different moment in the story, one close to the moment described above but not explicitly mentioned in the text; this would be a fairly ordinary supplementation. Or the picture may show a later moment that *is* mentioned in the text, the important moment when Alice and the Knight part, soon after the end of his song:

> As the Knight sang the last words of the ballad, he gathered up the reins, and turned his horse's head along the road by which they had come. "You've only a few yards to go," he said, "down the hill and over that little brook, and then you'll be a Queen—But you'll stay and see me off first?" he added as Alice turned with an eager look in the

38. Hodnett, 179. It is true that when "Alice looked all round the table . . . there was nothing on it but tea"; but an English tea would include milk. Hodnett criticizes a few other illustrations for oversights (177, 189).

direction to which he pointed. "I shan't be long. You'll wait and wave your handkerchief when I get to that turn in the road? I think it'll encourage me, you see."

"Of course I'll wait," said Alice: "and thank you very much for coming so far—and for the song—I liked it very much."

"I hope so," the Knight said doubtfully: "but you didn't cry so much as I thought you would."

So they shook hands, *and then the Knight rode slowly away into the forest.* [Emphasis added.]

On this reading, what the frontispiece shows at the start of *Looking-Glass* is the end of the relationship between Alice and the White Knight—that is, between Alice and Lewis Carroll—just before Alice grows up and becomes a Queen. Carroll thought this image less threatening than Tenniel's drawing of the Jabberwock, which it displaced from the front of the book, but it represents an equivalent crisis.

There is, as we have seen, one strikingly contradictory aspect of the frontispiece: the White Knight's advanced age. However, what that detail contradicts is not what the text says but rather Carroll's conception of the story, communicated privately to Tenniel, which is something else again.

Although in the last analysis neither frontispiece really contradicts its text, both do contain supplementary imagery that is remarkable and calls for interpretation. The bewigged eagle and parrot of figure 3.1 probably convey legal satire as well as refer to Alice Liddell's sisters, Edith and Lorina. The White Rabbit's miniscule trumpet may make fun of the outsized one in Carroll's inept drawing (fig. 3.2). The Knave's red nose may incriminate him.

The other frontispiece contains a more elaborate kind of referential supplement. Most of the paraphernalia that Tenniel loads onto the White Knight's horse is mentioned at some point during the eighth chapter, but some of it is not: the turnips; the bottle of wine hung upside down from the saddle; the wooden sword; the bell strapped to the horse's forehead; even the watchman's rattle discussed above. It is true that the turnips go with the carrots that Carroll *does* mention; and a wooden sword suits the childish and inept Knight; but there is more to these supplements than that. Janis Lull has shown, in a remarkable essay, that every item of the White Knight's equipment refers by synecdoche to past or future events in the story. For example, the fire irons hanging from the horse's saddle, mentioned by Carroll, refer to the White Knight's arrival in chapter 1, sliding down the fire poker; and the dangling bell, not mentioned, refers to the doorbell that Alice, as Queen Alice, will ring at the end of the book. The wooden sword is the sword that Tweedledum used in chapter 4. (Tweedledee's makeshift sword, a furled umbrella, is on the other side of the horse, not visible in the frontispiece, but conspicuous as a supplement to the text in figure 11.7.) And the bottle of wine prefigures the banquet of chapter 9. The *Looking-Glass* frontispiece, that is, is a synopsis of the whole book, a mirror of the looking-glass world.[39]

In burdening the White Knight's steed with miscellaneous, dangling paraphernalia, even including some fireplace equipment, Tenniel adapted an old *Punch* cartoon by his colleague John Leech, titled "The Chatelaine; A Really Useful Present" (fig. 11.8). That cartoon sat-

39. Janis Lull, "The Appliances of Art: The Carroll-Tenniel Collaboration in *Through the Looking-Glass,*" *Lewis Carroll: A Celebration,* 101–11.

FIGURE 11.7. Tenniel. The White Knight in the ditch. From *Through the Looking-Glass.*

FIGURE 11.8. John Leech. "The Chatelaine; A Really Useful Present." From *Punch,* 13 January 1849.

Laura. " OH ! LOOK, MA' DEAR ; SEE WHAT A *LOVE* OF A CHATELAINE EDWARD HAS GIVEN ME."

irized a women's fashion, supposedly a medieval revival, for wearing what has been defined as "a number of short chains attached to the girdle or belt, etc., bearing articles of household use and ornament, as keys, corkscrew, scissors, penknife, pin-cushion, thimble-case, watch, etc., according to taste" (*OED* s.v. *Chatelaine*). The absurd miscellany dangling from the lady's waist in the Leech cartoon is hardly less cumbersome than the array borne on the side of the White Knight's horse.

In so caparisoning the White Knight's horse Tenniel mocks the heroism of the chivalric iconography that was outlined in chapter 7 above. As Roger Simpson and Frankie Morris have noted, Tenniel and his colleagues at *Punch* often ridiculed the pretentious side of the Victorian neo-medieval revival. A favorite butt was the elaborate jousting tournament that was held at Eglinton castle in Scotland in August 1839. (Fate rained heavily upon it, and umbrellas were better needed than swords, at least for the thousands of spectators.) Many of Tenniel's early drawings for *Punch* cheerfully belittled the silly side of chivalry.[40] His White Knight belongs to that satiric tradition as well as to the earnest tradition of Dürer's heroic knight. Having it both ways, negotiating both modes at once, was characteristic of the artist's success.

OF COURSE, not all supplementary details signify; that is, not all relate to the text. The unmentioned ivy that flourishes throughout the pictures of the two books carries no interpretative value. Neither does the clump of foxglove that looms behind Alice and the pig-baby, and that grows next to the Cheshire Cat's tree (figs. 11.9, 1.12).

Carroll himself felt that the foxglove in the illustrations called out for interpretation: in *The Nursery "Alice"* he made it the subject of "a little lesson" in etymology. He claimed, erroneously, that *fox-* derived from *folk's*—*folk* being a name for fairies. Pharmacology may seem to offer a better ground for interpretation: foxglove is the source of digitalis, a lethal poison and, in the early nineteenth century, something of a panacea, prescribed at times even for madness. But for Tenniel foxglove is just an ordinary plant in the European landscape; it gives a decorative touch to three of his landscape drawings for *Æsop's Fables*, drawn decades earlier (for example, fig. 11.10). In their insignificance both the foxglove and the ivy differ from the conventionally emblematic straw on the March Hare's head, which adds to the words of the text to enforce their meaning.

Tenniel adds a detail to his picture of Humpty Dumpty which, unlike the straw, is not conventionally emblematic, but which has the same effect of reinforcing the text: the pointed coping on top of the wall, conspicuously shown in cross-section to the right of the picture (fig. 8.3). This detail is not mentioned in Carroll's text, nor the nursery rhyme; by introducing it, Tenniel highlights the danger of Humpty's position.

Some supplementary details are equivocal. The haberdashery that Tenniel gave the Jabberwock may underline the mock-heroic tone of "Jabberwocky," or it may mitigate too much the terrible nature of the beast. And what of the clothes that Tenniel gave to the terrible Queen of Hearts? Do they make her even more terrible, as the Queen of Spades? Or do they merely give a useful pattern to the picture? The careful variation of the roundedness of the characters in the garden scene seems a clearly significant supplement to the text, but what of the ideal dome in the background?

At least it is safe to say that Tenniel's Queen of Hearts does *not* symbolize Queen Gertrude, despite the resemblance; neither does the White Queen in *Through the Looking-Glass* signify the Pope; nor the Cheshire Cat, Abraham Lincoln. Although as a political cartoonist Tenniel was an allegorist by profession, as an illustrator he did not "allegorize on his

FIGURE 11.9. Tenniel. Alice and the pig-baby. From *Alice's Adventures in Wonderland.*

40. Simpson, 99–107. Morris, *Artist of Wonderland,* 28–29.

FIGURE 11.10. Tenniel. "The Fox and the Stork." From *Æsop's Fables* (1848).

own hook" (to give a literal twist to Rossetti's figurative phrase). Most of the prototype figures discussed in the earlier chapters are prototypes only, not symbolic referents. In general Tenniel operates more like Hunt than Rossetti, gamely trying to provide an equivalent in his own graphic language for a text necessarily different.

The normal metaphor for the process of illustration, which is the mimetic metaphor of the mirror, may seem especially appropriate for the *Alice* books in all their many symmetries; but the metaphor is flawed, like the mirror itself. Imitation always drifts and differs—a truism as old as Plato. It follows that no illustration can simply "reflect" a text. But it does not follow that text and illustration are fundamentally at odds. Though an illustration cannot copy a text, it can—indeed, as an illustration it must—recreate part of the same world that the text creates.

It has been said that Lewis Carroll liked only a single one of Tenniel's illustrations, the well-known picture of Humpty Dumpty.[41] The story is not convincing; why, if he was so disappointed, did Carroll ask Tenniel to illustrate the second book? But Tenniel's image of Humpty Dumpty, implausibly steadying himself between the impossible backward fall into mere copy and the inevitable forward fall into mere difference, is a happy emblem for the dangerous poise of his creator.

41. Furniss, "Recollections," 50.

CHAPTER 12

Coordinating Text and Illustration

*I*t is notorious that Lewis Carroll was finicky about the printing of his books. He acknowledged

having . . . inflicted on that most patient and painstaking firm, Messrs. Macmillan and Co., about as much wear and worry as ever publishers have lived through. The day when they undertake a book for me is a *dies nefastus* for them. From that day till the book is out—an interval of some two or three years on an average—there is no pause in "the pelting of the pitiless storm" of directions and questions on every conceivable detail.[1]

Carroll's correspondence with Macmillan, published in 1987, amply documents that "pitiless storm."[2] From the first printing of *Alice's Adventures in Wonderland* (1865) to the third edition of *Three Sunsets and Other Poems* (1898), Macmillan published more than a dozen books and pamphlets, some in several editions, for Carroll. They did so not independently but on commission from him; in each case Carroll bore the main financial risk. In each case he was also solicitous of his reputation as an author—or, rather, authors, for Macmillan published books not only by "Lewis Carroll" but also by "Charles L. Dodgson, M.A., Senior Student and Mathematical Lecturer of Christ Church, Oxford," as he is styled on the title page of *Euclid and His Modern Rivals* (1870). Carroll's attentive supervision of the publication of his books and pamphlets covered all kinds of details: page layout, title-page wording and layout, page dimensions (to within a quarter of an inch), binding material and design, paper quality, kind of ink, presswork, electrotypes, advertising and other forms of publicity, international rights, translations into foreign languages, relations with readers, permissions to use or cite his work, commercial arrangements with booksellers: in sum, "every conceivable detail." In his last letter to Macmillan, dated 15 December 1897—a month before he died of pneumonia—Carroll complained of

1. From a lost pamphlet by Carroll, "The Profits of Authorship," as quoted by Collingwood, *Life and Letters*, 228.
2. *Lewis Carroll and the House of Macmillan*.

the apparent paleness of the ink used to print the recently published ninth edition of *Alice's Adventures in Wonderland* and fourth edition of *Through the Looking-Glass.* Although he often sought the professional advice of Alexander Macmillan and his successor Frederick Macmillan, Carroll was usually decisive in instructing them how to proceed.

Although he tended to express his concerns with the same degree of earnestness, some were of greater importance than others. As regards the Tenniel illustrations to the *Alice* books, Carroll's most significant concerns had to do with the layout of the illustrations on the page and the quality of the presswork. Presswork will be discussed in some detail in chapter 14; the present chapter will examine layout in the *Alice* books, which proved to be highly successful in the early editions under Carroll's fastidious control, less successful in cheaper editions that Macmillan published with his consent in later years, and often careless in later editions by other publishers.

Carroll designed the early editions of *Alice's Adventures* and *Through the Looking-Glass* so that the text and illustrations would be significantly juxtaposed on the page. Typically, textual references stand next to their pictorial referents, and the narrative moments of text and illustration are visually synchronized. In some later editions, care was taken to preserve such significant juxtapositions. But for some other, cheaper editions, Carroll allowed the text and illustrations to drift apart. And most modern editions show too little concern for this aspect of the *Alice* books, which greatly contributed to their distinction as illustrated books. The unusually complementary relationship of Tenniel's illustrations to Carroll's text has often been remarked, but the strength of that relationship cannot be fully appreciated in casually laid-out editions. To see how fully the Tenniel illustrations respond to Carroll's text, it is necessary to see them as they were originally presented on the page.

The important illustration of Alice confronting the Queen of Hearts in the garden is a good case in point (fig. 6.1). The strongly expressive postures of the Queen and Alice suggest that the drawing captures a specific moment in the dialogue. But readers of recent editions of *Alice's Adventures* might well wonder *which* moment is being illustrated; any of several highly charged moments in the scene might seem to apply. Discussing the *Alice* books with college students, I have found that they are easily misled by the layouts of modern editions.

A reader of the Oxford English Novels edition might connect Tenniel's picture to the following passage, which appears below it there:

> . . . she stood where she was, and waited.
>
> When the procession came opposite to Alice, they all stopped and looked at her, and the Queen said, severely, 'Who is this?' She said it to the Knave of Hearts, who only bowed and smiled in reply.
>
> 'Idiot!' said the Queen, tossing her head impatiently; and, turning to Alice, she went on:
>
> 'What's your name, child?'
>
> 'My name is Alice, so please your Majesty,' said Alice.[3]

A reader of either the Modern Library edition of Carroll's *Complete Works,* or of the first edition of *The Annotated Alice,* might concentrate on the Queen's gesture of pointing, described in those books not far below the illustration: "'And who are *these?*' said the Queen, pointing to

3. *Alice's Adventures in Wonderland and Through the Looking-Glass and What Alice Found There,* ed. Roger Lancelyn Green, Oxford English Novels (London: Oxford University Press, 1971), 71. The layout of this edition is perpetuated in the Oxford Paperbacks edition of 1975, and in the World's Classics edition published by Oxford in 1982.

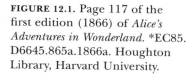FIGURE 12.1. Page 117 of the first edition (1866) of *Alice's Adventures in Wonderland*. *EC85. D6645.865a.1866a. Houghton Library, Harvard University.

The Queen turned crimson with fury, and, after glaring at her for a moment like a wild beast, began screaming, " Off with her head! Off—"

the three gardeners who were lying round the rose-tree; for, you see . . . they were lying on their faces, and the pattern on their backs was the same as the rest of the pack."[4] (These three cards can indeed be seen in the lower right-hand corner of the illustration—to which the explanation "for, you see" refers.) But a reader of the Puffin edition could too easily connect the Queen's obvious shouting in the picture to the command that is quoted immediately below it: "'Leave off that!' screamed the Queen."[5]

For all such readers, Tenniel's illustration would carry less force than it would for a reader of the first edition, published late in 1865 (with the date "1866" on the title page). That reader would find the picture underwritten by a single sentence of the text, which doubles as a precise caption: "The Queen turned crimson with fury, and, after glaring at her for a moment like a wild beast, began screaming, 'Off with her head! Off—'" (fig. 12.1).[6] Clearly this passage best matches the Queen's demeanor.

That the original arrangement is the best arrangement finds support, in this case, in some external evidence. A preliminary list in Carroll's hand of all the illustrations to *Alice's Adventures* refers to each one

4. *The Complete Works of Lewis Carroll* (New York: Modern Library, 1936), 87. *Annotated Alice*, 108.

5. *Alice's Adventures in Wonderland and Through the Looking Glass* (1962; rpt. Harmondsworth, Eng.: Puffin-Penguin, 1976), 108.

6. Lewis Carroll, *Alice's Adventures in Wonderland* (London: Macmillan, 1866), 117. This edition, referred to here as the "first edition" or "original edition" of *Alice's Adventures*, is the first edition to be published, but the second to be printed. As was mentioned in chapter 10, and as will be further discussed in chapter 14, the first printing, dated 1865, was suppressed because of defects, on Tenniel's advice. The second printing was entirely reset, but the layout of the two printings is essentially the same. The minor differences in layout, which chiefly involve the removal of "widows" at the tops of some pages, are described by Harry Morgan Ayres, "Carroll's Withdrawal of the 1865 *Alice*," *The Huntington Library Bulletin* 6 (1934): 153–63. Selwyn H. Goodacre amplified Ayres's observation that several of the changes "permitted a better placing of the picture"; see "The 1865 *Alice*: A New Appraisal and a Revised Census," *Soaring with the Dodo: Essays on Lewis Carroll's Life and Art*, ed. Edward Guiliano and James R. Kincaid (Silver Spring, MD: Lewis Carroll Society of North America, 1982), 78–79.

in a short phrase sufficient to distinguish it from all the others; for example, "Rabbit & watch," "cucumber frame," "caterpillar," "Duchess & Alice." Carroll refers to this particular illustration as "Queen of Hearts," and then adds a line in somewhat smaller script, "(off with her head)."[7] Whether this addition was meant to clarify matters for himself or for the printer, it is clear that Carroll understood the illustration to refer to this particular passage of the text. When he first commissioned the drawings he may have told Tenniel to illustrate this particular moment. In any case Carroll's memorandum shows that the layout of the 1866 edition reflects his sense of the illustration better than any of the modern layouts cited above.

Of course, the passage that served as a caption in 1866 describes the Queen's behavior only. To appreciate the way that Tenniel has drawn Alice here—head cocked upward in mild defiance and arms protectively crossed in front, boldly standing her ground—the reader can recall what he has just read at the bottom of the opposite page, when Alice repulsed the Queen's inquiry into the identity of the gardeners:

> "And who are *these?*" said the Queen, pointing to the three gardeners who were lying round the rose-tree. . . .
> "How should *I* know?" said Alice, surprised at her own courage. "It's no business of *mine.*"

Alice's defensive posture in the illustration persists from this moment in the dialogue. The illustration is bracketed by passages that together specify the demeanor of the main characters.

The same kind of precise bracketing by the text informs Tenniel's famous illustration of the Wonderland tea-party. After the Hatter has remarked to Alice, "Your hair wants cutting" (a milder version of the Queen's threat of execution), there is this brief passage at the foot of page 96: "'You should learn not to make personal remarks,' Alice said with some severity: 'it's very rude.'" The reader next sees, at the top of the opposite page, the tea-party illustration: there Alice is still glowering at the Hatter, her left hand gripping the arm of her chair. And then, immediately below the illustration: "The Hatter opened his eyes very wide on hearing this; but all he *said* was, 'Why is a raven like a writing-desk?'" (fig. 12.2). Apparently the illustration depicts the precise moment when, wide-eyed, the Hatter put his famous riddle to Alice.

But that implication is lost in some later editions, including one published with Carroll's approval. In 1887 Macmillan published a "People's Edition" of *Alice's Adventures,* along with one of *Through the Looking-Glass.* These books were less than half the price of the standard editions, and were less luxurious: plain edges rather than gilt, no gilt ornamentation on the covers, thinner paper, and fewer pages. To reduce the number of pages it was necessary to reset the type; and inevitably that resetting disturbed the careful arrangement of text and illustrations that had been worked out for the original editions. One result was the juxtaposition of the tea-party illustration with:

> "Do you mean that you think you can find out the answer to it [i.e., the riddle]?" said the March Hare.
> "Exactly so," said Alice.
> "Then you should say what you mean," the March Hare went on.[8]

7. Crutch, plate X; 211, no. 13.

8. *Alice's Adventures in Wonderland,* People's Edition (London: Macmillan, 1887), 88.

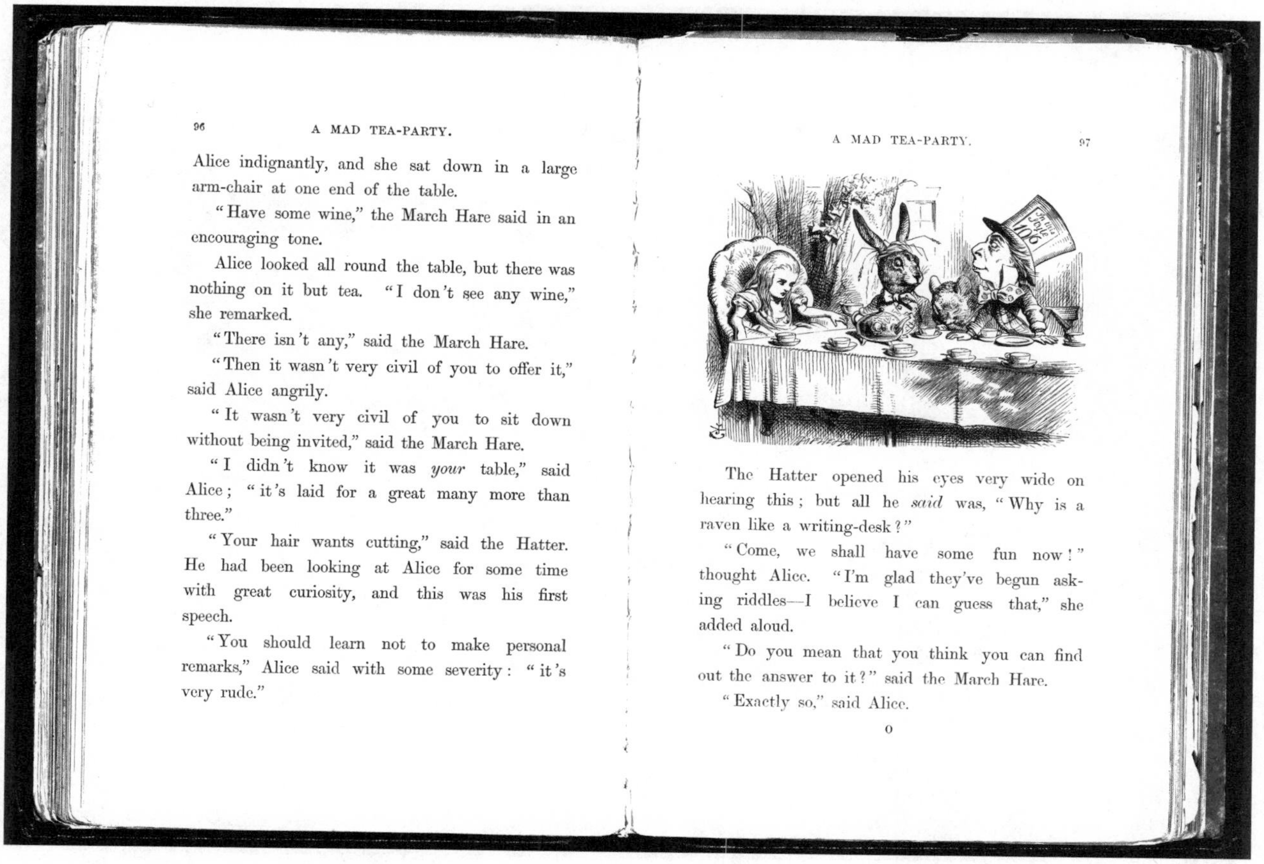

96 A MAD TEA-PARTY.

Alice indignantly, and she sat down in a large arm-chair at one end of the table.

"Have some wine," the March Hare said in an encouraging tone.

Alice looked all round the table, but there was nothing on it but tea. "I don't see any wine," she remarked.

"There isn't any," said the March Hare.

"Then it wasn't very civil of you to offer it," said Alice angrily.

"It wasn't very civil of you to sit down without being invited," said the March Hare.

"I didn't know it was *your* table," said Alice; "it's laid for a great many more than three."

"Your hair wants cutting," said the Hatter. He had been looking at Alice for some time with great curiosity, and this was his first speech.

"You should learn not to make personal remarks," Alice said with some severity: "it's very rude."

A MAD TEA-PARTY. 97

The Hatter opened his eyes very wide on hearing this; but all he *said* was, "Why is a raven like a writing-desk?"

"Come, we shall have some fun now!" thought Alice. "I'm glad they've begun asking riddles—I believe I can guess that," she added aloud.

"Do you mean that you think you can find out the answer to it?" said the March Hare.

"Exactly so," said Alice.

O

FIGURE 12.2. Pages 96–97 of the first edition (1866) of *Alice's Adventures in Wonderland* *EC85. D6645.865a.1866a. Houghton Library, Harvard University.

Such an arrangement weakens the immediate relationship of picture to text. That relationship is further weakened in the even cheaper "Sixpenny Series" edition that Macmillan published in 1898, less than a year after Carroll's death. There the illustration is delayed until the riddle topic has lapsed from the conversation and then revived. It comes in the middle of, and seems to illustrate, this paragraph:

> Alice sighed wearily. "I think you might do something [*illustration here*] better with the time," she said, "than waste it asking riddles with no answers."[9]

This arrangement ascribes "weariness" to the Alice of the illustration, where the original arrangement ascribed a certain "severity."

Only in the original arrangement does the text accurately represent the picture. Or, rather, only in the original arrangement does the picture actually represent the text. Despite the fact, noted in chapter 10 above, that Tenniel allowed that this illustration of "the Hatter asking the riddle . . . will do equally well for any other question that he may ask, and can go anywhere," Carroll honored his first suggestion and placed it where it belongs.

In three successive Norton Critical Editions of *Alice in Wonderland* this drawing has floated free of any mooring in the text, appearing at the very head of the chapter as a kind of résumé of the whole rather than as an illustration of a specific moment. The reader is denied any clue to its dramatic immediacy. The same arrangement, and the same

9. *Alice's Adventures in Wonderland,* Macmillan's Sixpenny Series (1898; rpt. London: Macmillan, 1903), 72; the same tea-party illustration decorates the paper front cover. For some features of the Sixpenny Series edition see Crutch, 235.

Within the reproduced book page:

CHAPTER IV.

TWEEDLEDUM AND TWEEDLEDEE.

THEY were standing under a tree, each with an arm round the other's neck, and Alice knew which was which in a moment, because one of them had 'DUM' embroidered on his collar, and the other 'DEE.' "I suppose they've each got 'TWEEDLE' round at the back of the collar," she said to herself.

They stood so still that she quite forgot they were alive, and she was just looking round to see if the word 'TWEEDLE' was written at the back of each collar, when she was startled by a voice coming from the one marked 'DUM.'

"If you think we're wax-works," he said, "you ought to pay, you know. Wax-works weren't made to be looked at for nothing. Nohow!"

"Contrariwise," added the one marked 'DEE.' "if you think we're alive, you ought to speak."

"I'm sure I'm very sorry," was all Alice could say; for the words of the old song kept ringing through her head like the ticking of a clock, and she could hardly help saying them out loud :—

F 2

FIGURE 12.3. Pages 66–67 of the first edition (1872) of *Through the Looking-Glass.* *EC85.D6645.872t. Houghton Library, Harvard University.

defect, are to be found in the handsome edition of *Alice's Adventures* designed by George Salter with the Tenniel illustrations colored by Fritz Kredel, which achieved a wide distribution after World War II. The two Broadview Editions are similar in this respect also.[10]

Page layout matters too in the sequel, *Through the Looking-Glass.* When Alice encounters Tweedledum and Tweedledee, Tenniel shows her in an awkward, startled posture because she has just been described in the text as "startled"—

> startled by a voice coming from the one marked 'DUM.'
> [*the illustration appears here*]
> "If you think we're wax-works," he said, "you ought to pay, you know. Wax-works weren't made to be looked at for nothing. Nohow!"

This arrangement, set out by the original edition (1872), can be seen in figure 12.3.[11]

The drawing shows Alice's startled response to Tweedledum's behavior. (Realistically, perhaps, Tenniel should have shown Tweedledum as in the course of speaking; but it was preferable to show him closemouthed, the same as his twin brother—perhaps between sentences.) In later editions this illustration too drifts away from its locality. It is delayed for two pages in the Sixpenny Series edition, and ascends to the top of the chapter in both the Oxford English Novels and Puffin editions, where it illustrates the general title of the chapter, "Tweedledum and Tweedledee," but where Alice's arrested posture loses its motivation.

10. *Alice in Wonderland*, ed. Gray, 54; 2nd ed., 54; 3rd ed., 52. *Alice's Adventures in Wonderland* (New York: Random House, 1946), 76. *Alice's Adventures in Wonderland*, ed. Richard Kelly (Peterborough, Ont.: Broadview Editions, 2000), 103; 2nd ed., 112.

11. Lewis Carroll, *Through the Looking-Glass, and What Alice Found There* (London: Macmillan, 1872), 66–67.

Then they all crowded round her once more, while the Dodo solemnly presented the thimble, saying, "We beg your acceptance of this elegant thimble;" and, when it had finished this short speech, they all cheered.

afraid that he really *was* hurt this time. However, though she could see nothing but the soles of his feet, she was much relieved to hear that he was talking on in his usual tone. "All kinds of fastness," he repeated : "but it was careless of him to put another man's helmet on——with the man in it, too."

"How *can* you go on talking so quietly, head downwards?" Alice asked, as she dragged him out by the feet, and laid him in a heap on the bank.

Many other full-width illustrations in both books show to best advantage in their original settings, with the immediately relevant passage of text strategically placed as a caption; for example, Alice and the Dodo (fig. 12.4), or Alice dragging the White Knight out of the ditch (fig. 12.5).

Rarely in the original settings does any illustration, large or small, seem to have been displaced from its proper location without some good typographical reason. It may be that an error was made (and overlooked by Carroll) in placing the picture that shows Alice and the two remonstrating Queens (fig. 12.6). The simultaneous gestures of the Queens, and Alice's withdrawn appearance, suggest that this illustration belongs on the opposite page, just below the thirteenth line, "'we *are* talking!'" No typographical constraint would prevent such an arrangement, which by bracketing the picture with two relevant sentences might better define the moment that Tenniel was illustrating.

In the working list that he prepared of the illustrations to *Alice's Adventures*, Carroll distinguishes between the illustrations meant to be centered on the page (marked κ on the list), and the usually narrower ones meant to be "let in," or run flush to the margin, set alongside a narrowed column of the continuing text (marked λ on the list). In some cases Carroll even specified from which margin, left or right, the illustration was to be let in.[12] The early editions place many of these let-in illustrations precisely next to the relevant passage in the text. So the references to "a low curtain she had not noticed before, and behind it . . . a little door about fifteen inches high," occur immediately next

FIGURE 12.4. Page 35 of the first edition (1866) of *Alice's Adventures in Wonderland*. *EC85. D6645.865a.1866a. Houghton Library, Harvard University.

FIGURE 12.5. Page 172 of the first edition (1872) of *Through the Looking-Glass*. *EC85.D6645.872t. Houghton Library, Harvard University.

12. Crutch, facing 196. For a discussion of the corresponding list for *Looking-Glass* see Edward Wakeling, "The Illustration Plan for *Through the Looking-Glass*," *Jabberwocky* 21:2 (Spring 1992): 27–38.

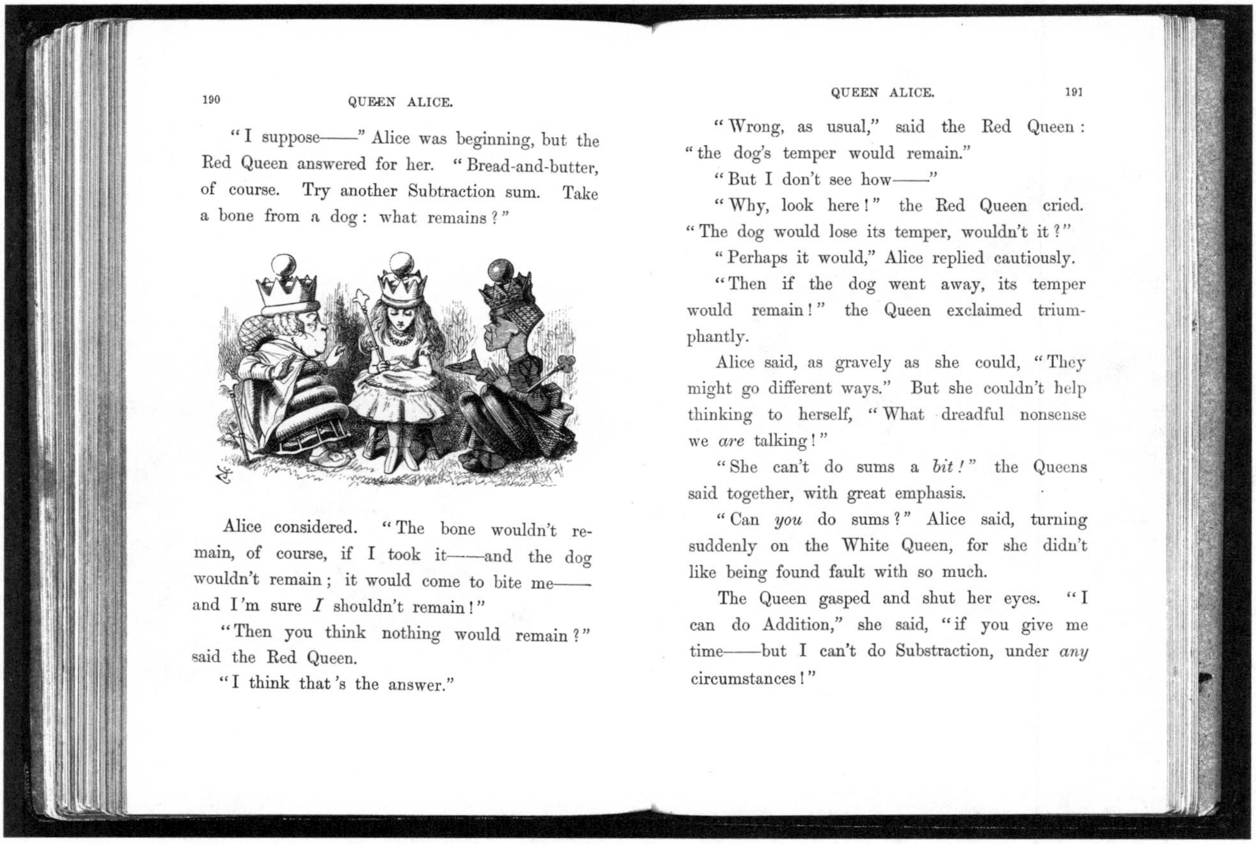

"I suppose——" Alice was beginning, but the Red Queen answered for her. "Bread-and-butter, of course. Try another Subtraction sum. Take a bone from a dog: what remains?"

Alice considered. "The bone wouldn't remain, of course, if I took it——and the dog wouldn't remain; it would come to bite me—— and I'm sure *I* shouldn't remain!"

"Then you think nothing would remain?" said the Red Queen.

"I think that's the answer."

"Wrong, as usual," said the Red Queen: "the dog's temper would remain."

"But I don't see how——"

"Why, look here!" the Red Queen cried. "The dog would lose its temper, wouldn't it?"

"Perhaps it would," Alice replied cautiously.

"Then if the dog went away, its temper would remain!" the Queen exclaimed triumphantly.

Alice said, as gravely as she could, "They might go different ways." But she couldn't help thinking to herself, "What dreadful nonsense we *are* talking!"

"She can't do sums a *bit!*" the Queens said together, with great emphasis.

"Can *you* do sums?" Alice said, turning suddenly on the White Queen, for she didn't like being found fault with so much.

The Queen gasped and shut her eyes. "I can do Addition," she said, "if you give me time——but I can't do Substraction, under *any* circumstances!"

FIGURE 12.6. Pages 190–91 of the first edition (1872) of *Through the Looking-Glass*. *EC85.D6645.872t. Houghton Library, Harvard University.

FIGURE 12.7. Page 8 of the first edition (1866) of *Alice's Adventures in Wonderland*. *EC85.D6645.865a.1866a. Houghton Library, Harvard University.

doors of the hall; but, alas! either the locks were too large, or the key was too small, but at any rate it would not open any of them. However, on the second time round, she came

upon a low curtain she had not noticed before, and behind it was a little door about fifteen inches high: she tried the little golden key in the lock, and to her great delight it fitted!

Alice opened the door and found that it led into a small passage, not much larger than a rat-hole: she knelt down and looked along the passage into the loveliest garden you ever saw. How she longed to get out of that dark hall, and wander about among those beds of bright

CHAPTER II.

THE POOL OF TEARS.

"Curiouser and cu-
riouser!" cried Alice
(she was so much sur-
prised, that for the
moment she quite for-
got how to speak good
English); "now I'm
opening out like the
largest telescope that
ever was! Good-bye,
feet!" (for when she
looked down at her
feet, they seemed to
be almost out of sight,
they were getting so
far off) "Oh, my poor
little feet, I wonder

FIGURE 12.8. Page 15 of the first edition (1866) of *Alice's Adventures in Wonderland.* *EC85. D6645.865a.1866a. Houghton Library, Harvard University.

to the illustration of these things, indeed in the same vertical sequence (fig. 12.7). So tall Alice's interjection, "Oh, my poor little feet," occurs at the very foot of the page, directly next to her distant feet (fig. 12.8; note too how Alice's height is enhanced by her vertically filling the page). So the references to "a snatch in the air" and "a crash of broken glass" in what might be "a cucumber-frame," run in parallel with the depiction of those things (fig. 12.9). There are other examples in both books of such nice matching of marginal illustrations with the text. This finesse suffers more or less in later editions.

Tenniel seems to have modeled the illustrations in figures 12.7–12.9, like several of his other illustrations for *Alice's Adventures,* on drawings that Carroll had himself made in the gift manuscript for Alice Liddell (see chapter 2). Of the thirty-seven drawings in that manuscript, four-teen are full-page "plates," so to speak, each one opposite the relevant page of text (most of them sideways—an awkward but not unconven-tional arrangement); and twenty-three are let-in, marginal illustrations. None is centered on a page of text, though many of Tenniel's were to be later. Conversely, Tenniel designed few full-page illustrations—ver-tical ones—and those only for special purposes. (Two are the frontis-pieces; and a third, the "Jabberwocky" illustration, had originally been intended for a frontispiece. The remaining two, which show the Red Queen being shaken back into the black kitten, are actually small draw-ings, though displayed alone on the page; and they mark an important transitional moment in the *Looking-Glass* narrative.)

Because of the quantity of full-page "plates," Carroll's manuscript is less closely integrated than either of the published *Alice* books. Nonetheless, the manuscript set an important precedent for the treat-

waiting till she fancied she heard the Rabbit just under the window, she suddenly spread

out her hand, and made a snatch in the air. She did not get hold of anything, but she heard a little shriek and a fall, and a crash of broken glass, from which she concluded that it was just possible it had fallen into a cucumber-frame, or something of the sort.

Next came an angry voice—the Rabbit's— "Pat! Pat! Where are you?" And then a voice she had never heard before, "Sure then I'm here! Digging for apples, yer honour!"

"Digging for apples, indeed!" said the Rabbit angrily. "Here! Come and help me out of *this!*" (Sounds of more broken glass.)

how she was ever to get out again: suddenly she came upon a little three-legged table, all made of solid glass, there was nothing lying upon it, but a tiny golden key, and Alice's first idea was that it might belong to one of the doors of the hall, but alas! either the locks were too large, or the key too small, but at any rate it would open none of them However, on the second time round, she came to a low curtain, behind which was a door about eighteen inches high: she tried the little key in the keyhole, and it fitted! Alice opened the door, and looked down a small passage, not larger than a rat-hole, into the loveliest garden you ever saw How she longed to get out of that dark hall, and wander about among those beds of bright flowers and those cool fountains, but she could not even get her head through the doorway, "and even if my head would go through" thought poor Alice, "it would be very little use without my shoulders Oh, how I wish I could shut

6

FIGURE 12.9. Page 48 of the first edition (1866) of *Alice's Adventures in Wonderland.* *EC85. D6645.865a.1866a. Houghton Library, Harvard University.

FIGURE 12.10. Page 6 of *Alice's Adventures under Ground* (1886).

13. Carroll, *Alice's Adventures under Ground* (Macmillan, 1886), 6.

14. Charles Dickens, *The Haunted Man and The Ghost's Bargain* (London: Bradbury & Evans, 1848), 53—a proleptic image, however, not tied to the adjacent text in the quadrant.

15. Use of the L-shaped block had affinities with fashionable Germanic page design in which a neo-medieval ornamental and storiated engraved image would entirely frame an inset block of text. John Buchanan-Brown, *Early Victorian Illustrated Books: Britain, France and Germany, 1820–1860* (London: The British Library, 2005), 115–35.

ment of the smaller illustrations. With only one exception, all the let-in illustrations in the manuscript stand next to the passages that they illustrate. Figure 12.10, which includes the prototype of Tenniel's drawing in figure 12.7, is a good example.[13] Tenniel improved the illustration by adding the door mentioned in the text, but the placement of the illustration in the book maintains an integration that the manuscript had already achieved. Much the same can be said of figure 12.9 and Carroll's prototype for the illustration in it. Similar care in placement was extended to most of Tenniel's "new" let-in drawings for *Alice's Adventures* (that is, those that Carroll had not attempted himself), and to the series for *Looking-Glass.*

One special kind of let-in illustration is the L-shaped kind, in which Tenniel did some of his most memorable work. The top or base of the illustration runs the full width of the page, but the other end leaves room on one side for a quadrant of the text. There are none like this in Carroll's manuscript, but at least since the 1840s engraved L-shaped wood blocks could intensify the juxtaposition of text and image. Tenniel made occasional use of the device more or less effectively in *Undine* (1845), *Aesop's Fables* (1848), Dickens's *The Haunted Man* (1845),[14] and Tupper's *Proverbial Philosophy* (1854; fig. 3.6).[15] The placement on a recto page of Tenniel's L-shaped drawing of Alice talking with the Cheshire Cat is especially subtle. Dependent from the very top of the page (even with but one line of text below it) the long side of the image emphasizes the elevation of Alice's gaze. Like Alice, the reader sees the Cat's curled, dark tail silhouetted against a white back-

"Well then," the Cat went on, "you see a dog growls when it's angry, and wags its tail when it's pleased. Now *I* growl when I'm pleased, and wag my tail when I'm angry. Therefore I'm mad."

"*I* call it purring, not growling," said Alice.

"Call it what you like," said the Cat. "Do you play croquet with the Queen to-day?"

FIGURE 12.11. Page 91 of the first edition (1866) of *Alice's Adventures in Wonderland.* *EC85. D6645.865a.1866a. Houghton Library, Harvard University.

ground—appropriately emphasized, for in the adjacent textual quadrant he draws attention to it by warning, "I . . . wag my tail when I'm angry. Therefore I'm mad" (fig. 12.11). And when the reader turns the page she will see the Cat, or rather some of it, in the same location at the top of the next recto page, fading away just as the text below it says: "ending with the grin, which remained some time after the rest of it had gone." Such page-turning legerdemain anticipates an even more dramatic moment of transition in *Looking-Glass,* which will be discussed later.[16]

In the L-shaped illustration of the King of Hearts, the King points out the tarts on the table in front of him. In the original edition, the textual quadrant of this illustration begins, "'Why, there they are!' said the King triumphantly, pointing to the tarts on the table." (In his list of illustrations, Carroll referred to this one as "There they are!") In the rest of the quadrant, the King continues to read from the letter that Tenniel has put in his right hand (see fig. 12.12); compare the immediacy of this arrangement to the irrelevancy of that in the People's Edition (fig. 12.13). So in the original edition of *Looking-Glass,* Humpty Dumpty and Alice join hands in both the illustrations and the textual quadrant (fig. 12.14), but not in the People's Edition.

Finally, the most remarkable example of felicitous picture placement occurs near the start of *Through the Looking-Glass.* In the original edition, the first picture of Alice passing through the mirror appears at the top of a right-hand page, captioned by the lines that describe the dissolving of the mirror and Alice's passing "through" it (fig. 12.15).

16. The careful sequencing of these two images in the same location on consecutive recto pages was noted by Morris, *Artist of Wonderland,* 178. The device may have been influenced by Carroll's appreciation of "dissolving views" in contemporary magic lantern shows.

"Why, there they are!" said the King triumphantly, pointing to the tarts on the table. "Nothing can be clearer than *that*. Then again—'*before she had this fit*—' you never had fits, my dear, I think?" he said to the Queen.

"Never!" said the Queen furiously, throw-

ing an inkstand at the Lizard as she spoke. (The unfortunate little Bill had left off writing on his slate with one finger, as he found it made

using the ink, that was trickling down his face, as long as it lasted.)

"Then the words don't *fit* you," said the King, looking round the court with a smile. There was a dead silence.

"It's a pun!" the King added in an offended tone, and everybody laughed.

"Let the jury consider their verdict," the King said, for about the twentieth time that day.

FIGURE 12.12. Page 186 of the first edition (1866) of *Alice's Adventures in Wonderland*. *EC85. D6645.865a.1866a. Houghton Library, Harvard University.

FIGURE 12.13. Page 169 of the People's Edition (1887) of *Alice's Adventures in Wonderland*.

FIGURE 12.14. Page 118 of the first edition (1872) of *Through the Looking-Glass*. *EC85.D6645.872t. Houghton Library, Harvard University.

fell off the wall in doing so) and offered Alice his hand. She watched him a little anxiously as she took it. "If he smiled much more, the ends of his mouth might meet behind," she thought: "and then I don't know what would happen to his head! I'm afraid it would come off!"

"Yes, all his horses and all his men," Humpty

there.   And certainly the glass *was* beginning to melt away, just like a bright silvery mist.

In another moment Alice was through the

glass, and had jumped lightly down into the Looking-glass room.   The very first thing she did was to look whether there was a fire in the

Such captioning is not itself unique. But at the very moment when the text has Alice pass through the looking-glass the reader is made to turn the page, and to discover on the left what is largely a mirror image of the illustration that he has just been looking at, now presented as a view, from the *other* side of the looking-glass, of Alice's passing through it (fig. 12.16).[17] These two complementary images are printed on opposite sides of the same leaf, in close registration with each other. The leaf, in effect, is the glass. Even the monogram of the artist fills the same space on the different sides of the leaf; and so does the signature of the engraver. Tenniel thoughtfully reversed his monogram left-to-right, so that in the second illustration it is seen as if through the leaf. The Dalziel signature, unfortunately, defies reversal on the other side of the looking-glass; commercial interests, unlike artistic ones, resist imaginative transformation.

The People's Edition preserves the superimposition of these two illustrations on opposite sides of the same leaf, but below them the "captions" of text have drifted irrelevantly. The Norton Critical Edition recovers the intended effect fairly well, given the different typographical requirements of its standard page. (However, the two images differ noticeably in size.) The Oxford English Novels edition, by placing these illustrations on facing pages, enables the reader to study the reflective symmetry of the two pictures; but it prevents her from experiencing with Alice the transition from one side of the looking-glass to the other.

BESIDES THE People's Edition of the *Alice* books, to which reference has already been made, there were several other relevant editions pub-

FIGURE 12.15. Page 11 of the first edition (1872) of *Through the Looking-Glass*. *EC85.D6645.872t. Houghton Library, Harvard University.

FIGURE 12.16. Page 12 of the first edition (1872) of *Through the Looking-Glass*. *EC85.D6645.872t. Houghton Library, Harvard University.

17. Davis mentioned this effect in his introduction to *The Illustrators of Alice in Wonderland*, 9.

lished during Carroll's lifetime. Macmillan published translations of *Alice's Adventures* in 1869 (German and French) and 1872 (Italian). Despite the elasticity that translation imposes on a text, these books preserve much of the rapport between text and illustration that marks the original edition. Carroll took a special interest in the matter; two weeks after complaining about some page proofs of the German edition that were each "a line too short, and ½ an inch too narrow . . . [throwing] most of the pictures out of proportion," he spelled out a general requirement for that edition that obviously applies as well to the layouts of both the original edition of *Alice's Adventures* and the forthcoming edition of *Looking-Glass* (as yet unwritten): "I forgot to say, with regard to the German *Alice,* that they need not trouble themselves to get into each page the *same* matter as is in the corresponding page in the English. Let them run it on as they like, so long as they *place the pictures as near as possible to the text to which they refer.*"[18] As a result of such attention the Macmillan editions of the three translations are more accurately laid out than most modern editions of the English text.

Of at least equal interest are the so-called ninth edition of *Alice's Adventures* and the so-called fourth edition of *Looking-Glass,* both published in 1897, which, aside from the People's Edition, were the only editions of the English texts to be published in Carroll's lifetime that actually involved resetting. Except for small verbal revisions, these new editions, unlike the People's Edition, were page-for-page and line-for-line replicas of the original editions, and so they preserved the same subtleties of layout. Macmillan reprinted these editions many times, both in London and New York, at least into the 1940s.[19]

The early layouts have survived, too, in photofacsimile editions of the original editions. In 1941 the Book League of America published a facsimile edition of "the first edition" of *Alice's Adventures*—the edition of 1866, judging from internal evidence.[20] There was some effort to reproduce the original binding, and a general literary introduction (by Kathleen Norris) was added. The half-title page bears the signature of C. L. Dodgson, but no textual note identifies the provenance of the copy that this edition reproduces. The following year, in 1942, the same book was issued by Doubleday, Doran in New York. It appeared again in 1957, with Dodgson's signature on the half-title page but without Norris's introduction, this time distributed by Crown Publishers in New York, as part of a boxed set of four long-playing records containing a reading of the text by Cyril Ritchard. (The cover of the box, published by Riverside Records in New York, says that the facsimile is "of the rare 1865 edition of the book," but it is actually 1866.) At some unidentified later date the same facsimile was issued in an imitation-leather binding by Avenel Books, in New York, a subsidiary of Crown. The same signature of C. L. Dodgson appears on the half-title, in the same location. Indeed, the same half-title, signature and all, puts in an illegitimate second appearance, just before the first chapter.

A parallel facsimile edition of *Looking-Glass,* apparently the 1872 edition, was also published by Avenel. It too is somewhat casually made up: pages 217 (devoted to Tenniel's illustration of the kitten, held in Alice's hands) and 218 (the start of chapter 12), which are unnumbered sides of the same leaf, have accidentally changed places. This error persists in the combined edition of these two facsimiles that was published in 1979

18. *Lewis Carroll and the House of Macmillan,* 65 (17 June 1868); 66 (3 July 1868; emphasis added). The three translations are: *Aventures d'Alice au pays des merveilles,* trans. Henri Bué (London: Macmillan, 1869); *Alice's Abenteuer im Wunderland,* trans. Antonie Zimmermann (London: Macmillan, 1869); and *Le avventure d'Alice nel paese delle meraviglie,* trans. T. Pietrocòla-Rossetti (London: Macmillan, 1872).

19. Crutch, 36, 64–65.

20. A few features that distinguish the setting of 1866 from that of 1865 were reported by Flora Livingston, *The Harcourt Amory Collection of Lewis Carroll in the Harvard College Library* (Cambridge, MA: privately printed, 1932), 12–14; Ayres provides more detail. So far as I know, the 1865 *Alice* (London: Macmillan) has never been reproduced in a facsimile edition. But many copies of the 1865 setting were outfitted with new title pages and published by D. Appleton and Co., New York, in 1866; these copies constituted the first American edition, and Appleton published a facsimile of *that* edition in 1927. The foreword to that facsimile aptly characterizes the original layout: "No format was ever better conceived, more consistent with the spirit of the text than the original edition illustrated by Tenniel."

by Derrydale Books, another Crown subsidiary, under the title *Journeys in Wonderland*. However, the autographed half-title has been confined to its proper location.

The foreword to this book, by Patricia Horan, is uninformative; but whoever wrote the dust-jacket copy understood in general what I have tried to specify: "These two masterpieces . . . are reprinted here with the original text and the magnificent John Tenniel illustrations, the ones approved by Lewis Carroll himself. All ninety-two illustrations are here, *in their proper places*" (emphasis added). All, that is, except for the picture of Kitty meant for page 217. And many of the illustrations in this reprint were poorly reproduced, with a loss of fine detail.

In 1982 I proposed to Michael Wace, then the editorial director of Macmillan Children's Books in London, that the firm reprint the two *Alice* books in their "original formats," to preserve the significant placement of Tenniel's illustrations. Two years later that project was realized by Macmillan and also by A. A. Knopf in New York. Under each publisher's imprint the books appeared in a boxed set, accompanied by an explanatory pamphlet that I wrote, and they were also issued as separate volumes. Macmillan took great care in preparing these facsimiles, even replicating the original gold-stamped red cloth bindings that Carroll had designed, as well as the pages as they were first published in 1866 and 1872.[21] A notice of this edition mentioned that Geoffrey Baker, Wace's colleague at Macmillan, spoke in 1985 about challenges faced in producing the volumes, which included the difficulty of reproducing "that strange black paper" used for the original end papers.[22] Carroll would have appreciated the thoroughgoing care and the results.

In succeeding decades Macmillan have continued to publish many additional editions of the *Alice* books, formatting them with apt attention to the placement of the image on the page. Particularly commendable in this respect is the boxed set issued in 1995, which, although printed on a large page and adding color to Tenniel's illustrations throughout, scrupulously respected the original layout of text and illustration. "As far as possible this edition follows the original positioning of the text and illustrations as agreed by Tenniel and Carroll for the very first edition in 1866" ("Publisher's Note").[23] The same care was taken in preparing the even larger pages for *The Complete Alice*, a deluxe sesquicentennial volume published in 2015. Again the publisher's note points out that "as far as possible this present edition follows the original positioning of text and illustrations as agreed by Carroll, Tenniel and Macmillan." Carroll might have disliked some of the flashier elements of the design of this bulky book and binding (all edges red foil!), but not the careful layout.[24]

The same care for Carroll's original page design was shown by the publishers of a boxed set that was issued by Books of Wonder and distributed by William Morrow in New York in 1992: "THE DEFINITIVE ILLUSTRATED EDITIONS," as stated on the front cover of the box.[25] What made them "definitive" was not just their tacitly respectful layout, following Carroll's guidance, but also their reproduction of Tenniel's black-and-white illustrations not as they were first published from electrotypes but as carefully printed from the original wood blocks. The source prints that were photo-reproduced in these volumes had been issued by Macmillan in a deluxe limited edition in 1988. The history of those prints and those wood blocks is part of the chapter that follows.

21. Macmillan: ISBN 0333370090; individual volumes, 0333370058, 0333370066. Knopf: ISBN 0394869362; individual volumes, 039486915X, 0394869168. Copies of the first editions of *Wonderland* (London: Macmillan, 1866) and *Looking-Glass* (London: Macmillan, 1872) held by Gettysburg College Library can now be consulted online at https://archive.org/details/alices-adventur00carr and https://archive.org/details/throughlooking00carr. For the copy of the suppressed first printing of *Wonderland* (1865) held by the Lilly Library at Indiana University see https://iucat.iu.edu/catalog/5883355.

22. *Bandersnatch: The Newsletter of the Lewis Carroll Society* 51 (April 1986): [4], reporting a meeting of the Society. See also 47 (April 1985): [1].

23. ISBN 0333679563; individual volumes: ISBN 0333640497, 0333651103.

24. Lewis Carroll, *The Complete Alice* (London: Macmillan's Children's Books, 2015), 466. ISBN 9781447275992. As with the editions of 1995, the exceptions had to do with L-shaped images that were promoted to full-page plates as colored by Harry Theaker for an earlier edition of the combined books (discussed below in chapter 16); but even "these plates sit as close as possible to the position of original illustrations" (467).

25. ISBN 0688120504; individual volumes: ISBN 0688110878, 0688120490.

CHAPTER 13

Engraving

In 1985, the same year that the first edition of this book was published, the secretary of Macmillan Publishing was in the process of inventorying items stored in a London bank vault when he was surprised to discover a pair of locked metal boxes, one of which was marked simply "Alice." "Keys in the Accounts Department," proclaimed an accompanying label. When forced open, without keys, the boxes proved to contain virtually all the original wood blocks that the Brothers Dalziel engraved for the two *Alice* books.[1] (The single missing block, which was replaced in the set by an electrotype replica, was that of Alice and the Dodo.) Michael Wace, who joined in this discovery, later supposed that these valuable wood blocks had long been kept by Macmillan in the safety of the vault, and were taken out from time to time only when it was necessary to make fresh electrotypes. When offset photolithography displaced letterpress at Macmillan—"well after the Second World War"—they were forgotten, no longer being needed.[2] An alternative possibility, suggested by Leo John De Freitas, is that the blocks were "carefully wrapped" and consigned to the vault—instead of being discarded, the usual fate of such blocks—out of respect for their historical importance, when it was realized that they were obsolete relics, no longer needed for any practical purpose.[3]

The Rosenbach in Philadelphia holds a typewritten memorandum of agreement between the executors of the Dodgson estate and Macmillan and Co., Ltd., dated "the seventh day of February 1898" and carrying the handwritten endorsement "Dated the 1st day of June 1898 for the Executors | Wilfred L. Dodgson," which set the terms for Macmillan to continue to publish Dodgson's (that is, Carroll's) books. It included the specification that "the EXECUTORS shall hand over to the PUBLISHERS all electros of the text and illustrations and also woodblocks of the illustrations free of charge." However, ownership of the blocks is deemed to be held by the Dodgson estate, which arranged for them to be deposited in the British Library, where they are available for consultation upon application.

1. Martin Fletcher, "Alice's Original Engravings Found in Vault," *The Times,* 18 October 1985, 32.

2. Michael Wace, "From Carroll to Crompton: The Work of a Children's Publisher," *Macmillan: A Publishing Tradition,* ed. Elizabeth James (Houndmills, Eng.: Palgrave, 2002), 242–55; 243–44.

3. Leo John De Freitas, *A Study of Sir John Tenniel's Illustrations to Alice's Adventures in Wonderland & Through the Looking-Glass* (London: Macmillan Publishers, 1988), 14.

At least twice during the twentieth century, before they were consigned to the vault, Macmillan had the blocks specially printed for collectors. In 1932, the Carroll centenary year, G. W. Phillips arranged for a correspondent to receive a set of proofs of the 42 *Wonderland* blocks, printed on three large sheets—"printed from the original wood blocks for the first (and only) time."[4] Also, the British Library holds sets of proofs of the original blocks for both books, printed several images to each large sheet of coated paper, the sheets preserved in an elaborate red leather case. These are catalogued as "c. 1955."[5] After that, the blocks do seem to have been neglected, until they were rediscovered.

In 1909, more than a decade after the Dalziel firm had wound up its engraving business, Gilbert Dalziel, a son of one of the founders, Edward Dalziel, presented a collection of 266 framed wood-engraving proofs to the Hampstead Central Library; these ranged in date from 1840 to 1890, and included proofs of fifteen engravings after Tenniel's designs, including three from *Wonderland* and two from *Looking-Glass*.[6]

A few years later, in 1912, the Dalziel family negotiated the sale of its vast archive of wood engraving proofs to the British Museum. "Contained in some forty-nine volumes there are about 54,000 impressions which show every image produced between 1839 to 1893."[7] Thanks to a recent digitization project these albums can now be inspected online. They include proofs made from the wood blocks of all the Tenniel illustrations for the two *Alice* books.[8]

Bethan Stevens, the principal investigator for this project, has begun to identify some of the many workers who engraved wood blocks for the Dalziel office and who signed each block anonymously with "Dalziel Sc" ("Sc" being the traditional abbreviation for the Latin *sculpsit*—that is, *he/she carved it*). She has recovered the names of 26 persons (mostly men, but including at least two women, Mary and Ann Byfield), who did such work at one time or another over the course of half a century—a fraction of an indeterminately large cohort. Though Stevens does not link any engraver to any particular wood engraving or illustrated book, retrieving such names from the Dalziel archives at least partially mitigates the personal oblivion that shadowed such fungible artistic labor in a thoroughly capitalistic system of production and reproduction.[9]

Stevens says little about other aspects of the working conditions under which these mostly anonymous artists plied their trade. She notes that more than one engraver might work on a given block, "with master engravers working the face and figure" (17). She also mentions that Mary and Ann Byfield did their work at home in Islington.[10]

As early as 1838 the industrious Henry Cole had recommended the skill of wood engraving as specially suitable for impecunious gentlewomen, as "a means of livelihood . . . which, without severing from home, without breaking up family assemblies, is at once more happy, healthy, tasteful, and profitable than almost any other of the pursuits at present practised by women."[11] This rosy forecast may have matched something of the Byfields' experience, but later accounts have painted a bleaker picture of the trade. Celina Fox and Michèle Martin emphasized the subordination and mechanization of the wood engraver's lot, toiling in abject, assembly-line, proletarian labor that earned trifling piecework wages, accomplished under inadequate, eye-straining illumination, in cramped, "squalid" and "unsalubrious" settings.[12] Leo John De Freitas, in an informative dissertation that traces the circum-

4. This set is now in the Houghton Library at Harvard (http://id.lib.harvard.edu/aleph/007182241/catalog).

5. General Reference Collection C.52.i.4.(1.) and C.52.i.4.(2.). Similar sets are held by the British Museum, catalogued in 1957: 1957,0308.1–5 (*Wonderland*) and 1957,0308.6–11 (*Looking-Glass*).

6. Anthony Burton, "Dalziel family (per. 1840–1905)," *Oxford Dictionary of National Biography* (Oxford University Press, 2004), online. Campbell Dodgson, "The Dalziel Brothers," *Dictionary of National Biography*, second supplement, vol. 1 (1912): 463–65; 465. Gilbert Dalziel, "The Brothers Dalziel," *Reader's Guide and Student's Review* 2:3 (1909): 74–76. Personal communication from Ingrid Smits, Camden Local Studies and Archives Centre, Holborn Library, London.

7. Paul Goldman, "The Dalziel Brothers and the British Museum," *The Book Collector* 45 (1996): 341–50; 349.

8. See *Woodpeckings: The Dalziel Archive, Victorian Print Culture, and Wood Engravings* (http://www.sussex.ac.uk/english/dalziel/).

9. Bethan Stevens, "Wood Engraving as Ghostwriting: the Dalziel Brothers, Losing One's Name, and Other Hazards of the Trade," *Textual Practice* (2017), DOI:10.1080/0950236X.2017.1365756. 1–33; 2.

10. Bethan Stevens, 17. Rodney Engen outlines the careers of Ann and Mary Byfield in *Dictionary of Victorian Wood Engravers* (Cambridge: Chadwyck-Healey, 1985), 39, 40. It is not known whether they did work for Dalziel when the *Alice* illustrations were being engraved.

11. Henry Cole (unsigned), "Modern Wood Engraving," *The London and Westminster Review* 7 (1838): 265–78; 278.

12. Celina Fox, "Wood Engravers and the City," in *Victorian Artists and the City: A Collection of Critical Essays*, ed. Ira B. Nadel and F. S. Schwarzbach (Oxford: Pergamon Press, 1980), 1–13. Celina Fox, *Graphic Journalism in England during the 1830s and 1840s* (New York: Garland, 1988). Michèle Martin, "Nineteenth Century Wood Engravers at Work: Mass Production of Illustrated Periodicals (1840–1880)," *Journal of Historical Sociology* 27 (2014): 132–50.

FIGURE 13.1. Wood engraver at work. Wood engraving by Dalziel Brothers. From Elisha Noyce, *The Boy's Book of Industrial Information* (1858).

stances of the "economical art" of wood engraving across almost two centuries, insisted on aspects and distinctions that Fox overlooked: engravings for book work and magazines were prepared more carefully than engravings for the illustrated press (242–43, 361, 369); no engraver referred to his place of employment as a "factory," instead "office" became the usual term (213, 338, 343, 345); work might comfortably be done at home (344); many well-known engravers were able to do excellent work into their seventies (315); the ideology of the trade, at least at the level of managerial artisans, was "petit bourgeois rather than proletarian" (376). Furthermore, working conditions would vary considerably, and rushed, large-scale work for the illustrated press was an extreme case, not typical of the trade as a whole.[13]

When George and Edward Dalziel wrote their memoir at the end of the nineteenth century they reported many anecdotes about their interactions with the more distinguished artists who designed many of the wood blocks that they produced, but hardly any information about the men and women who engraved them. It is not known how many workers were attached to their office at any given time, nor how the labor on a certain block might be divided up according to engravers' specialties, if at all. The most direct view they provide of an engraver at work—perhaps Edward Dalziel himself?—is an engraving that they prepared for *The Boy's Book of Industrial Information by Elisha Noyce; Illustrated with Three Hundred and Sixty-five Engravings by the Brothers Dalziel* (London: Ward, Lock, 1858)—a book that, in a characteristic practice, they produced themselves, although it appeared under a regular publisher's imprint (fig. 13.1). The engraving shows a man at his work desk, outfitted on his right with a variety of small wooden-handled engraving tools, a small pot of ink, a leather inking ball and wooden handle, a pencil, some wood blocks, a spatula used for taking proofs, some paper and wood blocks, lit by a sizeable lantern. The light from the lantern is focused by a water-filled glass globe upon the wood block that he steadies with his left hand upon a small leather pillow,

13. Leo John De Freitas, "Commercial Engraving on Wood in England, 1700–1880," dissertation, Royal College of Art, 1986; uk.bl.ethos.234734.

the surface of which he engraves with a sharp tool in his right hand. The basic account that accompanied this image presumably satisfied the Dalziels:

> In wood engraving a block of box wood is used, or several pieces are screwed or tongued together in order to make a block of the required size, for the box wood must be cut across the grain, therefore large blocks are not easily procured. These blocks are about an inch in thickness, so that they may range with type and be printed with it, they are made perfectly smooth on the face, which is rubbed with a little flake-white and Bath brick, to give it a whitish and slightly roughened surface. On this prepared surface the design is drawn with a black-lead pencil, and the block is then put into the hands of the engraver, who cuts away—to the depth of about one-twentieth of an inch—all those parts which have not been blackened by the pencil, leaving every line and dot of the drawing projecting, and this serves as a sort of stamp or type, to print from. (126–27)

Flake-white was the lead-based white paint dominant in many forms of art from ancient times until the present century, when concerns about the hazards of lead poisoning have discouraged its use. *Bath brick,* named after the city, was an abrasive powder scraped from bricks made from river silt. John Jackson mentions both applications, deprecating the use of the former (which might blunt fine cuts on the surface of the block), but encouraging use of the latter, if excess powder were wiped away with the palm of the hand.[14] A letter from Tenniel to Joseph Swain, whose workshop engraved Tenniel's weekly cartoons for *Punch,* reports Tenniel's opinion that of three trial preparations submitted for his approval, the one that combined "brick-dust" and "flake-white" proved to make the best surface for drawing on the block.[15]

Shortly after the discovery of the Tenniel–Dalziel wood blocks Macmillan announced plans to publish a limited-edition set of prints made from them; these appeared in 1988, carefully and handsomely printed by Jonathan Stephenson at the Rocket Press in Oxfordshire. In a separate publication Stephenson described the subtleties required to produce this edition, noting that "several engravings" had "suffered from having fine lines (particularly, for example, the artist's monogram) which had been battered and pushed well below type height," and speculating that "such damage may have been caused by careless handling when electrotypes were made."[16] (That process is discussed below, in chapter 14.) The prints were accompanied by an explanatory volume written by Leo John De Freitas, the author of the dissertation cited above. De Freitas provided a good deal of information about the production and use of these blocks, and the present account is substantially indebted to him.

The rectangular blocks that the Dalziels used to make the *Alice* engravings were sawn from cross-sections of the seasoned trunk of the box tree, close to type height (just over nine-tenths of an inch thick). Charles Wells, who supplied the blocks to Dalziel, was known in the trade for the high quality of his work, as well as for having invented a way of bolting blocks together when they had to support an engraved image larger than the small dimensions of a boxwood cross-section, which would usually be not more than a few inches in diameter. For the relatively compact *Alice* illustrations that proprietary expedient was not

14. Jackson in Chatto 1839, 643–44.

15. John Tenniel to Joseph Swain, 20 October, year not specified; Houghton Library. Written on heavy mourning paper from 10 Portsdown Road (in Maida Vale, London), where Tenniel moved with his wife Julia after their marriage in 1853. She died on 23 January 1856. According to Engen, Tenniel "continued to use black-edged mourning stationery" at least until 1864, when his mother died (*Sir John Tenniel,* 71–72).

16. Jonathan Stephenson, "The Printing of the *Alice* Engravings," *Matrix* 9 (1989): 136–45; 140.

FIGURE 13.2. Tenniel. Tracing of Alice at the little door, for *Alice's Adventures in Wonderland.* MS Eng 718.67. Houghton Library, Harvard University.

necessary, although a few of the illustrations (the frontispieces to the two volumes and also the Jabberwock illustration) were large enough to test the limits of a single slab of boxwood. Although the box tree was native to England, the local supply had been substantially depleted by the 1860s, and Wells maintained a reputation for the high quality of the blocks that he made from wood imported from Asia Minor and the Caucasus Mountains. As De Freitas notes, many of the *Alice* blocks are stamped on the back with Wells's name and Bouverie Street address. (He does not mention that many of the *Wonderland* blocks are also impressed on one or another edge with an enigmatic code, such as "11 D 1873"—always D, with the year ranging only from 1873 to 1875, and the days ranging from 1 to 17. Do these marks refer to dates when the electrotypes were made?)

Presumably, in keeping with his preference expressed to Swain, Tenniel arranged for the surface of the blocks supplied by Wells to be treated with a preparation of flake-white and brick dust. After drawing one or more preliminary sketches on paper, and then working up a detailed drawing on Bristol board, Tenniel would transfer the outlines of an image onto translucent tracing paper, which he would reverse before impressing those outlines onto the prepared surface of the block. The Houghton Library holds several of these tracings; for example, fig. 13.2.[17] He would then draw additional details directly on the block, using a hard pencil (6H) that marked very fine lines. Dalziel's responsibility was to carve away the surface of everything but those lines, leaving them to stand in relief on the surface of the block.[18] Dalziel would then print a proof of the block, which he would send to Tenniel for review. Tenniel would write penciled comments on the proof, sometimes adding bits of white or red paint to the image to clarify his intentions about lightening or cutting away details, and return it to Dalziel to make the corrections. ("Cut *away* red touches & *lighten* white ones," as he wrote on a proof of Alice and the White Knight unsteady on his horse.[19]) Copies were also often sent to Carroll for his approval.[20]

17. In his review of Garvey and Bond, *Jabberwocky* 9 (Autumn 1980): 104–07, Justin G. Schiller suggested that tracings for *Alice's Adventures,* unlike those for *Looking-Glass,* would have been done by Dalziel, not by Tenniel (105); and he repeated this suggestion ("probably") in his "Census" (56); but it is not clear on what grounds. For a list of the tracings at Harvard see Livingston, 15–16 (regarding *Alice's Adventures*), and 31, 32 (*Looking-Glass*); also MS Eng 718.6 (*Alice's Adventures*) and bMS Eng 718.7 (*Looking-Glass*) at http://oasis.lib.harvard.edu/oasis/deliver/~hou00171. Matt Demakos has studied tracings that Tenniel later made in the course of producing finished drawings for collectors, tracings evidently made from the published illustrations; see "'Once I Was a Real Turtle': Tenniel's Post-Production Drawings and Tracings in the Berg Collection—Part I," *Knight Letter* 100 (Spring 2018), 23–39. Possibly figure 13.2 was such a late instance, and not a tracing used in the production of the relevant wood block.

18. W. H. Bond, "The Publication of *Alice's Adventures in Wonderland." Harvard Library Bulletin* 10 (1956): 306–24; 316. Schiller proposed that the detailed drawings on Bristol board were done after publication, for collectors, as Tenniel often did for his *Punch* cartoons (62), but Morris thought that unlikely. Frankie Morris, "The *Alice* Drawings: Copies, Forgeries, and Tenniel's Originals," *Knight Letter* 77 (Fall 2006): 11–16; 12, 14.

19. Morgan Library and Museum.

20. In an undated letter Tenniel asks Dalziel to send Dodgson "another proof of the fight with the 'Jabberwock'— the one he has is damaged" (Morgan Library and Museum).

So far as I know, no surviving proof for a *Wonderland* illustration carries Tenniel's annotations. Although Morris just mentions "the touched proofs for both books," Schiller reports no corrected proof for a *Wonderland* illustration aside from a misleading ghost entry in a catalogue.[21] *Alice* was already famous when *Looking-Glass* was in production; not so when *Wonderland* was prepared—which probably explains the differential survival of annotated proofs. When the collector Harold Hartley sought some such proofs from Edward Dalziel in 1902, Dalziel replied that he was consigning them to "the Board of Education South Kensington" because Tenniel's "remarks on them are not only complimentary to my craft but are so purely technical in an Art Educational way as to make them invaluable."[22] Those materials are now in the National Art Library in the Victoria and Albert Museum. They include annotated proofs for *Looking-Glass*; and additional annotated proofs for that book are in the Morgan Library and Museum in New York, and in the Houghton Library at Harvard.

However, the proofs for *Wonderland* in the Dalziel collection at the British Museum do testify to a remarkable change in an illustration for that first book. Dalziel engraved two different blocks that show the White Rabbit dressed as a herald, first wearing a tunic ornamented with hearts that were unaccountably upside-down, and then in a tunic properly oriented. Other marked changes affect his gaze, the scroll that he holds, the seal that dangles from it, and the ground or platform that he stands on (figs. 13.3, 13.4). Michael Hearn suggested that the fault was Tenniel's, and that the correction was prompted by Carroll (16); it is hard to say. Preliminary and finished drawings of the second version are in the Amory Collection at Harvard.

Hearn also pointed out a marked change in several of the *Looking-Glass* illustrations, as Carroll rejected the puffy, crinoline skirt that Tenniel had originally drawn for Alice on the other side of the Looking-Glass and that Dalziel engraved accordingly. In each of these cases of revision Dalziel did not engrave a fresh block but corrected the one already made by sawing away the rejected portion, inserting a carefully shaped piece of boxwood to replace it, and reengraving that portion only. Similar large-scale repairs were made in two other *Looking-Glass* illustrations. Garvey and Bond and De Freitas have discussed one of these in some detail. The last illustration in *Looking-Glass* (fig. 13.5), which shows Alice coming to her senses after her dream, holding the Red Queen chess piece in her right hand and the black kitten in her left, underwent a major repair as Tenniel had Dalziel redo Alice's hair

21. Morris, *Artist of Wonderland,* 151. Schiller, 71–72. However, 28 unmarked proofs for *Wonderland* are held by The Rosenbach, and the Dalziel proof albums in the British Museum include a complete set.

22. Morris, *Artist of Wonderland,* 118.

to let it fall more fully behind her hair band. An early proof shows a pencil line drawn across her face, intersecting a vertical one at a right angle, with the annotation "Insert piece of wood" (Garvey and Bond, 74). De Freitas provides a photograph of the surface of the revised wood block that shows the horizontal seam of this insertion clearly (fig. 13.6)—a gap that is barely visible as a white line in the first and subsequent editions. Tenniel called for changes to some other details on a proof taken after this piece of wood was inserted and engraved, and added a lament, subsequently ignored by Dalziel: "The lines of the apron should not *all* have been cut away."[23] On the previous proof he had asked for the apron to be lightened—and so it was, evidently too much.

23. Morgan Library and Museum.

A similar change to the *Looking-Glass* frontispiece has not been explained before, although Schiller (87) lists most of the relevant materials. Traces of the change can be seen in the recent printings made from the original block. Figures 13.7, 13.8, and 13.9 show successive versions of Alice looking up at her White Knight on horseback, a significant detail of the important scene that is shown in full in figure 7.1. Figure 13.7 shows Alice's profile in an early sketch of the frontispiece (now at The Rosenbach); figure 13.8 shows how Dalziel first engraved her—and also how a correction was called for; straight and curved pencil lines, perhaps drawn by someone in Dalziel's shop, clearly outline the section to be replaced. Figure 13.9 shows the corrected detail as printed in 1872, and figure 13.10 reflects the recent condition of this part of the block as printed. Arguably Tenniel's sketch (fig. 13.7) puts Alice in the best light. In the proof (fig. 13.8) her hair band is misplaced, causing her hair to fall over her ears. The corrected engraving repairs that defect (fig. 13.9), but somehow makes Alice a more stolid figure than she was as Tenniel imagined her. The seam along the edge of the replacement block of wood was invisible in early printings but became noticeable in Stephenson's later printing from the original block (fig. 13.10). Another sketch, on tracing paper at Harvard (Amory Collection), falls somewhere between the Rosenbach sketch and the repaired engraving as regards the representation of Alice, but it uniquely outfits the White Knight with a folded umbrella carried over his right shoulder, and may not have been used in production (Garvey and Bond, 64).

In any case, the proposal to revise Alice's appearance on one of these blocks, or both, probably came from Carroll, who, as was noted above in chapter 10, objected at one point to "the face of the *hero-ine,*" leading Tenniel "to re-draw it, though this required the block to be 'plugged.'" None of the other blocks for either book shows such extensive reimagining of the heroine's face as was effected on these two blocks.

Two alterations involved the insertion of smaller, circular "plugs," to correct a minor detail. In *Alice's Adventures* the Mad Hatter was supposed to be shown as having taken a bite out of the teacup he held in one hand, as well as one from the slice of bread he was holding in the other. "In his confusion he bit a large piece out of his teacup instead of the bread-and-butter." (The visible bite out of the piece of bread had already been taken.) As first engraved the teacup appeared intact, and that detail had to be reengraved, on a replacement plug.

Later, in *Looking-Glass,* something was thought to be wrong with the shape of Alice's hand, spread out against the glass as she steadied herself to pass through it; the hand was therefore reengraved on a small circular plug inserted in the block at that point. (The proof in the Dalziel album, evidently taken before the change, shows nothing to complain of; the revision gave a slight crook to Alice's pinkie finger, but that can hardly have been the point.) The outline of the small circle is barely detectable in the early editions, but is more conspicuous in the recent prints made directly or indirectly from the block. It has an unintended, numinous appeal, highlighting the point of Alice's transition from one reality to another.

Four proofs selected from the many now at the Morgan Library and Museum carry penciled annotations that are representative of the detail with which Tenniel called for corrections. The simplest one, which shows the White Knight chess piece sliding down the poker, carries the simplest corrections: two small patches of white paint covering some adjacent shadow lines along either side of the Knight's profile, with the instruction, "Cut *away* white touches." More complicated is the proof of Alice holding the plum cake, flanked by the Unicorn and Lion (fig. 1.50 shows the final version), which is surrounded by a cloud of comments. Above a + mark pointing to the area of interest, Tenniel has applied a white wash to a dark patch in the sky directly over Alice's head, and commented: "The tint above the child's head to be reduced. I should think that [illegible word crossed out] cutting away alternate lines would about do it." In wood engraving, a *tint* was "the effect produced by a series of fine parallel lines more or less closely drawn so as to produce an even and uniform shading" (*OED*). Dalziel responded by cutting some of these lines away, lightening the patch as Tenniel requested. Below Alice Tenniel added a + mark and wrote below it: "Outer corner of eye too black. Ear. Finger. Left hand." He had just touched those details with white. "The large hand in the background to be less evident. It looks as if it belongs to the child. Lighten all round it." The hand, probably meant to belong to the gesturing White King, was duly effaced in the final print. "Outer line of R leg (& ankle) too black." These details were apparently not changed. Below the White King there is another + mark and the comment, "Outline of King's ankle too thick"—which seems not to have prompted an emendation either. In the lower left margin is a more general complaint, ending in three exclamation marks, which nonetheless seems to have prompted no improvement: "Every bit of *colour* has been cut out of the shadows & darker portions of the drawing!!!" (*Colour* was another term of the engraver's art, denoting variation of tone.)

The annotated proof of the large engraving of "the Jabberwock, with eyes of flame," originally intended to be the book's frontispiece, carries fine touches of white paint radiating downward from the monster's eyes, with this injunction written in the margin: "Light from eyes increased—but must be done very deliberately—Little more than *scratched.*" Hardly any glare from the eyes can be seen in the plain proof of this engraving pasted in the Dalziel album at the British Museum, but in the revised and printed version it is effectively rendered according to Tenniel's instructions here. (Tenniel knew what "eyes of flame" should look like, having given a similar pair of downward-focused lights to the demonic horse in his illustration to Barham's comic poem "The Smuggler's Leap."[24])

A proof of the Sheep's shop (Plate 1) bears many touches of white, marking details to be lightened; and many touches in red, marking areas to be cut away. Tenniel's comments include "Face should have been *darker,*" and "Left leg and foot. Outline too thick." The face may have been under-printed in this proof; it printed darker in the uncorrected proof in the Dalziel album, and also in the 1872 printing. All the other changes that Tenniel asked for here were duly made.

Most of the twenty-seven *Looking-Glass* proofs in this collection at the Morgan Library carry similar annotations by Tenniel, usually giving instructions to lighten or delete one detail or another, sometimes voicing particular complaints, such as "Eyes in flower seem to have been *fudged!* Make them quite clear." No compliments are evident in that set. However, as we have seen, Edward Dalziel remarked that the proofs he intended to give to the Board of Education, South Kensington, were not only "purely technical" but also "complimentary to my craft," and several of those proofs, now in the National Art Library, do show acquiescence, approval, and even praise. "All right. Please send complete proof," Tenniel commented on a rubbing of Alice (only) in the engraving of Alice and the Sheep in the boat—after changes that were called for in a previous proof had been made. "Very good. Please send a complete proof," regarding a detail of a slithy tove. "All right. Please send complete proof," regarding a detail of Tweedledum in his tantrum. Or, somewhat more expansively (though regarding designs for other books): "Very good. Should be printed very dark," on a proof for *The Ingoldsby Legends.* A proof for *Lalla Rookh* was "Very beautifully engraved" (yet still with this caveat, referencing a touch of red that Tenniel added on the proof atop a lamp: "This is a Persian candle. You have left out the flame.") And a simple compliment on another proof for that book: "Very beautifully engraved."[25] It was not always a matter of finding fault or making things better, though it was often that.

24. Richard Harris Barham, *Ingoldsby Legends* (London: Richard Bentley, 1865), 313.

25. For the last item see fig. 11.5.

CHAPTER 14

Electrotyping

On 28 October 1864 Lewis Carroll recorded in his diary a visit he made to the wood-engraving workshop of the Brothers Dalziel, 110 High Street, Camden Town, London, where he was shown fresh proofs of several engravings that the firm had made after drawings by John Tenniel to illustrate *Alice's Adventures in Wonderland*. "Mr. Dalziel showed me proofs of several of the pictures, including the 4 for 'Father William,' and decidedly advised my printing from the woodblocks" (*Diaries*, 5:22). The two principals of the firm, George Dalziel and Edward Dalziel, were both skilled wood engravers, and either of them could have given this advice. Probably one or more of their many employees did the actual work of engraving Tenniel's illustrations; the firm was a large one, and both brothers had managerial responsibilities. Such positive advice, coming from either brother, would carry some weight.

The alternative procedure, which Dalziel "decidedly" discountenanced, involved making electrotype facsimiles of the wood blocks and printing from them instead. By 1864 such an approach had become standard printing practice. It offered several advantages, chief among which was protecting the original blocks from damage in the print shop, which made them available in fine condition for producing later electrotype copies to use in printing later editions. "Electro saves your original wood blocks," as Carroll's publisher, Alexander Macmillan, pointed out in his first contribution to their surviving correspondence.[1] Carroll could hardly have guessed how many editions of *Alice's Adventures* would be published by Macmillan into the twentieth century from electrotype facsimiles made repeatedly from the original Dalziel wood blocks. However, by favoring electrotyping over direct printing, despite Dalziel's decided advice, Carroll helped to secure that printing and publishing bonanza.

Why did Dalziel recommend direct printing from the blocks rather than from electrotype replicas? Probably because he believed that prints

1. Edward Wakeling, *Lewis Carroll: The Man and His Circle* (London: I. B. Tauris, 2015), 54 (19 September 1864).

made from electrotypes were inferior to prints made from the original blocks. Electrotyping was good for reproducing images in large quantities: but how good was its quality? How good could it be? That question had been mooted since the early 1840s.

Replicating the carved surfaces of wood engravings by metallic electro-deposition, a process first demonstrated in England by Thomas Spencer in 1839, had by the 1860s become a practical and commercial printing routine. Most illustrated books of the period that was later to be celebrated as "the Sixties"—the heyday of wood-engraving illustration—were printed not from the original wood blocks but from electrotype replicas.[2] Certainly *Alice's Adventures in Wonderland* was such a book. We know that to be the case because Lewis Carroll recommended the 1897 edition of *Alice's Adventures* (then reaching 86,000 copies) in the following terms:

> For this eighty-sixth thousand, fresh electrotypes have been taken from the wood-blocks (which, never having been used for printing from, are in as good condition as when first cut in 1865), and the whole book has been set up afresh with new type. If the artistic qualities of this re-issue fall short, in any particular, of those possessed by the original issue, it will not be for want of painstaking on the part of author, publisher, or printer.[3]

In her book on Tenniel Frankie Morris has suggested that Carroll misreported Dalziel's advice, through a slip of the pen. "As the practice of printing from electrotypes . . . was fairly standard from around mid-century, it is probable that Carroll, meaning to write 'decidedly advised [against] my printing from the wood-blocks,' inadvertently left out the key word" (143).

How else can we understand what Carroll actually wrote? In 1864, the same year that Dalziel gave his advice, a handsome volume was printed at the Camden Press, which the Dalziel Brothers owned and managed, called *The Cornhill Gallery, Containing One Hundred Engravings from Drawings on Wood.* The publisher of this book, Smith, Elder & Co., had from 1860 published the monthly *Cornhill Magazine,* where the illustrations that were harvested in *The Cornhill Gallery* first appeared. Many of those illustrations had been engraved by the Dalziel Brothers, although most of them had been made by the competing firm of Joseph Swain. In a prefatory note to *The Cornhill Gallery,* Smith, Elder & Co. disparaged the adequacy of electrotype reproductions of original wood engravings, recommending the originals instead. The ambition of the firm in offering *The Cornhill Gallery* for sale at a considerable price (one guinea) was to do justice to the illustrations "as Works of Art."

> The impressions of the Pictures which have appeared in the various numbers of "The Cornhill Magazine" were unavoidably subjected to the disadvantage of being printed from electrotype casts taken from the Wood-blocks, and with the great speed necessary to insure the punctual publication of a Periodical Work which enjoys the favour of a very large circulation. *The Wood-blocks themselves have now been printed from for the first time,* in the production of the CORNHILL GALLERY; and the Publishers trust that, with the very careful and skilful aid of the Brothers Dalziel, the Pictures are now produced in a style which will place them in their proper rank as Works of Art.[4]

2. Geoffrey Wakeman, *Victorian Book Illustration: The Technical Revolution* (Detroit, MI: Gale Research, 1973), 74–76. Paul Goldman, *Beyond Decoration: The Illustrations of John Everett Millais* (London: The British Library, 2005), 35–36. Kooistra, 20–21.

3. "Preface to the Eighty-Sixth Thousand," dated "*Christmas 1896*," *Alice's Adventures in Wonderland* (New York: Macmillan, 1898). Regarding the London 1897 edition see Crutch, 36.

4. *The Cornhill Gallery, Containing One Hundred Engravings from Drawings on Wood* (London: Smith, Elder, 1865), preface; emphasis in the original.

Even discounted for the hyperbole of advertisement, the point made here matches Dalziel's advice to Carroll (and indeed the Dalziels were the printers in this special case): better to print the illustrations from original wood blocks than from electrotype replicas. A similar rationale motivated the publication of *The Graphic Portfolio* in 1876—*The Graphic* having become a fit rival to *The Illustrated London News* in the weekly publication of newsworthy wood engravings. In the course of regular business, it was explained,

> first of all there is a sketch, then a careful drawing on a boxwood block, then the engraving. From the engraving a wax mould is taken, then a copper electrotype from the wax mould, and finally in the press a ponderous machine takes *the unfortunate electrotype,* and hammers away impressions at the rate of a thousand an hour. . . . It is to show with what conscientious care the artist and engraver do their work that this book is published. These are the fair engravings of the engraved block *minus* the hurry essential to the publication of a newspaper.[5]

Joseph Pennell made the same case in his preface to *Some Poems by Alfred Lord Tennyson with Illustrations by W. Holman Hunt, J. E. Millais and Dante Gabriel Rossetti Printed from the Original Wood Blocks* (London: Freemantle, 1901)—a selection of the Pre-Raphaelite engravings in the Moxon Illustrated Tennyson:

> Now at last, the pictures and text of the Sixties will be seen on good paper, with care and attention devoted to every detail of the book, the drawings printed from the original wood blocks; and if, as a result, the illustrations prove almost unrecognisable, it will only be because of their increased, or rather their original beauty now fully revealed for the first time. (xvii)

However, the ordinary, not to say Platonic, presumption that replicas as such must be inferior to originals, which informs these advertisements, had been challenged from the outset by publicity that announced the invention of image electrotyping. James J. Mapes, a prominent American inventor, publicized the early success of electrotyping from wood blocks in a lead article for an issue of *The American Repertory of Arts, Sciences and Manufactures,* which he edited.

> From the time when the invention for obtaining metallic copies of works of art by galvanic precipitation was first made known, our constant desire has been to lay before the reader a specimen of printing from an electrotype the perfect copy of a wood cut. This wish is now realized. We present herewith an impression from the duplicate of a gem of art, so like the original that if there be any difference between them, it is not perceptible upon the closest scrutiny.[6]

Mapes displayed two illustrations apparently identical, one printed directly from a wood engraving and the other from an electrotype made from that block (fig. 14.1): The children here are like the implied reader of a bound volume of *The American Repertory,* studying an illustrated book. They are distinguishable by their haircuts—the boy ponders what the girl points out to him—but the two images are not so easily distinguished: they seem virtually identical, a doubleness

5. *The Graphic Portfolio: A Selection from the Admired Engravings Which Have Appeared in The Graphic* (London: The Graphic Office, 1876), preface; emphasis added. This book was printed by Edmund Evans, who would later print Carroll's *The Nursery "Alice"* (1890), discussed below.

6. "Electrotypes from Wood Engravings," *The American Repertory of Arts, Sciences, and Manufactures* 3 (1841): 161–63; 161.

Wood Engraving.

Electrotype Copy.

FIGURE 14.1. "Wood Engraving. Electrotype Copy." *The American Repertory of Arts, Sciences, and Manufactures* 3 (1841).

worth pondering. Mapes calls the electrotype "the perfect copy."[7] He credits both the engraving and the electrotype to Joseph A. Adams, a wood engraver who was drawn to the new electrotype process as a way to back-up and protect his work cutting engravings for "a pictorial Bible"—specifically, *The Illuminated Bible, Containing the Old and New Testaments,* published in parts from 1843 to 1846 by Harper & Brothers (New York), which featured numerous illustrations designed by J. F. Chapman and engraved on wood by Adams—a landmark in American book and Bible production.[8]

The year before *The Illuminated Bible* began to appear, the first book to be printed with electrotyped images was published in London by Longman, Brown, Green and Longman: a new edition of James Thomson's poem *The Seasons,* edited by the littérateur Bolton Corney. This edition featured seventy-seven wood engravings drawn by eleven members of a group called the Etching Club, and engraved by fifteen wood engravers. Wakeman (75), perhaps misled by the name of group, states that the electrotypes for this book were made from "intaglio plates," but the title page specifies "designs drawn on wood." The List of Illustrations identifies the wood engravers, many of them distinguished. The pictures were printed not directly from their wood blocks but from electrotype replicas, as Corney boasts in his preliminary Advertisement:

> It may be interesting to the scientific reader to know that the illustrations are printed from copper blocks formed by the electrotype process. This method has been found to be attended with several advantages in printing, besides the means which it affords of preserving the original blocks, and of renewing the electrotypes, thus forming a perpetual security against inferior impressions of the designs.

Such a strategy looked toward repeated editions of the book; and Longman did indeed publish a second edition in 1847, a third in 1852, and another (although still called "Third Edition") in 1863. By then the whole pages, which included the standing type as well as the engravings, would be printed from electrotypes—as may have been done also for the first American edition, published by Harper in New York (1842).

The innovation announced in the Advertisement was remarkable, and at least one notable American "scientific reader" celebrated the

7. A similar comparison had matched a printed copperplate engraving and a printed electrotype replica to illustrate the article "Electrotype" in *London Journal of Arts and Sciences* 16 (1840), plate VII, reproduced in Wakeman (74). Promotional, comparative prints from metal engravings and electrotype replicas also figured in Edward Palmer's *Illustrations of Electrotype* (London: E. Palmer, 1841).

8. Accounts vary in identifying the role that electrotyping played in the production of this book, some suggesting that only the ornamental frames were electrotyped, others implying that the whole pages were electrotyped.

perfection of these replicas: "the illustrations are from perfect electro-type copies of the most exquisite wood engravings."[9] A reviewer for *The Athenæum,* the prestigious literary weekly published in London, took a more guarded view of that interesting question: "The book is beautifully brought out; the vignettes are from copper blocks, produced by the electrotype process. This gives a certain peculiarity of effect to the impressions, more easy to perceive than to describe."[10] A writer for *The Art-Union* elaborated on this general difference, after noticing how "its singularly subtle imitation of the relief surface of wood-engraving is admirably shown in the recent edition of 'Thomson's Seasons.'"

It is true that in a comparison between an impression from the original wood cut and another from the electrotyped copy, there is a somewhat of hardness in the latter, but by no means so obtrusive as in comparing impressions of steel and copper-plates. We cannot, however, doubt, that still leaving something to be desired, the metal fac-simile will ultimately be made to yield cuts characterized by all the sweetness of those from the wood. The electrotype has arisen a giant at its birth, but this little finesse is wanting to its vast and creative power as far as concerns wood.[11]

By 1869 a London printer could claim that the word *reproduction* rather than *copy* was the right word to register the perfection of the electro-type process:

Every electrotype plate is so faithful to the original whence it is taken, that it is almost impossible for the human eye to detect the slightest difference between the original and its *reproduction,* for the term copy would scarcely be correct.

The electrotype plate is not only faithful in the most minute particulars, but for practical purposes it is vastly superior; the impressions from it being much clearer.[12]

A description of how electrotypes were made from wood engravings may help explain their uncanny similarity to and difference from the original blocks. "Electro-metallurgy," as the process was often called, was a dynamic field of amateur experiment and industrial production from its early period of discovery and invention in the late 1830s well into the twentieth century. As Gavin Bridson and Geoffrey Wakeman noted some years ago in their bibliographical guide *Printmaking & Picture Printing,* "despite the importance of electrotype to both letterpress and picture printing during the 19th century, no adequate history of the craft has yet appeared."[13] And, "although electrotype methods were a highly important element in 19th century graphic reproduction processes the subject is frequently passed over by historians of printmaking and picture printing" (29). That is still the case. It would be possible to list many recent studies of nineteenth-century book illustration that ignore the process altogether, or mention it only in the passive voice ("electrotypes were made," or "blocks were electrotyped"). To repair such amnesia Bridson and Wakeman paid special attention to the bibliographical history of electrotyping in England, identifying thirty-two relevant publications published before 1865 (when the Tenniel illustrations were first electrotyped). However, most of these publications were early announcements of the process or speculative refinements of it,

9. An editorial aside in *The American Journal of Science and Arts* 43 (1842): 390.

10. *The Athenæum,* 6 August 1842, 716.

11. "The Electrotype," *The Art-Union* 5 (1843): 109–11; 110.

12. William Collingridge, *Comprehensive Guide to Printing and Publishing* (London: City Press, 1869), 42; emphasis in the original.

13. Gavin Bridson and Geoffrey Wakeman, *Printmaking & Picture Printing: A Bibliographical Guide to Artistic & Industrial Techniques in Britain 1750–1900* (Oxford: The Plough Press, 1984), 55.

FIGURE 14.2. Brothers Dalziel. Electroplating workshop. Wood engraving. From Elisha Noyce, *The Boy's Book of Industrial Information* (1858).

and the interest in most cases is broader than the reproduction of wood engravings, sometimes focusing on reproduction of standing type and often having to do with the three-dimensional replication of sculptural objects.

Reproducing medals by electrolysis had been a popular experiment from the beginning, and reproducing elaborate sculptures became a routine practice. In 2011 the Metropolitan Museum of Art, in collaboration with the Victoria and Albert Museum, exhibited many fine sculptural objects that were reproduced in the nineteenth century by electrotyping, and a well-designed video displays the general process clearly.[14] The popularity of such large-scale three-dimensional work in the late nineteenth century anticipates the excitement that has been prompted in the twenty-first century by 3-D scanning and printing.

Elisha Noyce's *The Boy's Book of Industrial Information,* which the Dalziel Brothers produced and illustrated with wood engravings, and which provided technical information for the previous chapter about how wood engraving was done, duly included a section about "Electro-plating and Deposition of Metals." The three wood engravings by Dalziel that illustrated the process were themselves almost certainly printed from electrotype replicas. One of them illustrated part of a workshop for the gilding of rings by electrolysis. Another gave a schematic view of two vessels containing chemical solutions, zinc and copper plates suspended in them and properly connected by wires, and a "medallion or other object in plaster," the specially prepared surface of which would receive an even deposit of copper by electrolysis. The main illustration showed "troughs of depositing liquids [that] contain often many dozens of articles, which are all receiving a coating at once" (fig. 14.2). A workman holds a rod from which seven such objects are hung by wires. None of them is a wood block, but Noyce's general account of the process does mention "engraved surfaces" as suitable for "electrotyping"—the preferred term for "when a fac-simile of any surface is required" (179). For contemporary details about how engraved wood blocks were electrotyped we must turn to other sources.

Three accounts of electrotyping in the service of printing—accounts overlooked by Bridson and Wakeman—shed light on the processes that were probably used to make early electrotypes of Dalziel's *Alice* illustrations. A series of detailed articles, broadly titled "Electro-Metallurgy," began to appear in the first issue of *The Printer,* a weekly journal pub-

14. "An Art of Attraction: The Electrotyping Process" (www.youtube.com/watch?v=iTytvWs5nV8). See also scholarly presentations regarding the exhibition, "Victorian Electrotypes: Old Treasures, New Technology" (www.metmuseum.org/exhibitions/listings/2011/electrotypes).

lished in New York from 1858, which instructed American printers in the history, fundamentals, and latest refinements of their craft. Printers could learn about the early history of wood engraving by following a separate series of articles on that subject, which also started with the first issue. The articles on electro-metallurgy rather emphasized technique over history. Each installment was copyrighted by William Filmer, who was probably the most prominent expert in electrotype printing in his day.[15] According to the full-page advertisement that repeatedly appeared in *The Printer*, Filmer & Co., "electrotypers and manufacturers of electrotype materials," was the leading supplier of electrotype foundry equipment in the United States.

An Englishman by birth, Filmer had emigrated to the United States as a young man, where he became successful enough to endure bankruptcy.[16] Although, like earlier and later writers on electro-metallurgy, he described some applications of the process that had little to do with printing (even including such outré subjects as preparing tools for manufacturing carpets), the replication of letterpress and images by electrotype was the subject to which he devoted the most attention.

Despite its somewhat early date and its American provenance, Filmer's account probably applies to British workshop practice in the 1860s. American printing practices in the second half of the nineteenth century were often in advance of British custom; for example, British printers lagged some years behind their American colleagues in electrotyping whole pages of letterpress.

Filmer's 1858 account was quoted in a similar series that was published pseudonymously in London in 1864 (even as *Alice's Adventures* was being prepared for the press) under the title "Electro-Metallurgy, As Applied to Printing," by "Phosphorus." *J. & R. M. Wood's Typographic Advertiser*, where the series appeared, was the house journal of a firm of wood engravers located in West Smithfield, London. In many particulars the description of the process given by "Phosphorus" in twenty-five chapters, grouped in monthly installments from 1 September 1863 to 1 October 1864, parallels the account given by Filmer.[17] It, too, pays more attention to replicating letterpress than wood blocks, although some attention is paid to blocks in both accounts.

A third account of the process, substantially unpublished, is a set of thirty-two proofs of wood engravings prepared for the firm of Edward Badoureau, later Badoureau & Jones, headquartered at 14 St. Bride St., London, around 1890, perhaps for display at an exhibition. These proofs were donated to St. Bride Foundation and Library in 1957 by W. J. Bishop, whose father had worked in the business and who had done some work there himself; the son supplied a list of informative captions for all of the proofs. (The captions used in the illustrations below take the leading terms from that list.) Five proofs that showed different workrooms at Badoureau's—"Battery Room," "The Black Shop," "Electro Finishing Room," "Stereotype Room," and "Backing Up Shop"—were published in *The British Printer* in 1892 to illustrate an article about the firm.[18] Edward Badoureau, an engraver himself who made his name by manufacturing boxwood blocks of high quality, numbering prominent journals such as *The Illustrated London News* and *The Graphic* among his customers, entered the electrotyping and stereotyping business relatively late, in 1884. By 1892 the firm occupied some 10,000 square feet off Fleet Street and employed a hundred workers.

15. William Filmer, "Electro-Metallurgy," *The Printer* 1 (1858): 5–6, 22–23, 46–47, 72, 93–94, 115–16, 189–90, 213, 236–37, 259–60, 282–83. Cited by Rollo G. Silver, "Trans-Atlantic Crossing: The Beginning of Electrotyping in America," *Journal of the Printing Historical Society* 10 (1974): 84–103.

16. "Electrotyping Our Paper," *Scientific American* n.s. 1:16 (15 October 1859): 257. Luke North, "The Tale of Two Lives," *San Francisco Call*, 26 May 1895, 11. "Death of One of the First Electrotypers," *Inland Printer* 25 (1900): 253–54. Besides his series of technical articles for *The Printer*, Filmer wrote an historical account, "An American Art: The Electrotype—Its Application to Printing Purposes," *The Overland Monthly* 8 (1872): 524–29.

17. Phosphorus (pseud.), "Electro-Metallurgy, As Applied to Printing," *J. & R. M. Wood's Typographic Advertiser* 2 (1863–64): 30, 37, 42, 50–51, 62–63, 72, 86–87, 94–95, 100–01, 112–13; 3 (1864–65): 14–15; 34.

18. "Mr. Edward Badoureau (Badoureau and Jones)," *The British Printer* 5 (1892): 29–31. Later fortunes of the firm were detailed in "A Progressive House—Badoureau & Jones," *The British Printer* 13 (1900): 11–13.

19. For an illustrated account of electrotyping contemporary with the Badoureau engravings see "A Description of the Offices of The Strand Magazine," *The Strand Magazine* 4 (July–December 1892): 594–606, especially 601–04. Electrotyping, now applied to reproducing photomechanical plates as well as wood engravings, continued to be important into the middle of the twentieth century. Edward S. Pilsworth, *Electrotyping in Its Relation to the Graphic Arts* (New York: Macmillan, 1923); Arthur F. Winter, *Stereotyping and Electrotyping* (London: Sir Isaac Pitman and Sons, 1948).

20. Woolf, *Lewis Carroll in His Own Account,* 47.

21. Marianne Van Remoortel, *Women, Work and the Victorian Periodical: Living by the Press* (Houndmills, Eng.: Palgrave Macmillan, 2015), 110. Across the nineteenth century a firm might charge upwards of five pounds to eight guineas for a wood engraving, with the actual engraver receiving only a fraction of that. "The wood engraving costs of any book were always higher than the costs of the original art work, no matter who the artist was." De Freitas, "Commercial Engraving," 204.

22. *The History of Oxford University Press,* ed. Simon Eliot et al., 3 vols. (Oxford: Oxford University Press, 2013), 2:156–57.

23. Illustrated in "The Making of Alice" by Alysoun Sanders; *A View from the Bridge: Nature's Books and Arts Blog,* 19 November 2015; https://goo.gl/TmVWub.

24. "The multiplication of wood-cuts has been far more extensively carried on by Messrs. De la Rue than by any other firm. Their manufactory is reckoned, by those most competent to form an opinion, one of the most complete specimens of the union of art and science in mechanics, physics, and chemistry, that this metropolis, or perhaps even the entire world, can boast." Alfred Smee, *Elements of Electro-Metallurgy,* 3rd ed. (London: Longman, Brown, Green and Longmans, 1851), 316. Other firms advertised electrotyping in *The Printers' Journal and Typographical Magazine* in 1865 (volume 1): E. Plummer; B. Smith; J. and B. Dellagana; and Morel and Gowland, later Victor Morel.

Each electro that was made would typically "pass through something like fifteen hands before being finished. There is a great deal of skill required to make a duplicate as good as the original, and considering there are about twenty different stages for the electro to go through before being finished, it seems simply marvellous that it should pass through so many hands and come out without accident" (30).

In 1957 *The British Printer* again reproduced these scene-setting pictures (omitting the "Stereotype Room") to illustrate an article titled "Electrotyping in the Nineteenth Century." Neither article drew attention to the many other Badoureau wood engravings that illustrate consecutive steps in the electrotyping process. These have special interest in the present context because, unlike the accounts by Filmer and "Phosphorus," they particularly focus on making electrotype copies of wood engravings, not letterpress. Although this series was prepared well after the two *Alice* books first appeared, it fairly describes established electrotype practices that changed relatively little over several decades, aside from innovations in the mechanical generation of electricity.[19] Indeed, many of the steps that Filmer identified in the 1850s, and "Phosphorus" in the 1860s, are illustrated by the Badoureau proofs in the early 1890s. All three accounts will inform the following description of the manufacturing process.

First, however, before considering how the first *Alice* electrotypes were made, there is the question of who made them. It is just possible that the Dalziel Brothers did, despite their advice to print from the wood blocks instead. As has already been noted, in 1857 they had set up a printing and publishing office, The Camden Press, which specialized in fine art books; it may have included some facilities for electrotyping, although the firm's official history, taciturn about technique generally, does not mention the electrotype process at all. Perhaps Carroll's payment to Dalziel of £142 2*s.* for the 42 *Wonderland* wood engravings (a bit more than the £138 he paid to Tenniel) included the cost of electrotyping.[20] The Dalziels are known to have charged £12 10*s.* in 1868 for preparing just two wood engravings for a periodical, but they were relatively large.[21]

A more likely possibility is that the first printer of *Alice's Adventures,* Clarendon Press (Oxford University Press), produced the electrotypes in its workshop; early experiments with the technology had been renewed there in 1863, probably with the encouragement of Alexander Macmillan, who later arranged to publish Carroll's book.[22] The words "UNIVERSITY | PRESS | OXFORD," probably denoting origin of manufacture, are stamped into the floor of an electrotype that was made from standing type that spelled out the sinuous Mouse's Tale.[23] This electro is held by the Macmillan archives along with a large collection of electros made from the Tenniel *Alice* blocks (about which more later), and it may be that at least some of those electros were made at Oxford University Press.

It is also possible that either the Dalziels or (more likely) Oxford outsourced the production of the electrotypes to any of the several London firms that specialized in the new process, such as Thomas de la Rue.[24]

Whoever did make the electrotypes probably went through the several careful steps that Filmer detailed. The following summary notices the major steps but omits much of Filmer's abundant commentary; it also ignores details about the electrotyping of standing type, which

FIGURE 14.3. Edward Badoureau. "Pouring Boxes." Wood engraving proof. Circa 1890. Image courtesy of St. Bride Library.

was a standard practice in the United States by 1858. For the first printing of *Alice's Adventures* only the wood blocks were replicated by electrotype, and Filmer's account sheds ample light on how that was done.[25]

First, a wood block has to be cleaned of any ink adhering to it after proofing. For coarse engravings turpentine would do, but for fine work aqua ammonia would be used instead, "as it quickly dries and leaves no residue." "A fine tooth brush" should be used. "The molder cannot be too careful in this operation of cleaning. It is exceedingly annoying to the engraver to find a piece of work, on which he takes pride, injured by the carelessness of the electrotyper" (72).

Next, "the wood engraving . . . should be locked up with a type-high bearer [frame] all around," and the surface checked to make sure that it is type-high; if too low, it has to be built up with pasteboard or paper on the bottom until it stands at the correct height in the frame.

"Then, with the brush, put on a little blacklead"—finely powdered graphite—"brushing it over the whole block, and being careful that no particles remain in any of the lines of the cut" (72).

A liquid wax composition will have previously been prepared, to use in taking a cast from the blackleaded surface of the block. "The best unadulterated yellow wax" should be used "in summer time," but "in colder weather from two to twenty per cent. of crude or virgin turpentine is used to soften the wax, and prevent its cracking while cooling. . . . the best electrotypers prefer the wax, as pure and unmixed as the weather will permit." (72)

"New wax is better for being boiled several hours before molding. It improves after a few days' use," and can be recycled after use. "Care must, however, be used that too much heat is not put on," and that any water adhering to recycled wax is driven off as steam.

A molding pan—"a flat brass pan having a rim all round about a quarter of an inch high"—is now "slightly warmed" and "laid on a flat table . . . which has been accurately leveled," ready to be filled with the liquid wax. The wax should be poured from a tin dipper evenly across the surface of the pan, to make sure that it adheres evenly when cooled (fig. 14.3). Any bubbles that surface must be burst, one by one;

25. Handbooks published not long after *Looking-Glass* are consistent with Filmer's pre-*Wonderland* account: Frederick J. F. Wilson, *Stereotyping and Electrotyping* (London: Wyman and Sons, 1880, rpt. [1881]). J. W. Urquhart, *Electro-Typing: A Practical Manual* (London: Crosby Lockwood, 1881).

a heated, pointed iron tool called a "building iron" is hovered over each bubble, causing it to expand and break, "and thus leave a perfect surface when cooled." The same tool can be used to melt any new wax that "shrink[s] away from the edge of the pan."

> As soon as the wax is sufficiently cool that its surface cannot be injured by the brush, apply a little blacklead to its surface, and brush it thoroughly but gently over. The wax should not be left until quite cold, especially in winter, before the blacklead is brushed on, as when cold it attains a glassy surface and the powder does not stick so well. Always blacklead the wax when a little warm.
>
> The wax is now ready for the impression. The pan after the setting of the wax should not be allowed to get cold before molding. (94)

The room temperature should be "about 85 or 90 degrees Fahrenheit." Much below that temperature the edges of the mold will be "depressed"; much above, the wax will be too fluid to take the image, or the surface will be rough. The press used to impress the image into the wax—ideally, a hydraulic press—has to exert, for wood cuts, more than one thousand pounds of pressure per square inch (fig. 14.4). Melted by a heated iron tool, wax is next built up by hand on areas that will print as blank spaces (fig. 14.5).

> Sometimes wax has to be built on to very narrow spaces. A little slip, or a little extra heat to the iron, will run the melted wax down . . . on to the face of a cut. No instruction can be given in this process, the necessary skill being obtained solely by practice. . . . In case of a mold not being good, the wax should be re-melted. . . . A cut may be made good by two or three impressions, but the practice should be deprecated, for frequently the electrotype will show the effect of the double impression. (115)

The block is then carefully pried from the pan, and the molded surface of the wax in the pan brushed with blacklead, which "must be pure, free from grit, of a bright luster, and ground very fine" (fig. 14.6). Filmer even specifies that the "the brush is made of badger hair, from two to three inches square"—brushes made of badger hair tending to spread out rather than taper.[26] (Mechanical brushes might be used in larger workshops from the mid-1850s on.) Any excess blackleading must be carefully brushed away, and then blown away with a pair of bellows, hand-powered or steam-powered, depending on the size of the establishment.

> Care must be taken to remove every particle of the powder, which is sometimes packed very tight into the fine lines, as the deposited copper will go over the surface of the blacklead and not incorporate with or under it, and thus give an imperfect plate.
>
> By holding the mold in a position where the light can strike it, the operator can see if the face is clean or otherwise; when clean the light will be reflected from the polished face of the mold, even from the finest hair lines. (150)

After the molded surface is thus blackleaded, the back and edges of the pan are "plaster[ed] over" with "some melted wax" to isolate it

26. W. Williams, *The Art of Landscape Painting in Oil Colours,* 17th ed. (London: Winsor and Newton, 1863), 13.

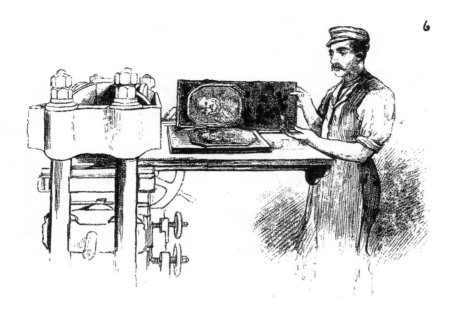

6

FIGURE 14.4. Edward Badoureau. "Moulding Press." Wood engraving proof. Circa 1890. Image courtesy of St. Bride Library.

8

FIGURE 14.5. Edward Badoureau. "Rising." Wood engraving proof. Circa 1890. Image courtesy of St. Bride Library.

9

FIGURE 14.6. Edward Badoureau. "Blackleading." Wood engraving proof. Circa 1890. Image courtesy of St. Bride Library.

FIGURE 14.7. Edward Badoureau. "Pumping out." Wood engraving proof. Circa 1890. Image courtesy of St. Bride Library.

FIGURE 14.8. Edward Badoureau. "Copper Bath." Wood engraving proof. Circa 1890. Image courtesy of St. Bride Library.

from the electrolytic solution. However, a few spots on the rim will be left exposed, for attaching a wire connected to the electrical battery or other power source.

> In order that copper may not be wasted, a heated building iron should be passed over all those parts of the wax which are not wanted. This melts the wax and destroys the blacklead surface of those parts. (190)

Next, the mold is wetted in a solution of alcohol or alcohol mixed with water, to prevent the formation of bubbles in fine lines, which would distort the deposition of copper. The surface is then rinsed under a fine, pressured water spray that dislodges any remaining bubbles (fig. 14.7).

The electrotyping process follows, which involves electrolysis in a specially prepared solution of copper sulphate, sulphuric acid, and water (fig. 14.8). The best proportion of these ingredients will vary with the season and workshop temperature; it also must be monitored and adjusted after repeated use, to offset chemical imbalances caused by the process itself. In use the solution tends to stratify, and should be stirred each day to prevent uneven deposition.

13

FIGURE 14.9. Edward Badoureau. "Stripping." Wood engraving proof. Circa 1890. Image courtesy of St. Bride Library.

Filmer takes the electrochemical aspect of the electrotype process largely for granted, except for an incidental discussion on page 237; but it can be briefly described: A sheet of copper is suspended in the prepared solution of copper sulphate, and is connected with a wire or metal strip to the positive pole of a battery or other source of electricity; the prepared blackleaded mold is connected to the negative pole and suspended in the solution; the voltage difference generated in the battery between its poles tends to draw copper ions from the solution to attach to the surface of the mold, which are replenished in the solution by ions leached from the copper source (Urquhart, 5, 7). During the process the liquid battery that powers it must be monitored; it should emit bubbles briskly, otherwise the battery solution needs to be replenished.

When the process has run long enough—often overnight—it is time to remove the copper shell from the wax (see fig. 14.9).

When the mold has received sufficient thickness of copper, it should be placed in a slightly slanting position; then pour some boiling water over it; at the same time, lift gently one corner of the shell. The heat of the hot water melts the surface of the wax immediately in contact with the under part of the shell, and, by carefully raising it, it will come off without difficulty, leaving a film of wax on its face—the amount of which, depends on the skill of the manipulator in pouring and lifting at the same moment. (213)

Filmer strongly recommends removing any residual film of wax by cleansing it with hot lye, followed by a rinse in water, to prevent wax from carbonizing at the next stage of the process—which is "tinning the back, preparatory to backing." A preliminary coating of tin is needed to bond the thin copper to a strong type-metal backing and support. To prepare for that coating the back of the shell is washed with a solution of "muriate of zinc [now known as zinc chloride], to which a little salammoniac [i.e., ammonium chloride] has been added." After that coating has been dried, the shell is raised "to a nearly perpendicular position" on a gridiron support and a molten blend of tin and lead is

FIGURE 14.10. Edward Badoureau. "Backing up." Wood engraving proof. Circa 1890. Image courtesy of St. Bride Library.

ladled across the top edge. "It will readily flow over and leave the copper with a good layer of tin, which has chemically combined with it."

Tinning the shell like this will usually warp it, and it will have to be made flat before it is backed with metal. Any tin that may have leaked through small holes has to be "carefully cut away," and any residual wax "should be removed with a rag dipped in turpentine."

> After having seen the shell perfectly free from any foreign matter, lay it on a perfectly clean flat plate of iron, or marble slab, and beat it over gently with a brush made of hair, about the stiffness of a blacking brush. Care must be used to beat around any large *built up* places or they will be beaten in. If this process is carefully attended to, the plate, when backed up, will be free from shrinkages. (259, emphasis in the original)

The copper shell now has to be backed and strengthened with type metal, an alloy of tin, antimony, and lead mixed and melted in a precise proportion by weight (4:5:91) at 700 degrees Fahrenheit. The molten metal is carefully ladled into the back of the shell (fig. 14.10), allowed to cool, and mechanically trimmed and shaved to a uniform thickness.

The plate is then cleaned and brushed, first with lye, to remove any traces of wax, then with turpentine, to remove any blacklead, and mounted on a wooden block. Filmer says the blocks used were the same as for the older stereotype process (which electrotyping was rendering obsolete): mahogany blocks (preferred for its tight grain), or cheaper blocks such as cherry.[27]

In 1918 an American textbook pointed out that "in practice more than twenty different operations are necessary to make a finished electrotype."[28] Filmer's account in 1858 details well more than a score of such steps. The summary given here has mentioned many of them, but omits many of the details of the finishing stage. It also hints at the qualitative subtext that runs throughout Filmer's remarks: there are not only many different things to do, but they must be done with care and understanding. A certain "precaution" must be taken in pouring the wax; then bubbles must be removed to avoid "imperfections in the mold" (93). "Considerable judgment is required in the molder during

27. C. S. Partridge, *Stereotyping, The Papier Mache Process* (Chicago: Mize & Stearns Press, 1892), 119. Urquhart, 139.

28. Harris B. Hatch and A. A. Stewart, *Electrotyping and Stereotyping* (Chicago: United Typothetae of America, 1918), 5.

this part of the process" (94). "This operation requires considerable practice and a steady hand. . . . A little slip, or a little extra heat, will"—cause trouble (94). "Care must be taken to remove every particle of the powder" (190). "The practiced workman" will have less trouble than "the unpracticed workman" (213). "No instruction can be given in this process—the necessary skill being obtained solely by practice" (94). Adverbs are frequent and often hortatory: "gently" (72, 190 twice, 213, 259, 260) "gently but thoroughly" (94), "firmly" (259, 260), "perfectly" (72, 189 twice), "immediately" (115, 190 twice), "thoroughly" (189, 190, 213, 282), "slowly" (189, 190), "completely" (190 twice), "carefully" (259), "sufficiently" (190, 260), "slightly" (213, 260), "smartly" (282). Mistakes will happen, at every stage of the process. Work may be wasted, and have to be done over again. Certain hazards particularly threaten the integrity of the image. The wood block may not make a clean and fully detailed impression on the wax mold if the wax is of the wrong consistency or at the wrong temperature, or if the wrong amount of pressure is applied. When the copper shell is stripped from the mold it will be more or less twisted, and the printing surface may not be rectified—made perfectly flat—if the molten metal backing is not properly manipulated. Filmer does not say how often such failures occur, but perfect replication of the surface of an engraved wood block is an ideal not easily realized.

"Phosphorus," too, dramatizes the uncertainty of the process, especially at one critical moment:

> The form [consisting of standing type] or woodcut must be moulded while the wax is yet warm; but, nevertheless, it must be perfectly set. Upon the experience of this simple fact depends, to a great extent, the success of the whole process; yet, simple though it seems, and really is, from some cause inherent in many people, it is the greatest difficulty to get men to mould the form or cut when the wax is at the exact temperature; but—like swimming—when proficiency is once obtained, it comes so natural, that a spoilt mould from this cause is a rarity, even with an inebriated moulder. I have known clever, steady, and assiduous men practice for weeks—nay, months,—and only succeed by chance, and never with certainty.[29]

Despite such practical difficulties, electrotyping achieved success on an industrial scale in the United States, Great Britain, and Europe. *The Illustrated London News*, a major source for visual culture for the Victorian middle-class reader, had adopted the process by 1856, after some years of hesitation; and other journals had done the same.[30] That commitment by the leading British illustrated magazine was exemplary. By the middle of the 1850s electrotyping of wood engravings had become the dominant medium for the printing of imagery—a function that lasted until photographic "process" reproduction displaced it, four decades later.[31]

Although *The Illustrated London News* was understated in describing its engagement with the electrotype process, in 1860 a French counterpart, *Le Monde illustré*, printed a full page of wood engravings, presumably themselves electrotyped, which illustrated men at work at several stages of the process—only a few years before the process was applied to Tenniel's illustrations for *Alice's Adventures*. The article "L'Électrotypie ou la Galvanoplastie" (*galvanoplastie* being the French word for the pro-

29. Phosphorus (pseud.), "Electro-Metallurgy, as Applied to Printing," chapter 11, *J. & R. M. Wood's Typographic Advertiser*, 1 April 1864, 94.

30. Charles Knight, "On Class XXVI, Drawing and Modelling, Letter-Press and Copper-Plate Printing, and Photography," *Reports of the Paris Universal Exposition, Part I* (London: H. M. S. O., 1856), 354, 365. *The Illustrated London News* had publicized and pondered over the process on several occasions, especially around the time of the Great Exhibition, when the Imperial Court and Government Printing Office of Vienna exhibited some specimens. 10 May 1851, 400; 17 May 1851, 437; 28 June 1851, Supplement: 627; 5 July 1851, Supplement: 26. According to H. R. Bradbury, the precipitating factor was "the enormous demand by the public for copies" of the journal during the Crimean War (1853–56), which "could not have been supplied, but by the reduplication of the cuts, only by the agency of the electrotype." *Printing: Its Dawn, Day & Destiny* (London: Bradbury & Evans, 1858), 23.

31. Gerry Beegan, *The Mass Image: A Social History of Photomechanical Reproduction in Victorian London* (Houndsmill, Eng. Palgrave Macmillan, 2008).

FIGURE 14.11. Émile Bourdelin. "Ateliers d'electrotypie." Wood engraving. *Le Monde illustré*, 7 January 1860.

cess), written and illustrated by Émile Bourdelin, is generally consistent with Filmer's account.[32] The several illustrations that appear there (fig. 14.11) were then synthesized by the wood engraver Ulysse Fournier to provide a single, idealized view of a French electrotyping workshop for a book that celebrated technical innovations past and present, starting with Gutenberg (fig. 14.12).[33] In that illustration the electrotyping vat, ringed with ranks of Bunsen cells, has been relocated to the right. Some interested visitors stand nearby, who represent us.

Neither they nor the workers are in a healthful space. In many ways electrotyping was a hazardous business. "Phosphorus" gives this precautionary advice:

It is almost unnecessary here to mention that the copper solution is highly poisonous, and that great care should be taken that none of it gets into the mouth or mucous parts of the body, or into any sore place on the hands. It is always advisable to have a pan of clean cold water close at hand, so that in the event of any of the sulphuric acid or

32. Émile Bourdelin, "L'Électrotypie ou la Galvanoplastie, appliquée a la reproduction du texte et des gravures au bois," *Le Monde illustré*, 7 January 1860, 11, 13–14.

33. Louis Figuier, *Les Grandes Inventions anciennes et modernes dans les sciences, l'industrie et les arts* (Paris: Hachette, 1861), 317.

FIGURE 14.12. Ulysse Fournier. "Atelier de galvanoplastie." Wood engraving. Louis Figuier, *Les Grandes Inventions anciennes et modernes* (1861).

FIGURE 14.13. Edward Badoureau. "Battery Room." Wood engraving proof. Circa 1890. Image courtesy of St. Bride Library.

blue solution [copper sulphate] getting on any part of the person, you may be enabled immediately to dilute the same by bathing or plunging the part affected into the water. I once saved a little boy's eyesight by adopting this precaution.[34]

Similar advice figures in G. Gore's *The Art of Electro-Metallurgy* (London: Longmans, Green, 1877) under the heading "REMEDIES FOR ACCIDENTS, ETC., IN PROCESSES OF ELECTRO-METALLURGY": "As various poisonous substances are employed in the art, it would be well for the operator to know their best antidotes" (366). Health hazards specific to electrotyping included the inhalation of graphite dust and the nitrogen dioxide generated from volatile batteries, not to mention the risk attendant upon manipulating molten metal. "Noxious fumes" were common.[35]

Badoureau's proofs show what such a workshop looked like in London as late as 1890; "Battery Room" in particular highlights a concentration of liquid-chemical batteries and deposition vats filled with volatile sulphuric acid, which shared with several workers tight quarters that

34. "Electro-Metallurgy," chapter 8, *J. & R. M. Wood's Typographic Advertiser*, 1 January 1864, 62.

35. J. H. Croucher, *A Popular Guide to the Electrotype; Containing Concise & Simple Instructions in the Various Processes of Electro-Metallurgy* (London: T. & R. Willats, 1847), 15. Hatch and Stewart, 4, 15. "Electro-typing cannot be considered a healthy occupation," Wilson remarked in 1880 (113).

were not particularly well ventilated despite some open windows (fig. 14.13). The claustrophobia that Alice suffered in the White Rabbit's house could easily have been renewed in an electrotyping workshop in Oxford or London.

How good could the results be of such careful and hazardous labor? How well did electros actually print on the page of a book? The most detailed contemporary account is that of Theodore Low De Vinne, who was the leading American printer of the 1870s and 1880s, particularly renowned for his skill in printing wood engravings and electros made from them to illustrate *Scribner's Monthly, St. Nicholas* (the leading American magazine for children, which was launched in 1872, the year *Looking-Glass* was published), and *The Century Illustrated Monthly Magazine,* which succeeded *Scribner's.* De Vinne, like Carroll later in his life (after the "fiasco" of the 1865 *Alice,* which is chronicled in the next chapter), brought the highest standards to judge the results of printing, and in the light of those standards even wood engravings could be problematic when managed in a commercial print shop, no matter how well they might look when the engraver carefully proofed them by hand. Electros presented additional difficulties, which De Vinne begins to enumerate in response to an imagined engraver's complaints:

> Why do you not give me a print that is like my proof, or something like it, at least? Why do you make the blacks so dull, the middle tints so muddy, and the greys so harsh? Why do you spoil my work? What is the use of cutting finely when the printing will almost certainly be done so rudely?[36]

In 1867 Carroll made similar demands of Macmillan, invidiously comparing fine proofs supplied by Dalziel to Richard Clay's printing of the illustrations and recent proofs supplied by Clay. The occasion for this complaint was a request from a friend, who had "seen the impressions rubbed from the woodblocks (on French paper I think it is)" and requested "a copy of 'Alice playing croquet' done in that way." Macmillan evidently intended to comply by having Clay print off some copies of the illustration. Carroll would have none of that:

> I fear from your saying you have "asked Clay to *print* a copy of 'Alice playing croquet,'" that you misunderstood my note. What Dalziel did, I believe, was to rub impressions, from the wood blocks, on soft French paper, the result being much more delicate than any prints from the electro-types.[37]

In a subsequent letter Carroll used the high quality of Dalziel's proof to impugn the illustrations in "the printed book":

> I have compared the 3 proofs of "Alice playing croquet" with the original one I had from Dalziel—they are completely inferior to it, and in fact are not at all better than those in the printed copies. . . . Dalziel called the process "rubbing off by hand." I don't know what that means exactly, but the result contains delicacy of detail to which there is no approach in the printed book, nor in the 3 proofs you have sent me.[38]

36. Theodore Low De Vinne (unsigned), "Woodcuts: Concerning the Taking of Proofs and Prints: Part I," *The Printing Times and Lithographer,* 15 October 1878, 197–99; 197.

37. *Lewis Carroll and the House of Macmillan,* 54 (18 June 1867).

38. *Lewis Carroll and the House of Macmillan,* 55 (24 June 1867).

De Vinne's response to his imagined engraver's challenging questions might as well have been addressed to Carroll. He contrasts the many favorable circumstances in which an engraver's proof is custom-made, to the many unfavorable ones that constrain a commercially printed image. What follows here is only the beginning of De Vinne's litany of contrasts in "Woodcuts" (198), and it is notable that the ones first mentioned have to do with the essential limitations of an electrotype, characterized as an "imperfect duplicate."

ENGRAVER'S PROOF.	PRESSMAN'S PRINT.
From the original wood; of faultlessly smooth surface.	From the imperfect duplicate of an electrotype, always of wavy and uneven surface, often marred by raised or cupped edges, and sometimes bruised by hammering on the back of the plate.
White lines as engraver made them, of full depth.	White lines more or less shallow, and clogged through wax, blacklead, dust, and the uncleansed ink of the proof adhering to the block before the block was moulded.
Black lines clean, sharp, and usually ungapped, even when they are undercut or without a supporting base.	Black lines often grimy, with rounded edges, bent, thickened, or gapped from too hard or too soft wax, or from undue pressure in moulding.
The wood is porous, imbibing, storing, and shedding ink readily.	The electrotype is solid, impervious, and takes a thin film of ink on the surface only.
The wood is measurably elastic and compressible, and does not spread or splurge ink when slightly overloaded with colour.	The electrotype is inelastic, and always spreads or splurges ink when it is in any way overcoloured.

This rehearsal of the limitations of electrotypes begins to explain why Clay's prints were inferior to Dalziel's proofs. (De Vinne also adduced additional, more general causes for deficiencies in printing, not specific to electrotypes, which will be noticed in the next chapter.) De Vinne's apology here runs counter to the rhetoric of perfect replication, or at least indiscernible difference, that greeted the advent of the electrotyping process in the 1840s; and it gives some substance to the previously cited "peculiarity of effect" and "hardness" of impression noticed by reviewers of the pioneering electrotypes made for Thomson's *Seasons*.

As regards the second disability mentioned in this list—"white lines more or less shallow"—and consequent defects, De Vinne elsewhere remarks that a channel present in the surface of an electrotype will be shallower (just by the thickness of the deposited copper) than the original channel cut into the wood block, and that shallow channels are too easily clogged with ink. To compensate for this deficiency the engraver who expects his work to be electrotyped must carve more deeply—and so, less finely: work that is destined to be electrotyped should be carved more coarsely than work intended for fine printing.[39]

De Vinne does concede two "great" advantages to "the electrotype, defective as it is in other features." Being "harder than the wood," it

39. Theodore Low De Vinne (unsigned), "A Printer on the Limitations of Engraving on Wood; In Three Parts—Conclusion," *The Printing Times and Lithographer,* 15 May 1879. 94–96; 94.

"will yield hundreds of thousands of fair impressions;" being "tough," it "will not crack nor warp from changes in the weather."

Several decades later Timothy Cole, whose finely toned reproductions of European paintings had helped to make the reputation of *The Century Illustrated Monthly Magazine* for its fine wood engravings, remembered only the subtle advantages of printing from electrotypes, and the disadvantages of letting printers handle the original wood blocks. When, in 1883, Cole started sending his blocks to Paris to be electrotyped, his blocks

> now were saved from the tender mercies of the printer (!) who, with their benzine and rags always succeeded in cleaning away their original bloom. . . . The wood block is a delicate thing, and the printers cannot realize this. I have had blocks ruined—in my estimation—in the more delicate parts by the printer's manipulations in washings and rubbings.[40]

De Vinne was Cole's merciful printer. One wonders whether they ever debated the merits of printing from wood blocks or electrotypes.

The history of electrotyping Tenniel's illustrations became more complicated in 1868, when Clay printed the sixth Macmillan edition not from standing type but from electrotypes. It is not known whether these electros were made just from letterpress, with electros of the illustrations then juxtaposed to them for printing; or whether an electro was made of an entire page, including a wood engraving—or even including an electro of a wood engraving. All subsequent Macmillan editions of *Alice's Adventures,* and all editions of *Looking-Glass,* were printed not from standing type but from electrotypes.[41]

Electros were made to be durable, and many of the Tenniel electros survive. The Macmillan archives hold complete sets for both the *Alice* books, including some duplicates. Most of these are unmounted, but at least one (the third illustration showing Father William) is mounted on a block made of composition wood, suggesting a later date. It is hard to tell which, if any, of these Macmillan electros were used to print the first editions of the two books. Many other such electros have surfaced from time to time at auction or in private collections. On 9 November 1995 Phillips in London offered for sale a

> set of original printing plates for Tenniel's illustrations to 'Alice,' comprising c. 90 original printing-plates for both *Alice's Adventures in Wonderland* and *Through the Looking-Glass and What Alice Found There:* steel-plated copper, some showing wear with the copper showing through, in an attractive accordion case [?early twentieth century].[42]

Facing copper electros with "steel" (actually, iron) by electro-deposition was practical by 1881 at least, so Phillips's guess about the date of manufacture is indeed uncertain.[43] In 1996 Mark Arman published a limited-edition brochure that included prints from twelve electrotype blocks, duplicates that were given to him before the lot described above was sent to auction at Phillips.[44]

In 2001 another set of electrotypes was sold at auction by Christie's in London, comprising "39 copper-plated lead printing blocks electro-

40. Letter from Timothy Cole to S. A. Hutchinson, 5 August 1922, quoted by Hutchinson in "Prints among the Recent Accessions," *The Brooklyn Museum Quarterly* 9 (1922): 194–98; 195–96.

41. *A Bibliographical Catalogue of Macmillan and Co.'s Publications from 1843 to 1889* (London: Macmillan, 1891), 130, 233. Clare Imholtz, "Notes on the Early Printing History of Lewis Carroll's 'Alice' Books," *The Book Collector* 62 (2013): 255–70; 264.

42. *Books, Autograph Letters, Manuscripts, Photographs & Maps to be Sold by Auction Thursday 9 November 1995* (London: Phillips, Son & Neale, 1995), lot 436.

43. Urquhart, 2, 32, 35–36.

44. Mark Arman, *The Story of the Electrotypes Used to Illustrate Sir John Tenniel's Drawings for Alice's Adventures in Wonderland & Through the Looking Glass* (Thaxted, UK: The Workshop Press, 1996).

typed from the wooden blocks cut by Dalziel Brothers after John Tenniel" for *Wonderland*; specifically, "36 illustrations (of 42, including 3 duplicates)"; and also thirteen electros for *Looking-Glass*, "for 10 illustrations" including two duplicates, and the "Jabberwocky" text in reverse. Though called "blocks," these were evidently electros backed with metal but not mounted on wood blocks (see below). They came to auction from the estate of Donald William Barber, who had been employed by the firm of Richard Clay, Son, and Taylor—Clay having printed the official first edition of *Alice's Adventures* after Carroll rejected the Clarendon Press printing as deficient, on Tenniel's advice. Christie's suggested that the *Wonderland* blocks were used in both of those important, early printings.[45] This lot of electrotypes realized £30,550 at auction.

In 2005 Christie's sold at auction, for £600, a single electro that had been prepared for use in printing the People's Edition of *Through the Looking-Glass* (1887), identified as "Toves, Borogroves, and Mome Raths and the Wabe."[46] As has already been mentioned, another singleton, reproducing Tenniel's *Wonderland* illustration of Alice and the Dodo, survived in Macmillan's bank vault along with the ninety-one original Dalziel wood blocks, replacing the only block that had been lost from that double set.

In 2016 Christie's again offered at auction the set of electros that they had previously auctioned from the Barber estate. When I saw them they were metal plates not mounted on wood blocks. The catalogue described them as "a superb collection of original printing plates for Tenniel's celebrated illustrations to Alice's Adventures in Wonderland, used in the production of the early editions including the legendarily rare first edition." The estimated bidding range for the lot was £35,000–45,000, but it did not sell.[47] In 2018 Christie's in New York sold the Barber electrotypes at auction for $81,250, well above the estimated range of $20,000 to $30,000. They were described in terms repeated from the 2001 sale:

> The present set of electrotype blocks was presumably prepared for the book's first printing in June 1865 by The Clarendon Press, and were then transferred to Clay for use in the first published edition (with letterpress text and electrotype illustrations). It is certainly unlikely that they were employed for the sixth edition of October 1868 (or subsequent editions), which were printed from electrotype plates of the text and illustrations.[48]

Altogether more than one hundred and fifty electrotypes of the Tenniel illustrations survive, the actual origin and use of which cannot readily be determined.

45. *Valuable Illuminated Manuscripts, Books and Autograph Letters* (London: Christie, Manson & Woods, 2001), lot 60. Although described as "copper-plated lead printing blocks" they were probably copper electrotypes backed by type metal (a blend of antimony, tin, and lead), as described above.

46. *The Nicholas Falletta Collection of Lewis Carroll Books: 30 November 2005* (London: Christie, Manson & Woods, 2005), lot 24.

47. *Valuable Books and Manuscripts: Thursday, 1 December 2016* (London: Christie, Manson & Woods, 2016), lot 152.

48. *Fine Printed Books & Manuscripts Including Americana: Tuesday, 4 December 2018* (New York: Christie, Manson & Woods International, 2018), lot 88. https//www.christies.com/lotfinder/books-manuscripts/dodgson-charles-lutwidge-and-6173148-details.aspx.

CHAPTER 15

Printing

"There's certainly too much pepper in that soup!" Alice said to herself, as well as she could for sneezing.

"It is wrong from beginning to end," said the Caterpillar decidedly, and there was silence for some minutes.

"Why, the fact is, you see, Miss, this here ought to have been a red rose-tree, and we put a white one in by mistake."

Lewis Carroll arranged for Macmillan & Co. to publish *Alice's Adventures in Wonderland* at his own expense: he would cover any loss, and share in a portion of any profit.[1] Details of the printing process and most details of the publishing process were for him to decide, after weighing any professional advice that Macmillan or Tenniel might offer. An important but uncontroversial question was who should print the book. Carroll chose the Clarendon Press at Oxford University Press, a richly experienced enterprise located barely a mile from his rooms in Christ Church. There were close ties between the press and the college. Henry George Liddell, the dean of the college (and Alice's father) was a member of the board of delegates (Wakeling, 72). Thomas Combe, the printing director, was a personal friend of Carroll's, and it was he who on 19 October 1863 introduced Carroll to Alexander Macmillan (*Diaries*, 4:258)—the Macmillan firm having become a distribution agent for Oxford University Press earlier that same year.[2] Combe had already printed two of Carroll's mathematical pamphlets (Crutch, 22–23). The Clarendon Press was an obvious choice.

It is not known what kind of printing press was used to produce the book. Oxford owned several machine-powered, manually fed flatbed presses, suitable for high-quality book work.[3] The book was constructed as an octavo: aside from the preliminaries, twenty-four sheets were printed, bearing eight pages on each side. Each electrotyped image called for special adjustment in the press: to sharpen the imprint a block might have to be raised a bit by inserting one or more sheets of paper underneath ("underlaying"); and areas of a block that might print too faintly in proof could be given sufficient pressure by inserting one or more shaped bits of paper at corresponding points on the tympan that pressed the sheet onto the forme. Such was the standard routine. After all the sheets were printed some were bound to Carroll's specifications by the London firm of James Burn & Co., who worked

1. By such an arrangement Macmillan typically would receive "a fixed ten percent of the receipts"; introduction to *Lewis Carroll and the House of Macmillan*, 15.

2. Eliot, "The Evolution of a Printer and Publisher," *The History of Oxford University Press*, 2:95–96.

3. Among the machines at the Clarendon Press, at least by late in the 1870s, were four double-feed presses introduced by David Napier by 1846, which "became the standard for bookwork throughout the nineteenth century," especially work involving "delicate typefaces or complex engravings"; Allan C. Dooley, *Author and Printer in Victorian England* (Charlottesville: University Press of Virginia, 1992), 80. Eliot inventories these machines and others in "Chapter 3: Machines, Materials, and Money," *The History of Oxford University Press*, 2:164. See also James Moran, *Printing Presses: History and Development from the Fifteenth Century to Modern Times* (Berkeley: University of California Press, 1973), 116–17, 120.

closely with Macmillan and would eventually bind all the books that Carroll published with them.[4]

Carroll was satisfied with the results, and on 15 July 1865 he set about inscribing "20 or more copies" to give to friends (*Diaries*, 5:93). But he had hardly finished distributing them before disaster struck. Tenniel opened a copy and found the printing of the book to be unsatisfactory. He complained to Carroll, who reported the problem to Macmillan and immediately canceled publication, making it necessary to recall the gift copies that had already been dispatched, and also to find a new printer. Macmillan was able to unload many of the remaining defective copies, outfitted with new title pages, to the publishing firm of Appleton and Co. in New York (the precise number is in dispute). Americans presumably had lower printing standards, and selling the books there would help pay for a new printing.

Only twenty-two copies of the original edition are known to survive, most of which are held by institutional libraries; six are in private hands. One copy sold at auction in 1998 for $1,540,000; another, offered in 2016 did not sell, although (or because) it was valued at between two and three million dollars.[5] All in all, an 1865 *Alice* is the most valuable book published in England in the nineteenth century.

Carroll chose the firm of Richard Clay in London to print the book all over again, presumably after having consulted with Macmillan and with Tenniel. As was noted above in chapter 7, Tenniel's first illustrated book, Fouqué's *Undine,* had been reprinted by Clay. The firm acquired a distinguished reputation for producing books that were handsomely illustrated with electrotyped wood engravings; a celebrated instance was the recent edition of Thomas Moore's *Lalla Rookh,* for which Tenniel supplied sixty-nine illustrations. *Macmillan's Magazine,* though not illustrated aside from the title page, had been a success since 1859; it was printed by Clay. The Dalziel brothers had worked closely with Clay, whom the publisher Routledge had chosen to electrotype and print their engraved illustrations for the five-volume *Illustrated Natural History* by J. G. Wood (1861–63). Clay was also chosen by Henry Bohn to print the leading contemporary history and manual of wood engraving, *A Treatise on Wood Engraving* (1861).[6] Charles Kingsley's *Water-Babies,* which Macmillan published as a book in 1863 after it appeared in *Macmillan's Magazine,* and which Alexander Macmillan had recommended as a prototype for the format of *Alice's Adventures,* was also printed by Clay.

Furthermore, Macmillan's contemporary advertisements display a network of continuing connections to the Clay firm. On 29 October 1864 their full-page ad in *The Athenæum* publicized a "New List of Books for The Season"—that is, the Christmas season. The list was headed by the Globe Edition of Shakespeare's *Complete Works,* edited by W. G. Clark and W. Aldis Wright—a landmark edition that was printed by C. J. Clay in Cambridge. Charles James Clay, then managing partner of Cambridge University Press and University Printer, was the elder son of Richard Clay and a veteran and protégé of Clay's printing establishment in Bread Street Hill, London.[7] Not far below was a notice of F. T. Palgrave's *Golden Treasury of the Best Songs and Lyrical Poems in the English Language* (1861), a book already established as the canonical lyrical anthology of English poetry—and a book that had been well printed by Richard Clay in Bread Street. At the bottom of the middle of the three

4. Robert J. Milevski, "A Note on Macmillan's Lewis Carroll Bindings," *Knight Letter* 92 (Spring 2014): 9–11.

5. "Auction Record for an Original 'Alice,'" *The New York Times,* 11 December 1998. *Alice's Adventures in Wonderland: The Extremely Rare 1865 First Edition* (New York: Christie's, 2016). Barbara Basbanes Richter, "First Edition of 'Alice in Wonderland' Fails to Sell at Auction," *Fine Books and Collections* blog, 17 June 2016.

6. James Moran, *Clays of Bungay* (Bungay, Eng.: Richard Clay, 1978), 48–52, 88–89.

7. Michael H. Black, *Cambridge University Press, 1584–1984* (Cambridge: Cambridge University Press, 1984), 152–53.

notice columns was an announcement, which has not previously been cited, of a "NEW ILLUSTRATED BOOK FOR CHILDREN. | *ALICE'S ADVENTURES IN WON-* | DERLAND. By LEWIS CARROLL. Illustrated by John | Tenniel, &c." The "&c." is perplexing, as if the copy-writer thought that Tenniel was only the most prominent among several illustrators for the book. In any case, this ad sold no books that season. On 20 November 1864, Carroll told Macmillan "I fear my little book *Alice's Adventures in Wonderland* cannot appear this year. Mr. Tenniel writes that he is hopeless of completing the pictures by Xmas"—partly because his mother had recently died. The book, printed by the Clarendon Press, was not ready for distribution until July 1865—when its publication was canceled at Tenniel's instigation.

To the left of the premature *Athenæum* ad for *Alice's Adventures,* at the bottom of the first column, was a large notice advertising "*SERIES* of *BOOKS* for the *YOUNG,* | Handsomely and uniformly bound in cloth, gilt leaves, | price *3s. 6d.* each." They included the third edition of Charles Kingsley's *Heroes, or Greek Fairy Tales*; the first edition of *My First Journal: A Book for the Young,* by Georgiana M. Craik, daughter of George Lillie Craik, a partner in Macmillan & Co.; and *Our Year: A Child's Book, in Prose and Verse,* by Dinah Maria Mulock, who would soon marry Georgiana's father. These and other children's books on the list were illustrated with wood engravings and printed by Richard Clay.

When the Clarendon Press failed to print *Alice's Adventures* to Tenniel's satisfaction the next printer to employ for the task was an obvious, almost inevitable, choice.

Clay reset all the letterpress for the new printing (this time in quarto signatures, four leaves—eight pages—to a sheet), but apparently used the same electrotype blocks of Tenniel's illustrations as the Clarendon Press had used. Again, the machine was probably a steam-powered but hand-fed platen press, preferred for "high quality work."[8] The book was bound by Macmillan's regular bindery, James Burn & Co. (Milevski, 9–11), and Carroll was pleased with the result, which Macmillan duly published in November 1865, in time for the Christmas season, though dated 1866 on the title page.

Different ads announcing the book, all under the rubric "This day is published," appeared in *The Spectator* on 11 November 1865 (page 1267); in *Notes and Queries* on 18 November 1865 (page [430]); and in *The Publishers' Circular* on 8 December 1865 (page 95 of the Illustrations section). The last-mentioned ad, which took up a full page, displayed two of Tenniel's illustrations: the head of the Cheshire Cat looming over the courtiers' consultation (fig. 6.8), and the White Rabbit running away from Alice in the corridor. All three ads represented the book as carrying the subtitle "A Tale for Children"—which had been a common subtitle for moralistic children's stories but was not the actual subtitle of this book nor the right genre for it. Early in 1866 Macmillan dropped that misleading subtitle from its advertising.

The book was well received, and many more editions followed.

In 1891 Macmillan and Co. listed the editions to date in its *Bibliographical Catalogue*: six separate editions, plus some twenty-eight reprintings. The most intriguing entry was the first: "First edition printed 1865."[9] In 1898 Ernest Dressel North, a dealer writing for *The Book Buyer* (New York), reported that this puzzling entry had been corroborated by the recent "sale of Mr. Dodgson's books in Oxford, where

8. "Clays used a number of makes— Napier, Rich, and Hopkinson"; Moran, *Clays,* 83.

9. *A Bibliographical Catalogue of Macmillan and Co.'s publications from 1843 to 1889* (London: Macmillan, 1891), 130.

a copy with the date 1865 was sold."[10] In fact two such copies were auctioned at the sale of Carroll's belongings in May 1898, both of them specially bound copies that Carroll had presented as gifts (to Alice Liddell and Marion Terry) but later reclaimed because Tenniel objected to the edition.[11] In an earlier report of the auction North had mentioned only the Terry copy.[12] Apparently informed directly or indirectly by one of these copies North listed eleven distinctive features of the suppressed 1865 edition that would distinguish it for collectors from the authorized edition of 1866. Two of the points that he mentioned would prove relevant to a lasting dispute about what was wrong with the suppressed edition: "10. The paper is a trifle thicker and whiter. 11. The illustrations are far more brilliant."

Why *did* Tenniel object to the 1865 printing? The record is equivocal. On 20 July 1865 Carroll wrote in his diary, "Called on Macmillan, and showed him Tenniel's letter about the fairy-tale, he is entirely dissatisfied with **the printing of the pictures**, and I suppose we shall have to do it all again" (*Diaries*, 5:97; emphasis added here, as in the following quotations).[13] On 3 August Carroll wrote to Tom Taylor, "I write to beg, that if you have received the copy I sent you of *Alice's Adventures in Wonderland*, you will suspend your judgment on it till I can send you a better copy. We are printing it again, as **the pictures** are so badly done" (*Letters*, 1:77). On 14 November he asked Georgina Balfour to exchange her gift copy for a better one: "The fact is, **the book was so badly printed, or rather the pictures**, that I have had it all done again, and the new ones are *far* better than the old" (*Letters*, 1:80). Probably in November Tenniel wrote to Dalziel, "Mr. Dodgson's book came out months ago, but I protested so strongly against **the disgraceful printing** that he *cancelled the edition*" (Ayres, 158). Carroll's first biographer, his nephew Stuart Dodgson Collingwood, summarized the matter in 1898: "The first edition, which consisted of two thousand copies, was condemned by both author and illustrator, for **the pictures did not come out well**."[14] (Collingwood's book appeared in December 1898—just a few months after the writer for *The Book Buyer*, with unwitting contrariness, characterized the illustrations of 1865 as "far more brilliant.") Many years later Frederick Macmillan was cited as holding the opinion that the book was withdrawn "because of dissatisfaction with **the way the printing was done**."[15] Frederick was fourteen years old when the book was printed; presumably he got his information from his uncle, Alexander Macmillan, whom he eventually succeeded in managing Carroll's continuing business with the firm.

What *was* wrong with "the printing of the pictures" / "the pictures" / "the book . . . so badly printed, or rather the pictures" / "the disgraceful printing" / "the pictures" / "the way the printing was done"? A critical industry has pursued this question for a century. In 1921 G. H. Sargent noted in *The Bookman's Journal*, regarding the two printings, "the woodcuts . . . appear to be identical, though the 1866 impressions are lighter and less inked."[16] Three years later the press that published that journal issued the first substantial Carroll bibliography, *A Bibliography of the Writings of Lewis Carroll (Charles Lutwidge Dodgson, M.A.)*, by Sidney H. Williams. Describing the situation in more detail, Williams added to the perplexity:

As for the defects said to be found in the woodcuts of this 1865 edition, I must say that I have been at a loss to find them; indeed, in many

10. Ernest Dressel North, "Notes of Rare Books," *The Book Buyer* 17:3 (October 1898): [223].

11. Lots 681 and 680, respectively; *Lewis Carroll's Library,* ed. Jeffrey Stern (Silver Spring, MD: Lewis Carroll Society of North America), 12; described in detail by Selwyn H. Goodacre, "The 1985 'Alice': A Revised and Augmented Census," in Schiller, 33–53; 37–39.

12. Ernest Dressel North, "Notes of Rare Books," *The Book Buyer* 16:6 (July 1898): 506.

13. In a later summary of events concerning the book, Carroll repeated this formula: "heard from Tenniel, who is dissatisfied with the printing of the pictures. July 19. (W). 1865" (*Diaries* 5:10).

14. Collingwood, *Life and Letters*, 104.

15. Williams and Madan, [225].

16. G. H. Sargent, "American Notes," *The Bookman's Journal and Print Collector* 5 (1921): 38.

instances the woodcuts are sharper, and more defined than those in the next edition, which was supposed to remedy the defects. Certainly in the second edition, they are more lightly printed, and less ink has been used: so sparingly in some cases, that portions of the edges of the woodcuts and Tenniel's monogram are not reproduced. (11)

The last point is the first mention that I have seen of a defect that often appears in the printing of Tenniel's *Alice* illustrations in many of Macmillan's nineteenth-century editions: because of indifferent makeready the edges of the images are often so weakly printed as to damage the Dalziel signature in one lower corner, or the JT monogram in the other—sometimes both. This defect, which the Clarendon Press largely avoided in the more heavily printed version of 1865, is common in the supposedly superior Clay printing of 1866—as it is also in many later editions published by Macmillan. Tenniel probably let it pass without objection because it was a defect to be expected in the machine printing of wood engravings—or, rather, of electrotype replicas of wood engravings—as, for example, in Clay's printing of his own illustrations to *Lalla Rookh,* where the signatures and monograms of more than a dozen illustrations are faint or broken.

Williams continued:

> Altogether there are well over one thousand small typographical differences between the two printings, mainly owing to lines commencing and ending with different words. The woodcuts in the first (1865) edition are more lightly printed than in the second (1866) edition, and they are in the Appleton issue, which is known to be the same printing. This would seem to accord with the reason given for the suppression of the first edition. (17–18)

This is confusing on its face, since only a few pages earlier Williams had (correctly) identified 1866 as the more lightly printed of the two editions. When Williams revised this passage for the second edition of the *Handbook* he rather compounded than resolved this problem, favoring the suppressed 1865 edition by changing "lightly printed" to "clearly printed," and canceling the final sentence, perhaps as nonsensical.[17]

So the matter stood until Harry Morgan Ayres reopened it in 1934, two years after Carroll's centennial. Surveying details of both editions, Ayres noted that the impressions were somewhat lighter in 1866, making Alice herself somewhat more attractive, but he doubted that difference alone would have warranted the bother of a reprinting. Instead, he found that it was the layout of the letterpress that was greatly defective in the 1865 edition and was largely amended in 1866: some fourteen typographical "widows" (a partial line at the top of a page) marred the 1865 printing; repairing them had the incidental benefit of improving the placement on the page of several pictures. But on balance it was the "printing," not the "pictures," that was the problem, according to Ayres.

In 1937 Oliver Wilson asserted that "the plates were brighter and clearer in the First than in the Second edition," and paraphrased North's list of distinctive points, including the remark that "the paper [in 1865] is a trifle thicker and whiter, with the illustrations definitely more brilliant."[18]

In 1952 R. G. Lyde, writing in *The British Museum Quarterly,* reported on his examination of the Museum's recently acquired copy of the

17. Williams and Madan, 229. In an additional note Williams states, "the preceding notes . . . are printed verbatim from the first edition of the Bibliography" (232); but evidently changes were made.

18. Oliver Wilson, *Alice's Adventures in Wonderland: A Survey of the Important Editions and Issues of One of the Outstanding Book Rarities of Nineteenth Century Literature* (Seattle, WA: Rara Libri Publishing, 1937), 10, 12.

1865 *Alice*. He focused on two neglected aspects, paper quality and print-through:

> A careful examination of the British Museum's recently acquired copy of the first edition reveals the probable grounds of Dodgson and Tenniel's objection. As a result of heavy inking and the use of an inferior paper, the type is in some places visible on the other side of the leaf, thereby impairing the appearance of the illustrations which are printed in the middle of the text. This defect was completely removed in the second edition, which Macmillan and Co. printed shortly after the suppression of this first issue of the first edition.[19]

Lyde was on to something, as we shall see.

When W. H. Bond came to review the whole question in 1956, he generally endorsed Ayres's opinion that the layout of the letterpress (that is, "the printing") was a major flaw in 1865, and he brought several other aspects of the printing under consideration. For one thing, the letterpress for the Clarendon Press *Alice* was set from "a foul case," in which letters from similar but different fonts were indiscriminately mixed: Clay did not repeat this careless mistake. Close comparison of the illustrations in 1865 and 1866 with surviving proofs that had been taken directly from the wood blocks showed subtleties of shading in certain proofs that were degraded in 1865 but retained in 1866, presumably thanks to Clay's more experienced management of makeready (underlays and tailored overlays for each block). Finally (although he takes this question up earlier) there is the matter of what Bond calls "offset":

> At a hasty glance the effect is of dirtiness in properly white spaces and around some of the pictures. A closer look shows that the "dirt" is offset, generally not from facing pages but from the reverse side of the sheets involved, probably occurring when the sheets were stacked as they came off the press. (316)

Bond does not mention Lyde's article, which noticed the same defect, explained in somewhat different terms.

In 1971 Warren Weaver, who was familiar with Lyde's article and had corresponded with Bond, summarized the "dirt" problem: "The press work on the Oxford Press 1865 edition was . . . faulty, there being various examples of over-inking and too much pressure, resulting in 'dirtiness' of spaces which should properly be entirely white."[20] And in his detailed descriptions of the surviving copies of the suppressed edition that he was able to examine (nineteen in all) he noted the presence of such dirt on each page where it occurred—an aspect that varied considerably from copy to copy, with some repetition.

What to make of all this? Is the first printing "brighter and clearer," more "brilliant," than the later one—or overprinted and dirty? Bond showed that sometimes excessive pressure or over-inking or both could detract from Alice's appearance in an engraving—making her look "disorderly, dissipated, with circles under eyes and mascara running, after one too many 'Drink Me's,'" as William Appleton later put it.[21] But many of the illustrations printed in 1866 are too lightly printed in some copies, fading at the edges, erasing Tenniel's monogram among other marginal details.

19. R. G. Lyde, "The Harmsworth 'Alice,'" *The British Museum Quarterly* 17:4 (December 1952): 77–79; 77. I have examined this copy and find that show-through, although present, is relatively less conspicuous in it than in some other copies of the first printing.

20. Warren Weaver, "The First Edition of *Alice's Adventures in Wonderland*: A Census," *The Papers of the Bibliographical Society of America* 65 (1971): 1–40; 4.

21. "In Alice's Footsteps at the Spring Meeting," *Knight Letter* 50 (Summer 1995): [3]. "The shadows about eyes and mouth, a heavy, sullen expression," as Bond more mildly put it in discussing certain 1865 impressions of the "DRINK ME" image, finding them inferior to results in 1866 (319). Jaques and Giddens make the same comparison at page 28.

As regards any particular illustration, which impression is better, 1865 or 1866? That will depend on the copies examined; for it is true, as Bond noted in a different context, that a defect "varies from copy to copy, as conditions of inking may vary during the run of the press" (316).

The defect that Bond had in mind as he made that point was "offset," the supposed transfer of ink from one freshly printed sheet to another, piled on it to dry. Later he withdrew that hypothesis, responding to some apt objections made by Selwyn Goodacre:

> The defect is not "offset" at all; it is due to "show-through," and is probably due to the use of a poor ink, containing too much vehicle for the pigment—the vehicle carries the pigment too far into the paper, so that it soaks in to the extent that it partially comes through the paper to show on the reverse side. It could not be offset from sheets stacked as they came off the press, as an examination of the pages shows that the "dirt" corresponds exactly with the type on the reverse side of the page.[22]

Bond later conceded the point, and went one step further: "I believe that Mr. Goodacre is correct in stating that the 'dirtiness' of the letterpress is caused by ink penetrating the leaf, rather than offset as I had conjectured." A copy at Harvard "clearly shows penetration of ink and excessive pressure in printing, almost breaking through the paper in places." Bond now conjectured that "the Oxford University Press, inexperienced in printing electros of complex wood engravings, tried extra pressure rather than elaborate makeready.[23]

Here Bond does not mention the quality of the paper. Jaques and Giddens emphasize that 1865 was printed on "poorer paper" than 1866 (30)—a point already made by Lyde ("an inferior paper"). I will suggest below that that inferiority involved a deficiency in sizing, which left the paper too absorbent.

If one takes the paper into account, there are three possible variables that may cause defects apparent on one or another page of the 1865 edition: the ink (sometimes excessively applied), the paper (sometimes too absorbent), and the pressure of the press (sometimes excessive, to compensate for inferior makeready). Two kinds of defect will then show themselves, depending on particular circumstances. The lines of some illustrations in some copies may be disfigured by overprinting. There will also be occasional, even frequent print-through, a vague splotchiness that may be noticeable behind letterpress on a given page, but that may be especially conspicuous in large white spaces, such as surround or appear within Tenniel's illustrations. Given all the variables (ink, paper, pressure) such defects will vary from page to page and, even more importantly, from copy to copy.

As has already been mentioned, Warren Weaver identified much variability in the "dirtiness" of the 1865 Macmillan *Alice*. More or less dirt would appear on certain pages in different copies of the nineteen copies that examined. And the pages often are different: a page that is marred with dirt in one copy will be unobjectionable in another. I have examined several of these copies myself, and also several copies of the 1866 Appleton edition, which was printed by Oxford at the same time with the same disabilities. Copies of that Appleton edition, too, vary in the same way, a page or illustration sometimes showing more or less dirt, sometimes not. The upshot (to rehearse the terms of the sev-

22. Goodacre, "The 1865 *Alice*," 79.
23. W. H. Bond, review of *Soaring with the Dodo: Essays on Lewis Carroll's Life and Art*, ed. Edward Guiliano and James R. Kincaid, *The Papers of the Bibliographical Society of America* 77 (1983): 518–20; 520.

FIGURE 15.1. *Alice's Adventures in Wonderland* (New York: Appleton, 1866), page 97 (detail). Children's Literature Research Collections, University of Minnesota Libraries.

FIGURE 15.2. *Alice's Adventures in Wonderland* (New York: Appleton, 1866), page 188 (detail). Children's Literature Research Collections, University of Minnesota Libraries.

eral early complaints that are quoted above) is that Oxford's "printing" of *Alice* in 1865, including the printing of the "pictures," would be seen as more or less "disgraceful" depending on which copy one happened to look at, and which illustrations.

Figures 15.1 and 15.2 show two details of the copy of the Appleton 1866 edition that is held in the Children's Literature Research Collections at the University of Minnesota. Raking illumination throws into relief the embossing of the paper caused by excessive pressure used in printing the other side of the sheet, and also the surface "dirt" that could result. These images are not atypical: other copies of Macmillan 1865 and Appleton 1866 show similar clutter in the background of several illustrations, varying from copy to copy.

Acknowledging that some copies of 1865 were "flawed," and that others were not, Morton Cohen and Edward Wakeling once suggested that "perhaps bad luck played a part in the drama" of the suppressed edition. "Could Tenniel have been sent one of the flawed copies?"[24] I

24. *Lewis Carroll & His Illustrators*, 6.

suspect that is indeed what happened, and that the objectionable flaw was a matter of "dirt" or show-through, a defect of printing that defaced some of Tenniel's illustrations in the particular, unfortunate copy that he was given. If, for example, his copy showed as much dirt on page 1 (the White Rabbit), or page 77 (the Frog-Footman), or page 97 (the Mad Tea Party), as appears in several surviving copies of the Oxford printing, he had good reason to object, and Carroll good reason to honor his objection. Commenting recently on one of the surviving copies of the 1865 edition, Selwyn Goodacre noted that show-through compromising the image of the White Rabbit on page one was "a point that would not have escaped Tenniel's notice."[25]

There were, as we have seen, other flaws than dirt that marred the first edition. Typographical flaws such as a foul case or incidence of widows might be regrettable, but did not affect the pictures. Morris follows Bond in emphasizing faults of tone or shading in the illustrations that were caused by overprinting, incident upon inadequate makeready, and she makes much of the fastidiousness that Tenniel repeatedly showed in this regard as he annotated proofs of wood engravings for Dalziel, invoking a high standard—and implying, perhaps, a low threshold for objection. However, Rodney Engen, Tenniel's other recent biographer, remarked that Tenniel could be indulgent about such matters: "He rarely gave his *Punch* engravings a second glance, never proofed them, and even accepted the poorly printed overall grayness of his early anthology drawings as part of commercial publishing."[26] Indeed, as will be explained below, such regrettable flaws of tone were endemic to the commercial printing of wood engravings, and might well be expected and overlooked, no matter how high were one's standards and hopes. However, the "dirt" that showed in some copies of the 1865 *Alice*—caused by excessive pressure forcing excessive ink through inferior paper—was not to be expected, and was objectionable.

Only when Tenniel criticized the printing of the 1865 *Alice* did Carroll find fault with it: before then, he had been happily inscribing copies to give to friends. He learned a lot about printing from that "fiasco" (as Carroll later called it, more than once); and he continued to be tutored, or hectored, by Tenniel. Carroll's later correspondence with Macmillan is filled with complaints about perceived deficiencies in printing, especially the printing of illustrations. Since Clay continued to be Carroll's printer, most of these faults were blamed on Clay. Print-through was no longer a problem; Clay was not as careless as the Clarendon Press. But adjusting the overall tone of an illustration continued to be a tricky business. Matters approached a crisis once more as Clay began to print the first copies of *Through the Looking-Glass,* in December 1871. Tenniel criticized the results, and Carroll took the matter up with Macmillan, who at first supposed that the problem came from the way that the sheets were being dried after printing, to hasten production for the Christmas market. Carroll responded to Macmillan:

> I have been thinking a good deal about the pictures, and the best way to secure their being really artistically done: I have no doubt that what you told me of, the pressing between sheets of blank paper in order to dry for binding, is the real cause of all the "inequality," which has so vexed Mr. Tenniel in the copies already done: indeed I can see for myself that several of the pictures have in this way quite lost all *brilliance* of effect.

25. Selwyn Goodacre, "One of the Greatest Rarities in the Book World," in *Alice's Adventures in Wonderland: The Extremely Rare 1865 First Edition*, 9, apropos the Kitchen copy, no. 9 in Goodacre's revised census in Schiller (43).

26. Morris, *Artist of Wonderland,* 151–52; Engen, *Sir John Tenniel,* 82.

I have now made up my mind that, whatever be the *commercial* consequences, we must have no more artistic "fiascos." . . . My decision is, we must have *no more hurry,* and *no more sheets must be pressed under blank paper.*[27]

Instead, the necessary time and care should be taken "to give the pictures their full artistic effect." Total sales were a matter of no consequence to Carroll: "the only thing that I *do* care for is, that all the copies that *are* sold shall be artistically first-rate."

Whether the drying process was to blame or not, the objectionable fault is captured in a word that Carroll evidently got from Tenniel: "all the 'inequality,' which has so vexed Mr. Tenniel in the copies already done." In certain printing contexts the term *inequality* denoted unevenness of impression, originally as regards letterpress (caused in part by literal inequality of height in pieces of metal type), and later as regards the printing of wood blocks or electros. In 1839 John Jackson pointed out that a certain kind of "inequality in the impression" was a constant hazard for wood engravings: "an impression from a wood-block, taken by a common press, without overlaying, or any other kind of preparation, is generally lighter in the middle than towards the edges."[28] Some "kind of preparation"—careful makeready: underlaying or overlaying or both—was needed to prevent that. Oxford obviously had neglected or mismanaged such preparation in printing the 1865 *Alice.* Tenniel evidently thought Clay guilty of similar neglect, if not to the same degree, in the first printing of *Looking-Glass,* though Macmillan at first preferred to blame the way that the paper was dried after printing. In any case, makeready and inequality were always matters of concern in printing wood engravings or the electros made from them.

In a subsequent letter, now lost, Carroll must have reported in more detail Tenniel's complaint about the *Looking-Glass* illustrations. Macmillan, in reply, almost lost patience:

> I think Mr Tenniel hardly realizes all the conditions needful for producing a book like Looking-Glass. He gets Bradbury & Evans to print his admirable Cartoons [published each week in *Punch*] in large numbers. But then see how those are cut. I don't suppose that more than one line in five in the same space is given in the Cartoon that is given in Alice.[29]

Here Macmillan may have been speaking from a vague memory of some of Tenniel's *Punch* cartoons, which, occupying a large page, might seem to have large passages of white space; but in fact Swain's cross-hatching for dark areas in the cartoons could be as densely detailed as any similar passage by Dalziel for the *Alice* books. Still, Macmillan's general point holds true: printing wood engravings was a demanding business.

Shortly thereafter Macmillan updated Carroll about how things were going, referencing as he did so another aspect of Tenniel's complaint: "They [Clay] have 6 presses on it . . . using utmost care. I have also got the paper made with less size for those new copies, and I think this will obviate a good deal of the rottenness which Mr. Tenniel complained of."[30] Here "rottenness" is another technical term of the printer's art. It denotes discontinuity in a printed line, which could be caused by a defect in the surface of the wood block (or electro), or by

27. *Lewis Carroll and the House of Macmillan,* 97 (17 January 1871); Carroll's emphasis.

28. Jackson in Chatto 1839, 736.

29. Imholtz, 266 (21 December 1871). See also *Lewis Carroll and the House of Macmillan,* 99n5.

30. Imholtz, 266 (23 December 1871). The almost illegible manuscript word "rottenness" was tentatively rendered as "[*wooliness*]," but Imholtz has since discarded that reading. Clare Imholtz, "Carroll's Publishing History with Macmillan: A Publishing Narrative," *Knight Letter* 100 (Spring 2018): 14–18; 17.

something amiss in the printing, such as inadequate makeready. In this case Macmillan now suggests that the fault was in the preparation of the *paper*—specifically, its sizing. The manufacture of paper for books usually involved incorporating into the rag or wood pulp some organic substance such as starch, which would prevent impressed ink from soaking into the paper. Too little sizing, and the ink would blur—or show through, as in the 1865 *Alice*; too much sizing, and the ink might not fully adhere, breaking up the impression. In printing wood engravings there were several paths that could lead to objectionable *inequality* or *rottenness,* and at one time or another Tenniel's *Alice* illustrations evidently traveled them all.

Carroll remained alert to such vagrancy. In 1893, when the third edition (1887) of *Looking-Glass* was again reprinted (the 60th thousand), he was alarmed by how the pictures looked. Evidently Clay blamed the electrotypes, as excessively worn. Carroll again complained to Macmillan:

> My own suspicion is, now, that Messrs. Clay have been laying on the electrotypes, the blame they ought to have taken on *themselves*: that the electrotypes are *not* worn-out but that the "making-up" for printing had been very carelessly done—probably they did not make new cushions at all, but used the old ones: and these probably got quite dry and hard, and were practically useless.[31]

As a result of his dissatisfaction, Carroll had the entire printing—about a thousand copies—withdrawn from the market—once more making surviving copies scarce collector's items. And, looking back at the 84th thousand of *Alice,* he found similar disappointment, though only in certain illustrations.

Three years later Carroll proposed to Macmillan that fresh editions of both *Alice* books be prepared, "with new type, and new electros of the pictures, and the *better* quality of paper (as originally used)"—books that he hoped would be "fully equal, from an artistic point of view, to the original issue"—adding the doubtful question, "Do you think we may fairly expect this result from Messrs. Clay? I own it is with a rather heavy heart that I contemplate the entrusting so important a task to *them,* but I am much inclined to be guided by *your* opinion."[32]

Receiving a positive response from Macmillan (no other "printer . . . would be likely to do the job better or even so well as Messrs. Clay") Carroll sought assistance from Tenniel, inviting him to approve proofs of the illustrated pages as they were made up. "Certainly," Tenniel replied; "I will do what you wish, in regard to supervising the pictures, with much pleasure: of course everything will depend on the *printing*" (Carroll's somewhat ominous italics—probably quoting Tenniel's).[33]

When Macmillan countered that such an arrangement would be impracticable, and proposed instead that Tenniel merely be sent proofs taken from the new electros, with Clay being held responsible for the results, Carroll angrily recalled Clay's "most discreditable behaviour as to the spoiled 1000 *Looking-Glass,* where he calmly ignored being in *any* degree responsible for the 'fiasco.' . . . 'Once bit, twice shy.' After the heavy money-loss entailed on me by Mr. Clay's misconduct, I cannot afford to run *any* further risks, in dealing with so untrustworthy a man."[34]

31. *Lewis Carroll and the House of Macmillan,* 295 (24 November 1893).

32. *Lewis Carroll and the House of Macmillan,* 340 (27 August 1896).

33. *Lewis Carroll and the House of Macmillan,* 341 (6 September 1896).

34. *Lewis Carroll and the House of Macmillan,* 342 (10 September 1896).

However, after certain negotiations, the details of which are not known, Carroll, Macmillan, and Clay—and Tenniel also?—proceeded with this project, which resulted in the last authorized editions of the *Alice* books that were printed in Carroll's lifetime. They would be reprinted for many years to come.

In Carroll's last recorded letter to Macmillan, written a month before he died, he expressed misgivings about this new edition, "the general look" of which an expert friend had judged to be "*too pale,*" and the ink "not really *black.*"

> He tells me inks differ greatly in blackness. Now Clay, on the other hand, writes that it was the very *best* ink (I presume they mean the *blackest*) they could procure. Do you know of any independent authority—someone who is an undoubtedly good judge of artistic effect—to whom you could submit copies of the books, without telling him of any opinions already given?[35]

So Carroll remained anxious about the printing of Tenniel's *Alice* illustrations until the very end.

TENNIEL AND CARROLL were not the first nor the last observers to find disappointment in the commercial printing of wood engravings. Complaints were made from the dawn of the medium, late in the eighteenth century, until at least a century later. In 1841, on behalf of overworked printers, William Savage complained that wood engravers presented an impossibly high standard for the printing of their work. In effect, they cheated:

> The engravers always show an impression . . . [that] is taken in a manner . . . such as to produce a superior effect to what a printer can with a press, when he has a number to do, which are generally worked in a form with types, and his price so low for printing, as not to enable him to do justice to the subjects. . . . the engraver's proof is obtained by means of a burnisher, with one thickness of paper in addition to that printed on, so that he can examine each part to bring it up where it is required, and leave the others as delicate as he pleases: he thus obtains an impression from the surface only, perfect in all its parts, with the best ink that can be procured; while the printer gives dissatisfaction, because he cannot, in the way of trade, perform impossibilities.[36]

Macmillan could have quoted this paragraph to answer Carroll's complaints about the inferiority of Clay's printing of the illustrations compared to Dalziel's proofs (page 204 above).

As Savage noted, the point had been made before, in one of the first treatises on wood engraving, Jean-Michel's *Traité historique et pratique de la gravure en bois* (1766). And the same apology would be elaborated by Theodore Low De Vinne only a few years after *Looking-Glass* was published. Besides the special deficiencies of electrotypes, detailed in the previous chapter, De Vinne acknowledged a series of problems that hampered commercial printing from any block at all, whether wood block or electro. Paper used for commercial printing was typically inferior to paper used for proofs. Printing on both sides of a sheet risked

35. *Lewis Carroll and the House of Macmillan*, 364 (15 December 1897).

36. William Savage, *A Dictionary of the Art of Printing* (London: Longman, Brown, Green and Longmans, 1841), 214.

print-through. Ink for machine printing had to be more fluid than the best, viscous inks used for proofing. Printing a block on a machine next to letterpress forced the printer to compromise optimum pressure for the block. Mechanical inking with rollers did not permit subtle variations across the surface of the block. Printing machines ran at high speed, printing upwards of a dozen blocks on a sheet, at upwards of 900 sheets per hour. "Four seconds for the print; thirty minutes for the proof."[37] In a later article De Vinne emphasized that "woodcuts made to show light and shade cannot be properly printed without a great deal of pressure"—upwards of "three to ten times as much" as for standing type; also that pressure would have to vary across the surface of a particular cut. Overlays carefully designed and carefully applied by an expert printer could mitigate some of these difficulties; but "there are limits to overlaying and the graduation of irregular pressure." All in all, the printing of wood blocks or electros on commercial presses was a challenging business, doomed to compromise.[38]

Electrotyped wood engravings were *the* mass reproductive medium for images and illustrations for more than half a century in England and the United States. But for De Vinne, a thoroughly experienced printer who valued the highest production standards, they were at best an exasperating challenge, and at worst a nuisance.

Given such practical realities, which occasioned Carroll's habitual fault-finding with Clay's work, it is heartening to note the earnest compliment with which the publisher Henry G. Bohn concluded his preface to the second edition of W. A. Chatto's *A Treatise on Wood Engraving*, the handsomely printed history and manual that registered much of the importance of wood engraving in the nineteenth century, which was lavishly illustrated with fine wood engravings, and which was printed by Richard Clay. "I think it due to Mr. Clay," Bohn remarked, "to acknowledge the attention and skill which he has exercised in 'bringing up' the numerous and somewhat difficult cuts to the agreeable face they now present. A good engraving without good printing is like a diamond without its polish."[39]

Though Bohn does not say so here, the "cuts" that Clay managed so well were probably electrotype replicas, not original wood blocks. As he noted later in the book,

> since the former edition of this work considerable improvements have been made in the mode of taking casts, of which the principal is *electrotyping*, by the galvanic precipitation of copper. By this process all the finer lines of the engraving are so perfectly preserved, that impressions printed from the cast are quite undistinguishable from those printed from the original block.[40]

Bohn (like others before him) may overstate the merits of electrotypes, but he does not exaggerate Clay's skill as a printer of them in difficult circumstances.

37. De Vinne, "Woodcuts," 198.

38. De Vinne, "A Printer on the Limitations of Engraving on Wood; In Three Parts—Conclusion," 95.

39. Henry G. Bohn, preface to Chatto 1861, iv.

40. From a new paragraph about electrotyping (638) that was added, perhaps by Bohn, to Jackson's chapter about the practice of wood engraving, which was reprinted from Chatto 1839.

CHAPTER 16

Coloring

*W*hen Lewis Carroll prepared the gift manuscript of *Alice's Adventures under Ground* for Alice Liddell he wrote the text and drew the illustrations in black ink (now faded to brown) on cream-colored paper.[1] All the illustrations function as black-and-white except for the one near the end that shows the Queen of Hearts in a rage: "'Hold your tongue!' said the Queen." There Carroll added touches of red ink, not to make the Queen's face florid, but to highlight the hearts that ornament her costume. Carroll had already used red ink to rubricate the initial letter and the Roman numeral of each of the chapter headings (<u>C</u>hapter <u>I</u>, <u>C</u>hapter <u>II</u>, <u>C</u>hapter <u>III</u>, and <u>C</u>hapter <u>IV</u>), in a manner consistent with centuries of practice in the production of important manuscripts and printed books. (Single underlining marks characters that Carroll illuminated in red; double underlining, in the next sentence, characters in blue.) When he prepared the title page and dedication page for the manuscript, he rubricated entire words as well as the first initial letter, and inked other words in blue, as well as black: <u>Alice's</u> <u>A</u>dventures under <u>G</u>round; <u>A</u> Christmas <u>G</u>ift to a <u>Dear Child</u> in <u>M</u>emory of a <u>S</u>ummer <u>D</u>ay. All these words are shadowed in gray. Surrounding the inscription on the dedication page Carroll added vignette tendrils in green, enclosing the whole in a double-ruled red Oxford frame. Ivy leaves in olive green also surround the words on the title page, and brighter green leaves ground the purple flowers that ornament the initial letter A. Outside the inner frame, which is made up of bands of the two shades of green, Carroll has used two additional colors, blue and yellow, to complete an outer frame of forget-me-not flowers, which ornament a background stippled in black and punctuated with small red flourishes (Plate 2).

T<small>HE FORGET-ME-NOTS</small> are significant. They are motivated by two mentions in the text, both of which have to do with the pool that was formed

1. Lewis Carroll, *Alice's Adventures under Ground: A Facsimile* (London: The British Library, 2008). "'Alice's Adventures Under Ground,' The Original Manuscript Version of *Alice's Adventures in Wonderland*," https://goo.gl/KR1Ust. Although the British Library describes the manuscript as "written in sepia-coloured ink" it was originally black, now "faded to a brownish colour." Edward Wakeling, "Take Pen & Ink & Write It Down," *Knight Letter* 91 (Fall 2013): 20–22; 20, 22.

by the flood of Alice's tears. "The pool had by this time begun to flow out of the hall, and the edge of it was fringed with rushes and forget-me-nots." "Everything seemed to have changed since her swim in the pool, and her walk along the river-bank with its fringe of rushes and forget-me-nots." When Carroll first told his Alice story to the three Liddell sisters during their boat excursion on the river Isis on 4 July 1862, that river, too, would have been fringed with rushes and forget-me-nots. The very name of the flower asks for lasting attachment—a pretty sentiment for Carroll to extend to his child friend Alice Liddell, who was growing older each year. A reputable Oxford botany, written by a fellow of Magdalen College, rehearsed an explanation for the name that would have given Carroll pause, had he thought about it:

> Two lovers, loitering on the margin of a lake one summer's eve; the maiden desired some flowers of the plant growing close to the bank of an island, at a distance from the shore. The lover plunged into the water, and gathered the wished-for prize. On his return, unable to regain the shore, though very near it, he threw the flowers on the bank, and, as he sank to his watery grave, his last words to the beloved lady were—*Forget-me-not*.[2]

When he finished the manuscript of *Alice's Adventures under Ground* Carroll had made use of nine colors altogether: *white* (the color of the page), *black* (the dominant ink), *red, blue, gray, green* (two shades), *pink, purple,* and *yellow*. Seven of these colors are named directly or indirectly at least once in the text: *white* (eight times—not counting eight more uses to name the white rabbit, who has not yet had his name capitalized); *green* (four); *red* (two—also *crimson*, once); *blue* (one); not *yellow* but *golden* (one—not counting four references to the metal); *grey* (one); and *pink* (one). Not named in the text, although used as pigments on the page, are *black* and *purple*.

Taken together, the color palette and the color nomenclature of Carroll's *Alice* manuscript closely match the colors that have been identified as "the basic colour terms for English . . . white, black, red, green, yellow, blue, brown, grey, purple, pink and orange."[3] This list reduces to a nutshell the ambitious and influential project that was launched in the 1960s by Brent Berlin and Paul Kay to identify cross-cultural linguistic universals thought to govern hierarchically the sequence by which colors accrue to the repertoire of any language. That hierarchy was summarized by I. C. McManus in these terms:

> If a language has only two colour terms these are black and white; if a third is added it is always red, and the fourth and fifth will always be green and yellow, although the order varies in different languages. The sixth term is always blue, and the seventh always brown. Finally, if further basic colour terms are used these will be selected from purple, pink, orange and grey.[4]

The details of this hierarchy have been subjected to criticism and revision since Berlin and Kay first framed their account, but their repertoire of basic color terms in English has been broadly confirmed by studies in corpus linguistics.[5] It is not surprising that, in a story written for a child, Lewis Carroll would largely restrict his color terminology

2. Richard Walker, *The Flora of Oxfordshire and Its Contiguous Counties* (Oxford: Henry Slatter, 1833), 47, citing Charles Mills, *History of Chivalry* (London: Longman, Hurst, Rees, Orme, Brown and Green, 1825).

3. Joris Bleys, *Language Strategies for the Domain of Colour* (Berlin: Language Science Press, 2015), 5.

4. I. C. McManus, "Basic Colour Terms in Literature," *Language and Speech* 26 (1983): 247–52; 247.

5. Brent Berlin and Paul Kay, *Basic Color Terms, Their Universality and Evolution* (Berkeley: University of California Press, 1969); 2nd ed. (1991). Ian C. McManus, "Note: Half-a-Million Basic Colour Words: Berlin and Kay and the Usage of Colour Words in Literature and Science," *Perception* 26 (1997), 367–70; 367–68. Anders Steinvall, "English Colour Terms in Context," Ph.D. dissertation, Umeå Universitet (2002), 67.

to such basic terms. For *crimson* and *golden,* the two outliers in his manuscript, he could appeal to poetic license. "Crimson with fury" was a literary formula for emotion, not a literal descriptor. (So Dickens at one point figured Oliver Twist as "crimson with fury.") "Golden scale," too, has a literary pedigree. Alice's deranged recitation "How doth the little crocodile / Improve its shining tail, / And pour the waters of the Nile / On every golden scale!" echoes a popular translation of Ovid by Laurence Eusden , "He glitter'd soon with many a golden scale, / And his shrunk legs clos'd in a spiry tail."[6] Allowing for these minor exceptions, Carroll's color terminology in *Alice's Adventures under Ground* is pretty basic.

Perhaps more significant is the fact that Carroll does not make much use of such terminology—neither in *Alice's Adventures under Ground* nor in its more developed version, *Alice's Adventures in Wonderland.* This fact is an aspect of the general truth that Carroll does not describe things much in either book, preferring to leave such details to the reader's imagination, if not indeed to the illustrator's imagination. As regards the color of things the reader gets little help from the text, and even less from the illustrator, whether Carroll or Tenniel, who works as an illustrator in black and white.

The textual color information in *Alice's Adventures in Wonderland* is slight. There are eight instances of the word *white* (not counting twenty-two nominal mentions of the White Rabbit, now formally distinguished with capital initials); four of *green;* three of *red;* now two of *crimson* (the King's crown rests on "a crimson velvet cushion"); two of *brown* (a basic color term missing from *Under Ground*); and one each of *golden* (substituting for yellow), *pink, grey,* and *purple.* Two basic color terms are still not used: *black,* and *orange.* The empty jar labeled "ORANGE MARMALADE" that Alice does briefly hold near the start of her adventures in both versions of the story names not a color but a kind of fruit. Still, orange marmalade is *orange* in color; perhaps it should be counted, leaving *black* as the one color in deficit.

Although the basic color terms can thus be largely accounted for, they are not much used in *Wonderland,* and no other color terms are used there. Altogether colors are named some thirty times in a book that is more than 26,000 words long—not a highly colored story. We are not even told what color dress Alice wears. For such information we have to wait for Carroll's next version of that story, *The Nursery "Alice"* (1890), which Tenniel again illustrated, this time in color.

In the Preface to *The Nursery "Alice,"* which is "ADDRESSED TO ANY MOTHER," Carroll states that the book itself is addressed to "Children aged from Nought to Five"—but not for them to read, for they are assumed to be "illiterate, ungrammatical." Instead, he expects the book "to be thumbed, to be cooed over, to be dogs'-eared, to be rumpled, to be kissed" by them. The actual reading would be done aloud by the mother, or someone substituting for her. The mother's voice would merge with that of the narrator, who frequently addresses the child directly, quizzing it about what it knows and expects, and directing its attention to the pictures for information about what things look like in the story.

The very title of the book privileged Tenniel's pictures over Carroll's text: *The Nursery "Alice" Containing Twenty Coloured Enlargements from Tenniel's Illustrations to "Alice's Adventures in Wonderland" with Text*

6. *The Works of the English Poets from Chaucer to Cowper,* ed. Alexander Chalmers, 21 vols. (London, 1810), 20:461.

Adapted to Nursery Readers by Lewis Carroll. That priority acknowledged not only the peremptory power of illustrations in general but also the chronological priority of Tenniel's pictures over this version of Carroll's text.[7] Tenniel colored the twenty illustrations for Carroll in 1885 (who selected them?), but Carroll did not begin to write the corresponding text until 1888.[8] In many ways *The Nursery "Alice"* would be a picture book.

Carroll greatly abridged and simplified Alice's adventures to fit them within *The Nursery "Alice"*—only about one-fourth as long as the previous book, using a more restricted vocabulary (not quite 1000 different words—some 800 fewer than in *Wonderland*). The color terminology here is only slightly reduced: twenty-eight mentions of colors (not counting eleven of the White Rabbit), not much down from thirty; but these color terms are reduced to six only, all quite basic: *red* (ten times), *white* (seven), *pink* (four), *green* (three), *blue* (three), and *brown* (one). For detailed color information, such as the color of Alice's dress, it is necessary to look at the pictures—which were reduced in number from forty-two to twenty.

The pictures in *The Nursery "Alice"* were, as advertised on the title page, "enlargements" of those originally used in *Alice's Adventures in Wonderland*—perhaps pantographically or photographically enlarged—to befit the larger page size of the new book (10 × 7.75 inches). They were also altered in some significant details, especially the trimmer style of Alice's dress.[9] Complex cross-hatching in backgrounds was replaced by plain patches of color. John Tenniel hand-colored the revised images, which served as models for reproduction. He was a skilled watercolorist, in 1874 admitted to membership in the Institute of Painters in Water Colours. Five *Alice* illustrations colored by Tenniel (White Rabbit, Cheshire Cat, Ugly Duchess, Terrier, and the flying pack of cards) were exhibited at the Carroll Centenary in London in 1932.[10] It is not known whether they were colored in preparation for *The Nursery "Alice,"* and none is reported in Schiller's recent "Census." Nor is either of two inked and watercolored illustrations, of the *Wonderland* frontispiece and of Bill the Lizard, which Goodacre once saw in a private collection, both "signed on the back by Dodgson, and in brown ink on the pictures in the usual Tenniel monogram." Their colors closely matched those in the second, preferred printing of *The Nursery "Alice."*[11]

Tenniel's colored models were sent to Edmund Evans, the leading color printer of the day, who was especially renowned for his work with children's books. Evans engraved multiple wood blocks for each illustration, each block adding a different ink color to each stage of printing—with each overlaid impression carefully registered in the printing (a delicate task), contributing its share to the fully realized color image.[12]

Proofs of the multiple blocks used to print the image of Alice upsetting the jury box survive at the Houghton Library at Harvard; each print is labeled and numbered in pencil with the name of the color that was used: "Brown 1" (the base color), "Pink 2," "Blue 3," "Buff 4" (a kind of yellow), "Red 5," "Light Grey 6," and "Dark Grey 7" (noted as "Complete").[13] The disturbed lizard in the center of the picture was mostly blue at stage 3, with a pinkish-brown underbelly, until overprinting with the buff/yellow ink at stage 4 changed the blue to green. Orange similarly resulted from overprinting buff/yellow with pink or red (the White Rabbit wears an orange jacket with a red handkerchief in its left pocket, over a yellow waistcoat). Purple is largely absent, unless it, instead of

7. Morton N. Cohen, "Another Wonderland: Lewis Carroll's *The Nursery 'Alice,"' The Lion and the Unicorn,* 7/8 (1983–84): 120–26; 120, 122.

8. *Diaries,* 8:181 (29 March 1885), 439 (28 December 1888); *Lewis Carroll and the House of Macmillan,* 191 (8 July 1885).

9. Brian Sibley reports some of these changes in "The Nursery 'Alice' Illustrations," *Jabberwocky* 4 (1975), 92–95.

10. Madan, 100, nos. 602, 603.

11. Selwyn H. Goodacre, "The Nursery 'Alice': A Bibliographical Essay," *Jabberwocky* 4 (1975): 100–19; 101.

12. *The Reminiscences of Edmund Evans,* ed. Ruari McLean (Oxford: Clarendon Press, 1967). Ruari McLean, *Victorian Book Design and Colour Printing* (Berkeley: University of California Press, 1972), 156, 178–88. John R. McNair, "Chromolithography and Color Woodblock: Handmaidens to Nineteenth-Century Children's Literature." *Children's Literature Association Quarterly* 11 (1986): 193–97.

13. Without consulting these proofs Ruari McLean identified the same seven colors used in printing the pictures, though he named them differently: "red, flesh tint, blue, yellow, pale-grey, blue-grey, and brown." Reported by Goodacre in "The Nursery 'Alice,'" 109.

grey, tinges the flecked ermine that lines and decorates the costumes of the Queen and King of Hearts. Take the "Buff" ink as yellow, the "Dark Grey" as black, and the "Light Grey" as grey, and the resulting palette is: *white* (the paper), *black, pink, blue, yellow, red, grey, orange, brown,* and, perhaps, *purple*—the basic color terms in English.

As colored by Tenniel and printed by Evans, however, certain tones strongly dominate: red, brown, and olive green. The text names *red* more often than any other color, and the pictures comply. Shades of red dominate the frontispiece (Plate 3): the drapery behind the King and Queen of Hearts on their elevated thrones, and the drapery hung below that platform; the bright red outer cloak of the King and pantaloons, belt, and sleeve gore of the Knave of Hearts; the red hearts on the costumes of the White Rabbit and an armed guard—and the King's face, a bright pink, contrasting with his pale hands and his wife's face and hands.

THAT CONTRAST of complexions is not figured in the text of *Wonderland,* which merely remarks the King's discomfort: "The judge, by the way, was the King; and as he wore his crown over the wig, (look at the frontispiece if you want to see how he did it,) he did not look at all comfortable, and it was certainly not becoming." This remark is expanded in *The Nursery "Alice"* without explaining why the King is so red in the face:

> Now, if you look at the big picture, at the beginning of this book, you'll see what a grand thing a trial is, when the Judge is a King!
> The King is very grand, *isn't* he? But he doesn't look very *happy.* I think that big crown, on the top of his wig, must be *very* heavy and uncomfortable. But he had to wear them *both,* you see, so that people might know he was a Judge *and* a King. (50)

Matters are more subtly managed in a hand-colored frontispiece tipped into a regular copy of *Alice's Adventures in Wonderland* (Macmillan, 1866), once owned by Harcourt Amory and now in the Houghton Library, which may have been colored by Tenniel—perhaps in preparation for *The Nursery "Alice"* (Plate 4).[14] There the King's face is a light shade of pink, suggesting some discomfort appropriate under the awkward circumstances, but not indignation. If that is the effect that Tenniel wanted, Evans did not deliver it.

In *The Nursery "Alice"* garden scene (Plate 5) the royal facial colorations are quite reversed: the King's physiognomy looks as normal as Alice's, but the Queen's face is fully red: "crimson with fury," as she was described at this moment in *Wonderland,* but simply, and rather inadequately, "angry," here.

WHEN CARROLL saw copies of the first printing of *The Nursery "Alice"* he wrote to Macmillan and canceled it:

> The pictures are *far* too bright and gaudy, and vulgarise the whole thing. *None must be sold in England*: to do so would be to sacrifice whatever reputation I now have for giving the public the *best* I can. Mr. Evans must begin again, and print 10,000 *with Tenniel's coloured pictures*

14. "A frontispiece, colored evidently under Tenniel's direction for 'Nursery Alice,' is inserted," according to Livingston, 14. Here Livingston follows a surmise that Amory penciled onto the verso of the front flyleaf in 1915: "The colored frontispiece evidently done under Tenniel's direction for the new edition of 'The Nursery Alice'—which see." The image is a regular frontispiece from an early edition of *Wonderland,* not something enlarged and altered for *The Nursery "Alice."* Assuming that Tenniel colored it, he may have done so as a preliminary trial—or after the fact.

The notion that the coloring of the pictures for *The Nursery "Alice"* was done not by Tenniel but "under Tenniel's direction" was aired by Martin Gardner in his introduction to the facsimile edition of *The Nursery "Alice"* published by Dover Publications (New York) in 1966, though without mentioning Livingston or Amory (vii). Sibley discredited it (92), without mentioning Gardner; seconded by Goodacre, "The Nursery 'Alice,'" 101. See also note 7 above and Carroll's letter of 23 June 1889 quoted below.

One conspicuous difference between the hand-colored frontispiece (1866 or later) and the *Nursery "Alice"* frontispiece (1890) is the insignia worn by the guard at the upper right: black Clubs in 1866, but red Hearts in 1890.

before him: and I must *see* all the proofs this time: and then we shall have a book really fit to offer to the public.[15]

Like the suppressed 1865 *Alice,* this rejected printing was off-loaded to America.[16] Successive printings published in England evidently satisfied Carroll, although none was as subtle in its tones as the Amory frontispiece.

Many of Evans's blocks for The Nursery *"Alice,"* along with black-ink proofs taken from them at some point, survive in the collection of The Newberry Library in Chicago. The blocks for the Tenniel illustrations are "key" blocks only, that is, those used in the first color impression; supplementary blocks for each of these images are not included in this collection. However, the drawing of the White Rabbit by Carroll's friend E. Gertrude Thomson, which was used to decorate the back cover of the book, is represented by five wood blocks, each cut for a different color.

Thomson also designed the front cover, which synthesizes several scenes in the story as the content of a dream that hovers above a sleeping Alice. Next to Alice, lying open on the ground, is a book that she has been reading, which displays full-page colored illustrations left and right, with the verso of a leaf, apparently letterpress (ideally conversations to supplement the pictures), showing between them. Blocks for that front-cover image are not included in the Newberry collection. I have been told that the St. Bride Foundation in London holds a large collection of blocks from Edmund Evans's workshop, which have yet to be catalogued; perhaps some blocks from The Nursery *"Alice"* will turn up among them.

AND ALICE'S DRESS? What color? The text does not say. Tenniel made it gold, to match Alice's hair (the color of which the text does not specify, either), though with blue accents: a blue border on her white pinafore covering the front of her dress and her shoulders, a large blue bow or ruffle tied behind her, matching blue stockings and a matching hairband tied in a bow. Thomson follows suit for the front cover, though with fewer blue accents: we see a white pinafore worn over a golden dress, with blue stockings, and a glimpse of the blue hair band bow. Tenniel's color scheme appears also in two *Alice* products that Carroll or Macmillan authorized, *The "Wonderland" Postage-Stamp-Case* (1890), and the *Wonderland* playing cards published by De la Rue with guidance from Gertrude Thomson (c. 1900).[17]

In 2010 Mark Burstein pointed out that Macmillan first showed Tenniel's Alice in a blue dress in 1903, when it published a small-format condensation titled *Alice's Adventures in Wonderland, Adapted for Very Little Folks from the Original Story by Lewis Carroll, with Thirty-two Coloured Illustrations by Sir John Tenniel* (1903). Judging from Macmillan's 2016 facsimile reprint of the Little Folks edition of *Looking-Glass* (1903), the dress was blue in that sequel also. Burstein also noted that in the second edition of the Little Folks version of *Wonderland* (1907), the dress has turned from blue to red; and so it appears in Macmillan's parallel *Looking-Glass* facsimile (2016), which is based on that second edition.

In 1911 Macmillan published a combined edition of the two *Alice* books that included sixteen colored plates after Tenniel, supplement-

15. *Lewis Carroll and the House of Macmillan,* 257 (23 June 1889).

16. For an account of the unusually complex history of the several printings of this book see Goodacre, "The Nursery 'Alice.'"

17. Mark Burstein, "Am I Blue?" *Knight Letter* 85 (Winter 2010): 27–30; see also his forward to Catherine Nichols, *Alice's Wonderland: A Visual Journey Through Lewis Carroll's Mad, Mad World* (New York: Race Point Publishing, 2014), vii–viii. "Beyond Wonderland: Wonderland Stamp Case," https://goo.gl/G2wwVv. Selwyn Goodacre, "The De La Rue Alice Card Game," *Jabberwocky* 22:3 (Summer 1993): 28–33.

ing and indeed upstaging the other, black-and-white illustrations. The artist who colored the plates, not credited at the time, was Harry G. Theaker (1891–1938), a design instructor and administrator at Regent Street Polytechnic, London.[18] Burstein sees Theaker's Alice as dressed in blue, so strengthening what was becoming the dominant tradition. Recently issued Macmillan editions of the *Alice* books reproduce Theaker's plates, supplemented by the other Tenniel illustrations as colored by the contemporary children's-literature artist Diz Willis. These books appeared in different editions, in 1995 and 1996, and 2015, and the editorial matter that accompanied them saw the Theaker plates differently.[19] In 1995 and 1996: Theaker's images "were the first pictures to establish the enduring image of Alice in her lilac [sic] dress and stripy stockings" (Publisher's Note, n.p.). In 2015: Theaker's images "were the first to establish the enduring image of Alice in her blue dress and stripy stockings" (Publisher's Note, 466). What's the difference? Generally in the original Theaker plates the dress does look blue, but sometimes the blue has a lavender tinge, and in a few of the *Looking-Glass* plates—especially the ones that show Alice and the White Knight in the forest, and Alice disrupting the table at the end—blue is the color of Alice's hair band, back-bow, and stockings, but her dress is a lighter, contrasting shade of lilac. Macmillan's several reprints of the Theaker plates mute this lilac aspect, despite the editorial remark quoted above. (And Willis's coloring of the images that Theaker left untouched, as printed in these recent volumes, strongly favors blue.)

Eight years after Theaker's plates first appeared in print, the musical comedy *Irene,* written by James Montgomery and Joseph McCarthy, with music composed by Harry Tierney, opened on Broadway to enjoy an unprecedented run. "Alice Blue Gown" was the musical hit of the first act. The first stanza, about the loss of innocence, went:

> I once had a gown, it was almost new,
> Oh, the daintiest thing, it was sweet Alice Blue;
> With little forget-me-nots placed here and there,
> When I had it on,—I walked on the air.
> And it wore, and it wore, and it wore,——
> Till it went and it wasn't no more.[20]

"Alice Blue" here referenced not the color of Carroll's Alice's dress (despite the "little forget-me-nots placed here and there") but rather a dress fabric and color that had been made famous by Alice Lee Roosevelt, later Alice Roosevelt Longworth, the pampered and independent daughter of president Theodore Roosevelt, who at one time or another in the first decade of the twentieth century displayed a gown made of a fabric dyed a color soon popularized as "Alice blue"—"a light greenish-blue colour" (*OED*). The reinforcing vogues of Alice Roosevelt's signature color and Irene's waltz can only have increased the likelihood that Alice's dress would be blue.

Certainly that was the color that Fritz Kredel chose when he was commissioned to color the Tenniel illustrations for a handsomely produced and popular gift-box edition of the two *Alice* books that Random House published in New York late in 1946. In both books Alice's dress is a bold blue, both in and out of her dreams, except for the interval near the end of *Looking-Glass,* when she assumes the dignity of Queen

18. "Harry George Theaker," *Mapping the Practice and Profession of Sculpture in Britain and Ireland 1851–1951,* https://goo.gl/Nzr1Rj. That same year, 1911, Macmillan published Theaker's illustrations for the *Ingoldsby Legends,* including fifteen color plates. Most of his later illustrated books were children's books published by Ward, Lock & Co.

19. *Alice's Adventures in Wonderland* (London: Macmillan Children's Books, 1995). *Through the Looking-Glass and What Alice Found There* (London: Macmillan Children's Books, 1996). *The Complete Alice,* foreword by Philip Pullman (London: Macmillan Children's Books, 2015). Between 1911 and the recent Theaker revival Macmillan also issued, in 1927, a "Children's Edition" of *Alice's Adventures* and *Looking-Glass,* which included fifteen and twelve colored plates, respectively; these books were often reprinted in later years.

20. Harry Tierney, James Montgomery, and Joseph McCarthy, *Irene: A Musical Comedy in Two Acts* (London: Francis, Day & Hunter, 1920), 11–13.

Alice—a transition that Tenniel marks by fashioning a more adult dress for her, which Kredel renders as white, just touched with light blue shadows. A confident colophon at the end of this volume (echoing a similar one at the end of *Wonderland*) reads, in part, "*This edition of* THROUGH THE LOOKING-GLASS *was designed by George Salter. The John Tenniel illustrations from the original edition were colored in the manner of the period by Fritz Kredel.*"

George Salter, who was born in Bremen, Germany, in 1897, was a successful stage designer before he taught and administered at the Municipal Graphic Arts Academy in Berlin—a situation that he gave up in 1934 to move to New York, where he quickly became an influential designer of book covers and dust jackets, working closely with Alfred A. Knopf and Random House. Fritz Kredel, three years younger than Salter, also fled Germany for New York in 1938, where he reestablished his career as a prolific and highly respected book illustrator.[21] In a retrospective letter, now untraced, Kredel is said to have remarked, "I never saw the 'Nursery Alice' but it would interest me, of course, very much."[22] He probably would have been surprised by Alice's yellow dress.

Was Kredel's coloring "in the manner of the period"? Mid-Victorian publishers did not typically issue such books with hand-colored wood engravings. Hand-colored copperplate engravings or etchings had brightened many books with limited print runs in preceding decades, indeed for more than a century, and technological advances made direct color printing from wood engravings possible from the 1850s on; but black-and-white wood engravings used to illustrate books would be published just as they were first printed, in black and white. In that respect Kredel's fine work was belated, anachronistic. His watercolor washes tend to pale pastels, as if reluctant to challenge—willing to acknowledge—the dominant black lines of the engravings (e.g., Plate 6).

Some of his color choices were subtly effective—as when he rendered the squares of the chess-board landscape in *Looking-Glass* in alternating tones of green and golden yellow, distinguishing unharvested from harvested parcels of land (Plate 7).

Salter admired that result enough to repeat it as a vignette anchoring his title page for the book, previewing the game to come. (Full disclosure: my copy of this boxed set was given to me by my parents when I was about Alice's age.)

Kredel exercised less restraint when he hand-colored twelve of the Tenniel engravings for an abridged version of *Alice* that Nelson Doubleday in Garden City, New York, issued in 1958 as part of a forty-two-volume series, *Best in Children's Books*.[23] Conforming to the economical house style, he also highlighted twenty-two other illustrations to that story with monochromatic patches—crimson for this story. Each of the dozen multicolored illustrations is given a full page, and in that larger space Kredel allows himself to apply bold primary colors with convincing effect. Alice's dress is, of course, again blue, now solid blue. More subtle is Kredel's use of white for the drapery and tablecloth in the trial-scene frontispiece, which brings the other colors forward and makes for a brighter scene than what Tenniel imagined (Plate 8; cf. Plates 3, 4).[24]

21. For a comprehensive bibliography of Kredel's work see Ronald Salter, *Fritz Kredel: Das buchkünstlerische Werk in Deutschland und Amerika* (Rudolstadt: Burgart-Presse, 2003).

22. Charles C. Lovett and Stephanie B. Lovett, *Lewis Carroll's Alice: An Annotated Checklist of the Lovett Collection* (Westport, CT: Meckler, 1990), 213.

23. *Best in Children's Books,* 12 (Garden City, NY: Nelson Doubleday, 1958), 1–66.

24. Kredel's frontispiece to the Random House edition of *Alice's Adventures* (discussed above) had used white to similar effect, but the pastel colors employed there are less vivid.

WHEN THE DESIGNERS of Walt Disney's animated version of *Alice in Wonderland* (1951) chose blue for Alice's dress they confirmed an orthodoxy so persistent that it even controlled Tim Burton's first movie for Disney, *Alice in Wonderland* (2010), though he did stray from it in the second, *Alice Through the Looking-Glass* (2016), at one point assigning Alice a dress of many colors.

Coloring books recently regained popularity, and *Alice* coloring books have been popular for some time. Although artistic license would seem to define the genre, the coloring book that The Walt Disney Studios issued to accompany its movie in 1951 began with colored samples or models to follow, based on the movie. (Alice of course wears blue.) An ambivalent note on the inside front cover explains the advantages: "Some parts of the outline pictures are already colored. This will suggest ways to complete the pictures and yet leave the young artist free to use his own experience and imagination."[25]

When Macmillan Children's Books published *Alice's Adventures in Wonderland: A Colouring Book* in 2015 it, too, betrayed some ambivalence about the freedom of the artist. The inside fold of the front cover gamely declares, "the iconic illustrations in this book . . . invite you to be playful and imaginative as you explore scenes from the classic book and colour them in however you choose." However, the last page of the book draws attention to the "new image of Alice" that Harry Theaker devised for Macmillan in 1911, "wearing a blue dress and stripy stockings"—the image which "is the one most recognized as *the iconic Alice.*" So, we are further told, in 1995 Diz Wallis was commissioned "to create coloured versions of the rest of Tenniel's original artwork, following *the classic colours established by Theaker*" (emphases added). Enough to give a colorer pause.

The book is handsomely produced, but also over-designed; it is tightly bound, several pages are more black than white, and ornamental borders and patterns often overwhelm the images. The heavily sized paper does not invite a crayon, although a felt pen would work.

If I wanted to color a Tenniel coloring book, and it were still in print, I would buy *The Colorful Alice in Wonderland,* published by Determined Productions in San Mateo, California, in 1961. Printed on absorbent paper in a large format (14.5 × 20 in.), in a perfect binding with the verso pages left blank, the Tenniel illustrations are bold, uncluttered even by text, and ready to be colored. The title page gives unconfining instructions: "Here is the magic Alice in Wonderland for you to color and paint. You will want to tear out the pages and frame them . . . they make wonderful wallpaper, too . . . or send them to someone you like very much."

In some respects the question of how to color the *Alice* books merely intensifies the general question of how to illustrate Alice's stories—or any story, for that matter. If it is true that any narrative or verbal description will under-determine any visualization of the text (and Carroll's discreet descriptions do demonstrate that general truth), it is also true that any pictorial representation will over-determine the scene represented by the text, to the potential annoyance of the writer, or the reader, or both. The additional detail that color brings to any illustration can easily be criticized as unmotivated or peremptory, or both.

25. Bob Grant, *Walt Disney's Alice in Wonderland Coloring Book* (New York: Simon and Schuster, 1951).

Some people sometimes dream, or say they dream, in black and white; other people, or the same people at other times, dream in color, or say they do. Alice's dreams, as reported by their narrator, are only occasionally colorful; most of the time Tenniel's black-and-white style serves them well. Although Tenniel long earned a comfortable living as a master of that style he did earn distinction for another kind of accomplishment, achieving membership in what eventually became the Royal Institute of Painters in Water Colours. It would not have been out of keeping for Alice, too, to dream in color, more than her narrator knew.

CHAPTER 17

Reengraving

One of several major projects that were launched to celebrate Lewis Carroll's centenary in 1932 was the publication of a special edition of *Alice's Adventures in Wonderland* by the Limited Editions Club in New York. Founded by George H. Macy in 1929, the Limited Editions Club published classic texts by subscription in deluxe editions that were usually limited to 1500 copies—a number not very limited, but sufficiently profitable. The usual price for a copy was $10 (roughly $170 today). Advertisements identified the audience for these books as men and women who wished to display their literate good taste and, by implication, their considerable social status. The advertisement for the *Alice* edition that appeared in *The New York Times* on 25 September 1932 was accompanied by testimonials from subscribers that spoke to this aspect: "the membership offers me the chance for 'appreciation' so desirable nowadays and so difficult of attainment"; "the presence in one's library of a complete set of these books is, in a sense, a badge of respectability."[1]

Little of the cost of producing these books went to their authors, most of them being dead, and their texts safely out of copyright. Instead, Macy paid contemporary artists, designers, and typographers to produce books of real distinction. Although machine-made in the modern way, not printed on a hand press from hand-set type, they were handsome books, and collectible.

Macy made his edition of *Alice* particularly collectible by persuading Alice Hargreaves, née Alice Liddell, who was approaching eighty years of age, to sign her name on sheets that were bound into many copies of the book. "The original Alice" crossed the Atlantic to participate in the much-publicized centenary celebration that was held at Columbia University in New York in 1932; the new edition of her book was timed to benefit from that celebration. Indeed, arrangements were made for Alice to sign the sheets during her visit to New York.[2]

1. Megan L. Benton highlights this aspect of the Limited Editions Club, though not this ad, in *Beauty and the Book: Fine Editions and Cultural Distinction in America* (New Haven: Yale University Press, 2000), 225–28.

2. "Alice," *The Monthly Letter of the Limited Editions Club* 40 (September 1932): 3. George Macy to Frederic Warde, 26 April 1932: "Mrs. Hargreaves arrives on Friday, and we ought to have the sheet ready for her signature, since she will only stay two weeks." George Macy papers, Harry Ransom Humanities Research Center, The University of Texas at Austin.

From a collector's standpoint a copy that Alice signed became one of the most desirable books published by the Limited Editions Club (referred to below as LEC). When such a copy comes to market it usually realizes several thousand dollars—roughly ten times what a copy that she did not sign would sell for.

Usually Macy commissioned distinguished artists—such as Matisse, Picasso, Thomas Hart Benton, and Rockwell Kent—to supply new illustrations for his books, which enhanced their appeal. *Alice* was a different case. There was no point in commissioning someone to do new illustrations of the book; that had been done already, many times, after Carroll's copyright lapsed in 1907, and there was no need for yet another novelty. Tenniel's illustrations were generally acknowledged to be an essential part of the book: they could not be replaced. But they could be treated with appropriate respect, and thereby improved upon.

The *New York Times* display ad quoted above just touches, somewhat mysteriously, upon that aspect: the book "has the original illustrations by Tenniel, all carefully cut in wood especially for this edition after the *original drawings*." The repetition of "original" perhaps protests too much. Macy did not have access to "the original drawings." He did, in a mediated way, have access to "the original illustrations."

The designer and general editor of the LEC *Alice* was Frederic Warde, a distinguished typographer and book designer who had served as director of printing at Princeton University Press and then worked closely with William Edwin Rudge, who printed several titles for the Limited Editions Club. Today Warde is best remembered for the italic typeface Arrighi, which he designed under the supervision of Stanley Morison, and also for his marriage to Beatrice Warde, a skilled typographical historian who, as publicity manager for the Monotype Corporation, was an effective advocate for Morison's modern design aesthetic.

On 15 September 1931 Warde wrote to Macy, providing cost estimates for the production of *Alice's Adventures,* including two possible scenarios for the illustrations, the preferred one involving the preparation of fresh woodcuts ($600) and electrotypes ($80), and the less expensive one involving line-cuts (photo-engravings; $200). In both cases there would also be an expense of $80 to take photographs of the forty-two illustrations—presumably from a copy of an early edition of *Alice.*[3]

Two days later Macy agreed to move the project forward. He authorized Warde to commission the new wood engravings from "your correspondent in Germany" for $600 (roughly $10,000 today), and also addressed the questions of electrotyping and photography. "I am surprised that you want to have electrotypes made, since I thought the woodcuts would be available for printing." As regards photographs, Macy assumed that they would be made at "the Library"—the New York Public Library, which owned copies of several early editions of *Alice.* He had spoken to Philip Hofer, who was Keeper of the Spencer Collection there, and recommended that Warde allow him to make the necessary arrangements, at a lower cost.[4]

The artisan whom Warde had selected to make the new wood engravings from those photographs—Warde's "correspondent in Germany"—was Bruno Rollitz, of Berlin, who was virtually unknown in the United States at the time, and is hardly recognized today. He was, however, an extraordinarily accomplished wood engraver, in an era when

3. *Believe Me, I Am: Selected Letters of Frederic Warde, 1921–1939,* ed. Simon Loxley (Lavenham, Eng.: Lavenham Press, 2015), 173–74.

4. George Macy to Frederic Warde, 17 September 1931; Harry Ransom Humanities Research Center, The University of Texas at Austin. Regarding Hofer's role at the Spencer Collection see William Bentinck-Smith, "Prince of the Eye: Philip Hofer and the Harvard Library," *Harvard Library Bulletin* 32 (1984): 317–47; 335–36.

FIGURE 17.1. Bruno Rollitz. Self-portrait. Wood engraving. *Gebrauchsgraphik* 6:1 (January 1929).

wood engraving had completely lapsed from the field of commercial book manufacture (displaced by cheaper "process" technology) and had taken refuge in the ateliers of fine printers. Most of his work was done for the Officina Serpentis, a press in Berlin that produced genuinely limited editions of the highest quality.[5] A case in point is the hand-printed edition (limited to 265 copies) of Dante's *Divina Commedia* published in 1925, beautifully produced with illustrations engraved on wood by Rollitz after celebrated drawings by Sandro Botticelli, with rubricated initials engraved by Rollitz after designs by Hanns Thaddäus Hoyer. Though virtually unknown in the United States, Rollitz was accustomed to illustrate and ornament books that were finer than those published by the Limited Editions Club. For a period during the 1920s Warde worked closely with Hans (Giovanni) Mardersteig, who produced choice books in limited editions at the Officina Bodoni in Switzerland, and it may be that Warde became acquainted with Rollitz's work at that time.

An engraved self-portrait of Rollitz at work at his bench, peering with one eye through a magnifying cylinder at the carving under way, profiled before a crowded bookcase, many wood-engraving tools at hand, was published in 1929 (fig. 17.1), along with a bookplate that he had engraved for Max Berti Lorusch.[6] Rollitz also carved a portrait of Marcus Behmer intent on *his* work as a wood engraver, in the same pose and posture, in similar surroundings, lit much the same.[7]

Why did Warde bother to have the Tenniel illustrations reengraved? As a matter of course the Limited Editions Club reprinted texts but

5. Arnulf Backe and Hedda Köppen, "Die Officina Serpentis," *Philobiblon* 39:2 (1995): 94–169.

6. "Der Holzschneider | The Wood Engraver | Bruno Rollitz," *Gebrauchsgraphik* 6:1 (January 1929): 43.

7. The Miriam and Ira D. Wallach Division of Art, Prints and Photographs, New York Public Library; accessible at https://goo.gl/PrXEVa.

not illustrations; the artwork that made a book especially attractive had to be new. Although Tenniel's illustrations, an essential part of *Alice,* were not new, they could be made new by commissioning an artist to renew them. A subscriber to the Limited Editions Club would expect a contemporary artist to be involved in the production of the book, and Bruno Rollitz would be that artist. Such was the unstated rationale.

Macy's stated rationale was different, and alluded to the demerits of electrotyping and Tenniel's notorious dissatisfaction with the results:

> The same electrotypes were used year after year in making reprint after reprint of that book. Never were Tenniel's illustrations reproduced so excellently that it might be felt he would be satisfied with them although, in the Christmas season of 1896, Macmillan issued a new edition in London, with a new preface explaining that the type had been reset and new electrotypes had been made. Never were the original wood-cuts used.[8]

Ambitious "to arrange for the proper printing of the Tenniel illustrations for the first time," Macy and Warde turned "to Bruno Rollitz in Berlin, a wood-cutter famed throughout Central Europe." Warde sent him "a series of fine prints of the original electrotypes" (presumably the photographs that Hofer had made of the illustrations in a copy of some early edition in the New York Public Library), "and Herr Rollitz proceeded to cut all of the Tenniel illustrations, lovingly and faithfully, into new wood-blocks. . . . This occupied him for nine months of joyous but continuous labor."

As we have seen, Warde's budget for this project included the cost of making electrotypes from Rollitz's blocks—a provision that puzzled Macy, who in the passage quoted above implicitly discredits the early Macmillan editions because they were not printed from "the original wood-cuts." A subscriber who read this *Monthly Letter* might suppose that the LEC *Alice* would be printed directly from Rollitz's own lovingly crafted wood blocks,[9] but it is not certain that that was the case. Electrotypes must have been made at some point to facilitate the reuse of the Rollitz engravings, such as will be documented below; and they may have been made and put to use at the outset.

Thirty-eight of Rollitz's forty-two wood blocks for *Alice* survive in the Robert B. Haas Family Arts Library at Yale University. They are accompanied there by a bound set of prints that were made from them by the firm of A. Colish, Inc., in 1979, when it was mistakenly believed that they were the original Dalziel wood blocks.[10] Close comparison of those wood blocks, the prints that Colish made from them, and the illustrations that were printed in the Macmillan 1866 *Alice* make clear that Rollitz had marvellous skill as a facsimile wood engraver. In virtually every detail, line-by-line, Rollitz replicates the look of the early Dalziel engravings—or, rather, the details of (photographs of) published prints made from electrotypes of those engravings—even including the particular configuration of the "Dalziel Sc" signature in each engraving. In most cases it is hard to tell the difference between a Rollitz illustration in 1932 and a Dalziel illustration in 1866. When *The Saturday Review of Literature* reviewed the LEC *Alice* it tersely alluded to the uncanny accuracy of Rollitz's work: "In this new edition Mr. Warde has printed the book as it ought to have been printed in the sixties, and to complete the

8. "Alice," *The Monthly Letter of the Limited Editions Club* 40 (September 1932), 1.

9. Such a supposition would be reinforced by "The Looking-Glass," *The Monthly Letter of the Limited Editions Club* 71 (April 1935): 1–4; 1: "Immediately upon the issue of this first edition, Lewis Carroll recalled the entire printing. The illustrations were drawn to be cut on wood. But they were never reproduced from the wood blocks. The wood blocks were cast into moulds and the editions were printed from electrotypes. Every subsequent edition was printed from electrotypes; despite Carroll's suppression of the first printing, subsequent editions were made from the same electrotypes. John Tenniel's illustrations for *Alice in Wonderland* were never properly printed. Until when? Until The Limited Edition Club issued its own edition, in 1932."

10. *Illustrations by John Tenniel for Lewis Carroll's Alice in Wonderland Engraved in Wood by the Dalziel Brothers, London, 1865* (A. Colish, Inc., "one copy printed directly from the original wood engravings for the Yale University Library, December 1979").

illusion he has had Tenniel's drawings reengraved by a diabolically clever German wood engraver."[11] The painstaking project of replication was a *tour de force,* which must have given Rollitz some satisfaction, if not joy.

At least he was proud enough to sign his work, almost invisibly, in minuscule block letters that he secreted in Dalziel's busy surface patterning on four of the blocks. Hidden in the grass at the lower right corner of the engraving that shows Alice coping with the enormous puppy, flush with the right margin, is the signature "B. ROLLITZ." When the Queen of Hearts confronts Alice in the garden "B ROLLITZ SC." can barely be seen in the same corner. When Alice overturns the jury box she does not notice the inscription "ROLLITZ SC." carved into the wood in the lower-right corner, next to Tenniel's monogram (fig. 17.2). Rollitz signed the final and climactic illustration also, in which the playing cards explode into the air, by inscribing "B. ROLLITZ SC." along the edge of the playing card that barely shows behind the six of spades. However, Rollitz's cleverest signature on these blocks was not his own, but Tenniel's characteristic JT monogram, which he neatly placed in the lower-right corner of the trial scene frontispiece, where it belonged, but where Tenniel or Dalziel had not bothered to put it. (This block is not among the thirty-eight that survive at Yale.)

Ironically, any edition of *Alice's Adventures in Wonderland* that bears Tenniel's monogram on the frontispiece was printed not from electrotypes of the original Dalziel wood blocks but from Rollitz's reproductions of them—and probably not from the original Rollitz blocks but from electros made from them. Many such editions were published after 1932, only some of which were produced directly under Macy's control.

In 1936 the Modern Library in New York published *The Complete Works of Lewis Carroll,* which evidently used electros for the *Alice* illustrations made from the Rollitz wood blocks, if not the actual blocks themselves. The Rollitz signatures appear on all four illustrations (the puppy, the Queen of Hearts, the jury box, the cards), and the tell-tale Tenniel monogram appears on the frontispiece. Alexander Woollcott, who wrote the introduction to this Modern Library edition (which was later often reprinted in other editions), had entered into what Frederic Warde's biographer describes as "a prolonged and sometimes explosive friendship and collaboration with Warde";[12] probably they arranged together for this reuse of the Rollitz blocks.

In the 1930s Macy established The Heritage Club and The Heritage Press to publish well-made books in unlimited editions. At first these were original productions; later, many were reprints of LEC titles, in a less expensive format.[13] For *Alice's Adventures* Macy chose not to reuse Warde's design but to commission a new one from W. A. Dwiggins, who was arguably an even more prestigious graphic designer.[14] Dwiggins used a larger type face than Warde and made free use of rubrication, applying Indian red to the title page, to the chapter headings, to the (large) page numbers—and most emphatically to double-lined frames anchored with small rosettes at the corners, which he imposed around all the illustrations save one, rather upstaging than enhancing them. According to the colophon, "The illustrations by John Tenniel have been copied faithfully from wood-engravings cut from his original

FIGURE 17.2. Detail of wood engraving by Bruno Rollitz showing Rollitz's signature and Tenniel's monogram. *Alice's Adventures in Wonderland* (New York: Limited Editions Club, 1932), 160.

11. "R.," "*Batouala* and *Alice,*" *The Saturday Review,* 29 October 1932, 214.

12. Simon Loxley, *Printer's Devil: The Life and Work of Frederic Warde* (Boston: David R. Godine, 2013), 113.

13. Carol Porter Grossman, *The History of the Limited Editions Club* (New Castle, DE: Oak Knoll Press, 2017), 104–06.

14. Rudolph Ruzicka, "W. A. Dwiggins, Artist of the Book," *More Books: Being the Bulletin of the Boston Public Library* 23 (1948): 203–11. Wendy Bowersock, "William Addison Dwiggins: Knopf's Master of Book Design," *The Library Chronicle of the University of Texas* 22:4 (January 1992): 84–101. Bruce Kennett, *W. A. Dwiggins: A Life in Design* (San Francisco, CA: Letterform Archive, 2017).

drawings."[15] When this book was reissued in 1969 the accompanying issue of the *Sandglass* leaflet gave more detail:

> The Tenniel illustrations are printed from plates carefully photographed from fine pulls of the wood-blocks created for The Limited Editions Club. In the Heritage edition, these illustrations may not be quite so meticulous or so perfect as they are in The Limited Editions Club's edition; but they are only once removed from perfection, and are far superior to the comparatively indistinct prints of the illustrations which appear in other editions of *Alice*.[16]

There is no specific mention of Rollitz here, whose signature appears on the usual four illustrations and who added Tenniel's monogram to the frontispiece.

Also in 1941 Macy published *Alice* in two even cheaper formats, as an independent title and combined with *Looking-Glass,* in both cases under the Heritage Reprints imprint. The joint edition included a prefatory note explaining that it and other Heritage Reprints had been "made necessary by the government's wartime regulations that, whenever a book is reprinted, *less* paper must be used in the reprint." In this case the pages were not fewer but thinner, the layout maintaining Dwiggins's page design—including the Rollitz illustrations.

In 1946 the World Publishing Co. in Cleveland, Ohio, published *Alice's Adventures in Wonderland* combined with *Through the Looking-Glass* in the Rainbow Classics series of children's literature. The black-and-white illustrations for *Alice,* which were those engraved by Rollitz, as well as those for *Looking-Glass,* were heightened by Miróesque patches of pale gold. The editor of the Rainbow Classics series, and the editor of this book, was May Lamberton Becker, the mother of Beatrice Warde, Frederic's wife.

In 1960 the firm of Clarkson N. Potter, Inc., in New York, published one of the most popular and influential editions of the *Alice* books ever to appear, *The Annotated Alice,* edited by Martin Gardner. All four of the signed Rollitz engravings were used in that book, as well as the frontispiece distinctively signed with Tenniel's monogram by Rollitz. These could have been electros; more likely they derived from photographs. Conceivably the whole set of illustrations descended from Rollitz's work for the LEC. This early edition of *The Annotated Alice* was often reprinted, in hardcover and paperback, in the United States and England, carrying the Rollitz illustrations along with it.[17]

Among other editions that reproduce Rollitz's engravings the most noteworthy are the Signet Classic mass-market paperback edition of the two *Alice* books combined (New York: New American Library, 1960); a later edition of that Signet Classic, introduced by Martin Gardner (2000); and, most curiously, the first edition of the Norton Critical Edition of *Alice in Wonderland,* ed. Donald J. Gray (1971), which does not bear Rollitz's signature on any of its illustrations but does carry Rollitz's Tenniel monogram at the lower-right corner of the trial-scene frontispiece, where Dalziel did not put it.

The Limited Editions Club *Alice* proved to be a great success, the demand for copies signed by Alice far exceeding the supply.[18] Overall the book "outstripped" all other LEC products in popularity, prompting Macy to undertake the obvious sequel, a Limited Editions Club pro-

15. Lewis Carroll, *Alice's Adventures in Wonderland* (New York: The Heritage Press, 1941), [174].

16. "Lewis, Alice, and John," *The Heritage Club Sandglass* No. VII R: 39 (1969): 1–4; 4; copy accompanying *Alice's Adventures in Wonderland* (Avon, CT: Heritage Press, 1969). Michael C. Bussacco reports a third edition of this book also (1983); *An Annotative Bibliography of the Heritage Press,* 2nd ed., 3 vols. (Bloomington, IN: Author House, 2008), 1:155.

17. In the third edition of *The Annotated Alice* (New York: Clarkson N. Potter, 2000), Gardner himself noticed that "in many editions of *Alice in Wonderland* . . . the card hidden by the six of spades has on its left margin the mysterious letters 'B. ROLLITZ,'" and he speculated that Rollitz might have been an employee of the Dalziel Brothers. In the current edition of *The Annotated Alice,* edited by Mark Burstein (New York: W. W. Norton, 2015), credit for that image is reassigned to the Limited Editions Club (146).

18. *The Monthly Letter of the Limited Editions Club* 39 (August 1932): 4.

duction of *Through the Looking-Glass*, again designed by Frederic Warde, again enhanced with the signature of the original Alice. This time, however, Warde chose "to reproduce the Tenniel illustrations . . . himself."

> Mr. Warde got hold of fine prints of the original wood blocks in which Tenniel's illustrations were cut; he had these photographed onto heavy zinc; then he proceeded to tool all of the lines in the metal himself. From such hand-tooled zinc blocks, the reproduction of John Tenniel's illustrations becomes perfect: every dot, every line which came from the illustrator's pen, will be found in the printed sheets of our edition of *Through the Looking-Glass*.[19]

This account should not be taken too literally. "The illustrator's pen" is obviously a figment of Macy's imagination. Warde may well have had the illustrations "photographed onto heavy zinc"—but what then? "He proceeded *to* tool all of the lines in the metal *himself*"; the zinc blocks were "hand-tooled." Phrasing it like that implies an intaglio engraving process, common enough for traditional copperplate engraving but not for modern zinc, which might be etched with chemicals but not engraved with tools. Furthermore, wood engravings (and electros made from them) were printed in relief, along with letterpress; it would be strange for a project that pretended to regain "original" authenticity, instead to resort to an intaglio process, which would require a separate press and a printing process altogether different. The remaining logical alternative, that Warde did not incise the lines of the illustrations, as if he were making an intaglio copperplate engraving, but rather cut away the blank spaces around the lines, as if the zinc block were a wood block, letting the lines stand in relief—is barely credible.[20]

So what did Warde do with the illustrations? He certainly did something. On 8 August 1934 Macy wrote to Warde, "I am glad to know that you have finished your work on the illustration plates for our edition of Through the Looking Glass. I attach our check for two hundred and fifty dollars in payment."[21] On 19 December 1934 Warde wrote a letter to Macy seeking payment for autographing the colophon of each copy of *Looking-Glass*, in addition to the other tasks he had performed in connection with that book, which were these:

> Upon looking over the estimate and the correspondence that has to do with *Through the Looking Glass*, I am obligated to do only the work on the illustrations, nothing else, and that I would be paid by you the sum of $250 for this work. I spent weeks over the illustrations. You paid me the $250.
>
> In your interest, and in making the book as good as possible, I went to the paper mill and supervised the making of the paper. I also made the plan for the book, the typography, and the placing of the illustrations. I worked on the prospectus for the book. I spent some time in trying to find a suitable leather for the binding. I checked the color of the inking and the printing of book.
>
> Now do you think me very greedy if I ask you to consider paying me at the rate of twenty cents each for signing the colophon? I am not in any way comparing myself to 'Alice.' At the same instance, if Alice's signature is worth something, do you not think my signature might be of modest worth? It is about all I have. (*Selected Letters*, 203)

19. "The Looking-Glass," *The Monthly Letter of the Limited Editions Club* 71 (April 1935): 1–4; 2.

20. The official LEC bibliography *Quarto-Millenary* (New York: Limited Editions Club, 1959) reports that *Looking-Glass* had "original illustrations by John Tenniel re-engraved in metal by Frederic Warde" (247). Warde's biographer comments, "that Warde re-engraved all the illustrations for *Though the Looking Glass* seems a task of stupendous magnitude requiring phenomenal skill"; still, he gives Warde the benefit of the doubt (Loxley, 137). In her recent history of the LEC Grossman amplifies the account given in *The Monthly Letter:* after having had the images photographed onto zinc plates, Warde "used a graver to recut these engravings. He did a superb job." Subsequent mention of a later project seems more accurate: there, "much as he had done" for *Looking-Glass*, Warde "touched up" zinc plates (Grossman, 75, 89). As regards the LEC edition of *Alice's Adventures*, to which she devotes a paragraph that emphasizes the Hargreaves connection, Grossman omits to name the "German engraver" who cut the illustrations (44).

21. George Macy papers, Harry Ransom Humanities Research Center, The University of Texas at Austin.

Let me hope that you will not think I am unreasonable, and that you will grant that I have done a good share on my part for the book, beside the stipulated work upon the illustrations.[22]

The surviving correspondence does not explain what that "stipulated work upon the illustrations" amounted to.

On Warde's account, he "spent weeks over the illustrations." Compare that to the "nine months of joyous but continuous labor" that, according to Macy, Rollitz invested in the *Wonderland* engravings. It is unlikely that Warde was able "to tool all of the lines in the metal himself" in anything like the same way. But it *is* believable that "Mr. Warde got hold of fine prints of the original wood blocks in which Tenniel's illustrations were cut" and that he "had these photographed onto heavy zinc." That would be the first step in preparing relief zinc blocks of the images by a process known as photo-zincography, which involved not cutting away but etching away with nitric acid the adjacent zinc surface of the protected lines of a photo-transferred image. That Warde was familiar with the process is suggested by his casually mentioning, as regards a project of his colleague Bruce Rogers, the making of a "reduced zinc block which was to be employed in the actual printing."[23] Photo-zincography was a complicated process, which required some skill[24]—but much less skill than the impossible task of carving relief images in zinc. Preparing zinc plates of all fifty *Looking-Glass* illustrations could well have kept Warde busy for several weeks. Perhaps he outsourced some or all of that labor (the $250 that he charged Macy for it corresponds proportionally to the $200 that, he had previously estimated, the less preferred option of "line-cuts" would cost for the LEC *Alice*). Whoever did the actual work, the fact that zincography was essentially a photographic process would explain the precise matching of details in the illustrations in the LEC *Looking-Glass* to those in Macmillan's first edition of that book.

Because the LEC *Looking-Glass* illustrations lack distinctive features such as Rollitz's signature or other anomalies, it is hard to say which if any later editions of the book perpetuate Warde's photo-zincography, either directly through reuse of the zinc plates or indirectly through the manufacture of electrotype replicas or photographic copies. It would not be surprising if later editions of the combined *Alice* books that carry the Rollitz illustrations for *Wonderland* should carry, invisibly, the Warde illustrations for *Looking-Glass* also.

22. Warde, *Selected Letters*, 203–04. Macy, "distressed" on reading this letter, sent Warde a check for $100 the next day, relieving him of any obligation to sign copies of *Looking-Glass* (which he did nonetheless), and concluding, "I don't know why there should not be some revenue in the graphic arts for a man of your enormous knowledge and ability." Loxley, 138.

23. Frederic Warde, *Bruce Rogers, Designer of Books* (Cambridge, MA: Harvard University Press, 1925), 28.

24. W. T. Wilkinson, *Photo-Mechanical Processes: A Practical Guide to Photo-Zincography, Photo-Lithography, and Collotype*, 2nd ed. (London: Hampton, 1897).

CHAPTER 18

Retrospect

Looking with Alice

"'What is the use of a book,' thought Alice, 'without pictures or conversations?'" *Alice's Adventures in Wonderland,* which opens as Alice thinks this thought, has plenty of pictures and conversations, and not a few pictures *of* conversations—or at least moments in conversations; for conversations take place in time and standard pictures do not. The conversational verb *said* is the most common verb in the book—more common even than the name *Alice.* But *looking* is also important, in *Wonderland* as well as in the *Looking-Glass* sequel: in *Wonderland* the words *look* (as verb and noun), *looked,* and *looking* occur more than a hundred times altogether, averaging once in every double-page opening—more than twice as often as pictures appear. Wonders are typically seen as well as wondered at. Picaresque Alice is an inquisitive child, sometimes willing to ask questions in conversation, even more likely to look about her with her eyes wide open.

People, animals, things, and scenes are what Alice looks at, however, not pictures. She hardly notices the "maps and pictures" that she glimpses hanging on hooks as she falls down the rabbit-hole. She does not notice, and the narrator does not mention, the framed picture hanging on the wall in a room that she fills while growing too large (fig. 1.48). But the narrator does think in terms of pictures. The Dodo "sat for a long time with one finger pressed upon its forehead, (the position in which you usually see Shakespeare, in the pictures of him)."[1] In the last sentence of *Alice's Adventures* he says, "she pictured to herself" how in future days she would share with nieces and nephews the delight of tales of Wonderland. An even more fully framed picturing grounds the vision near the end of *Through the Looking-Glass,* as Alice contemplates the White Knight astride his horse, singing his song (the scene discussed in chapter 11, pages 156–57). "*All this she took in like a picture,* as with one hand shading her eyes, she leant against a tree, watching the strange pair, and listening, in a half dream, to the melancholy music of the song." That scene is more causal, more musical, more evocative,

1. Perhaps referring to a mezzotint by James Faed (1859) after a portrait by John Faed, which shows the thoughtful bard as seated, fingers of the left hand pressed to the forehead. National Portrait Gallery, London: D41647 and D41648; also an albumen carte-de-visite, Ax39783.

more sentimental than the one that Tenniel drew as the frontispiece to *Through the Looking-Glass*, which gives more determined agency to both the Knight and his horse as they exit from the scene and the story; but in that scene too Tenniel shows Alice gazing at what she sees, as if it were not close at hand but already distant, in the past (fig. 7.1).

Several illustrations in *Alice's Adventures* and *Looking-Glass* depict Alice more as a startled spectator than as a participant in the scene she looks at. When she opens the kitchen door in *Alice's Adventures* and walks in, this is what she sees: "a large kitchen, which was full of smoke from one end to the other: the Duchess was sitting on a three-legged stool in the middle, nursing a baby; the cook was leaning over the fire, stirring a large cauldron which seemed to be full of soup" (fig. 4.2). The picture shows all that and also Alice arrested in a startled posture, looking at what she has just come across, there in front of her eyes.

The posture is typical:

> There is an eye blink, a forward movement of the head, a characteristic facial expression, a raising of the shoulders and moving them forward, a motion of the upper arms somewhat away from the body, a bending of the elbows so as to raise the forearms and hands, a rotation of the forearms inward so that the palms more or less face each other, a clenching of the fingers, a motion of the upper body forward from the hips, a tightening of the abdominal muscles, and a bending of the knees.[2]

Aside from the fleeting eye blink and the inscrutable tightening of the abdominal muscles, most of these typical features, gleaned by psychologists in the 1930s from laboratory photographs of startled subjects, are apparent in Tenniel's depiction of Alice's bodily response to discovering the kitchen scene. Such an ensemble of involuntary gestures could, of course, be mimicked in theatrical display. "A start or recoil was an important part of the repertoire of gestures learnt by actors in the nineteenth century, a rehearsed 'point' through which the performer made visible moments of sudden perception or crises of recognition."[3] In "An Essay on Gesture" (1820) the painter Michael William Sharp had observed that "the elevation of the hand turned outward must always bespeak astonishment." (He cited a cartoon by Raphael in which both tell-tale gesture and astonishment accompanied "looking.")[4] Two years later the actor and theater manager Henry Siddons, who had read Sharp's essay, repeated that observation in *Practical Illustrations of Rhetorical Gesture Adapted to the English Drama* (based on an eighteenth-century German treatise by Johann Jakob Engle), noting also that "astonishment, like thought, stops suddenly short when an object of interest presents itself unexpectedly to the view."[5] So Tenniel's Alice stops suddenly short as she discovers the strange kitchen scene and its ugly Duchess. There is indeed something theatrical about Alice's arrested posture at this moment, and we know that Tenniel frequented the theater, where Siddons's repertoire of eighteenth-century gestures had a long half-life. However, the point of the picture is not its melodramatic theatricality but the "[moment] of sudden perception" that Alice's posture legibly illustrates. Alice perceives and reflexively responds in much the same way that Robinson Crusoe did in many eighteenth- and nineteenth-century illustrations of his discovering Friday's surprising footprint.[6]

2. Ronald C. Simon, *Boo! Culture, Experience, and the Startle Reflex* (New York: Oxford University Press, 1996), 9, summarizing work reported by Carney Landis and William A. Hunt, *The Startle Pattern* (New York: Farrar & Rinehart, 1939), especially 21.

3. Tiffany Watt Smith, *On Flinching: Theatricality and Scientific Looking from Darwin to Shell Shock* (Oxford: Oxford University Press, 2014), 17.

4. Michael William Sharp, "An Essay on Gesture: Part II," *Annals of the Fine Arts* 4 (1820): 84–102; 88.

5. Henry Siddons, *Practical Illustrations of Rhetorical Gesture Adapted to the English Drama*, 2nd ed. (London, 1822), 74. "The man struck with sudden astonishment ought to remain fixed like a statue to his posture for a time" (79). Compare Landis and Hunt: "the primary response . . . persists while the individual remains immobile" (140).

6. David Blewett, *The Illustrations of "Robinson Crusoe, 1719–1920* (London: Colin Smythe, 1995), 43, 54, 60, 218 (Cruikshank, 1831), 83 (Grandville, 1840). 47 (John Gilbert, 1853), 119 (Griset, 1869).

FIGURE 18.1. The live flowers startle Alice. From *Through the Looking-Glass*.

FIGURE 18.2. Tenniel. Sketch for chess-board landscape, tipped in opposite p. 38 of *Through the Looking-Glass* (1872). *EC85. D6645.872t. Houghton Library, Harvard University.

Alice responds similarly in *Looking-Glass* when she is startled by what she sees, or, rather, hears. When the live flowers suddenly speak to her in chapter 2 she is caught by surprise, stopped in her tracks, her arms typically flexed and upper body slightly bent forward (fig. 18.1). Later she responds similarly to the surprising voice of Tweedledum, who interrupts her looking—her staring—at the strange pair she has just come across: the spectator suddenly observed and challenged (fig. 1.1, discussed in chapter 1 above, page 6). Forgetting that they are human, Alice treats the twins as wonderful objects open to intimate inspection—for which impoliteness she is properly rebuked. "'I'm sure I'm very sorry,' was all Alice could say."

In chapter 8 Alice responds in the same startled and watchful way whenever the White Knight begins to fall off his horse "sideways . . . on the side on which Alice was walking"—which happens repeatedly, Tenniel making one illustration do for all the instances (fig. 7.3). Shortly after her encounter with the live flowers Alice comes upon a strange scene spread out at a distance before her eyes. Again she pulls herself up short, startled by what she sees and then gazes upon, which is an agricultural landscape so crisscrossed by rectilinear hedgerows and brooks that it is no longer agricultural but purely cultural: the artificial layout of a chess-board. Or so she would appear in Tenniel's sketch of this scene (fig. 18.2).

> For some minutes Alice stood without speaking, looking out in all directions over the country—and a most curious country it was. There were a number of tiny little brooks running straight across it from side to side, and the ground between was divided up into squares by a number of little green hedges, that reached from brook to brook.
>
> "I declare it's marked out just like a large chess-board!" Alice said at last. "There ought to be some men moving about somewhere—and so there are!" she added in a tone of delight, and her heart began to

FIGURE 18.3. Tenniel. Chess-board landscape. From *Through the Looking-Glass.*

beat quick with excitement as she went on. "It's a great huge game of chess that's being played—all over the world—if this *is* the world at all, you know. Oh, what fun it is!"

By now the startlement has relaxed into a kind of awe.

And yet Alice the spectator, though present both in this narrative and in Tenniel's sketch, is absent from Dalziel's engraving (fig. 18.3). When Carroll saw a proof of the engraving, he thought to revise it. Tenniel wrote to Dalziel, on 27 December 1870, "Mr. Dodgson said something about one of the blocks 'The Chessboard Landscape' being done over again. Please send me another proof of it—he has the other—and don't send the blocks to Messrs. Macmillan till you have heard from me" (Livingston, 30). But Carroll changed his mind, as Tenniel let Dalziel know in an undated letter: "Dear Dalziel, Mr. Dodgson now says that he doesn't care about 'Chessboard Landscape' being re-engraved. Sorry you had the trouble to take proof—but it will do for my set."[7] It is not certain how Tenniel would have used the proof to revise the picture, had Carroll persisted in his desire to have the block "done over again." Perhaps he would have added to that proof the startled figure of Alice gazing at the landscape, as shown above.

Although the chess-board landscape presents a strange vista, in some ways it is wholly conventional. "The notion of a distant view from a high terrace" is typical of landscape painting and dates back to the origins of the genre.[8] It became common to frame such prospects with massed foliage—in this case, a sturdy oak, emblem of England. Sometimes the view to the far horizon would be organized by central or single-point perspective, a device that Tenniel emphasizes in the convergent hedgerows. Furthermore, early and late landscape paintings and prints often included one or more spectators gazing at the prospect before them, modeling for the viewer how to look at that scene and appreciate its significance. As Alice takes in the landscape in Tenniel's sketch, so we should observe the picture, whether she is present in it or absent.

The vacillation of Alice in this landscape, present or absent, marks her equivocal role in her stories as both observer and observed. Although Carroll's omniscient narration of the stories tends to objec-

7. *The Library of Jerome Kern, New York City* (New York: The Anderson Galleries, 1929), lot 246. Making an extra proof would indeed have involved some trouble, a half hour or more of hand labor.

8. Kenneth Clark, *Landscape Into Art* (London: John Murray, 1941), 21.

tify Alice as well as the phenomena that she encounters, those phenomena are sometimes depicted, in Carroll's manuscript and in Tenniel's illustrations, from Alice's point of view. In such cases of what might be called "free indirect observation" (the vanishing Cheshire Cat, the White Knight sliding down the poker, the sleeping Red King) they are what she sees. Although often we look at Alice, sometimes we identify with her and share her point of view.

In its very title *Through the Looking-Glass* thematizes looking. Before Carroll settled on that title at the suggestion of a friend, Henry Liddon, alternative possible titles had been *Looking-Glass World* or *Behind the Looking-Glass* (Jaques and Giddens, 41). *Mirror* is an older term than *looking-glass* (the words date from the fourteenth and sixteenth centuries, respectively); and by the nineteenth century *mirror* had established itself in British English as the dominant term.[9] However, *looking-glass* survived as a synonym, peaking at about the time that Carroll wrote his book.[10] Furthermore, although the terms were used interchangeably in "silver-fork" novels by Disraeli, Bulwer-Lytton, and Mrs. Catherine Gore, the frequent use of *looking-glass* in those works suggests that it was the preferred if not the default term in the sociolect of the elite—a distinction that has been remarked in twentieth-century British English also.[11]

Both terms had long been used in the titles of didactic, often moralizing books, pamphlets, and broad sheets, with the sense of "thing regarded as giving a true description of something else";[12] for example:

> *The Mirror for Magistrates* (1559)
> *A Looking-Glass for Drunkards* (1627)
> *The Mirror of Architecture; or, The Ground-Rules of the Art of Building* (1671)
> *Green's Useful Knowledge for Little Children: Being a Looking Glass in Which They May See the Dangers of Childhood Without Feeling Their Effects* (1850?)
> *A Looking Glass for Brewers, Wherein They May See Their Origin and Dignity, Together with the Curious Customs of Their Ancient Craft* (1860)
> *A Looking-Glass for the Young Men of the Period, Wherein All Their Vices and Follies are Clearly Reflected* (1871)[13]

As the last example suggests, many titular uses of *looking-glass* are self-oriented as well as world-oriented: the lesson to be learned is not just about what the world is like, but also about what one's own behavior in that world is like. Though it is available to *Mirror* titles, that doubleness of perspective is more marked in some *Looking-Glass* titles because the term *looking-glass* foregrounds the agency and self-interest of a person looking. The most popular such book for children was *The Looking-Glass for the Mind; or, Intellectual Mirror: Being an Elegant Collection of the Most Delightful Little Stories and Interesting Tales, Chiefly Translated from That Much Admired Work, "L'Ami des enfans; or, The Children's Friend"* (1787), which was translated from the French of Arnaud Berquin and achieved dozens of editions in the eighteenth and nineteenth centuries, many of them illustrated with wood engravings by John Bewick, the younger brother of Thomas Bewick—often with the pictures indifferent to or at cross-purposes with the earnest conversations they were supposed to represent.

Despite her well-schooled disposition, Alice is not particularly eager to learn about the ordinary world as it is, nor even about herself as it is; instead she wants to see what is in that other world, the world behind

9. https://goo.gl/Rk7RGR.

10. https://goo.gl/suL1qt.

11. Alan S. C. Ross, "Linguistic Class-Indicators in Present-Day English," *Neuphilologische Mitteilungen* 55 (1954): 20–56; 45.

12. *OED* s.v. *Mirror* n. 3a.; cf. *Looking-glass* n. 1b.

13. These examples are drawn from Copac, the online British union catalogue. Discussing "the looking-glass book for children" in *The Making of the Alice Books: Lewis Carroll's Uses of Earlier Children's Literature* (Montreal: McGill-Queen's University Press, 2000), 52–54, Ronald Reichertz cites Herbert Grabes, *The Mutable Glass: Mirror-Imagery in Titles and Texts of the Middle Ages and English Renaissance*, trans. Gordon Collier (Cambridge: Cambridge University Press, 1982).

the looking-glass, and to do so she rashly or bravely passes through that glass. "Then she began looking about, and noticed that what could be seen from the old room was quite common and uninteresting, but that all the rest was as different as possible. For instance, the pictures on the wall next the fire seemed to be all alive"—motion pictures *avant le lettre*. Once through the looking-glass Alice watches or looks about her, repeatedly, often "with great interest," "with great curiosity," or (sometimes the same thing) "a little anxiously." Looking is not always easy; in the Sheep's shop "Alice rubbed her eyes, and looked again." Things are hard to make out there: "The shop seemed to be full of all manner of curious things—but the oddest part of it all was, that whenever she looked hard at any shelf, to make out exactly what it had on it, that particular shelf was always quite empty: though the others round it were crowded as full as they could hold." One of the things that Alice finds in the quantum world behind the looking-glass is that looking can be problematic. Ocular proof can be no proof at all.

Aside from the uncertainty of veridical looking, excessive looking has long been stigmatized, first as "the lust of the eyes" (1 John 2:26), then, more clinically, as *Schaulust* or *scopophilia*. The pioneering and persistent photographer Lewis Carroll, for some decades Freud's contemporary, might have shared St. Augustine's anxiety about excessive visual attachment to the things of this world. ("*Curiosity, the lust of the eyes,*" is the headline for the page in St. Augustine's *Confessions* that deals with that anxiety, as that book was published in Carroll's Oxford by Parker.[14]) Alice is made anxious as she looks at the world, both in Wonderland and behind the looking-glass, but it is the world, not her looking at it, that is at fault. "Curiosity killed the cat" is a discouraging formula that matured just after *Looking-Glass* was published.[15] Alice is the exception that proves that rule. Nothing if not curious ("Alice looked at it with great curiosity"[16]), Alice learns by looking, as does the reader, the other eye-witness of both her books.

14. *The Confessions of S. Augustine: Revised from a Former Translation, by The Rev. E. B. Pusey, D. D.* (Oxford: John Henry Parker, 1853), 213. Pusey was a founder of the Oxford Movement. The Parker firm was Carroll's academic publisher.

Jasmine Jagger discusses *seeing* to good effect in "The Child's Eye-View in the Illustrated Texts of Lewis Carroll," *The Carrollian* 25 (2010, published 2014): 38–63.

15. First listed as an Irish proverb by James Allan Mair, *A Handbook of Proverbs* (London: George Routledge and Sons, [1873]), 34; derivative from "Care will kill a cat" and variants.

16. *Looking-Glass*, 162.

BIBLIOGRAPHY

A Bibliographical Catalogue of Macmillan and Co.'s Publications from 1843 to 1889. London: Macmillan, 1891.

"Alice." *The Monthly Letter of the Limited Editions Club* 40 (September 1932): 1–3.

Alice's Adventures in Wonderland: The Extremely Rare 1865 First Edition (New York: Christie's, 2016).

Altick, Richard D. *"Punch": The Lively Youth of a British Institution, 1841–1851.* Columbus: Ohio State University Press, 1997.

Ayres, Harry Morgan. "Carroll's Withdrawal of the 1865 *Alice*." *The Huntington Library Bulletin* 6 (1934): 153–63.

Bond, W. H. "The Publication of *Alice's Adventures in Wonderland*." *Harvard Library Bulletin* 10 (1956): 306–24.

Brooker, Will. *Alice's Adventures: Lewis Carroll in Popular Culture.* New York: Continuum, 2004.

Brown, Sally, ed. *The Original Alice: From Manuscript to Wonderland.* London: The British Library, 1997.

Carroll, Lewis. *Alice in Wonderland.* Ed. Donald J. Gray. New York: W. W. Norton, 1971. 2nd ed., 1982. 3rd ed., 2013.

———. *Alice's Adventures in Wonderland.* Ed. Richard Kelly. Peterborough, Ont.: Broadview Press, 2000. 2nd ed., 2011.

———. *Alice's Adventures under Ground, Being a Facsimile of the Original MS. Book Afterwards Developed into "Alice's Adventures in Wonderland."* London: Macmillan, 1886.

———. *The Annotated Alice: Alice's Adventures in Wonderland & Through the Looking-Glass.* Ed. Martin Gardner. New York: Clarkson N. Potter, 1960. 3rd ed., 2000. 4th ed., ed. Mark Burstein, 2015.

———. *The Letters of Lewis Carroll.* Ed. Morton N. Cohen. 2 vols. New York: Oxford University Press, 1979.

———. *Lewis Carroll & His Illustrators: Collaborations & Correspondence, 1865–1898.* Ed. Morton N. Cohen and Edward Wakeling. Ithaca: Cornell University Press, 2003.

———. *Lewis Carroll and the House of Macmillan.* Ed. Morton N. Cohen and Anita Gandolfo. Cambridge: Cambridge University Press, 1987.

———. *The Lewis Carroll Picture Book.* Ed. Stuart Dodgson Collingwood. London: T. Fisher Unwin, 1899.

———. *Lewis Carroll's Diaries: The Private Journals of Charles Lutwidge Dodgson (Lewis Carroll).* Ed. Edward Wakeling. 10 vols. Luton, Eng.: Lewis Carroll Society, 1993–2007.

———. *The Nursery "Alice."* London: Macmillan, 1890.

———. *The Russian Journal and Other Selections from the Works of Lewis Carroll.* Ed. John Francis McDermott. 1935; rpt. New York: Dover Publications, 1977.

Chatto, W. A. *A Treatise on Wood Engraving, Historical and Practical, With Upwards of Three Hundred Illustrations, Engraved on Wood, by John Jackson.* London: Charles Knight, 1839. 2nd ed., London: Chatto & Windus, 1861.

Clark, Anne. *Lewis Carroll: A Biography.* New York: Schocken Books, 1979.

———. *The Real Alice: Lewis Carroll's Dream Child.* London: Michael Joseph, 1981.

Cohen, Jane R. *Charles Dickens and His Original Illustrators.* Columbus: Ohio State University Press, 1980.

Cohen, Morton. *Lewis Carroll: A Biography.* New York: Alfred A. Knopf, 1995.

Collingwood, Stuart Dodgson. *The Life and Letters of Lewis Carroll (Rev. C. L. Dodgson).* London: T. Fisher Unwin, 1898.

Crutch, Denis. *The Lewis Carroll Handbook.* 4th ed. Folkestone, Eng.: Dawson-Archon, 1979. (See also Williams and Madan; Green.)

Dalziel, Edward, and George Dalziel. *The Brothers Dalziel: A Record of Fifty Years' Work in Conjunction with Many of the Most Distinguished Artists of the Period, 1840–1890.* London: Methuen, 1901.

Davis, John. Introduction to *The Illustrators of Alice in Wonderland and Through the Looking Glass.* Ed. Graham Ovenden. London: Academy Editions, 1972.

De Freitas, Leo John. "Commercial Engraving on Wood in England, 1700–1880: An Economical Art." Ph.D. thesis, Royal College of Art, 1986. uk.bl.ethos.234734.

———. *A Study of Sir John Tenniel's Illustrations to Alice's Adventures in Wonderland & Through the Looking-Glass.* London: Macmillan Publishers, 1988.

De Maré, Eric. *The Victorian Woodblock Illustrators.* London: Gordon Fraser, 1980.

De Vinne, Theodore Low (unsigned). "Woodcuts: Concerning the Making of Proofs and Prints: Part I." *The Printing Times and Lithographer,* 15 October 1878, 197–99.

Eliot, Simon, et al., eds. *The History of Oxford University Press.* 3 vols. Oxford: Oxford University Press, 2013.

Empson, William. *Some Versions of Pastoral.* London: Chatto & Windus, 1935.

Engen, Rodney. *Sir John Tenniel: Alice's White Knight.* London: Scolar Press, 1991.

Ewing, Elizabeth. *History of Children's Costume.* New York: Charles Scribner's Sons, 1977.

Fairholt, F. W. *Costume in England.* London: Chapman & Hall, 1846.

Filmer, William. "Electro-Metallurgy." *The Printer* 1 (1858): 5–6, 22–23, 46–47, 72, 93–94, 115–16, 189–90, 213, 236–37, 259–60, 282–83.

Furniss, Harry. *The Confessions of a Caricaturist.* 2 vols. London: T. Fisher Unwin, 1901.

———. "Recollections of 'Lewis Carroll.'" *The Strand Magazine* (British edition) 35:205 (January 1908): 48–52.

Garvey, Eleanor, and William H. Bond. *Tenniel's Alice.* Cambridge, MA: Houghton Library, 2005.

Goodacre, Selwyn H. "The 1865 Alice: A New Appraisal and a Revised Census." *Soaring with the Dodo: Essays on Lewis Carroll's Life and Art.* Ed. Edward Guiliano and James R. Kincaid. Silver Spring, MD: Lewis Carroll Society of North America, 1982. 77–96.

———. "The 1865 'Alice': A Revised and Augmented Census." Schiller, 33–53.

———. "The Nursery 'Alice': A Bibliographical Essay." *Jabberwocky* 4 (1975): 100–19.

Green, Roger Lancelyn, ed. *The Lewis Carroll Handbook.* Folkestone, Eng.: Dawsons of Pall Mall, 1970. (See also Williams and Madan; Crutch.)

Grossman, Carol Porter. *The History of the Limited Editions Club.* New Castle, DE: Oak Knoll Press, 2017.

Guiliano, Edward, ed. *Lewis Carroll: A Celebration—Essays on the Occasion of the 150th Anniversary of the Birth of Charles Lutwidge Dodgson.* New York: Clarkson N. Potter, 1982.

Hargreaves, Caryl. "Alice's Recollections of Carrollian Days, As Told to Her Son, Caryl Hargreaves." *The Cornhill Magazine* 73 (1932): 1–12.

Harvey, J. R. *Victorian Novelists and Their Illustrators*. New York: New York University Press, 1971.

Hatch, Harris B., and A. A. Stewart. *Electrotyping and Stereotyping*. Chicago: United Typothetae of America, 1918.

Hearn, Michael Patrick. "Alice's Other Parent: John Tenniel as Lewis Carroll's Illustrator." *American Book Collector* n.s. 4:3 (May–June 1983): 11–20.

Hodnett, Edward. *Image and Text: Studies in the Illustration of English Literature*. London: Scolar Press, 1982.

Hudson, Derek. *Lewis Carroll*. London: Constable, 1954. 2nd ed., 1976.

Imholtz, Clare. "Notes on the Early Printing History of Lewis Carroll's 'Alice' Books." *The Book Collector* 62 (2013): 255–70.

Jaques, Zoe, and Eugene Giddens. *Lewis Carroll's "Alice's Adventures in Wonderland" and "Through the Looking-Glass": A Publishing History*. Farnham, UK: Ashgate, 2013.

Kooistra, Lorraine. *Poetry, Pictures, and Popular Publishing: The Illustrated Gift Book and Victorian Visual Culture, 1855–1875*. Athens, Ohio: Ohio University Press, 2011.

Landis, Carney, and William A. Hunt. *The Startle Pattern*. New York: Farrar & Rinehart, 1939.

Layard, George Somes. *Tennyson and His Pre-Raphaelite Illustrators*. London: Elliot Stock, 1894.

Leary, Patrick. *The "Punch" Brotherhood: Table Talk and Print Culture in Mid-Victorian London*. London: The British Library, 2010.

Lennon, Florence Becker. *Victoria through the Looking-Glass: The Life of Lewis Carroll*. New York: Simon and Schuster, 1945.

Life, Allan R. "'Poetic Naturalism': Forrest Reid and the Illustrators of the Sixties." *Victorian Periodicals Newsletter* 10 (1977): 47–68.

Livingston, Flora V. *The Harcourt Amory Collection of Lewis Carroll in the Harvard College Library*. Cambridge, MA: privately printed, 1932.

Lovell-Smith, Rose. "The Animals of Wonderland: Tenniel as Carroll's Reader." *Criticism* 45 (2003): 383–415.

Lovett, Charlie. *Lewis Carroll among His Books: A Descriptive Catalogue of the Private Library of Charles L. Dodgson*. Jefferson, NC: McFarland, 2005.

Loxley, Simon. *Printer's Devil: The Life and Work of Frederic Warde*. Boston: David R. Godine, 2013.

Lull, Janis. "The Appliances of Art: The Carroll-Tenniel Collaboration in *Through the Looking-Glass*." *Lewis Carroll: A Celebration*, ed. Edward Guiliano. New York: Clarkson N. Potter, 1982. 101–11.

Madan, Falconer, ed. *The Lewis Carroll Centenary in London 1932*. London: J. & E. Bumpus, 1932.

Mespoulet, Marguerite. *Creators of Wonderland*. New York: Arrow Editions, 1934.

Milevski, Robert J. "A Note on Macmillan's Lewis Carroll Bindings." *Knight Letter* 92 (Spring 2014): 9–11.

Monkhouse, Cosmo. *The Life and Work of Sir John Tenniel, R.I.* London: The Art Journal Office, 1901.

Moran, James. *Clays of Bungay*. Bungay, Eng.: Richard Clay, 1979.

Morris, Frankie. *Artist of Wonderland: The Life, Political Cartoons, and Illustrations of Tenniel*. Charlottesville: University of Virginia Press, 2005.

Muir, Percy H. *Victorian Illustrated Books*. New York: Praeger Publications, 1971.

Noyce, Elisha. *The Boy's Book of Industrial Information . . . Illustrated with Three Hundred and Sixty-Five Engravings by the Brothers Dalziel*. London: Ward & Lock, 1858.

Phosphorus (pseud.). "Electro-Metallurgy, As Applied to Printing." *J. & R. M. Wood's Typographical Advertiser* 2 (1863–64): 30, 37, 42, 50–51, 62–63, 72, 86–87, 94–95, 100–01, 112–13; 3 (1864–65): 14–15; 34.

Prager, Arthur. *The Mahogany Tree: An Informal History of "Punch."* New York: Hawthorn Books, 1979.

Price, R. G. G. *A History of "Punch."* London: Collins, 1957.

Pudney, John. *Lewis Carroll and His World*. New York: Charles Scribner's Sons, 1976.

Reid, Forrest. *Illustrators of the Eighteen Sixties*. 1928; rpt. New York: Dover Publications, 1975.

Rossetti, Dante Gabriel. *Letters of Dante Gabriel Rossetti*. Ed. Oswald Doughty and John Robert Wahl. 4 vols. Oxford: Clarendon Press, 1965–67.

Ruskin, John. *The Works of John Ruskin*. Ed. E. T. Cook and Alexander Wedderburn. 39 vols. London: George Allen, 1903–12.

Sarzano, Frances. *Sir John Tenniel*. English Masters of Black-and-White. New York: Pellegrini & Cudahy, 1948.

Schiller, Justin G. *Alice's Adventures in Wonderland: An 1865 Printing Re-Described and Newly Identified as the Publisher's "File Copy."* Kingston, NY: privately printed, 1990.

Sibley, Brian. "The Nursery 'Alice' Illustrations." *Jabberwocky* 4 (1975): 92–95.

Spielmann, M. H. *The History of "Punch."* London: Cassell, 1895.

Steig, Michel. *Dickens and Phiz*. Bloomington: Indiana University Press, 1978.

Stephens, Frederick George, and Mary Dorothy George. *Catalogue of Political and Personal Satires*. 11 vols. London: The British Museum, 1870–1954.

Stern, Jeffrey. "Lewis Carroll the Pre-Raphaelite: 'Fainting in Coils.'" *Lewis Carroll Observed*. Ed. Edward Guiliano. New York: Clarkson N. Potter, 1976. 161–80.

Stevens, Bethan. "Wood Engraving as Ghostwriting: The Dalziel Brothers, Losing One's Name, and Other Hazards of the Trade." *Textual Practice* (2017). DOI: 10.1080/0950236X.2017.1365756. 1–33.

Surtees, Virginia. *The Paintings and Drawings of Dante Gabriel Rossetti (1828–1882): A Catalogue Raisonné*. 2 vols. Oxford: Clarendon Press, 1971.

Urquhart, J. W. *Electro-Typing: A Practical Manual*. London: Crosby Lockwood, 1881.

Vaughan, William. *German Romanticism and English Art*. New Haven: Yale University Press, 1979.

Wakeling, Edward. *Lewis Carroll: The Man and His Circle*. London: I. B. Tauris, 2015.

Warde, Frederick. *Believe Me, I Am: Selected Letters of Frederic Warde, 1921–1939*. Ed. Simon Loxley. Lavenham, Eng.: Lavenham Press, 2015.

Williams, Sidney Herbert, and Falconer Madan. *A Handbook of the Literature of the Rev. C. L. Dodgson (Lewis Carroll)*. London: Oxford University Press, 1931. (See also Green; Crutch.)

Wilson, Frederick J. F. *Stereotyping and Electrotyping*. London: Wyman and Sons, 1880; rpt. [1881].

Woolf, Jenny, ed. *Lewis Carroll in His Own Account: The Complete Bank Account of The Rev. C. L. Dodgson*. London: Jabberwock Press, 2005.

Wright, Thomas. *A History of Caricature & Grotesque in Literature and Art*. London: Virtue Brothers, 1865.

INDEX

Cecilia, Saint, 3, 146, 147

Charles VI (king of France), 97

Chartism, 9, 10

chatelaine, 157, 158

Chatto, William Andrew. *See* Jackson, John

Cheshire Cat (*AW*): foxglove, 159; an image colored by JT, 226; not Lincoln, 170; as observed by Alice, 245; placement of illustration, 211; precedent designs, 10, 13

chess. *See* chess-board landscape, Staunton pattern

chess-board landscape (*LG*), 230, 243–44. *See also* landscape

children's literature, 79, 103, 106–7, 125, 211

Children's Literature Research Collections (University of Minnesota), 216

Christ Church, Oxford: doorway, 31; John Ruskin, colleague at, 40, 63, 99, 114; LC borrows book from deanery, 44; LC Collection at, 129, 130; LC student and lecturer at, 3, 132, 161, 209; Queen Victoria visits, 80

Christie's, 57, 59, 62, 122, 206–7

Clarendon Press: available printing presses, 209; chosen by LC to print *AW*, 209; defects of printing, 212–17; LC rejects printing, 211; may have prepared electrotypes for *AW*, 194. *See also* Oxford University Press

Clark, Anne, 93, 133, 155

Clark, Kenneth, 61, 244

Clay, Richard: Bohn commends Clay's skill, 221; differences between Clay and Clarendon printings of *AW*, 211–17; electrotypes possessed by Clay employee sold at auction, 206–7; JT faults printing of first edition of *LG*, 218; LC chooses Clay to print *AW* afresh, 210; LC deprecates image print quality compared to proofs, 204; Macmillan defends Clay against LC's complaints, 218, 219; prints books containing early JT illustrations, 95, 96–97; prints sixth edition of *AW* from page electrotypes, 206; relevant expertise and experience, 210–11

Clubs (playing card suit, *AW*), 227

Cohen, Morton, 40, 133, 216

Cole, Henry, 178

Collingwood, Stuart Dodgson: faults Clarendon Press printing of *AW*, 212; JT advises LC re *LG* illustrations, 137, 138–39; LC advises JT re: *LG* illustra-

tions, 133, 135; mentions prototype for Hatter, 132; quotes from "The Profits of Authorship" (LC), 161

color: *Alice* coloring books, 231–32; "basic color terms," 224–25; color in Alice's dreams as LC reports (*AAuG, AW, NA*), 152–54, 223–26; color printing of *NA* by Edmund Evans, 226–28; colors of Alice's dresses, 228–31; in gift manuscript of *AAuG*, 223–25; JT colors illustrations for *NA*, 52, 67, 226

Comic Almanack, 23, 24

cook (*AW*), 52, 243

costume: court figures for *AW* adapted from playing cards, 77, 84–85; headdress of Duchess (*AW*), 62; medieval headdresses, 64, 65, 66; medieval, JT student of, 2, 64; nineteenth-century history of, 10, 11. *See also* Alice's costume; armor; crinoline fashion; Hatter; Jabberwock; "Punch's Book of British Costumes"; skeleton suit; White Rabbit

Crimean War, 8, 34, 72, 201

crinoline fashion, 15, 135, 182

cross-hatching (engraving), 52, 141, 155, 218, 226

crown, Saint Edward's, 79, 80

Cruikshank, George: *Comic Almanack*, 23, 24; *Jack Sheppard* (Ainsworth), 72–73; *Oliver Twist* (Dickens), 146, 148, 149; *Robinson Crusoe* (Defoe), 242

"Crystal Palace" exhibition, 82, 83, 131–32, 201

Dali, Salvator, 5

Dalziel Brothers: commended by LC, 147; criticized by D. G. Rossetti, 146; and electrotyping, 187, 194; engrave illustrations for *AW* and *LG*, *passim*; engrave illustrations for other books, 56, 126 (Tupper), 126 (*Æsop's Fables*), 146 (Tennyson), 149 (Moore), 179, 192 (Noyce), 188 (*Cornhill Gallery*); engraved signature, 173, 213, 236; engraved wood blocks for *AW* and *LG* at British Library, 177, 181; and engraving process, 179–88; letter from JT to, 244; proof albums at British Museum, 136 (*LG*), 178, 182 (*AW*); proofs by, 204; proofs of LC illustrations, 182, 184, 186; reuse of wood block, 148–49. *See also* Dalziel, Edward, and Dalziel, George

Dalziel, Edward, 142, 178, 179, 182, 186, 187

Dalziel, George, 142, 179, 187

Davies, Martin, 60–61, 62

Davis, John, 133, 151, 173

De Freitas, Leo John: cost of wood engraving, 194; last illustration in *LG,* 182, 183, 184; supposed disposition of Dalziel wood blocks, 177; wood-engraving technique, 180–81; working conditions for wood engravers, 178–79

de la Rue, Thomas, 77, 84, 85, 194, 228

De Vinne, Theodore Low, 204–6, 220–21

Demarteau, Gilles-Antoine, 62, 63, 64, 66

description in *AW,* 150–51, 154

Dickens, Charles: and George Cruikshank, 146, 148, 149; and Hablot Browne, 142; and illustration, J. Hillis Miller on, 149; JT illustrates *The Haunted Man,* 170; Mrs. Gamp and Mrs. Harris (*Martin Chuzzlewit*) 15, 16; Oliver Twist "crimson with fury," 225; on "skeleton suit," 8; Q. D. Leavis on, 151; and Robert Seymour, 148

differences between text and illustration, 143–60

"dirt" (printing), 214–17

Disney, Walt, 74, 231

Disraeli, Benjamin: cartoons of, with Gladstone, 116–18; and man "dressed in white paper" (*LG*), 115–16; possible successor to Palmerston, 15; silver-fork novels by, 245; and Unicorn (*LG*), 116, 118; and Walrus (*LG*), 116

Dodgson, Charles Lutwidge. *See* Carroll, Lewis

Dodo (*AW*), 32, 34; electrotypes, 177, 207; placement of illustration, 167; and Shakespeare, 241

Dormouse (*AW*), 131, 156

Doyle, Richard, 89, 90, 91, 112, 134

dragons, 103, 106, 108, 109, 110, 112

dreams: *AW,* 77, 78, 143, 153, 155; color in, 152, 153, 232; *A Dream of the Past* (Millais), 99, 100; *Interpretation of Dreams* (Freud), 106; *LG,* 144, 156, 182, 241; *NA* (E. G. Thomson), 228; point of view in (Moser), 152. *See also* "A Little Christmas Dream"

du Maurier, George: caricatures *Punch* staff, 91, 92, 93, 94; reports JT eschewed models, 9. *See also* "A Little Christmas Dream"

Duchess (*AW*): an image colored by JT, 226; and Margaret, duchess of Carinthia and countess of Tyrol ("Maultasch"), 57, 59, 60, 61, 64; and medieval headdress, 64–66, 154; men-

tioned in LC's list, 164; "sharp little chin," 154; startles Alice in kitchen scene, 242

Duckworth, Robinson, 5, 40

Dürer, Albrecht, 94, 95, 96, 98, 159

Dwiggins, William Addison, 237, 238

eagle, eaglet (*AW*), 55, 157

eel bucks, eel weir (*LG*), 29, 30

Egg, Augustus Leopold, 119, 121, 122

electrotypes of *AW* and *LG* wood blocks: Alice and the Dodo, 177; damage to block, 180; deprecated by Dalziel, 187, 189; "fresh" ones made, 188; Macy deprecates, 236; surviving, 194, 206–7; Warde budgets for, 234

electrotyping process, 187–206; difficulties of, 194, 200–201; equivocal quality of printed images, 189–91, 205–6; hazards of, 202–3

Empson, William, 46, 60, 115, 116

Engen, Rodney: biography of JT, 2; fresco projects, 3; JT as White Knight, 93, 94; JT joins *Punch* staff, 132; JT visits Oxford, 180; JT's mourning stationery, 217; other works by, 122, 123, 178

ermine in robes and heraldry, 86, 226–27

Evans, Edmund, 189, 226–28

executioner (*AW*), 52

facsimile editions: of *AAuG,* 39; of *AW,* 174–75; of *LG,* 174–75

Fairholt, F. W., 10, 11, 64, 66, 112, 113

fairy tales, 106, 107, 211, 212

fantasy and the fantastic, 1, 5, 19, 49, 107, 153

Father William (*AW*), 28, 29, 153, 156, 187, 206

Fawn (*LG*), 98

Ferdinand II ("Bomba"), King of the Two Sicilies, 8, 33, 34

Figuier, Louis, 106, 107, 108, 202, 203

Filmer, William, 193–96, 199–202

Fish-Footman (*AW*), 15, 131, 217

flamingo (*AW*), 43

foreshortening (*AW*), 52, 53, 56, 77

forget-me-not (*AAuG*), 223–24

Forster, Edward Morgan, 76

Mapes, James Jay, 189–90

March Hare (*AW*), 67, 71, 74

Margaret ("Maultasche"), duchess of Carinthia, countess of Tirol, 57, 59–60

Massys, Quinten: *The Misers,* 64; subject of romance by Pichler, 64; *An Old Woman ("The Ugly Duchess"),* 57–64, 66

Matsys, Quentin (*also* Quinten). *See* Massys, Quinten

Mayhew, Horace ("Ponny"), 87–92, 94

medieval motifs: architecture, 31; chatelaine, 157–58; chivalry, 159; costume, 2, 11, 64, 65, 66; verse, 99. *See also* armor; George, Saint; layout; ornamental initials

Melzi, Francisco, 60, 61–62

Mespoulet, Marguerite, 5, 6, 12

messenger (*LG*), 12, 14, 153

Metsys, Quentin. *See* Massys, Quinten

Millais, John Everett: commends quality of Dalziel engraving, 148; *A Dream of the Past: Sir Isumbras at the Ford,* 98–101; *My First Sermon,* 122

Miller, Joseph Hillis, 149–50

mimesis, 149, 150, 160

mirror. *See* looking-glass

Modern Library, 162–63, 237

monogram (JT), 6, 69, 226, 237; added by Rollitz (*AW*), 237, 238; damaged, 180, 213, 214; reversed (*LG*), 173

Moore, Thomas; see *Lalla Rookh*

Morgan Library and Museum. *See* Pierpont Morgan Library

Morris, Frankie: biography of JT, 2, 5; JT's drawing of knight on horseback, 93; JT's drawings on Bristol board, 181; red nose of Knave of Hearts, 52

Moser, Barry, 152

Mouse (*AAuG, AW*), 46, 49, 194

Moxon, Edward. *See* Moxon illustrated Tennyson

Moxon illustrated Tennyson (*Poems*), 142–48, 189

Mr. Punch: distributes volumes of *Punch,* 30, 31; and fashionable young women, 121; as Greek warrior, 109, 110; as knight in graffito, 91; picnicking with his family, 28; and Prince Albert, 82; as schoolmaster, 8

Müller, William, 29

Mulready, William, 85, 143

Museo Fournier de Naipes de Álava, 77, 84, 85

mushrooms, 19, 20, 44

mutton, leg of (*LG*), 21, 22, 23

Newberry Library, 228

Nicholas I, czar, 72, 73

North, Ernest Dressel, 211, 212

Noyce, Elisha, 179, 192

Nursery "Alice": Alice's dress, 228; cancelled edition, 227–28; color palette, 226–27; cover illustrations by G. E. Thomson, 228; foxglove, 159; frontispiece (trial scene), Plate 3; garden scene, Plate 5; illustrations (JT), 225–27; JT colors illustrations, 52, 67; King of Hearts, 52; Knave of Hearts, 52; Kredel and, 230; March Hare and straw, 67; narrator comments on illustrations, 44, 52, 67, 150, 159; printed by Edmund Evans, 189, 226; proofs, 228; wood blocks, 228

Ophelia (*Hamlet*), 68, 69, 72

ornamental initials (*Punch*), 64, 65, 108, 109, 124

ostrich as croquet mallet (*AAuG*), 43

Oxford. *See* Carter, Theophilus; Christ Church; Clarendon Press; Oxford University Press; Sheep's shop

Oxford University Press, 129, 194, 209, 215. *See also* Clarendon Press

Oysters (*LG*), 19, 20, 24, 25

Palmerston, third viscount (Henry John Temple), 15, 31

"Papal Aggression." *See* Pius IX; Wiseman, Nicholas

Parliament: debates, 37; decoration of Houses of, 2; Schleswig-Holstein affair, 31. *See also* Seymour, Henry Danby

parrot ("lory," *AW*), 49, 55, 151

Paton, Joseph Noël, 134

"Phiz." *See* Browne, Hablot Knight

"Phosphorus," 193, 194, 201, 202–3

photographs: Alice Liddell, 133, 134; *AW* illustrations for Rollitz to reengrave, 234, 236, 238; daughters of fourth marquess of Bath, 123; Horace Mayhew, 89, 90; of JT, 93; JT studies portraits, 92; LC as photographer, 40, 99,

Rowlandson, Thomas, 72, 148

Royal Institute of Painters in Water Colours, 139, 232

Ruskin, John: becomes Mock Turtle (*AW*), 99; classmate of Henry Danby Seymour, 63, 64; criticizes labor of facsimile wood engraving, 141–42; criticizes Millais's *Sir Isumbras,* 99, 100; criticizes two Dalziel Tennyson engravings, 147; criticizes Rosa's *Saint Anthony,* 113–14; deems illustrating poetry impossible, 144, 146; discourages LC's ambitions for drawing, 40; drawing instructor for Liddell daughters, 99; satirized, 100

Sandys, Frederick, 100, 101, 148

Sarzano, Frances, 5, 87, 116, 135

Saturday Review (London), 98, 99

Schiller, Justin: census of *AW* and *LG* drawings, 118, 135, 142, 226; drawings on Bristol board, 181; *LG* frontispiece, 184; no surviving annotated proof of *AW* engraving, 182; tracings, 181

science, fabulous aspect, 107, 108

Seymour, Alfred, 59, 62–63

Seymour, Henry Danby, 61, 63

Seymour, Robert, 148

Shakespeare, William, 68–72, 82–84, 210, 241

Sheep (*LG*), 186

Sheep's shop (*LG*), 132, 153, 156, 246, Plate 1

show-through (printing), 215. *See also* "dirt"

Simpson, Roger: JT and fresco, 3; medieval satire, 159; ornamental initials, 109; papacy, 15; Romanesque doorway, 31; straw sign of madness, 48

Sir Isumbras at the Ford (Millais), 98–101

sizing (paper), 215, 219

skeleton suit, 6–8

Spades (playing card suit, *AW*): Ace of, 79, 80; gardeners as pips of, 77; Queen of, 85, 86, 159; six of (Rollitz), 237

Spielmann, Marion Harry: Edward Bradley, 21; Frank Bellew, 21; Horace Mayhew, 87–92; JT disdained models, relied on memory, 9, 92; JT illustrated "Punch's Book of British Costumes," 10; JT self-portrait, 93; JT's stock imagery, 8; *Morning Herald* and *Evening Standard,* 15; Royal Academy

Schools, 2; wood engraving process, 142

St. Bride Foundation and Library, 193, 195, 197–200, 203, 228

Staunton pattern (chess pieces), 135

Stern, Jeffrey, 27, 55, 134, 144, 212

Stevens, Bethan, 178

straws as sign of madness (*AW, NA*), 67–74

Swain, Joseph, 55, 180, 181, 188, 218

swords, wooden (*LG*), 154, 157

tarts (*AAuG, AW*), 52, 53, 54, 76, 171

Taylor, Tom: author of "Metrical Romance of Sir Ysumbras," 99, 100; connects LC with JT, 5, 39–40, 129; LC recalls copy of 1865 *AW* from, 212; sketch of, 90

tea-party (*AW*): Alice's body language in illustration, and its placement, 131, 164–65; "dirt" mars illustration in copies of 1865 *AW,* 217; JT requests text of chapter, 88, 130–31; layout of illustration, 164–65; milk jug missing from illustration, 156; straws on March Hare at, 67–68, 71–72

Tenniel, John: annotates wood block proofs, 182–83, 185–86; biographical sketch, 2–3; cartoons for *Punch,* 5–124 *passim;* portraits of, 93; consults with LC, 130–31, 136–40. *See also* books illustrated in whole or part by JT; monogram

Tennyson, Alfred: his concept of illustration, 144, 149, 152; "The Lady of Shalott," 143–44, 147, 152, 154; Moxon illustrated edition of *Poems,* 142–48, 144, 154, 189; "The Palace of Art," 144–46, 147; "The Vision of Sin," 144

Theaker, Harry G., 175, 229, 231

Thompson, John, 143

Thompson, John Gordon, 118, 120

Thomson, Emily Gertrude, 133, 228

Thomson, James, 118, 190, 191, 205

Thornbury, Walter, 139, 148–49

Through the Looking-Glass: Annotated Alice (Gardner), 31, 116, 154; facsimiles of early editions, 174–75; Heritage Club, Heritage Press, Heritage Reprints, 237–38; Limited Editions Club, 238–40; Macmillan 1872 (first edition), 166–68, 172, 184–86, 243; Macmillan 1887 (People's Edition), 3, 164, 171–73, 74, 207; Macmillan 1897 (fourth edition), 162, 174; Macmillan 1898